2004

Reconsidering Roosevelt on Race

Reconsidering Roosevelt on Race

How the Presidency Paved the Road to *Brown*

Kevin J. McMahon

THE UNIVERSITY OF CHICAGO PRESS

CHICAGO & LONDON

Kevin J. McMahon is associate professor in the Department of Political Science at the State University of New York, Fredonia.

The University of Chicago Press, Chicago 60637
The University of Chicago Press, Ltd., London
© 2004 by The University of Chicago
All rights reserved. Published 2004
Printed in the United States of America
13 12 11 10 09 08 07 06 05 04   1 2 3 4 5

ISBN: 0-226-50086-1 (cloth)
ISBN: 0-226-50088-8 (paper)

Library of Congress Cataloging-in-Publication Data

McMahon, Kevin J.
    Reconsidering Roosevelt on race : how the presidency paved the road to Brown / Kevin J. McMahon.
        p.   cm.
    Includes bibliographical references and index.
    ISBN 0-226-50086-1 (cloth : alk. paper)—ISBN 0-226-50088-8 (pbk. : alk paper)
    1. Roosevelt. Franklin D. (Franklin Delano), 1882–1945—Views on race. 2. Roosevelt, Franklin D. (Franklin Delano), 1882–1945—Relations with African Americans. 3. United States—Race relations—Political aspects. 4. African Americans—Civil rights—History—20th century. 5. African Americans—Legal status, laws, etc.—History—20th century. 6. United States—Politics and government—1933–1945. 7. United States. Supreme Court—History—20th century. 8. Segregation in education—Law and legislation—United States—History—20th century. I. Title.

E807.M38 2003
323.1′196073′009043—dc21   2003008350

⊗ The paper used in this publication meets the minimum requirements of the American National Standard for Information Sciences — Permanence of Paper for Printed Library Materials, ANSI Z39.48-1992.

For
My Mom and Dad
&
For
Stephanie

CONTENTS

ACKNOWLEDGMENTS

The effort to forge a civil rights mission on the Supreme Court involved many individuals and years of work. While hardly comparable, the same was true in the research and writing of this book. Early on, Shep Melnick, Sid Milkis, and H. W. Perry, Jr. provided invaluable guidance about how to shape the project and helped me refine the skills necessary to pull it off. Beginning in my graduate school days, and continuing until today, numerous friends have spent many hours discussing my arguments, reading my work, or just providing support. They include: Brad Clarke, Pearson Cross, Rick Dewine, Mike Hausenfleck, Amy Higer, Elena Kolesnkikova, Millette Shamir, and Mauri Ziff. Chris Kirkey deserves a special note of gratitude in this regard.

Bob Duffy and K. C. Johnson read substantial parts of the manuscript and provided critical advice on how to sharpen its focus. Others who read and commented on portions of the manuscript assisted me in significantly improving its quality. They include: Howard Ball, Amy Bridges, Mark Graber, Jim Hurtgen, Ken Kersch, Bill Leuchtenburg, Carolyn Long, George Lovell, Mark Peterson, Dick Pious, Suzanne Samuels, Stephen Skowronek, and Keith Whittington. The anonymous reviewers made excellent comments and were especially helpful in working out the kinks of the manuscript. Charlie Derber, Howard Gillman, and John K. White offered encouragement and important advice at various points along the way.

Karen Orren was exceedingly generous in helping me to prepare my article "Constitutional Vision and Supreme Court Decisions: Reconsidering Roosevelt on Race" for publication in *Studies in American Political Development*. Much of that article appears in the pages of this book. Don Beachler read and reread most of the manuscript. Beyond providing invaluable feedback about the work, he has become a close friend with whom I often discuss ideas and thoughts about politics and the law. I owe a special thanks to Mike Paris for his continuing support of this project since its inception. I met Mike in graduate school at Brandeis University, and ever since he has read and commented on much of what I have written, always with his mixture of compassion and constructive criticism.

My colleagues at SUNY, Fredonia, have been very supportive and have provided me with a nourishing environment for finishing the research and writing of this book. A grant from the Franklin and Eleanor Roosevelt Institute facilitated my weeks with the primary documents at the FDR Library. A grant and invitation to attend the Supreme Court Historical Society's 2001 Summer Seminar allowed me to complete my research at the Library of Congress and the U.S. National Archives and to share my work with other scholars in my field of interest. In the course of researching and writing this book, I have benefited greatly from the resources of many libraries and archives. I thank their staff members for the aid they provided me. Stephanie Frederico also assisted me during one summer under the Dana Intern Program at Ithaca College, helping me track down some of the more obscure sources I rely on in making my arguments.

I am indebted to my editor, John Tryneski, who took a chance on a first-time author he knew little about. His colleagues Anne Ford, Rodney Powell, and Leslie Keros were also very helpful in preparing the book for publication. Copyeditor Clair James and Joanne Foeller, who assisted with the index, deserve praise for their fine work.

My mom and dad, children of the New Deal, have of course been with me throughout the years it took me to finish this book. I thank them for their love and patience. I also owe thanks to my late grandparents and to the rest of my family for the care and warmth they have provided and continue to provide me.

And in the end, my wife, Stephanie, deserves a special place in this book. I met Steph in the midst of my writing, but without her love and encouragement I would have never completed the project.

ONE Introduction

The Day They Drove Old Dixie Down

"Shocked." That was the word Governor James "Jimmy" Byrnes of
South Carolina used to describe his reaction to the Supreme Court's
decision in *Brown v. Board of Education*. Byrnes had expected the
Court to uphold the "separate-but-equal" doctrine when it issued its opinion
on school segregation on May 17, 1954. But it didn't. Instead, Chief Justice
Earl Warren announced in a firm clear voice that in the area of education
the *Plessy* doctrine was no longer the law.[1] The South would have to comply.

As the leader of the first state to secede from the Union, the seventy-two-
year-old Byrnes was an uncommon man. Besides the sitting justices, only he
and one other person alive knew the experience of being on the nation's
highest tribunal.[2] Appointed as an associate justice by Franklin D. Roosevelt
on the eve of America's entry into World War II, Byrnes gave up his judicial
post after serving just over a year to head the war mobilization effort as the
"assistant president."[3] Elected governor in 1950, he sought to use his first-
hand knowledge of the Court by equalizing South Carolina's schools in an
attempt to undercut the National Association for the Advancement of Colored People's (NAACP) legal attack on *Plessy*. While recent Court action
clearly indicated a decision in favor of the civil rights organization, Byrnes
felt that he could still save segregation.

In turn, he sought to establish a record of rapid improvement in South
Carolina's treatment of African Americans and to counter the NAACP's
years of effort in the legal and political arenas. Along with his $75 million
school-building equalization program, Byrnes pushed through legislation
intended to end Ku Klux Klan activities in his state by outlawing "the public
wearing of masks by adults or the burning of crosses on private property
without the owner's consent." To challenge the NAACP in court, he convinced one of the most respected and politically influential attorneys in the
nation — John W. Davis — to argue the South's position before the justices.
Davis, the 1924 Democratic presidential nominee and a veteran of more
than 250 Supreme Court cases (more than any other twentieth-century

1

attorney), was confident that precedent was on South Carolina's side.[4] Having already broken with President Harry Truman, Byrnes also courted GOP presidential candidate Dwight Eisenhower in an attempt to set himself up as the South's power broker in the 1952 election. With reestablished clout in Washington, he felt he could influence an Eisenhower administration's position on the desegregation cases. Finally, Byrnes visited the Supreme Court in the spring and summer of 1953, where he "lobbied two old friends," Chief Justice Fred Vinson and Associate Justice Felix Frankfurter. With all of this activity, the former justice sought to persuade the Court (and the new administration) that it was unnecessary to overturn *Plessy*, arguing that southern states were now upgrading black schools and a ruling against the South would unleash powerful forces of resistance. In other words, such a decision would end his brand of moderately conservative political leadership below the Mason-Dixon line.[5]

To many, despite Davis's confidence, Byrnes's effort to produce a decision sympathetic to the South seemed unlikely to end in success. Although the Court had never directly challenged the separate-but-equal standard in its previous rulings, for years it had consistently sided with the NAACP position in a range of cases concerning race. As early as April 1941, guided by a Justice Department brief, a Court of eight — with five Roosevelt justices in place — united to support an African American congressman's complaint against the Interstate Commerce Commission. Never before had the Justice Department submitted an *amicus curiae* brief on behalf of a black defendant. In 1946 the Court, with only the newly seated Truman appointee Harold Burton dissenting, sided with a black woman who had refused to move to the back of an interstate bus. Two years later, again at the Justice Department's urging, all six participating justices concluded that racially restrictive covenants in housing could not be enforced in state court, virtually making them null and void.[6] In cases decided in 1948 and 1950, the Court turned to the question of school segregation in higher education, methodically and unanimously developing the precedent necessary to support *Brown*. "Discussions among the justices in the 1950s cases," moreover, showed "that they were ready to abandon" the *Plessy* doctrine.[7] Indeed, by 1944, it was clear that the newly created Roosevelt Court would practice a new style of progressivism when addressing the issue of race. In that year, the Court overturned a unanimous ruling just nine years old and invalidated the white primary, a device that was then thought to be *the* most effective legal measure for keeping African Americans out of the South's one-party political process.[8] With this ruling (*Smith v. Allwright*), the Court initiated a decade-long undertaking that called into question the constitutionality of the southern states' segregation statutes, culminating in *Brown v. Board of Education*.

Given this string of decisions, it is difficult not to wonder whether Byrnes feigned his amazement at the result in *Brown* — to question whether or not his shock was that of the Captain Louis Renault variety in the film *Casablanca*. Indeed, of all the southern leaders commenting on the decision the day of its announcement, Byrnes's surprise, coupled with his hope for a reversal, was a rare reaction. Most others expressed disappointment, outrage, even acceptance.[9] To the extent that southerners shared in Byrnes's surprise, it was due more to the unity of the Court than to the ruling itself. As the *Atlanta Constitution* put it, "the South has three representatives on the court in Justices Black of Alabama, Clark of Texas and Reid [*sic*] of Kentucky, which is a border commonwealth. Expectations had been that the South's traditional stand on segregation would be upheld by some of these at least."[10] In *Brown*, it wasn't.

But while Byrnes's reaction may have been odd, it should not be disregarded. With their decision in *Brown*, the justices completed a dramatic turn in American law that rejected the defining institutions of the South and endorsed the ideal of a more inclusive democracy. First as an influential senator, then as a justice, and finally as a member of both the Roosevelt and Truman administrations, Byrnes had been at the center of the political regime that created this Court. Perhaps more than any other elected southern official, it could be said that the Court's transformation on race had occurred on his watch. In this light, his surprise should not be surprising at all. Rather, his emotions as well as his efforts to save *Plessy* suggest a profound misunderstanding — if not denial — of the Court's institutional mission following the "constitutional revolution of 1937." Given this mission, Byrnes's search for a compromise was destined for failure. It represented the thinking of a skilled legislator, a status Byrnes had achieved in his twenty-four years in Congress, not of a successful jurist, a label few would attach to him. Thus, in *Brown* the justices unanimously rejected the governor's late-day attempts to save segregation by stressing that separate schools based on race could not be made equal — as South Carolina had sought to do — for they were "inherently unequal."[11]

The Origins of the Supreme Court's Civil Rights Decisions

How did this judicial transformation occur? How did *this* Supreme Court emerge as such a unified opponent of segregation? Countering conventional wisdom about their inability to significantly sway judicial interpretation, I argue that presidents, especially "reconstructive" presidents like FDR, are powerful agents of constitutional change. Under the influence of these presidents, Supreme Courts are predisposed to follow the command of the executive branch. In turn, I suggest that the civil rights decisions are the by-products of an institutional mission — embraced by the Court — that was significantly shaped by what I call the "judicial policy" of the Roosevelt administration, a policy that was itself a consequence of FDR's management of divisions within the Democratic Party and of his construction of the modern presidency.[12] Put another way, FDR's conclusion that "southern democracy" was incompatible with his vision of a thoroughly liberal Democratic Party and with his institutional design for an executive-dominated national government served as a mainspring for the Supreme Court's later commitment to federal civil rights protection.[13] To be sure, this assessment does not transform FDR into a radical reformer on race. His decisions were driven more by the demands of intraparty management and his own institutional desires than by a personal commitment to the African American cause. And while his administration laid the institutional foundation for the development of the Court's civil rights doctrine of the 1940s and 1950s, it must be made clear that others built the house.

In developing this argument, I focus on three inquiries made by southerners on the day of *Brown*'s announcement. First, why did a Court largely staffed soon after the constitutional crisis of the 1930s issue such an activist decision? After all, as the *New York Times* reminded its readers, "five of the nine Supreme Court Justices who today outlawed race segregation in public schools were appointees of President Franklin D. Roosevelt."[14] It had been only seventeen years since FDR's historic fight with that tribunal to ensure Congress's ability to regulate the economy as it saw fit. Now, all of the Court's members — even those who for years had preached judicial restraint — had, in the words of Georgia's Governor Herman Talmadge, "blatantly ignored all law and precedent." Echoing his governor's sentiment, Senator Richard Russell issued a declaration that reminded many of the late president's attempt to "pack" the Court. "Ways must be found to check the tendency of the court to disregard the Constitution and the precedents of able and unbiased judges to decide cases solely on the basis of the personal predilections of some of its members as to political, economic and social questions."[15]

While anger over the justices' activism stirred emotions, it masked the partisan makeup of the Court. And in the days following *Brown*, few southern voices had an answer to a second, more implicit, question. Why would

a court dominated by justices appointed by two Democratic presidents —
and approved with the overwhelming support of southern senators — issue a
ruling so harmful to southern democracy? Rather, southern leaders tended
to ignore the essence of this inquiry by fixing their sights on the new chief
justice, the only member of the Court appointed by a Republican president.
After all, as late as December 1952 — the time of the first oral arguments in
Brown — many in the South thought segregation would survive. For his part,
Byrnes predicted that the NAACP would lose decisively, with only Justice
William O. Douglas supporting *Plessy*'s demise.[16] Instead, despite the lame-
duck Truman administration's restrained attack on the separate-but-equal
doctrine in the government's brief, a Fred Vinson-led Supreme Court unanimously held the case over for reargument and invited the incoming Eisenhower administration both to take part in oral arguments and to submit a
brief.[17] Warren's addition to the mix following Vinson's death in 1953, coupled
with Eisenhower Attorney General Herbert Brownell's reserved support of
the NAACP's position in the government's "supplemental" brief, must have
upset the balance.[18] Only "under the duress" of these two men, South Carolina Senator Burnet Maybank concluded, could the Court have reached
this "shameful political edict." Simply stated, "had the Democrats been in
power, the decision would never have been made." Joining in this South
Carolina chorus, Senator Olin D. Johnston reasoned that with Warren and
Brownell in command, the Court had made "a flagrant, direct appeal for the
political favor of minority groups."[19]

In their assault on Warren, southern leaders took aim at not only his leadership but the nature of his opinion as well. Senator Russell, the self-
proclaimed voice of Georgia, underscored that "for the first time, the Court
admittedly substitutes psychology for law and legal precedent in construing
the Constitution." Other southerners, including Byrnes, accused the scholars
cited by the Court as being "members of Communist front organizations."[20]
These comments led to a third question. Why did the Court use social science — in its famed footnote 11 — to support its conclusion that segregated
schools violated the Fourteenth Amendment? To be sure, the use of this evidence was no small matter. Along with southern attacks, it opened the
Brown decision to significant criticism from members of an otherwise
friendly legal community. For example, Edmond Cahn noted in 1955 that
he would "not have the constitutional rights of Negroes — or of other Americans — rest on any such flimsy foundation as some of the scientific demon-
strations" cited in *Brown*.[21]

Nevertheless, the deed was done. Jimmy Byrnes's early efforts to prevent

President Truman's renomination as the Democratic candidate in 1952, combined with his support for the Republican Eisenhower over the Democrat Stevenson, had blown up in his face. Congressional sentiment held that such "bolting" southerners had been "badly hurt" by the decision. Senator Russell — described as "the most powerful southerner in the Senate" — did provide some political cover for the South Carolina governor. To him, the Court, dating back to the Truman administration, had formed into "a pliant tool" of the Attorney General, a mere "political arm of the Executive Branch of the Government."[22] Once the Eisenhower Justice Department decided to continue the Truman administration's stance on segregation, *Plessy's* fate was sealed.

Summary of the Argument

Since Russell's initial assessment of the origins of the Supreme Court's decision, many have followed. In the years since, *Brown* and the Court's civil rights decisions leading up to it have alternatively been understood as: (1) a reflection of the "current of history,"[23] (2) a consequence of the NAACP's effective organization and advocacy,[24] (3) an expression of the national political regime,[25] and (4) a result of an independent judiciary convinced of the evils of Jim Crow.[26] While each of these explanations offers insights into the origins of these decisions, none can fully answer the three concerns southern leaders articulated following *Brown*. Namely, why did a court supposedly committed to judicial restraint issue such an activist decision? Why did the *Democratic* white South suffer a dramatic loss before a court filled with eight justices appointed by *Democratic* presidents? And why did the Court employ social science in its unanimous ruling? These questions inform the focus of this book.

   In seeking to answer them, I pursue an approach influenced by historical institutionalist analysis. In contrast, the most dominant explanations in political science concerning the origins of the Court's civil rights decisions tend to place little emphasis on institutions and how they may shape the policy choices of the individuals who occupy them. Instead, in these Court-centered attitudinalist analyses, unconstrained judicial behavior garners the greatest attention.[27] In another Court-centered approach, proponents of the political systems model also place little emphasis on institutions, often reducing the presidency and the Court into mere intermediaries in an exchange between partisan "clients" and favorable judicial decisions. Other scholars have employed a bottom-up approach by highlighting the activities of rights-advocacy groups like the NAACP and the American Civil Liberties Union (ACLU), but they too disregard the importance of the Court's institutional setting. Yet another group of scholars, based mainly in legal academia, does place significant weight on the Court as an institution but often overlooks the role other institutions play in shaping judicial interpretation.

I pursue an approach that highlights the importance of institutional context across branches of government without disregarding the behavior of individual justices, the role of rights-advocacy groups, or the importance of legal principles in the making of Supreme Court decisions. I do so by focusing on and linking the institutional characteristics of the presidency, which affect how presidents influence judicial interpretation at particular historical moments, and those of the Court, which guide and constrain its rulings. This presidency-focused approach seeks to provide a more complete picture than the existing scholarship on the source of constitutional change for this period, while at the same time altering the terms of the analysis.

In examining the origins of the civil rights decisions, I argue that through its judicial policy, the Roosevelt administration aided in constructing the federal judiciary's institutional norms and commitments, especially with regard to the High Court. These norms and commitments conditioned behavior on that tribunal for the middle third of the twentieth century. Put simply, the executive branch's commitment to the expansion of civil rights — established by the Roosevelt administration and not, as is traditionally thought, by its successor — significantly influenced the development of the Court's doctrine. By asking the "Roosevelt justices" to intervene on the race issue, the Roosevelt Justice Department helped them resolve the apparent contradiction between their actions and the "mistaken" activism of the "old" anti–New Deal Court. In doing so, the Roosevelt administration established a common bond with the goals of legal reform groups such as the NAACP and the ACLU and at times fought hand in hand with them to legally sabotage the constitutionally protected system of southern white supremacy.

The Roosevelt Justice Department's promotion of an active Court on race also set an important precedent. Culminating with *Brown*, the Truman and Eisenhower Justice Departments carried on this practice of civil rights advocacy through *amicus curiae* briefs and further cooperation with the NAACP.[28] In doing so, as Cornell Clayton writes, "the executive branch originally supported — even drove — the Supreme Court in its new political role . . . welcom[ing] judicial activism of the Warren Court variety."[29] Indeed, the Truman Justice Department was the first party to argue before the

Court that it should overturn the *Plessy* doctrine. In its October 5, 1949, brief in *Henderson v. United States*, the department confessed error and supported Henderson's claim against the Interstate Commerce Commission to desegregate interstate travel.[30] In taking this action, it stressed: "so long as the doctrine of the *Plessy* case stands, a barrier erected not by the Constitution but by the courts will continue to work a denial of rights and privileges and immunities antagonistic to the freedoms and liberties on which our institutions and our form of government are founded. 'Separate but equal' is a constitutional anachronism which no longer deserves a place in our law. . . . It is neither reasonable nor right that colored citizens of the United States should be subjected to the humiliation of being segregated by law, on the pretense that they are being treated as equals."[31] Five years later, all nine justices agreed, a majority of whom had been appointed by FDR.

This argument does not diminish the importance of the NAACP attorneys in convincing the Court to author its civil rights decisions. Nor does it reduce Supreme Court justices into mere clones of the president when issuing their rulings from the high bench. Rather, the presidency-focused approach accents the previously underestimated contribution of the executive branch in helping to construct a Court decidedly inclined toward achieving racial equality under the law. Clearly, the presidency-focused approach cannot explain all forms of judicial behavior. Instead, it seeks to explain the development of an embedded mission on the Supreme Court at midcentury. Once ensconced in the Court, this institutional mission "structure[d] the identities, interests, opportunities, and (hence) the strategic choices of [its members] without fully determining them."[32]

The Basis for a Presidency-Focused Approach

Others have certainly highlighted the role nonjudicial institutions play in shaping constitutional interpretation. Bruce Ackerman argues that constitutional change emanates directly from democratic politics at certain "higher lawmaking" moments, not from nine justices walled off from the world.[33] Stephen Griffin stresses that "the course of constitutional change during the New Deal and other important periods of change in the twentieth century flowed through the President and Congress, not the Supreme Court and the legalized Constitution."[34] Keith Whittington calls for a political model of "constitutional construction" to understand the "significant aspects of our historical constitutional development [that] are not driven primarily by their fidelity to known textual meaning" but are the result of "ambitious political actors" who have "construct[ed] a vision of constitutional meaning that enshrines their own values and interests."[35] The presidency-focused approach builds on such research.

Too often, however, the efforts of these and similar scholars have been consumed by the age-old question of the legitimacy of judicial review, and by attempts to solve the countermajoritarian conundrum.[36] This is not my intent. I am not interested in the *ought* of Supreme Court decision making here. Forays into such normative discussions tend to cloud the historical portrait, whether deliberately or not. Thus, while my work may contribute to these valuable discussions, I leave it to the reader to decide how my conclusions about the origins of the Court's civil rights decisions fit into our democratic tradition. More importantly, while these scholars recognize the importance of the president and Congress as forces in constitutional change, they rarely explain the development of the forces advocating and constructing this change. While Whittington does, he spotlights areas of constitutional development where the Court's action has been limited, not those, such as civil rights, where its role has been central. Other "regime" scholarship has expanded our understanding of the origins of the Court's opinions by stressing "how the decisions of state actors reconstructed and empowered the institution of the federal judiciary," but to date few scholars have focused on the presidency as an agent of constitutional change.[37] None have explained how and why the Roosevelt justices came to be greater advocates of racial equality than were the progressive jurists of their formative years. I attempt to detail this development.

My main interests include uncovering the origins of court decisions and exploring the distinctiveness of the presidency as an institution. Here, I add to recent efforts by new historical institutionalists who "explore the broader cultural and political contexts of judicial decision making . . . [by] examining how judicial attitudes are themselves constituted and structured by the Court *as an institution* and by its relationship to other institutions in the political system at particular points in history."[38] First, I seek to understand why courts act at certain times on certain issues, and specifically why the Supreme Court, absent a sustained social movement, chose to preempt congressional action on civil rights with its desegregation decisions. I do so for two reasons. The first centers on my intention to add to the academic debate on Supreme Court decision making. Most political science scholarship in this area explains the Court's decisions as a response to certain stimuli, either societal pressures, the dominant political alignment of the time, or the personal policy preferences of the individual justices. Informed by the new institutionalism, I explore the institutional perspective of the Court. As Rogers Smith writes: "Political institutions appear to be 'more than simply mirrors of social forces.' They are themselves created by past human political decisions that were in some measure discretionary, and to some degree they are alterable by future ones. They also have a kind of life of their own. They influence the self-conception of those who occupy roles defined by them in ways that can give those persons distinctively 'institutional' perspectives. Hence such institutions can play a part in affecting the political behavior that reshapes them in turn — making them appropriate as units of analysis in their own right."[39] With this in mind, I argue that only by uncovering the political forces that forged the Court's institutional mission at mid-twentieth century can we understand why it upset the *Plessy* doctrine in the string of civil rights decisions leading up to and including *Brown*.

The second reason for uncovering the origins of the Court's decisions concerns the lasting effectiveness of those decisions. Put another way, the Constitution is a malleable document. Judges and justices have interpreted certain clauses, including the equal protection clause, to mean different things at different times. What upholds these interpretations is usually not the words themselves but the political forces supporting them. I seek to identify those forces that tore down *Plessy* and constructed *Brown*. By doing so, I argue that we can better understand why *Brown* was ultimately endorsed and extended by the democratically elected branches, despite the great difficulties with its implementation. Along the same lines, I argue that such insight reveals the truest meaning of *Brown*. In this account, *Brown* represented a drive to undermine southern democracy and end the worst abuses of southern white supremacy. Once African Americans achieved these goals of "simple justice," political support for more elusive goals — like school integration — waned.

Second, I seek to illuminate the power of the presidency. Based largely on the lasting influence of Richard Neustadt's work, *Presidential Power*, scholars have consistently underscored the institutional weakness of this institution. Rather than formal structure and power, political scientists have stressed, in a virtual academic mantra, "presidential power is the power to persuade."[40] This conclusion places significant emphasis on the personal leadership qualities of individual presidents. Simply stated, the degree to which a particular president has been effective has depended largely on his own abilities to lead.

Presidential weakness is commonly accentuated even more with regard to the judiciary. Despite strong evidence to the contrary, conventional wisdom asserts that presidents often fail in court. Specifically, as then Associate Justice William Rehnquist noted,

History teaches us, I think, that even a "strong" president determined to leave his mark on the Court, like Lincoln, or Franklin Roosevelt, is apt to be only partly successful. Neither the President nor his appointees can foresee what issues will come before the Court during the tenure of their appointees, and it may be that none had thought very much about these issues. Even though they agree as to the proper resolution of current issues, they may well disagree as to future cases involving other questions. . . . [T]he Supreme Court is an institution far more dominated by centrifugal forces, pushing towards individuality and independence, than it is by centripetal forces pulling for hierarchical ordering and institutional unity.[41]

Such conclusions are usually supported by well-worn anecdotes of presidents proclaiming frustration with certain judicial appointments. For example, many scholars employ President Truman's statement that putting that "damn fool from Texas," Justice Tom Clark, on the Court was one of the biggest mistakes of his tenure in the White House. Others prefer President Eisenhower's comments concerning Chief Justice Earl Warren and Associate Justice William Brennan. In response to a similar question about whether he had made mistakes as president, Eisenhower nearly echoed his predecessor. "Yes, two, and they are both sitting on the Supreme Court."[42]

Again, in contrast to this conventional thought, I argue that at times the presidency has served as the mainspring of constitutional change. In doing so, I rely on recent presidency research that emphasizes the institution's formal powers and the importance of the "political time" in which presidents rule. Building on these themes, I seek to highlight the capacity of the presidency to reorder the judiciary at particular historical moments. In doing so, I move beyond the mere selection of justices to an examination of the institutional levers of influence and the dissemination of ideas. While my study concentrates on FDR, in chapter 6, I consider the impact of the judicial policies of the Truman and Eisenhower administrations on the Court's civil rights decisions. And in the conclusion, I briefly discuss the usefulness of this presidency-focused approach for explaining how other presidents have shaped legal orders.

FDR and Race

Along with highlighting the general power of the presidency to influence judicial interpretation, my work emphasizes the specific and extensive consequences of the Roosevelt administration's judicial policy on later Supreme

Court decisions. This argument has considerable consequences for scholarship about FDR's legacy on race. President Roosevelt has traditionally received scant praise for advancing the rights of African Americans. For instance, as Ira Katznelson and his colleagues have written, up until America's entry into World War II:

> Roosevelt and congressional leaders tailored New Deal legislation to southern preferences. They reached an implicit modus vivendi: southern civil society would remain intact and southern representatives would support the key elements of the administration's program. There would be no attempt to build a mass biracial base in the South; nor would even the most heinous aspects of regional repression, such as lynching, be brought under the rule of law. Further, sponsors fashioned key bills to avoid disturbing the region's racial civilization by employing two main policy instruments: the exclusion of agricultural and domestic labor, the principal occupational categories of blacks, from legislation, including the National Recovery Act, the Wagner Act, Social Security, and the Fair Labor Standards Act, and decentralized administration.[43]

This assessment of the Roosevelt administration's performance on civil rights is supported by other scholars who generally argue that FDR did not lack the opportunity to improve the plight of African Americans, just the will.[44] While still others dispute this interpretation of the Roosevelt record, their arguments tend to focus on the role FDR and his administration played in altering the atmosphere of race relations, on improving the economic predicament of Depression-ridden African Americans, and on transforming the partisan preference of black voters.[45] No extensive analysis exists that explores the actions of the administration in connection to the momentous changes in the way federal jurists approached the civil rights of African Americans in the 1940s and 1950s. This is seriously incomplete. I argue that had FDR allowed southern Democrats to shape his judicial policy in the same racially exclusive fashion in which they constructed key New Deal statutes, the Supreme Court would not have challenged segregation when it did (and may not have done so at all).

Thus, while customarily exaggerated — "the Court supinely transposes . . . the words of the briefs filed by the Attorney General and adopts the philosophy of the brief as its decision" — Senator Richard Russell's words about the centrality of the executive branch in *Brown* were not far off target. His charge in late 1953 that the appointments "of the last few years" were responsible for *Plessy*'s destruction, however, missed the mark entirely.[46] I argue that in seeking to reconstitute the courts to advance his intraparty and institutional interests, FDR's judicial policy helped create — at times intentionally and at times not — a legal order clearly in conflict with his legislative compromises on race.

Notably, then, Truman's Supreme Court appointments — often considered conservative "compromise" candidates — failed to follow in the progressive footsteps of the Roosevelt justices they replaced.[47] Few would argue with the proposition that if Chief Justice Harlan Fiske Stone and Associate Justices Frank Murphy and Wiley Rutledge had lived longer, segregation would have met its legal death earlier. In judicial behavior analyses, each was far more liberal than his replacement.[48] Before their deaths, Murphy and Rutledge had attained the status of being the two most liberal justices on the bench, beating out even the venerable Warren Court liberals, Justices Hugo Black and William Douglas. They had been the only two to support a 1948 NAACP motion on the implementation of *Sipuel v. Oklahoma* (higher education segregation case), with Justice Rutledge writing that the state had to "end the discrimination . . . at once, not at some later time, near or remote." Indeed, according to Richard Kluger, Thurgood Marshall thought the loss of these "two fast friends of the NAACP's legal crusade was obviously a blow" to the case against segregation.[49] For his part, Chief Justice Stone was undoubtedly a greater visionary on the Court's role in extending civil rights than was Fred Vinson. After all, Stone authored the celebrated *Carolene Products*, footnote 4, which outlined much of the Roosevelt Court's forthcoming work on individual rights.[50] Though Stone was more conservative than expected as Roosevelt's chief justice, behavioral scholars have still identified him as easily more liberal than Vinson on civil rights and civil liberties. In the final analysis, Morton Horwitz concludes, Stone, Murphy, and Rutledge, together with Black and Douglas, "formed the most solid pro–civil liberties block in the history of the Supreme Court."[51]

Perhaps more important than individuals sympathetic to civil rights claims, the nature of New Deal jurisprudence — with its commitment to deference — set up the Justice Department to significantly influence the norms of the Court following the constitutional crisis of the 1930s. Obeying the lessons of the immediate past, New Deal jurists generally thought, as Martin Shapiro writes, that "courts should defer to Congress, [and] Congress should defer to the President. So courts really were to defer to the Executive."[52] At times, this commitment conflicted with the principle of judicial restraint; but as I will show, Justice Department officials eased the justices' dilemma by arguing that the Court was clearing the blocked arteries of

American democracy not repeating the activism of the "nine old men." In turn, they convinced the Court to carve out a new course by establishing itself as the protector of the rights of African Americans and other "discrete and insular minorities"—as the defender of a more inclusive democracy. This was the mission of the Supreme Court—secured by embedded institutional norms and commitments—in the years following the "constitutional revolution of 1937."[53]

The Presidency-Focused Approach

Having previewed my conclusions, I now present my approach. As noted above (and as detailed in chapter 7), previous explanations of the origins of the civil rights decisions do offer some important insights into the Court's action. However, I argue that they fail to provide a full picture of the source of this doctrinal development. Beyond filling in the gaps, the presidency-focused approach changes the terms of the analysis by displaying how nonjudicial institutions and outside political forces at times structure decision making on the Court. Specifically, it seeks to uncover the political origins of Supreme Court decisions by examining the formulation of presidential judicial policy and assessing its influence on judicial interpretation.[54]

In pursuing this approach, it is essential to understand what motivates those who occupy the Oval Office. Recent scholarship on the presidency will help. While presidential motivations are complex and dependent on the historical period, Terry Moe and William Howell conclude that, along with reelection, "it is fair to say that most presidents have put great emphasis on their legacies and, in particular, on being regarded in the eyes of history as strong and effective leaders."[55] Moe's and Howell's theoretical conception of presidential motivations, while quite useful, needs more specificity. After all, presidents are reelected and leave their mark on the nation's politics through successful action. I argue that presidential motivations include (1) the consolidation or expansion of an electoral coalition; (2) the achievement of a president's immediate legislative policy preferences; and (3) the implementation of a president's "constitutional vision," defined simply as his image of an ideal institutional order.[56] While realizing a constitutional vision is most important for securing a lasting legacy, each of these motivations contributes to history's view of a president. Each is also at the center of a president's formulation of the administration's judicial policy. Therefore, understanding these motivations in the construction of a president's judicial policy is central to revealing the political origins of Supreme Court decisions and to evaluating the import of the presidency on the nature of those rulings.

First, I argue that more than reelection, presidents employ their administration's policy toward the judiciary in an attempt to create a lasting electoral coalition. Historically, presidents have fashioned their electoral coalitions with the leading "judicial" issues of the day serving as significant but secondary concerns. While these concerns typically do not generate widespread agreement in the alliance — and may threaten to disrupt it if emphasized — the president's position on them is often essential to attracting new groups of voters into his party. One might think of Richard Nixon's use of "law and order" and his skepticism toward some civil rights initiatives as a means for drawing white southern Democrats into the GOP, or of Ronald Reagan's stance on abortion as a vehicle for bringing social conservatives into the Republican fold.

At the same time, presidents must ensure that recruiting these coalition partners does not undermine the second presidential motivation of achieving the administration's legislative goals. Few presidents who have failed to enact significant legislative measures have been treated well by either the electorate or by history. Here, a president's skills as a party leader and legislative coalition-builder will come into play since groups focused on "judicial" concerns will likely pressure him to pursue legislative action for quick relief. If the president acquiesces, however, he may destabilize his electoral alliance and fray his governing coalition in Congress. The first will diminish chances of reelection and the construction of an enduring alliance; the second will disrupt the administration's primary legislative initiatives. It was with this conundrum in mind that FDR explained to NAACP executive secretary Walter White in 1934 why he could not support the organization's leading concern in Congress, antilynching legislation: "I did not choose the tools with which I must work. Had I been permitted to choose them I would have selected quite different ones. But I've got to get legislation passed by Congress to save America. The southerners by reason of the seniority rule in Congress are chairmen or occupy strategic places on most of the senate and house committees. If I come out for the anti-lynching bill now, they will block every bill I ask Congress to pass to keep America from collapsing. I just can't take that risk."[57]

In turn, presidents have employed their judicial policy in an attempt to simultaneously attract new voters and advance leading items on their legislative agenda. For instance, beginning in his second term FDR used his administration's policy toward the judiciary in part to appease newly Democratic African American voters while still avoiding conflict with southern Democrats — both voters and members of Congress — by not openly supporting civil rights legislation. Presidents must still weigh how this policy will affect electoral and legislative goals, but given the gradual way in which judicial interpretation is usually altered, the side effects will most often be less immediate and severe. More than the president's legislative approach, then, his judicial policy will involve the management of intraparty cleavages.

Presidents also use their judicial policy as a means for implementing their individual constitutional visions. As noted above, I define a constitutional vision as a president's ideal institutional order, an image of an institutional arrangement that would most effectively advance the president's values and interests. Typically, a constitutional vision comes in the form of a blueprint, a work in progress. It is unlikely to be the sole product of the president's thinking, especially concerning the role law and courts play in its attainment and design. Rather, a president usually serves as a leader of a larger political movement from which the ideas and ideals of his vision originate. Without such a movement, a president's constitutional vision — lacking the foundation of a body of intellectual and practical thought — will likely be blurred. In this sense, while reconstructive presidents may be the driving force behind constitutional change, other political actors, such as interest groups, other political leaders, and interpretive communities (i.e., leading jurists, judicial advocates, and constitutional scholars), significantly influence them.

FDR's constitutional vision was defined by a system of government with power centralized in Washington, concentrated in the presidency, and committed to a progressive agenda that highlighted newly articulated statutory rights and restored individual rights. As political scientist Sidney Milkis writes: "The New Deal Democratic party . . . was committed to a program of institutional reform that eventually would weaken the two-party system, and substitute for it a refashioned, modern executive as the principal instrument for organizing majorities and intermediating between the popular will and government. Whereas the two-party system was created to protect interest in society against the government, the 'modern presidency' and administrative agencies that emerged during the 1930s were molded to use government as an instrument for the attainment of positive public ends."[58] But if FDR's "modern presidency" were to replace the political party as the primary agent of democracy, the executive branch would have to wrest control of the traditional channels of political participation to open them up to the previously disfranchised. To secure a closer link between the president and the populace, civil rights and liberties would have to be protected in order to subvert the state and local parties' supremacy over the electoral process and to enable wider participation in the political arena as a whole.[59]

Otherwise, disfranchised citizens and newly activated groups supporting the New Deal—most importantly, unionized workers—would be denied their rightful voice. In other words, as parties became less important for mobilizing majorities with the implementation of FDR's institutional program, individual freedom would have to supplant the collective behavior required for a system of vibrant parties.[60]

This institutional program was particularly important with regard to the South. FDR had always felt that he was unduly constrained by the restrictive nature of southern democracy, and the conservative Congresses it produced.[61] For instance, in a speech in his "adopted" home state of Georgia delivered three months before he announced the 1938 purge campaign, the president called for the end of the South's "feudal" system. He then noted that there was "little difference between the feudal system and the Fascist system. If you believe in the one, you lean to the other."[62] Four years later, Roosevelt complained that Mississippi Representative John Rankin "would never last in his congressional district if his constituents voted, but they didn't vote on account of the [poll] tax." Consequently, "Rankin's total vote was only six or seven thousand out of a population close to a quarter of a million." At the same time, in a remarkable memo to Attorney General Francis Biddle, FDR called for a constitutional challenge to the poll tax. According to the president, the attorney general, as "the guardian of the Constitution," should test in court "unreasonable restrictions" imposed by states "on universal suffrage." After all, as FDR put it, "in the poll tax States a very large number of whites, as well as Negroes, are, in effect, denied the right to vote." To him, such action by those states seemed unconstitutional. (The memo apparently provoked enough concern about its potential political repercussions that a White House staff member asked the president whether he wanted it destroyed after it was returned from the Justice Department. Instead, Biddle kept a copy and twenty years later put it in his autobiography—were others destroyed?).[63]

Thus, beginning in FDR's second term, his judicial policy also sought to disrupt southern politics by attempting to create a new legal order that challenged the traditional localized structure of the American party system and emphasized a more inclusive democratic process. In doing so, the Roosevelt administration endeavored to construct legal doctrine that fit with the president's institutional program, namely, a style of interpretation that protected individual rights and liberties and advanced the theory of judicial deference toward the executive branch (so that it could properly craft policies to meet national needs). In helping to create what would become the Supreme

Court's institutional mission, the administration employed the ideas of theorists in the legal realism movement and the learned lessons of practitioners seeking to advance the rights of both organized labor and African Americans.

The reason why presidents look to the judiciary as means for securing their constitutional vision is best explained through comments made by and about President Nixon. On the domestic scene, Nixon stressed that "there is probably no more important legacy that a President of the United States can leave . . . than his appointments to the Supreme Court."[64] Second in importance only to foreign affairs, writes Nixon's assistant John Ehrlichman, was the president's "ability to change the domestic situation through the creation of a long-lived strict-constructionist Supreme Court, composed of young Justices who would sit and rule in [his] own image. . . . If he could get his Supreme Court nominees confirmed by the Senate, fundamental domestic changes could be effected by the third branch of the Federal Government." The Nixon example, then, underscores why presidents devote so much attention to changing the courts. In comparison to legislative achievement—which is often difficult to carry out, and which subsequent presidents and Congresses can wipe away—constitutional change is more permanent. Simply stated, constitutional revolutions are both rare and enduring.

Understanding presidential motivations underlying the construction of an administration's judicial policy is only part of the presidency-focused approach. It tells us nothing about which presidents will most effectively influence judicial interpretation. Here, Stephen Skowronek's alternative model to the study of the presidency—presented in *The Politics Presidents Make*—is essential. Skowronek studies the presidency by focusing on institutional/structural factors and by viewing it as the most disruptive institution in American politics. For him, a paradox is built into the institution because presidents enter office seeking to put their imprint on the nation's institutions and policies, but must still abide by the constitutional command of executive leadership. As a result, "presidential action in history is politicized by the order-shattering, order-affirming, and order-creating impulses inherent in the institution itself." Presidents with the most "political authority," like FDR, lead during a "politics of reconstruction" and have the greatest opportunity to institute change because they face a highly vulnerable pre-existing institutional order. Presidents "in all other situations" possess less authority and therefore have varying degrees of difficulty in marking "their moments in history and refashion[ing] legitimacy on their own terms." The presidency, then, "is a battering ram." Those who have been most successful have not necessarily been the most skillful, but rather "have been the best situated to use it forthrightly as such."[65]

The presidency-focused approach, then, understands that—by the nature of the office they command—presidents will seek to shape or secure a particular type of judicial interpretation. Those with the most political authority will be most effective since they will possess the greatest freedom over their electoral coalition while still advancing their legislative concerns and implementing their constitutional visions. In other words, their election coalitions will be cohesive, and their legislative measures and constitutional visions will have great credibility, despite the fact that the preexisting regime will most likely still be represented on the Supreme Court. Presidents with less authority will fall into two camps. The first will have little desire to install a new institutional order, preferring instead to advance or revive the established political arrangement. The second will have less influence on judicial interpretation since their ability to attract voters with their judicial policy will be limited by a fear of a legislative backlash, likely due in part to the presence of divided government. In addition, the constitutional vision of these presidents will likely be under consistent challenge since the preexisting institutional order will retain some level of force. Any attempt to install it on the Court will likely harm their electoral chances and result in a confrontation with the Congress.[66]

Thus, if provided the opportunity, presidents can significantly influence the shape of the legal order for years to come. This influence will be greatest on those issues most central to a president's judicial policy. On more distant political concerns, previously constructed legal principles or the unconstructed policy preferences of the justices may dominate the decision-making process, as alternative models of Supreme Court decision making posit (see chapter 7).

To be sure, the presidency-focused approach does not assume the success of a president's judicial policy. Clearly, the wisdom of a president's individual choices will affect the endurance of his judicial legacy. In other words, a president situated to reconstruct the courts may miss or misuse the opportunity the contours of the political time present him. On the other hand, a poorly situated president may affect judicial doctrine more profoundly than expected. To assess the level of success, it is necessary to analyze the Supreme Court's opinions and then work backward to examine whether or not a causal connection exists between them and a president's judicial policy. It is also possible to analyze a president's policy and predict its effect on later judicial interpretation. Even if successful, however, a president's policy toward the judiciary will not dictate the detail and timing of judicial action. The justices will work out these matters. Instead, it will help forge the institutional mission of the Court.

Influencing the shape of such a mission is no small matter. Scholars from a range of disciplines have displayed the powerful effects of environment on individuals. Similarly, new institutionalists argue that institutional environment strongly influences individual behavior in the political world. As Skowronek writes, "institutions do not simply constrain or channel the actions of self-interested individuals, they prescribe actions, construct motives, and assert legitimacy . . . any a priori notion of individual interest will very quickly succumb to historically derived and institutionally embedded rationalities of action."[67]

Overview of the Analysis

With the presidency-focused approach defined, I analyze — through a detailed examination of FDR's judicial policy — the development of a rights-expanding approach toward the law within the Roosevelt administration and discuss its effect on the Supreme Court's decision making. The three pillars of this policy were reconstructive legislation, appointments to the federal courts, and Justice Department efforts to extend federal protection of civil rights. My analysis reveals an active attempt by the administration to shape court decisions that not only advanced the civil rights of African Americans but transformed the role of the federal government in securing rights and liberties for all Americans. In other words, by exploring the three presidential motivations in the construction of this judicial policy, I uncover one of the mainsprings of constitutional change in mid-twentieth-century America, revealing the political/institutional origins of the Court's civil rights decisions and providing more complete answers to the three questions raised earlier. I do so by focusing on how the Roosevelt administration transformed the mission of the Court following the "constitutional revolution of 1937," making it into an advocate of what I refer to as rights-centered liberalism.[68]

Given New Deal jurisprudence's penchant toward deference, it is highly unlikely that the Court would have trod a progressive civil rights trail without the support of the executive branch. The Roosevelt justices were intimately aware of the institutional weakness of the judicial branch, its lack of the power of either the purse or the sword. Many of them had been FDR's field generals in his war against the "old" Court and understood that without the support of the executive their actions would be as problematic as were those of their anti–New Deal predecessors. In other words, along with a commitment to rights-centered liberalism, deference toward the executive was a central component of the Court's institutional mission as well. This combination resulted in a Roosevelt Court that was not only sympathetic to civil rights claims, but one that was constructed to be instructed by the executive branch on race. Once constituted, moreover, the Court's institutional mission found support in both the Truman and Eisenhower administrations. It reached its full expression in *Brown*.

In developing this argument, I take the reader on a tour of the Roosevelt administration's judicial policy. This tour is that of a skydiver's view, beginning with an examination of the union between the broad movements of rights-centered liberalism and legal realism and ending with an analysis of specific Supreme Court civil rights decisions. To preview, I argue that, while the 1932 election may have created an opportunity for constitutional change, it did not presage a revolution in the judiciary's attitude toward individual rights. Instead, the Court's institutional mission of the 1940s and early 1950s was a consequence of Democratic Party and institutional politics. As I show, a variety of forces influenced the development of this mission, but the combination of FDR's party leadership and his pursuit of the modern presidency — each defined by the three presidential motivations and shaped by his conclusion that southern democracy was inconsistent with his vision for the nation — ensured that the ideal of a more inclusive democracy was woven into the fiber of the Court's midcentury doctrine.

I begin in chapter 2 by focusing on the rights-advocacy groups that initially drove the movement to expand civil rights and liberties protection at the federal level. These groups included industrial labor unions, the NAACP, and legal reformers known as legal realists. Although each had reason to expect that their cause would garner more attention in the new administration, as I display, during FDR's first two years, social reform often took a back seat to the economic recovery of the nation. While both labor and legal realists enjoyed increased influence in New Deal Washington, their ideas for employing law to produce social change often found little sympathy in the Roosevelt White House. A turning point came when the Supreme Court struck down the heart of FDR's first New Deal. After this "Black Monday" in May 1935, the president was clearly more committed — in part through his support of the Wagner Act — to reconstituting the federal judiciary so that it would no longer be an overwhelming obstacle to progressive reform.

In chapter 3, I explain how this commitment reached new heights with the introduction of the Court-packing plan. Countering conventional wisdom, I argue that FDR's plan was not simply designed to "constitutionalize" the New Deal, but was rather part of a larger institutional program that would expand the influence of the presidency by ending enduring alliances between the Court's doctrine and certain sectional interests represented in Congress. For civil rights, the most important of these alliances was the one between the Court and the South. Given that the Court had for years provided constitutional cover for the South's system of white supremacy through decisions like *Plessy v. Ferguson,* southerners in Congress were openly skeptical of FDR's intentions in proposing a high bench of fifteen. Put simply, FDR's institutional design for a modern presidency threatened southerners' sense of security over the future legality of segregation. I argue that together with other forces opposed to the president's constitutional vision, southerners helped bring down the Court-packing plan. This argument challenges traditional interpretations of the plan's failure as the result of presidential mismanagement.

In chapter 4, I begin my focus on the construction of a reformulated federal judiciary by examining the creation of the Roosevelt Supreme Court, the second of the administration's three-pillared judicial policy. Here, I show that FDR's nominees were generally committed to rights-centered liberalism and legal realism. I also examine the politics surrounding each of FDR's nine appointments to the Court. In doing so, I explore the connection between FDR's attempt to purge (mostly southern) conservatives in the 1938 Democratic Party primaries and his choices for the Court (eight of which took place between 1937 and 1941). Finally, I consider the manner in which southern filibusters against civil rights legislation — especially the NAACP-supported antilynching bill — contributed to Roosevelt administration efforts to advance the federal protection of rights in the courts.

In chapter 5, I analyze the final pillar of the administration's policy toward the judiciary, namely, the Roosevelt Justice Department's program to extend federal protection of individual rights, most importantly for African Americans. In doing so, I pay particular attention to the creative efforts of the Justice Department's newly created Civil Rights Section (CRS) to revive — at times in cooperation with the NAACP — "dead-letter" Reconstruction-era civil rights laws through controversial prosecutions. I focus specifically on the Justice Department efforts in the areas of the white primary, the poll tax, lynching, and police brutality. I argue that through these prosecutions, the CRS aided in constructing rights-expanding norms on the Supreme Court. In developing this argument, I also consider the extent to which World War II enabled the Roosevelt administration to carry out a campaign in the courts that sought to make American democracy more inclusive and to punish those responsible for violent attacks against black Americans in the South.

In chapter 6, I analyze the activities of the Truman and Eisenhower administrations with regard to the expansion of African American rights. Here, I evaluate the importance of both domestic and international influences on the civil rights positions of these two administrations, with a special focus on their judicial policies. In doing so, I join in a scholarly debate about the importance of the ideological confrontation of the cold war in pressuring these administrations to advocate an end to *Plessy.* I also consider how the precedent set by the Roosevelt administration affected the participation of the Truman and Eisenhower Justice Departments in NAACP-sponsored school segregation cases before the Supreme Court.

In chapter 7, I return to the three questions about *Brown v. Board of Education* that frame the book. I begin by describing how conventional explanations of the origins of Supreme Court decisions would answer these three southern-inspired questions. Then, by drawing on the substantial literature about the development of the *Brown* decision from inside the Court, I answer the same questions in my own terms. In doing so, I reach conclusions about the influence of the judicial policies of the Roosevelt, Truman, and Eisenhower administrations on the high bench's institutional mission, a mission that drove its decision to constitutionally dismantle southern segregation. I conclude by considering the usefulness of the presidency-focused approach for understanding the origins of Supreme Court decisions of other eras.

TWO   The Incongruities of Reform

*Rights-Centered Liberalism and Legal Realism
in the Early New Deal Years*

Franklin Delano Roosevelt took command of the White House reins
with an abundance of political authority. This high level of authority
was the result of a severe legitimacy crisis of the preexisting governing order. That order placed the judiciary front and center; and for the better part of two generations federal courts regulated the nation's economic
development based on a particular conception of liberty that virtually can-
onized the protection of property rights. Aided by a two-party system designed to meet the interests of state and local organizations and ill-suited for
progressive action at the national level, federal jurists routinely nullified legislative attempts at social reform. Depression, however, utterly destroyed
faith in that manner of governing the economy and the nation. As a reconstructive president, FDR was at least theoretically empowered with the capacity to transform the judiciary in a fashion that advanced his ideal institutional arrangement — what I call his constitutional vision. This vision, as
it emerged over time, sought to place the presidency at the center of a restructured national government with unprecedented power and a commitment to expanding statutory rights and securing individual rights. In this
vein, in his notable 1932 campaign address to the Commonwealth Club,
FDR spoke of the need to revise the nation's "social contract" by calling for
"the development of an economic declaration of rights, an economic constitutional order." While assuring listeners that the government "must" respect "old" individual liberties "at all hazards," to him, this "re-definition" of
economic rights was essential to meet the demands of "a changing and
growing social order."[1]

But while incoming presidents may have blueprints in hand and ideas in
mind, they do not enter office with a solution to every problem, an answer
to every question. Initial promises are easily stated, but lasting legacies must
be made. Here, President Roosevelt was no different. If fact, more than most
presidents, FDR showed a willingness to experiment with a wide range of
policies during the early years of his administration before settling on a more

coherent governing philosophy. In this chapter, I examine this process of policy development during FDR's first term with respect to the new judicial order that emerged later in his administration. In doing so, I show how those groups most interested in attacking the preexisting judicial order often failed to realize high levels of influence in the opening years of the Roosevelt presidency. Instead, the president appeared more committed to appealing to a broad coalition of constituents in an effort to ensure legislative success and return the nation to economic prosperity. For the administration's judicial policy, this stance translated into an unwillingness to challenge the essence of the Supreme Court's philosophy and nearly a cross-your-fingers hope that the justices would let the New Deal stand.

But timidity no longer held sway once the Court constitutionally uprooted FDR's sapling of a recovery program in May 1935. In response, the president pushed through Congress a string of legislation that centered on the constitutionally questionable Wagner and Social Security Acts, seemingly setting up a confrontation with the High Court. To be sure, the enactment of the "second" New Deal did not ensure a complete turn toward a vision for the nation that emphasized new statutory rights and restored individual rights, and not all legal reformers welcomed such a shift.[2] Rather, it began the movement away from centralized planning toward rights-centered liberalism. While some have described this shift as the "taming" of New Deal liberalism, for the Roosevelt administration's judicial policy it meant a more coherent attack on the Court's continuing capacity to control the domestic political agenda.[3] In addition, it further linked labor and African American leaders in their efforts to ensure federal protection of basic individual rights and liberties, even if it did not unite them in support of the Wagner Act.

In examining this shift toward rights-centered liberalism, my focus is threefold. First, I explore the early New Deal efforts at legal reform to uncover the origins of the mission that later committed the judiciary to expanding the rights of black Americans. Here, I am especially interested in the emerging union between rights-centered liberalism and legal realism. Clearly, in these years, the focus of legal reform was not on safeguarding the rights of a racial minority but on securing a new level of influence for labor. Still, to many in the reform community, a common vision of the proper role of individual rights in a democracy linked these two efforts. Second, I display the importance of rights-advocacy groups outside of government and legal reformers inside of government in pressuring the administration to pursue a rights-centered approach to social, political, and economic change.

On this score, the role reformers played in challenging the cautiousness of the Justice Department was particularly significant given its later importance as an aggressive advocate of civil rights reform. Finally, I lay the foundation for my argument that FDR's commitment to the federal expansion and protection of rights hinged on the state of his vexing relationship with the South. My focus is similar to that of scholars who have identified the South's role in limiting the progressiveness of New Deal legislation.[4] I argue that FDR's interest in a restructured judiciary ripened as he moved toward a rights-centered agenda. In other words, as the underlying motivations of his administration's judicial policy shifted, his willingness to surrender to southern interests lessened significantly.

My larger argument about the Roosevelt administration's eventual commitment to protecting African American rights emphasizes the incongruities of reform and therefore necessarily challenges some conventional explanations about the importance of the 1932 election on later judicial interpretation. I begin with a discussion of this challenge.

The 1932 Election and the Expansion of Federally Protected Rights

Many political scientists have argued or implied that the Court's civil rights decisions were part of the dramatic consequences of the 1932 election.[5] While that realigning election clearly created a significant opportunity for constitutional change, scholars who jump to this conclusion make two faulty assumptions. First, they apparently assume that the election swept into power an administration firmly committed to reformulating the judiciary to protect individual rights for all Americans. During the 1932 election, however, there was little indication a Roosevelt administration would dramatically transform the nature of judicial interpretation. Nor did the New York governor eagerly employ anti–Supreme Court rhetoric to attract the votes of those most affected by the past generation's judicial decisions. Rather, Roosevelt ran a rather cautious campaign. Lacking any detailed program for recovery, his bid for the White House was largely void of the crusading progressive characteristics that would later describe his administration.

FDR's most controversial comment about the Court came toward the end of the campaign when he veered from his prepared text during a speech in Baltimore. The speech had ironically focused on the Four Horsemen of the Republican leadership — "Destruction, Delay, Deceit, and Despair" — and had called for Roosevelt to read: "After March 4, 1929, the Republican Party was in complete control of all branches of the Federal Government —

the Executive, the Senate, the House of Representatives." But the words on the page were not enough for this enthusiastic candidate, so he continued. "And, I might add for good measure, the Supreme Court as well."[6]

The fallout from the comment was quick and sharp. Republicans attacked FDR's "demagogue" appeal, calling it a "slur" on the Court and adding that "to weaken respect" for that institution "is to destroy the foundations of law and order." Roosevelt's opponent, President Herbert Hoover, questioned the "deeper implications" of the statement, asking, "Does [it] express his intention, by his appointments or otherwise, to attempt to reduce that tribunal to an instrument of party policy and political action for sustaining such doctrines as he may bring with him?"[7] For his part, FDR steered cleared of the GOP's rhetorical reef, telling one of the "ghost" writers of the original speech — even before Hoover's criticism — that he was not prepared to apologize for his addendum to the Baltimore address. The "ghost," whom FDR would later make a Supreme Court justice, was Jimmy Byrnes, then South Carolina's junior senator.[8]

The fact that FDR's most important statement about the Court came as something of a campaign blunder reveals his reluctance to directly challenge the judiciary as a candidate for the presidency. The fact that Jimmy Byrnes was a speechwriter and strategist aboard the campaign train in the race's final days displays the importance of the South in FDR's rise in presidential politics — a South not unsympathetic to much of the Court's doctrine. Significantly, FDR had relied on southerners to gain the presidential nomination and to secure his election to the presidency. In years leading up to his nomination, he had been, as historian Harvard Sitkoff describes, "a loyal Democrat, a Northern politician in a party that was overwhelmingly Southern." As its assistant secretary during the Wilson administration, he had participated, without objection, "in the Jim-Crowing of the Navy." As governor of New York, he had "ignored blacks in appointments and legislation." As a candidate for the presidency, he had focused on reuniting the once solid South rather than appealing to the small African American vote. In turn, despite his overwhelming victory, Al Smith — the 1928 Democratic presidential candidate — earned a greater share of the black vote in his devastating loss to Hoover than did FDR four years later.[9] Such a record did not bode well for advocates of rights-centered legal reform once the new president entered the White House. As the ACLU's Roger Baldwin noted on the eve of the 1932 election, "whoever is elected on November 8th will not make much difference to the cause of civil liberty."[10] Indeed, as I document in this chapter, in the early years of his administration President Roosevelt did not display a strong desire to restructure the courts to extend individual rights. That desire emerged later in his presidency, fed by FDR's need to manage divisions within the Democratic Party and his own sense of how judicial reform fit into his constitutional vision of a modern presidency. Simply stated, a single election did not settle the product of the so-called constitutional revolution of 1937. History is rarely so neat.

Scholars who stress the dramatic impact of the 1932 election also assume that there had been no attempt by the political branches to challenge the Supreme Court's doctrine before FDR's historic victory. But there had been such an effort, one that was notably bipartisan in tone. The Court's armor had most dramatically shown its cracks in 1930. In that year, President Hoover, seeking to build on gains made in the South during the 1928 election, nominated Judge John J. Parker of North Carolina to fill a High Court vacancy. Despite knowing that progressives were emboldened by their near defeat of Charles Evans Hughes's nomination to the Court's center chair barely a month before, Hoover selected the controversial Parker. Hughes, who had left the Court after six years of service as an associate justice to run for the presidency in 1916, returned to the high bench after the Senate confirmed him by a vote of fifty-two to twenty-six. It was the closest Senate vote for a chief justice nominee since the confirmation of Roger Taney in 1836.[11] Moreover, according to the *New York Times*, "it was strikingly clear that all, or nearly all, the twenty-six Senators who voted against him subscribed to the doctrine that our highest tribunal must be composed, in greater part, if not wholly, of men who would interpret the laws in a spirit that was not influenced entirely by strictly legalistic reasoning."[12] In other words, the wear and tear of legal formalism (explained below) was visibly on display during the Hughes confirmation. With the selection of the relatively unknown Parker, Democrats and progressive Republicans again sought to use the confirmation process as an opportunity to attack the Court's doctrine. As the battle took shape, opponents focused mainly on Parker's attitude toward labor and African Americans, but as one editorial noted, "in reality [it was] an attack upon the Supreme Court" itself.[13]

From the standpoint of the array of interests stung by the Court's doctrine, certain components of Parker's record symbolized the justices' hostility toward progressive reform. For example, as a judge on the U.S. Court of Appeals for the Fourth Circuit, Parker had supported the Supreme Court's *Hitchman* ruling when he enjoined the United Mine Workers (UMW) from unlawful organizing activities and upheld the companies' use of the yellow-dog contract. As a candidate for governor of North Carolina in 1920, he had proclaimed, "the participation of the Negro in politics is a source of evil and danger to both races."[14] In the end, one vote made the difference in his nomination. With seventeen Republicans joining twenty-three Democrats and one Farmer-Labor Party member, the Senate rejected the forty-five-year-old North Carolinian forty-one to thirty-nine.[15] Of the thirty-nine supporters, ten were Democrats. Of those ten, nine were southerners.[16] In short, the Parker vote showed that the question of what type of jurist should sit on the Court split both major parties and left some southern Democrats wondering whether the Senate had "decreed that any man who holds that the Negro has not the capacity to direct governmental affairs shall not serve on the Supreme Court."[17]

As the leader of this disparate Democratic Party, then, FDR's election did not portend a revolution in the judiciary's attitude toward individual rights, especially for African Americans. While the new president certainly came from the progressive wing of his party, he would still need to depend on the mainly southern leadership in the Democratic Congress to secure legislative success. Moreover, if the Parker nomination were any indication of future behavior, some southern Democratic senators seemed perfectly willing to split with their party to ensure the Supreme Court continued its antagonism toward organized labor and African American interests. Electorally, with the black vote seemingly in secure Republican hands, it appeared that FDR had little to gain by appealing to African American concerns and much to lose from the southern base of his own party. Finally, on the personal side, Roosevelt displayed little appreciation or sympathy for the plight of black Americans.

Yet by midway through FDR's third term, federal courts, along with their newly developed willingness to defer to the executive branch, were firmly committed to enhancing federal protection of civil rights and liberties — a coupling that was essential to the Supreme Court's later effort to revamp civil rights law. In 1942, as noted in chapter 1, the president himself sought to take advantage of this coupling by urging his attorney general to challenge state-imposed limitations, such as literacy tests and the poll tax, "on universal suffrage." By the final year of his presidency, the Justice Department was calling on the Supreme Court to certify its effort to "federalize" protection against police brutality and lynching, two violent pillars of the South's system of white supremacy. As part of that effort, the head of the department's Civil Rights Section emphasized: "Until minority rights are fully protected by both State and Federal governments, the Constitution which it is our special duty to uphold has not been made effective and the American dream has not been realized." Just four years after FDR's death, the Truman Justice Department asked the justices to put an end to segregation.[18] Five years later, the Court unanimously obliged. How did this Democratic transformation on race occur? And why was it aimed at the courts? In carrying out this conversion, why did federal judges and justices adopt tenets of legal realism, given FDR's obvious doubts about this reform movement? In this sense, what role did the president play in legal reform? And how did legal realism fit with the general pursuit of rights-centered liberalism? With these questions in mind, I explore the path of rights-centered legal reform during FDR's first term. As the story unfolds, the image that emerges is far more complicated than some conventional explanations about the origins of the Supreme Court's civil rights decisions suggest.

Transforming Ideas into Action: Legal Realism, Rights, and the New Deal

The account of the Roosevelt administration's commitment to securing rights for African Americans begins with the expansion of federally protected rights generally and with the development of an intellectual movement known as legal realism. Legal realism was the name attached to the work of a group of scholars who emerged in the early 1930s by offering a radical critique of the law. In issuing their challenge, realists rebelled against a nineteenth-century system known as legal formalism. As Edward Purcell explains, together with "a vague belief in natural law and a rigid theory of precedent, [formalists] claimed that reasoning proceeded syllogistically from rules and precedents that had been clearly defined historically and logically, through the particular facts of a case, to a clear decision. The function of the judge was to discover analytically the proper rules and precedents involved and to apply them to the case as first premises. Once he had done that, the judge could decide the case with certainty and uniformity."[19] To realists, however, by the 1920s this system of law had become too overburdened by societal changes to work in any logically coherent fashion. Law had become a rigid set of abstractions that were ambiguous, dangerous, and unchanging. Instead of using law to maintain social cohesiveness, those in power were using it as a legitimizing and coercive force to maintain the status quo. Jerome Frank — one of the cofounders of the realist movement — offered the harshest criticism of formalism, calling it "legal fundamentalism" and chastising it as a religion showing its "childish desire" for "the absurdly unrealistic notion that law is, or can be made, entirely and definitely predictable."[20] Along with this challenge to the predictability and objectivity of legal "rules," realists questioned the ability of formalists to properly attain the "facts" of a particular case. In their drive to have law better reflect the realities of American society, they in turn championed social scientific inquiry as a device that would provide a more accurate understanding of "social facts" and enable lawyers and judges to be guided by the social consequences of their actions.

While realists offered a strong critique of the inconsistencies of formalism, absent an alliance with political forces their writings would likely have amounted to little more than words on paper. Realist ideas gained prominence because they spoke to an ever-increasing frustration that progressive groups, most importantly labor unions, faced when they confronted a judiciary defined by formalist doctrine. In many ways, as the Parker fight displayed, the perceived stubbornness of the old legal order gave rise to the progressive movement against it. In particular, both realist scholars and union leaders attacked the formalist-dominated judiciary because — by invalidating both state and federal legislation — it had for years stifled labor's successful efforts in the political arena.[21] To many of the best young legal minds in America, law had become anything but neutral, natural, and apolitical. To many workers struggling to make a living, law represented an overwhelming obstacle to a better life.

Realist ideas fit well with an administration confronting an old orthodoxy and willing to experiment in creating a new one. Consequently, at the dawn of the New Deal many budding realists joined the Roosevelt administration, including Jerome Frank. For them, as Frank put it in a 1933 speech, "*if the old principles, which the high priests of the Old Deal worshipped, dictated the unhappiness that we call a depression, then . . . those principles are not divine but Satanic, barbarous and cruel.*" New principles, designed "*to produce happiness and security,*" would take their place in the form of the New Deal. President Roosevelt in turn was the "master" realist — "a great leader . . . trying to give the forgotten man a decent life, free of gnawing insecurity and with adequate leisure."[22]

Frank's acclaim for FDR displays the hope many realists felt with the onset of the Roosevelt presidency. But while welcomed onto many New Deal staffs, the president kept these young realists at arm's length during his first two years in office. More than advocating a new method of legal reasoning, as Frank's words suggest, many realists possessed a progressive streak that emphasized employing the law to advance the plight of the powerless. Yet, at the time, FDR's own sense of pragmatism pushed him to pursue economic recovery rather than commit to the kind of social and legal transformation that realism seemed to require. As noted New Deal historian William Leuchtenburg writes, in these years "Roosevelt presented himself not as the paladin of liberalism but as father to all the people . . . the unifier of interests and the harmonizer of divergent ideologies."[23] The result was a Roosevelt administration approach to the law that drew on realist ideas to implement and defend its recovery program, but not to ignite any systematic social reform.

In fact, following his landslide victory in which he captured 57.4 percent of the popular vote and all but six states, any concern FDR might have had over how the Court would treat his New Deal did not translate into a unified approach for dealing with a judiciary with a penchant for upending progressive programs. In writing legislation, implementing it, and arguing for its validity in court, the administration essentially had three possibilities to pursue. The first option emphasized the urgency of the emergency, a depression akin to a war, and implied that all would return to normal once the recovery was complete. The second possibility called for some revision of the existing legal order, as demanded by an "objective," disinterested review of the facts. Most importantly, this option called for the administration to emphasize its need to respond to the realities of a national economy by asserting that old formalist formulas like that of a "current of commerce" required revision. Finally, the administration could adopt a style of legal reform that endorsed some of the more radical ideas of legal realism. In general, through their critique of judge-made law, realists emphasized judicial restraint and result-oriented action by legislatures and administrative agencies better equipped with the social scientific expertise to solve societal problems. However, the more radical realists were "committed not to mere detached study but devoted to action on the basis of their tentative judgments." Inherent in their challenge to the old formalist alignment of courts and corporations was an eagerness to restructure the American economy: to rid, as Frank put it, the "profit system" of its "*evil* aspects" so that it can "*be tried, for the first time, as a consciously directed means of promoting the general good.*"[24]

Thus, while realism had many strands as an intellectual movement—almost one for every realist, noted one observer[25]—to many in early New Deal Washington, realism represented another form of political liberalism. In time, however, the demands of practical politics—especially as the Court dismantled the first New Deal—would require realists to de-emphasize their calls for radical reform. As the next sections show, as practitioners of New Deal policy, realists in the Roosevelt administration ultimately moved closer toward advocating a stronger conception of rights, joining other New Dealers in pursuing a more rights-centered agenda. Although this union was somewhat contradictory for realists, who in theory stressed remedies over rights, it fit within the scope of the rights-centered liberalism of the second New Deal.[26] This collection of legislation, which FDR eventually championed, highlighted advancing traditional individual rights by reformulating the definition of rights to meet the demands of an industrialized America. In other words, unlike the original conception of individual rights in America, which sought to limit federal power, the rights-centered second New Deal endeavored to employ an energetic centralized state to empower individuals by enlarging and protecting their rights in the pursuit of a more democratic society. For instance, along with expanding the rights of workers, successful implementation of the Wagner Act required that the government first secure the constitutional rights of speech, press, and assembly. Put simply, without the federal government actively protecting those traditional rights and liberties upon which the Wagner Act rested, opponents could easily render it impotent.

The willingness of realists to adopt a rights-centered approach highlights a central component of their critique. More than an effort to install a new legal method, realism challenged the wisdom of the *Lochner*-era doctrine and sought to diminish the role of the judiciary in constitutional construction. In this sense, the realist design sought to delegitimize constitutional authority based on the content of what was being protected (at the time, property rights) in favor of constitutional authority based on democratic sovereignty. In other words, content mattered less than who controlled the decision-making process — a position perfectly suited for a president seeking to take command of a domestic policy arena previously dominated by the judiciary.

Unmet Expectations in the Era of Experimentation (1933–35)

In exploring the trials and tribulations legal realists and rights-centered liberals faced in advancing their form of reform from 1933 to 1935, I show how, when push came to shove, their projects usually fell victim to the demands of conservatives within the Democratic Party. In this sense, the emergency and revision models of legal reform were the favored approaches of the early New Deal. To display FDR's desire for conciliatory change at this time, I discuss three examples where the winds of realist-type reform subsided in the face of conservative resistance (in the name of the business community and conservative southerners). In each of these examples, reformers incorporated —

even emphasized—the advocacy of rights expansion in their pursuit of social change. First, I deal with the difficulty reformers had in convincing the president and the Justice Department to maintain a strong commitment to the protection of workers' rights through section 7(a) of the National Industrial Recovery Act (NIRA) of 1933. More than demonstrating FDR's early resistance to union demands, this example highlights labor's growing influence in Washington as it developed grassroots support—particularly among industrial workers—to affect electoral politics and potentially disrupt the president's plans for economic recovery. Second, I examine an unsuccessful attempt by legal reformers to extend the rights of sharecroppers through executive action. It is perhaps the best example of the limits on legal reform—constricted by the powerful reach of southern senators—during the first two years of the Roosevelt administration. Finally, I discuss the difficulties the NAACP and other rights-advocacy groups faced when attempting to convince the Roosevelt White House and Justice Department to pursue the cause of extending African American rights. The details of this interaction display not only the administration's resistance, but the NAACP's aggressiveness in pursuing its cause. In exploring these events, I demonstrate both the New Deal's break from the previous order and the *beginnings* of the process of what Karen Orren and Stephen Skowronek call "regime formation," meaning "the consolidation of new governing arrangements."[27]

The Significance of Section 7(a)

Section 7(a) of the NIRA emerged out of a presidential-inspired attempt to forge a consensus on a plan that would restore the type of government-business cooperation that existed during World War I. Primarily concerned with eliminating cutthroat competition, the drafters of the industrial recovery bill focused on an approach that would relax antitrust laws and install a system of federal regulation over production and prices. In the words of General Hugh Johnson, the future director of the National Recovery Administration (NRA), the legislation was to create a system of "government supervision looking to a balanced economy as opposed to the murderous doctrine of savage and wolfish individualism." To form an impressive coalition of support, the NIRA contained something for nearly everyone. For its part, labor got section 7(a), with language designed to guarantee workers their right to "organize and bargain collectively through representatives of their own choosing, and . . . free from the interference, restraint, or coercion of employers."[28]

As with legislative successes of the progressive era, following the passage of section 7(a), labor leaders once again proclaimed that American workers had finally received their "Emancipation Proclamation"—their "Magna Charta."[29] But the UMW's John L. Lewis and the American Federation of Labor's (AFL's) William Green were well aware of the ambiguity of section 7(a), the assuaging political atmosphere that led to its inclusion in the NIRA, and the hostility many employers harbored toward it. They also understood that lingering questions about the NIRA's constitutionality exacerbated concerns about section 7(a)'s usefulness for the labor movement. Put simply, it was clear to them—as well as to leaders on the other side on the labor-management divide—that the actual interpretation of the section would mean more than its enactment.

For Lewis and the UMW—the union that spearheaded the drive to include a right to collective bargaining in the NIRA—labor would have to boost its political influence in order to get a sympathetic reading of section 7(a).[30] As the *United Mine Workers Journal* put it, "The bill will not be self-enforcing . . . [it] will only be helpful to those who help themselves." In turn, as head of the UMW, Lewis launched an organizing drive to increase membership. Even before FDR signed the NIRA into law, UMW organizers ventured out into the coalfields of West Virginia, Pennsylvania, Illinois, and Kentucky, in response to Lewis's charge to act quickly "before the employers woke up to the fact that there were ways of getting around the law." Given the temper of the times, organizers—with vague and intentionally misleading slogans like: "The President wants you to Unionize" and "The United States Government has said Labor Must Organize"—had little trouble signing up miners.[31] In the two years following section 7(a)'s passage, the UMW's membership rose more than 400 percent, from a little over one hundred thousand to well over four hundred thousand.[32]

But while the president of the UMW was eager to see the forces of industrial unionism rapidly expand, the president of the United States was not so sure. At this point in his presidency, FDR viewed developing a labor policy as secondary to economic recovery and was "somewhat perturbed at being cast in the role of midwife of industrial unionism."[33] Indeed, driven by a concern that labor might use its newly won rights to retard the recovery, Roosevelt did little throughout this period to secure a Magna Carta for workers.[34] To many progressive legal reformers, the president's attitude displayed a disappointing disregard for the theory that guaranteeing workers their rights would transform industrial relations and ensure a permanent recovery. To them, the best option for the administration lay in ensuring workers their right to bargain collectively, thereby marrying the ideals of rights-centered liberalism with the realist desire for a cure to labor unrest. To FDR, even if he preferred, the cleavages of the Democratic Party and the demands of a depressed economy did not allow for such a risky plan at this time.

Nevertheless, the growing number of strikes during the summer months of 1933—partially provoked by the administration's actions—did force the president to take steps to find a meaning of 7(a) suitable to labor.[35] In response to what would become the greatest strike wave in the United States since 1920 and the NRA's apparent inability to prevent or settle them, FDR formed the National Labor Board (NLB) on August 5, 1933. By using an "interest-group approach"—the board was composed of three representatives from industry, three from labor (including Green and Lewis), and New York's Senator Robert Wagner—President Roosevelt intended to settle labor disputes through mediation. After some initial success, however, the NLB, with a vague mandate, undefined procedures, and few enforcement powers beyond appeals to public opinion, quickly found itself essentially irrelevant. With a design centered on cooperation, the board simply stumbled when the more confrontational device of litigation was required to force delinquent employers to follow section 7(a). Moreover, it was unable to enforce its orders in court without the assistance of the Justice Department, whose "lawyers viewed the NIRA with ill-concealed distaste." In the end, the NLB simply failed to intimidate those employers who violated the law.[36]

In an attempt to simultaneously hold the board together and please disgruntled union leaders, FDR did issue an executive order supporting the prolabor principles of majority rule and exclusive representation on February 1, 1934. Taken together, these principles ensured that an "unscrupulous employer [did not have] an opportunity to play one group against another constantly," thereby undermining the collective bargaining process.[37] In fact, the president's failure to take such a stance earlier had led to the rapid rise in company unions. This in turn provoked labor leaders, who considered unions run under company supervision a form of "fake representation," to issue strike orders. FDR's newfound support for labor, however, did not last long. A short time later he altered course, endorsing the principle of minority representation in order to settle a strike in the automobile industry.[38] That shift effectively "sounded the death-knell for the NLB."[39] For soon after, "labor erupted." When employers interpreted the president's policy shift to settle the automobile strike as "a guarantee that they could avoid dealing with trade unions," labor leaders responded by again issuing strike orders.[40] Despite this result, FDR remained silent.

Instead, the president ordered administration lawyers to work with Congress to help draft what became Public Resolution 44, an agreement that sought to end the strikes by setting up a new labor board. Critics charged that FDR was conspiring with Republican and southern Democratic congressional leaders to use the resolution to squash the movement of Senator Wagner's Labor Disputes bill through Congress. Nevertheless, both houses passed the resolution.[41] And on July 9, 1934, the National Labor Relations Board (NLRB)—with Lloyd Garrison, the dean of the University of Wisconsin Law School, as its head—began operations.[42] Like the NLB, the NLRB was empowered to investigate controversies arising under section 7(a). Unlike their predecessors, however, the three members of this new board viewed their role not as mediators but as judges. While this change was a significant one, the new board still had to rely on the Justice Department to enforce its orders, a fact that soon proved detrimental to its work. Led by an unsympathetic Homer Cummings, the Justice Department resisted enforcing NLRB orders, signaling to employers that they could effectively ignore the board's will. The result, according to both Garrison and his replacement, Francis Biddle, was more strikes.[43]

At this point, with growing concerns about the NIRA's constitutionality, disputes over the administration's litigation campaign became immersed in the debate about the future direction of the New Deal. As usual, the Justice Department was on the side of caution, with the attorney general suggesting that he was unable to enforce the NLRB's orders (despite congressional and presidential language asserting otherwise). In turn, Biddle helped Senator Wagner push a revised Labor Disputes bill through Congress. Cummings and Justice Department lawyers countered by working with Senate Majority Leader Joe Robinson of Arkansas to first try to amend and then block Wagner's legislation, now known as the National Labor Relations bill.[44] As the battle waged on, labor's early struggle to secure the right to collective bargaining became an important influence on FDR's growing understanding of how a rights-centered approach fit into his maturing constitutional vision.

Ironically, the Supreme Court—with its 1935 decision striking down the NIRA—helped initiate the president's shift toward an agenda that emphasized rights-centered policies and realist ideas.[45] As explained below, after that decision in *Schechter*, FDR pursued a decidedly more progressive direction. To be sure, the Court's action was not the sole factor in shifting the focus of the Roosevelt administration's agenda. Progressive advances in the 1934 midterm elections, the continued threat of strikes, and FDR's desire to put in place a program more in line with his increasingly liberal aspirations for the 1936 election all contributed to the shape of the second New Deal.

Still, the judicial destruction of the first New Deal was critical to escalating the import of the union between legal realism and a rights-centered outlook in the formulation of the administration's judicial policy.

Recovery over Social Reform

Another failed attempt to advance the rights of labor by legal reformers during this period came from within the Agricultural Adjustment Administration (AAA). To be sure, when Jerome Frank arrived at the AAA with his realist perspective and hired a group of "experimentalists" from the best law schools in the country, aiding the farmer was not all he had in mind. The most telling example of his interest in achieving social reform through legal interpretation came when a group of Arkansas sharecroppers appealed to the AAA for support in their effort to unionize.

While always a concern to the progressives in the AAA, any action regarding the divisive issue of tenant labor threatened to disrupt their tenuous relationship with powerful southerners in Congress and with the many conservatives in their own agency. For instance, in September 1933 a young realist named Alger Hiss, on receiving widespread reports of fraud, attempted to send AAA rental checks for land taken out of cotton production directly to sharecroppers rather than to their landlords. In response, "Cotton Ed" Smith, the race-baiting senator from South Carolina, burst unexpectedly into the twenty-nine-year-old's office and announced: "You're going to send money to my niggers, instead of to me? . . . I'll take care of them."[46] While the AAA backed off its rental check scheme, it wasn't long before progressive reformers clashed again with conservatives both inside and outside the agency. This time the issue was tenant displacement. In particular, the controversy concerned the meaning of Section 7 of the 1934 and 1935 Cotton Acreage Reduction Contract. As the section read, producers should " insofar as possible, maintain . . . the normal number of tenants," and "shall permit all tenants to continue the occupancy of their houses" (rent-free). To replace a tenant, a producer would have to show that he was a "nuisance or a menace."[47]

Since the end of the Civil War, tenancy had grown year by year, as more and more farmers moved from ownership to dependency.[48] With few if any rights, miserable working conditions, and riddled with debt, sharecroppers lived in virtual peonage. Most of these workers rarely had more than a verbal agreement with their landlord and, therefore, usually worked in the quiet fear of being thrown off the farm if any conflict arose. Spurred on by the Socialist Party leader Norman Thomas, this environment gave rise to the Southern Tenant Farmers Union (STFU) and made a political controversy out of the AAA's definition of the ambiguous phrases of section 7. As a racially mixed group of thousands of sharecroppers from the cotton counties of Arkansas, the STFU elicited intimidation and evictions from landlords alarmed by its rapid growth. To combat the landlords' aggressive action, AAA progressives, led by Frank, challenged the legality of the evictions. Specifically, they charged that a landlord could not evict tenants who were on the farm at the time of the signing of the two-year AAA contract in 1933. As two of Frank's allies put it in a memo, "no 1933 tenant who wants to stay for the 1934–35 crop seasons shall be forced to leave, and no tenant shall have his status changed."[49]

Unfortunately for the progressives, conservatives who supported the landlords were the dominant group within the AAA. Led by Chester Davis, they asserted that membership in the STFU constituted "good reason" for eviction under the "nuisance" or "menace" clause of section 7. To them, the section did not require a landlord to keep the same tenants, just the same number of tenants. In the end, the dispute forced Agriculture Secretary Henry Wallace to choose between the two sides. Aware that Majority Leader Robinson's support was crucial for future AAA appropriations, Wallace concluded the reformers had gone too far. "I am convinced that from a legal point of view, they had nothing to stand on," he later noted, "and that they allowed their social preconceptions to lead them into something which was not only indefensible from a practical agricultural point of view but also bad law." Along with rejecting the progressive interpretation of section 7, Wallace reluctantly acceded to conservative demands that he fire Frank and several members of his staff who, according to Davis, were "interested in social revolution."[50] On the afternoon of February 5, 1935, Davis announced the "purge" of AAA progressives. Besides Frank, Wallace dismissed Lee Pressman, Francis Shea, Victor Rotnem, and Gardner Jackson. Soon after, Hiss resigned in protest.

News of the purge sent shock waves through progressive circles. Colorado Senator Edward Costigan expressed to FDR the "grave concern" on Capitol Hill over the "upheaval in the Department of Agriculture." In a telegram from Florida, Assistant Secretary of Agriculture Rex Tugwell informed the president that he was "being besieged by requests from Department of Agriculture people" who wanted to resign. Tugwell, who considered resigning himself, believed Frank had "followed the President's and Secretary's policy," and he feared the appearance of a "liberal desertion of the administration."[51] For his part, FDR explained the purge as just a part of the difficulties of governing, indicating no strong preference for either side.[52]

Indeed, those purged from the AAA did not have their careers noticeably harmed by the incident. Soon after the purge, Frank became special counsel to the Reconstruction Finance Corporation (RFC), and the others continued to advance progressive causes both in and outside of the federal government during the Roosevelt years. In fact, Shea and Rotnem eventually moved to the Justice Department, where they became leaders in its effort to expand the federal protection of African American rights during the 1940s.[53]

Still, the purge symbolized the president's early caution toward potentially divisive issues concerning the South and his uneasiness with a style of legal reform that combined realist ideas with the expansion of individual rights. While these attitudes would change later in his presidency, in the early months of 1935 FDR aptly summarized the administration's position himself. In a meeting with Norman Thomas, he told the Socialist leader: "I know the South and we've got to be patient."[54]

A Frustrated NAACP

Indeed, going slow with social reform, especially if it concerned the South, was a virtual creed of the first New Deal. Roosevelt figured he could not afford any sort of confrontation with the powerful southern senators, at least, if he wanted to proceed with his recovery program. As documented in chapter 1, when Walter White of the NAACP asked for the president's assistance in passing an antilynching bill, FDR's response was predictably negative. Despite White's tenacity in lobbying the White House (with the assistance of Eleanor Roosevelt), FDR thought that if he supported the bill, he would undermine his plans for the recovery.[55] Indeed, throughout this period, NAACP leaders usually had their requests rejected by the administration, and White House staff members typically dismissed their attempts to meet with the president.[56] Charles H. Houston, head of the NAACP's legal division, best summarized the organization's reaction to this insensitivity — exacerbated by the administration's sensitivity toward white southern interests — in a letter to Stephen Early, assistant secretary to the president: "We protest that the lives and physical protection of American citizens are just as important as any NRA program ever can be; and that the traditional policy of temporizing with injustice and disrespect of law is to a great extent responsible for the moral collapse and selfishness exhibited in so many quarters to-day. The law and constituted authority are supreme only as they cover the most humble and forgotten citizen."[57]

Along with brushing aside NAACP leaders (both personally and politically), White House staff members usually deferred the civil rights organization's constant flow of memos and informational reports to the Justice Department. The Justice Department, however, was hardly compassionate toward African American interests in these years. In an October 1935 *Crisis* article that he later sent to FDR, White tagged the department the "U.S. Department of (White) Justice," and denounced its inaction on racial concerns:

> The Department of Justice in Washington may lay claim to a 100 per cent performance in at least one branch of its activities — the evasion of cases involving burning questions of Negro rights. It side-stepped the issue of the exclusion of Negroes from southern elections on the ground that it was loaded with political dynamite. Other legalistic reasons were later added but the first orders to "Go Slow" were placed on purely political grounds. On the lynching issue the department has set a new record for its ability to dodge from one excuse to another. . . . The attorney general continues his offensive against crime — except crimes involving the deprivation of life and liberty and citizenship to Negroes.[58]

Indeed, throughout his tenure as head of the Justice Department, Homer Cummings showed little creativity in employing federal statutes to protect African Americans from racial attacks, despite reasonable arguments to support their use. Thus, when members of lynch mobs escaped state prosecution or conviction in the South during his time in office, the Justice Department never brought them to trial on federal charges. In keeping with tradition, the department would typically conclude, as it did after a 1936 investigation of a reign of terror targeted at striking STFU members, "that no federal law had been violated."[59] While rights-centered reformers complained bitterly about the politics of the Justice Department, FDR did little to respond to their calls for action (until after the 1938 elections, when he sacked Cummings).[60] Despite a host of social ills affecting African Americans during the Depression, reform would have to wait for another day.

Of course, the NAACP's difficulty with the Roosevelt White House and a Cummings-led Justice Department represented only part of what was a torrent of resistance toward African American concerns in the early New Deal days. More importantly, New Deal legislation, designed to meet the demands of southern Democrats in Congress, often excluded black Americans from its domain. As noted earlier, this exclusion occurred mainly though the outright omission of domestic and agricultural workers from legislation and through the decentralized structure of many New Deal programs, which led to blatant racial discrimination at the local level.[61] This disregard for African

American interests went to the core of the first New Deal. Indeed, in their evaluations of the New Deal's minimal benefits to blacks, most African American leaders reserved their "greatest volume of criticism" for its "cornerstones," the National Industrial Recovery Act and the Agricultural Adjustment Act, concluding that both were simply "a continuation of the same old raw deal."[62]

With the legislative and executive branches of the national government either openly hostile or destructively unconcerned with advancing the rights of black Americans, an effort to achieve change through the courts was a natural alternative for the NAACP. Even before FDR's election, the organization had initiated its litigation campaign to undermine the constitutionality of segregation. By 1931 Nathan Margold, a protégé of future Roosevelt justice Felix Frankfurter, had finished his report outlining the nature of the NAACP's litigation strategy, and its Legal Committee had methodically set about trying to fulfill its end goal.[63]

Unfortunately for the NAACP, in the mid-1930s the Supreme Court was hardly sympathetic to its argument that segregation was inconsistent with the Constitution. This is not to say that the Court was totally insensitive to the plight of African Americans at this time. Seven justices did side, for example, with the "ignorant and illiterate" black defendants in the 1932 Scottsboro case, declaring that the due process clause dictated the appointment of counsel for those facing a death sentence. But rather than representing a challenge to white supremacy, this and other decisions like it simply continued the Court's somewhat recent trend of rejecting the South's most blatant attempts to institutionalize racial inequality while still upholding the core structure of its color-coded system.[64] The Court's early and inchoate indications that it was altering its stance on the federal protection of some First Amendment freedoms — specifically speech and press — did provide additional optimism. But again, this civil liberties shift did not at the time translate into a willingness on the part of the Court to challenge the South's system of segregation.[65]

Indeed, in the midst of announcing its anti–New Deal decisions, the Court also diminished the hopes of the NAACP's nascent litigation campaign with a unanimous judgment upholding the legality of the white primary.[66] In response, Walter White informed FDR, as leader of his party, that "certain members of the Democratic Party in Texas" were "urging" state legislators "in other southern states" to "take advantage of this Supreme Court ruling and exclude Negroes." He then reminded the president, with supporting documentation from a *Literary Digest* poll, "of the potential influence of the Negro votes in states like Indiana, Missouri, Ohio, Illinois, Delaware and other border and northern states." While White called for no immediate action on the white primary issue, the message was clear. If the president wanted the black vote in the 1936 election, he should be a better ally in the group's effort to advance the rights of African Americans.[67] The evidence of such electoral clout — White implied that black Americans just might hold the balance of power in the upcoming election — no doubt influenced the judicial policy of a president seeking reelection and in the midst of a war with the Court. Indeed, in later chapters, I elaborate on the continuing importance of both the NAACP's advocacy efforts and the black vote in pushing the Roosevelt administration toward a more rights-centered judicial policy that encompassed greater federal protection of African American rights. As noted above, it was an effort aided by the Court's demolition of the first New Deal.

The End of the Beginning: The Supreme Court and the First New Deal

"Defendants do not sell poultry in interstate commerce." With those words, Chief Justice Charles Evans Hughes, speaking in his stentorian tones and for a unanimous Court, began reading the body of his opinion declaring the NIRA unconstitutional, and thus fulfilling FDR's and his New Dealers' greatest fears. On May 27, 1935 — so-called Black Monday — the Supreme Court delivered three major opinions against the administration, effectively killing the first New Deal. There were no dissents.[68]

Surprisingly optimistic signs had initially given the administration some hope that the NIRA might survive a constitutional challenge. Two early 1934 decisions appeared to show that the Supreme Court might be accommodating to arguments that the first New Deal's centerpiece was constitutional. With these promising indications, NRA lawyers, under the direction of Donald Richberg and his chief aide, Blackwell Smith, developed an aggressive strategy for a litigation campaign that would first enforce and then defend the NIRA in court. In a memo outlining their plan, Smith, a graduate of Columbia Law School (one of the birthplaces of realism), used language that surely would have made fellow New Dealer Jerome Frank proud: "Objective: Results; Methods in General: Machiavellian — the end justifies the means (almost)." The means of enforcement, Smith wrote, were based on a combination of "threat and persuasion" and "tricks" designed to "bring to swift justice locally well known chisellers." Moreover, when it came time to choose appropriate cases for prosecution (in late 1934), Smith made weekly trips to the White House to consult with President Roosevelt, who "looked at each case in detail."[69]

This litigation campaign, however, seemed to stall in its infancy, as the Justice Department once again moved to challenge the authority of the New Deal agencies. On the same day Smith circulated his Machiavellian memo (April 9, 1934), Attorney General Cummings issued one of his own. He addressed it to all New Deal agencies interested in enforcing their codes in court and stated that Justice Department lawyers would "assume full responsibility for the institution and prosecution of litigation." The NRA lawyers would be effectively shut out of the courtroom, relegated to simply "assembling the facts and law."[70] As might be expected, conflict over the scope, direction, and nature of the litigation campaign soon arose, as Justice Department lawyers pursued a far more restrained approach toward the law than that favored by their younger counterparts in the NRA. The result was a languid effort to enforce the NRA codes and to find a good test case to argue before the Supreme Court.

As lawyers within the Roosevelt administration continued to do battle with one another over the best defense for the New Deal, the justices' early signs of sympathy seemed to vanish into the night. In a string of decisions, the High Court went on a judicial rampage in the early months of 1935, striking down pieces of the Roosevelt program, and signaling — with its style of constitutional interpretation — that more trouble lay ahead for the administration. The Court began its New Deal dissection with its *Panama Refining Co. v. Ryan* decision (otherwise known as "the Hot Oil case"), invalidating a minor portion of the NIRA, with only Justice Benjamin Cardozo dissenting.[71] The government had argued that, given the chaotic condition of the industry and the futile efforts by the states to control production, federal regulations were both necessary and a valid exercise of the commerce power of Congress. But the justices sidestepped the commerce argument and instead voided Section 9(c) of the NIRA — which had authorized the president to prohibit the interstate transportation of oil produced in excess of state regulations — on delegation grounds. While the Court's next major action partially supported New Deal legislation, the three 5–4 decisions in the *Gold Clause Cases* were far too narrow and ambiguous to provide much comfort for the administration. FDR aptly expressed this uneasiness, noting: "I shudder at the closeness of five to four decisions in these important matters."[72] Nevertheless, the decisions did prevent him from making a speech attacking the Court. If the *Gold Clause Cases* had gone against the administration, he had planned, quoting from Lincoln's first inaugural address, to remind the Court of the realities of American democracy and to refuse to "stand idly by" as a set of decisions threatened to "imperil the [nation's] economic and political security."[73] But in the end, FDR never gave the speech.

The Court struck again on May 6, 1935, when it declared, again 5–4, that the Railroad Retirement Act of 1934 was unconstitutional. In overturning this New Deal social security system for the railroad industry, Justice Owen Roberts, writing for the Court, spoke in sweeping terms in asserting that the Congress had overstepped its authority to regulate interstate commerce. Justice Stone, who joined the dissent, later wrote that the decision was "the worst performance of the Court" since its notorious *Lochner* ruling in 1905.[74]

The next Supreme Court test for the New Deal was the *Schechter* case. In an atmosphere of relative harmony, Justice Department and NRA lawyers produced a brief that was shaped to favor the NRA's position, since the department lawyers had concluded after the Hot Oil decision that the administration stood little chance of succeeding. As a result, the brief focused more on political factors than legal ones, as the NRA lawyers sought to place the devastation of the Depression at the center of their argument. To begin, the brief drafters based their discussion of the commerce clause on the revision theory that "business in the U.S. had become a single integrated whole." To support their argument that the NIRA was within the commerce power, they developed an extensive analysis of the "emergency doctrine" with the confidence — despite warnings from the lower courts — that the Supreme Court would not strike down an act intended to relieve Depression-induced human suffering. Moreover, they featured the economic crisis in an attempt to resolve the delegation question that had been so detrimental to the government's position in the Hot Oil case. In their plea, the New Deal lawyers appealed to the justices' humanity rather than the need for consistency in legal doctrine. Read their words: "The delegation will be found justified by the unprecedented economic chaos existing in the spring of 1933, which compelled Congress to provide for the regulation of a subject of magnitude requiring great flexibility in dealing with different conditions and diverse elements in the various industries. . . . When Congress convened, the banks were closed, millions were unemployed, and business was stagnant. The nation was at the verge of panic; hope and confidence was based largely upon the belief that Congress would take immediate action. . . . The Recovery Act was an attempt to combat these evils." To add to this appeal, Donald Richberg concluded his oral argument by suggesting the Court not apply a "narrow legalistic construction of the Constitution" based on "medieval dialectics" solely to "preserve the theoretical liberty," which "has been very properly described as a 'liberty to starve.' "[75] The justices were unconvinced.

In a historic opinion, Chief Justice Hughes summarized the Court's objections to the administration's emergency doctrine with language in sharp contrast to realist thought: "Extraordinary conditions may call for extraordinary remedies. But the argument necessarily stops short of an attempt to justify action which lies outside the sphere of constitutional authority. Extraordinary conditions do not create or enlarge constitutional power." In dealing with the second question of delegation, Hughes asserted that the legislative powers provided to the president in section 3 of the NIRA were "without precedent" and "an unconstitutional delegation of legislative power." On the final question of the commerce clause, Hughes dismissed the government's claim that business had become a "single integrated whole." Instead, as in the case of the Schechter's poultry, the "flow" of interstate commerce could be broken. Congress could regulate the transportation of the "sick chickens" across state lines, but once they came to a "permanent rest" in New York, it could do no more.[76]

The Court's decision in *Schechter* represented a clear rejection of the administration's more modest legal models of emergency and revision. While realist ideas had clearly influenced their arguments, New Deal lawyers had not asked for a radical restructuring of the legal order. They had instead requested either a temporary reprieve or an update to the legal formulas that the Court employed to oversee the governing of the economy. But even these models of legal reform were too much for a Court steeped in the traditions of a passing age, whether formalist, Republican, or those of old-style "New Freedom" progressivism, which stressed the necessity of a decentralized polity.[77] Thus, on this day in late May 1935, the Court spoke in a unified voice, and it spoke clearly and affirmatively against the New Deal.

For FDR, "Black Monday" was an important turning point. In the first two years of his administration, he had clearly not been an advocate of rights-centered liberalism, legal realism, or the emerging union between the two. Following the Court's interring of the first New Deal, however, he seemed both ready and willing to take on the existing legal order. He seemed ready to become a realist in his own right. Indeed, his action two years later — with his introduction of the Court-packing plan — confirmed his willingness to attack judicial authority in order, as he put it, to have "the law catch up with life."[78]

Constitutional Uncertainty and the Second New Deal

As expected, *Schechter* provoked strong reaction from all sections of the nation. In Washington, the rapid passage of a second New Deal soon after the decision signaled a shift in emphasis for the Roosevelt administration, as it abandoned a constitutionally defunct system of national planning and adopted components of rights-centered liberalism. In this section, I focus on the meaning and significance of the second New Deal, particularly one of its two pillars, the Wagner (National Labor Relations) Act. More specifically, I consider the extent to which the Wagner Act represented the legislative arrival of the union between legal realism and rights-centered liberalism. The Wagner Act, after all, sought to install a new system of industrial relations by securing basic rights and liberties for workers through creating an independent agency and reducing the judiciary's authority over labor. Under this new system of labor relations, proponents asserted, legal rules created for a master and servant society would no longer control the workers of an industrialized society. Instead, a quasi-judicial agency — guided by expertise and committed to protecting workers' rights — would ensure industrial peace and economic prosperity by averting strikes.

In addition to representing realist and rights-centered principles, Congress passed the Wagner Act in an atmosphere emitting legislative contempt toward notions of judicial certainty. In other words, despite the clear expectation that the Court would swiftly upset the Wagner Act, Congress enacted the measure by overwhelming numbers. The Court's rejection of the first New Deal seemingly had a similar impact on the president's view of the law. When the Guffey Coal bill — a part of the second New Deal that included Wagner Act-style labor provisions — stalled in Congress, FDR urged Congressman Samuel Hill to defer all questions concerning its constitutionality to the courts. While Attorney General Cummings thought the Guffey bill was "clearly unconstitutional,"[79] the president took a different tone, asserting to Hill: "I hope your committee will not permit doubts as to constitutionality, however reasonable, to block the suggested legislation."[80] To be sure, there were a number of factors pushing FDR and the Democratic Congress to back the Wagner bill. Still, I argue that the president's support signified his willingness to adopt an increasingly realist approach toward the courts and foretold a more aggressive judicial policy. While it may be too much to say "a court-packing era . . . began immediately after *Schechter*," FDR's actions after the decision certainly laid the foundation for his dramatic attack against the justices less than two years later,[81] an attack that sought to place the executive as the leading institution in constitutional construction. Significantly, this more direct approach toward the courts coincided with the president's shift toward an agenda more in line with rights-centered liberalism.

In exploring the politics surrounding the passage of the Wagner Act, I also explore why southerners voted in favor of the measure in such strong numbers. Southern congressional leaders, after all, had successfully led the opposition to previous attempts by Senator Wagner to pass rights-expanding legislation for workers. I consider what might have accounted for this diminished effort. Finally, I examine the extent to which the Wagner Act advanced the cause of rights-centered liberalism more generally. In doing so, I explain why supporters considered the act a major victory for the expansion and protection of individual liberties, despite the fact that the NAACP and ACLU both initially opposed it.

The *Schechter* Decision, Legal Realism, and the Passage of the Wagner Act

With its far-reaching "Black Monday" decisions, the Court was clearly trying to send FDR into retreat. But instead, the president responded with a reinvigorated sense of purpose and somewhat shocking realist rhetoric. As noted above, he had prepared to take on the Court three months before in anticipation of the justices' disapproval of the gold clauses, but when they unexpectedly approved the administration's action, he had remained quiet. Now, with a unanimous Court constitutionally decapitating his first New Deal, he let loose. In a lengthy press conference on the Friday following "Black Monday," he issued his famous statement about the Court's decision in *Schechter*: "We have been relegated to the horse-and-buggy definition of interstate commerce." But he also stressed to the rapt reporters: "Make it clear this is not a partisan issue. It is infinitely deeper than any partisan issue." Indeed, although many may have disregarded this point, to him the conflict was not about Democrat versus Republican, but between those who understood the modern conditions of the nation and those who did not, between those who supported a more centralized federal state and those who did not.[82]

FDR's words confirmed to both Washington and the nation his commitment to transforming the federal government into an active agent of economic regulation. Thus, on June 1, 1935, the second Hundred Days began, with the Wagner Act and Social Security Act serving as the core pieces of the new Roosevelt program. The Wagner Act had been redesigned at the end of 1934 to deal with the legal difficulties surrounding section 7(a) and the enforcement problems they presented for the National Labor Relations Board. The bill picked up momentum following a federal district court judge's decision in *United States v. Weirton Steel Co.*, declaring section 7(a) unconstitutional, on February 27, 1935.[83] In turn, Senator Wagner, joined by

NLRB chairman Francis Biddle, urged Congress to pass the restructured bill, arguing that a permanent independent tribunal — one opponent called it a "supreme court of labor"[84]—designed to decide and enforce labor cases would prevent the judiciary from emasculating this attempt to aid workers.

With the *Weirton* decision, the threat of more strikes,[85] and a more favorable environment in Congress following the 1934 elections,[86] Wagner pushed for quick passage of his revised bill. Supporters focused on the need to enforce the principles outlined in section 7(a), reasoning that employer resistance to labor elections was largely responsible for the 1934 strike wave. By asking federal district courts to review the NLRB's orders, employers had effectively created "an insurmountable barrier of delay" for the board and tied its future enforcement effort to the outcome of those cases.[87] In addition, since the NLRB needed the approval of the unsympathetic Justice Department before filing suits against recalcitrant employers, the enforcement of section 7(a) had been virtually suspended. The Wagner bill represented a solution, since it provided "adequate powers" to a "single experienced agency to find out the facts and carry through enforcement of the law up to the point of review in the Circuit Court of Appeals."[88] In a clear break with the ambiguity of section 7(a), moreover, the bill outlawed company unions and endorsed the principles of majority rule and exclusive representation. Finally, the drafters of the bill gleaned lessons from the Court's actions, believing that "no New Deal statute could survive the judicial gauntlet without the armor of legislative specificity and procedural clarity."[89] While the legislation was dramatic in nature, Wagner was confident it could pass. But even before the *Schechter* decision, many were not so sure, citing the president's apparent lack of interest and the bill's dubious constitutionality.

Indeed, as the Senate began to consider it, many thought that, despite Wagner's own beliefs, the bill that bore his name could not withstand constitutional scrutiny. Standing on solid precedential ground, detractors argued that the combination of the Court's action toward previous labor legislation and its initial dismantling of the New Deal left little hope that the justices would uphold Wagner's legislation. To add further support to their position, detractors could also point to the general expectation that the Court would soon void the NIRA in its forthcoming *Schechter* decision. Indeed, by this time even Donald Richberg, considered one of the most optimistic New Dealers, was expressing "grave doubts" about the judicial fate the NIRA.[90] If this concern proved fateful, Wagner would seemingly have a more difficult argument to make about the constitutional validity of his bill, since it dramatically extended and strengthened section 7(a). On May 14,

1935, news from the Court finalized Richberg's fear. On that night, Felix Frankfurter relayed a message from Justice Louis Brandeis to FDR and a group of progressive senators that the first New Deal's "eleventh hour" had arrived.[91] Significantly, then, when senators voted on the National Labor Relations bill two days later, they did so under a cloud of constitutional uncertainty. As Republican Senator Daniel O. Hastings of Delaware put it, "one does not have to be anything more than a law student to reach the conclusion that the proposed act is unconstitutional."[92] Nevertheless, on May 16, 1935, the Senate passed the bill by the overwhelming margin of 63 to 12.

To a certain extent, the Senate's action fit with legal realism's skepticism about the certainty of law. The fact that the Court had consistently voted 5–4 to overturn federal law suggested that constitutional interpretation was decidedly uncertain: legal doctrine was as malleable as realists had asserted. Without an ability to know whether Wagner or his detractors were correct about the constitutionality of the bill, the Senate supported it. To do otherwise would have been politically problematic — since Democrats needed to enact a program for the upcoming presidential campaign — and economically destructive — that is, if labor leaders fulfilled their promise of more strikes. Facing these potentialities, as Irving Bernstein writes, "many senators, convinced that the bill was unconstitutional, wished to shift the onus of its defeat to the Supreme Court. They would gain labor's political support while certain that the measure would not take effect because employers would fail to comply until the court declared it void."[93]

This disregard for the constitutionality of the measure became even more discernible when — three weeks after the unanimous *Schechter* decision—the House took it up for consideration. During the debate, for example, Virginia's Howard Smith declared, "the Supreme Court will unquestionably declare it unconstitutional at the first opportunity." To applause, Indiana Republican Charles Halleck echoed this sentiment, wondering how any of his colleagues, whether sympathetic to "the merits of the bill" or not, could vote in favor of it "in light of the Constitution and the Supreme Court decisions thereunder, and under our oaths to support and uphold the Constitution." Speaking specifically on the Court's recent action, Georgia's Malcolm Tarver asserted that one of the bill's defenders had articulated a position on the commerce clause that was "directly opposed" to the justices' reasoning in *Schechter*.[94]

While not alone in anticipating a quick judicial voiding of the Wagner Act, this expectation seemingly clarifies why some southerners went along with such a radical departure from past labor legislation. Put another way, these southerners were continuing an old alliance with a Supreme Court that had consistently endorsed the states' rights creed, apparently assured that the justices would come through again in the end. This is not to say that southern congressional leaders did not attempt to block passage of the bill. They did. When Senate Majority Leader Robinson and Senator Pat Harrison of Mississippi met with FDR and Wagner before the Senate vote, they set out to persuade the president to intervene to stop (or delay) action on the bill.[95] While both thought it would be easy to gain FDR's approval — given his previous reservations about the measure and his instrumental role in defeating Wagner's Labor Disputes bill the year before — they were ultimately unsuccessful. FDR decided to remain neutral, and the Senate went ahead with its vote. Although most thought the tally would be close, the opposition's decision to focus on the constitutionality of the bill in earlier hearings before the Senate Education and Labor Committee severely limited its persuasiveness.[96] With similar arguments being made against legislation FDR publicly supported, including the Social Security bill, the call for the Congress to be constitutionally responsible apparently lost its potency. In a period of such constitutional doubt, many senators seemingly found Wagner's speech on the constitutional validity of the bill convincing enough and the rumblings from labor groups threatening enough to gain their support. Without Roosevelt's assistance, Robinson decided, "he didn't want to embarrass the members of the Senate with having to declare themselves" against Wagner's bill.[97] And in the end, both he and Harrison voted in favor of the measure.

Strikingly — and for very different reasons — the ACLU and the NAACP joined in the southern conservative distaste for the bill. To the ACLU's board of directors, the Wagner Act dangerously bound the rights of workers to the impulses of federal control. According to ACLU head Roger Baldwin, the board based its opposition on a concern about the fate of minority unions and the assumption that the NLRB could not "fairly determine the issues of labor's rights" when it intervened in employer-employee conflicts. To him, "only unions militant enough and strong enough to withstand many pressures have been able to achieve anything like an unrestricted exercise of their rights." Confronted by a swell of dissent from its membership, however, the board later rescinded — ironically on Black Monday — its opposition, deciding instead to take "no position" on the bill.[98] Joined by the National Urban League, the NAACP opposed the measure because it was unable to secure a clause "that would have denied the benefits of the legislation to any union which discriminated on the basis of race."[99]

Although some scholars have interpreted the combination of African American opposition and the number of southerners who voted in favor of the measure as an indication of southern acceptance of the Wagner Act, the bounty of evidence tells another story.[100] To begin, the backroom actions of Robinson and Harrison do not support this conclusion. Second, according to his chief aide Leon Keyserling, Wagner conceded — "much against his will" — to the elimination of the antidiscrimination clause not because of southern opposition but because the AFL "fought bitterly" against its inclusion.[101] In this sense, while a boon to union power, the closed shop allowed AFL unions to continue their practice of racial discrimination, thereby effectively shutting many African Americans out of the workplace. Finally, southern conservatives — especially those unbound by a relationship with the Roosevelt White House — clearly disliked the Wagner bill, concerned that it would further centralize power in an already morbidly obese federal state. Unlike the first New Deal, which embraced centralization in a temporary fashion and was largely a reaction to the economic crisis, the Wagner Act "was a *political* initiative by forces within and outside" the federal government, "which had the *effect* of reshaping and extending the state."[102] Thus, while a remarkable fifteen of the twenty-two southerners in the Senate backed the measure, of the six most conservative southerners, five either voted against it or did not cast a vote at all.[103] The largest threat to the act in the Senate, moreover, came in the form of a killer amendment offered by Millard Tydings of the border state of Maryland, the second most conservative of all the Senate Democrats serving from 1933 to 1939.[104] Representative Eugene Cox of Georgia best summarized southern conservative concern about the pending legislation. To him, the Wagner bill represented "the most terrible threat . . . to our dual form of government that has thus far arisen." Virginia's Howard Smith expressed similar unease about the potential loss of state sovereignty, appealing to his colleagues "not to further strip the States of their police powers in purely local matters by means of legislation of this character forced through under whip and spur of real or fancied emergency."[105] In sum, despite the Wagner Act's effective exclusion of African Americans, southerners voiced deep-seated distress about its potential threat to their "way of life."[106] Given the constitutional questions surrounding the measure, some members nevertheless voted in support when in truth they opposed its very foundation.[107]

While the Wagner bill had made it through the Senate on May 16, 1935, it still did not have the president's backing. It would take nine more days for FDR to publicly support the measure. By this time, a number of leading progressives had told him that he needed to move to the left to undercut the rising popularity of Senator Huey Long of Louisiana and the "radio priest," Father Charles E. Coughlin. According to these advisors, this required the president, like his distant cousin Teddy before him, to take on some members of his own party. To Senator Burton Wheeler of Montana, "it was all right" for FDR "to get all he could out of Senators Robinson and Harrison"—which had been a "great deal"—but he had to know "that neither man had any sympathy" for his program.[108] To Wheeler and the others in the room, it was necessary for the president "to take a firm stand on his progressive policies and force the fighting along that line." But while another attendee, Wisconsin's Senator Bob La Follette, thought the meeting represented "the best, the frankest, the most encouraging talk" leading progressives had "ever had with him," FDR still did not come out in support of the Wagner bill.[109] Two days later, May 24, 1935—after a meeting with labor leaders, members of his administration skeptical of the bill, and Wagner—the president finally stated that he agreed "in principle" with the measure. On the same day, word had come down from the Supreme Court that it would issue its *Schechter* decision on the following Monday.[110] In this sense, a complex set of factors drove FDR's decision to back the Wagner bill. Most prominent among these were, first, his willingness and ability to move in a more progressive direction and, second, the pressure that was brought to bear by labor, electoral concerns, and (in a negative sense) the Supreme Court.[111]

A week after *Schechter*, the president announced his list of "must" legislation for the 1935 session. By including the National Labor Relations bill, he all but assured its enactment.[112] Indeed, when the House opened debate on the bill in mid-June, no substantial opposition emerged. In the end, the House passed it by a voice vote. After only some minor compromises in conference committee, the bill was sent to the president for his signature in almost "pristine form." According to Philip Levy, the *Schechter* decision had "persuaded most lawyers and most members of Congress that the law was unconstitutional. The opposition just folded up. There was no reason for them to go on record and to go through a bruising battle on the floor."[113] They would let the Supreme Court do their deciding.

In one final plea, Attorney General Cummings urged the president to veto the measure because of its "rather doubtful constitutionality," but his effort was to no avail.[114] The Supreme Court had pushed FDR and the Congress into a zone of constitutional ambiguity, and both responded by challenging the Court over the meaning of the Constitution. Some in Congress clearly hoped to lose that battle, but fearing either labor's impact or the lack of a working program on which to wage the upcoming campaign, they supported the president. Others were devoted to charting a new course for worker's rights and challenging the nature of judicial interpretation. Many newspaper editorials throughout the nation declared that those in Congress who supported the measure were disregarding their oaths of office. But, as Harold Ickes noted, many in the administration believed that "the people will demand the right to determine for themselves whether the nation is to have a clear road to economic and social development, just as other civilized countries have that right, without the insistence of any court that we return to the strait jacket of fifty years ago." Indeed, if arguments about the constitutional validity of measures were taken seriously, all but the mildest parts of the second New Deal would have been delayed. Questions of constitutionality would have to wait not only because the president wanted a new program, but because many in the administration and in Congress believed that the Court was not behaving as it should — it was not, as Wagner had written, allowing law to "respond sensitively and rapidly to the social and economic problems created by the interpenetration of our modern industry."[115] By the end of the summer, then, the Congress had enacted the president's controversial second New Deal, and the nation moved into the next phase of constitutional limbo.[116] While many expected its judicial demise in short course, the enactment of the Wagner Act nevertheless represented something significant for legal reformers. In a matter of months, the aspirations of legal realists and rights-centered liberals had changed dramatically in the Roosevelt administration. It had been just a few months since the AAA purge and only several weeks since one of the president's most progressive aides had become so disenchanted with FDR's trend toward the right and big business that he concluded it might be necessary for progressives to wait "for ten or twelve years for Bob La Follette to come along."[117] But now FDR was pursuing a more aggressive approach toward legal reform that not only embraced realist doubts about judicial authority, but also championed legislation that reformulated the rights of workers by reducing court control over them.[118]

The Significance of the Wagner Act for Rights-Centered Liberalism

Constitutional doubts aside, the Wagner Act represented a clear departure from labor's previous position in the law and ignited the Roosevelt administration's drive to alter judicial interpretation via a rights-centered approach.[119] Before the act, as Joseph Rosenfarb wrote in 1945, "when labor sought to exercise its 'right' to organize or strike, the most fruitful soil was prepared for the wholesale violation of [workers'] civil liberties. Because of economic dependence of the community, particularly the smaller ones, upon the payroll of frequently a single enterprise, the employer was able to dragoon, directly or indirectly, the leading elements of the community against labor." To supporters, then, the Wagner Act attacked "the very source of anti-unionism" by extending the scope of First Amendment freedom protection to include violations by private persons in the field of labor relations. "It prohibited employers from abridging their workers' freedom of speech" and assembly and, according to Rosenfarb, "liberate[d] whole communities from the feudal control of the dominant economic interest." It was in this vein that in 1937 the ACLU again altered its position on the act, asserting that "in effect" it was "a civil liberties statute" and hailing the Supreme Court decision upholding it as "the year's outstanding victory in the struggle for civil liberties." A California state senator went even further, calling the Wagner Act "the greatest gain for civil liberties since Thomas Jefferson and the Democrats of his day forced the adoption of the Bill of Rights as an essential part of the Constitution."[120]

Indeed, many rights-centered liberals believed that by forging an alliance with the federal government, relations between industry and labor would be fairer and, by implication, provide unions with better outcomes. Others went further, believing that the Wagner Act could achieve the "industrial democracy" that left-leaning unions had long sought. To this end, FDR, members of his administration, and labor leaders — with varying levels of commitment to achieving industrial democracy — did not defend the Wagner Act in working-class terms. Rather, class was surprisingly absent from the discourse surrounding the act, as rights-centered liberals — both inside and outside of government — concentrated on the themes of fairness and democracy, regarding unions "as (potentially) representative institutions in a new political and social order." According to political scientist David Plotke, supporters thought unions "would encourage social stability and economic growth as well as embody democratic norms." Perhaps with this in mind, the ACLU's Baldwin noted in 1938 that "the struggle for the political rights of fifteen million Negroes . . . the defense of religious liberties, of academic freedom, of freedom from censorship of the press" are wrapped up in the larger "fight for the rights of labor" — in the battle for political democracy.[121]

In the final analysis, then, the act represented a victory for both legal realism and rights-centered liberalism. For years, *Lochner*-like thinking had dominated labor relations in the federal courts. Through the creation of a new institution filled with experts, labor gained some freedom from what realists considered was the whim of judges supposedly committed to legal formalism. In this sense, the passage of the Wagner Act displayed to legal reformers in Washington how realism could fit with the general New Deal effort toward an expansive understanding of rights.

Shifting Coalitions: The 1936 Election and the Path to Rights-Centered Liberalism

Like the passage of the second New Deal, the 1936 election also contributed to shifting the Roosevelt administration's attention away from the sensitivities of the South and toward a more rights-centered agenda. Three electoral concerns were most significant in this regard. The first centered on the potential of a third-party threat. Most notably, after they had successfully joined forces to defeat the president on the World Court treaty in January 1935, talk of an electoral union between Huey Long and Father Coughlin began to alarm some in the White House. In turn, the Democratic National Committee (DNC) commissioned a secret political poll in the spring. It showed that, as a third party candidate, Long could hold the balance of power in some large industrial states and just might tip the election to the Republicans. According to a surprised Jim Farley, chairman of the DNC, Long's "probable support was not confined to Louisiana and near-by states. On the contrary, he had about as much following in the North as in the South, and he had as strong an appeal in the industrial centers as he did in the rural areas." With this in mind, Roosevelt sought to mobilize a new constituency of voters to secure the states of Pennsylvania (which had voted for Hoover in 1932), Illinois, Ohio, Indiana, Michigan, California, and New York. With these states, FDR could not only repel the third-party threat, but fulfill his "hope to free the Democratic Party from its dependence upon the solid South."[122] In this sense, his second New Deal was in part designed to appeal to "the lower middle class," the primary Long constituency.[123]

A second, equally important (somewhat overlapping) concern involved FDR's ability to attract first-time voters from the growing industrial labor force now represented by John L. Lewis and his newly created Committee (later Congress) of Industrial Organizations (CIO). Many progressives rightfully thought that a rights-centered agenda would be the most effective way to appeal to these voters as well. Thus, in 1936, buoyed by the CIO's extensive assistance in the reelection effort and by the Supreme Court's continuing hostility toward New Deal labor policies,[124] Roosevelt's relationship with Lewis was closer than ever.[125] This closeness, moreover, further strained the president's increasingly frayed alliance with southern congressional leaders. Nevertheless, "the inclusion of labor" offered the best "possibility of broad rank and file support for a transformed Democratic party."[126]

The final electoral concern, which was most distressing to southerners, centered on the Roosevelt administration's planned attempt to increase African American support at the polls. If successfully carried forward, this effort would create a virtual fork in the road as the administration developed its second-term judicial policy. After all, as Walter White bluntly wrote in February 1936:

> The chief criticism of Negroes of the Roosevelt administration has been its too great deference to the second- and third-rate politicians who in most instances represent the South in the two houses of Congress. Between now and November the administration needs to determine whether it will continue to listen to anti-Negro senators and congressmen from the eleven southern states with an electoral vote of only 124, or whether it will pay attention to the wishes of thoughtful people of both races in the seventeen states with more than twice as many electoral votes. Of one thing the administration may be sure . . . these eleven southern states will not revolt despite the frothing at the mouth of men like Governor Talmadge of Georgia, as to do so would mean the loss to southerners of committee chairmanships in both houses of Congress, huge sums for relief, public works and other benefits from the national treasury and the *power which they hold in a Democratic administration, which in turn is based largely upon direct disfranchisement of Negro voters and indirect disfranchisement of many white voters in their states.*[127]

For White, the choice was clear. If the president truly wanted to reform the Democratic Party and reconstruct American democracy, he would have to cast off his previous devotion to alleviating southern unease. FDR saw the opening as well. He could transform each of these three electoral concerns into opportunities and, in turn, solidify popular support for his decision to pursue a more progressive, rights-centered agenda and a modernized presidency.

In the end, of course, the assassination of Long in September 1935 ended the third-party threat. Roosevelt went on to trounce Alfred M. Landon by collecting 60.8 percent of the popular vote and carrying every state save Maine and Vermont. Long's success in arousing and mobilizing voters, especially after the repeal of the Louisiana poll tax in 1934, nevertheless helped convince FDR that he had been constrained by a southern conservative–led Congress for too long: southern liberalism would never develop under the current political structures but would require federally induced reform.

Indeed, the conduct of the campaign emitted glimpses of forthcoming New Deal efforts to undermine southern democracy. During the Democratic convention, for example, delegates abolished the South's cherished two-thirds rule at the president's urging. To FDR, the rule was "archaic" and unnecessary, a potential brick wall in his effort to remake the Democratic Party by undercutting the power of conservative forces.[128] Essentially, the abolition of the rule sought to transfer control of the convention over to Democrats from the North and West, causing great alarm in southern conservative circles. In this vein, less than two years after the convention, North Carolina Senator Josiah Bailey agonized about the fate of his party: "Since the abolition of the Two-Thirds Rule, there is grave danger that it will fall into the hands of very objectionable men whose politics are entirely distasteful to Southern Democracy. They get elected by the negro vote . . . [and] are common fellows of the baser sort."[129]

In addition to Roosevelt's convention maneuvers, in the course of the campaign he displayed a clear desire to separate his reelection bid from the past practices of the party and to assert a new, more progressive vision for the future.[130] And at the urging of the first lady, the president went ahead with his southern-criticized effort to expand his share of the black vote. As part of this effort, the Democratic National Committee gave new life to its recently created "Colored Voter Division" and courted the African American constituency in a fashion unparalleled in the party's history. The reason for such action was clear. While long "captured" by the GOP, black voters had displayed a newfound independence in 1934. "For the first time in history, a majority of Afro-American voters went Democratic," helping to elect a decidedly progressive Congress.[131] Progressive Democratic forces understood this trend and sought to secure an even greater percentage of the black vote for their party in 1936. Describing the thinking of one such progressive, two reporters concluded: "At the end of a bright vista," he "saw millions of negro voters. Republicans no longer. Democrats all."[132]

Despite these actions and southern animosities toward the Roosevelt record, southern voters, with their long tradition of party loyalty, supported FDR by huge margins in 1936. In South Carolina, for example, the president won 98.6 percent of the vote. In Mississippi, his tally was somewhat smaller, 97.1 percent. (To be sure, this did not prevent conservative southerners in Congress from vociferously attacking FDR, his wife, and members of his administration for their increasingly cozy relationship with the African American community.)[133] But FDR's overwhelming victory in Dixie did not tell the story of the election for the South. As political scientist Howard Reiter writes, "with the unprecedentedly high (for a Democrat) percentages that Roosevelt won in 1932 and 1936, the southern proportion of the national Democratic vote was lower than it had ever been, with the sole exception of Al Smith's losing campaign in 1928. In 1936, it was barely 12 percent."[134]

Thus, while southern support remained strong, the rising popularity of the president and his party in the North gave him greater flexibility to govern the nation as he saw fit. Building on their 1934 gains, Democrats picked up twenty-two seats in the House and seven in the Senate, bringing their totals to three hundred thirty-one and seventy-six, respectively, or an astonishing 76 and 79 percent.[135] Not since James Monroe's Democratic-Republicans had one party so dominated the national legislature. Significantly, African Americans were at the center of Roosevelt's increased electoral strength in the North, as they radically altered their voting behavior from four years before. Then, fewer than one-third of black Americans had voted for FDR, remaining more loyal to the "Party of Lincoln" than any other single group. In 1936 that figure stood at 76 percent, representing perhaps the most dramatic shift in the history of presidential elections. Despite its small size, moreover, many political strategists considered the African American vote highly valuable because in a close election — especially if black migration northward continued to increase — it could be the margin of difference in the large northern states rich with electoral votes. Indeed, even before the 1936 election, FDR noted to White that he knew "how powerful" the black vote was in a tight race.[136]

While this victory gave Roosevelt the largest plurality in American history, the numbers nevertheless disguised "the incompatibility of the forces" that made up his coalition, most notably, white southerners and northern blacks.[137] To many progressives, this was unproblematic since it offered FDR a clear choice. Indeed, some even appeared to welcome it. Writing in 1937, Stanley High — a "close" presidential advisor and speechwriter during the 1936 campaign — noted that he had "never discovered any great alarm among New Dealers about" the "prospect" that "the New Deal and the solid South are wholly incompatible." To him, "the surrender, by the New Deal, of the solid South in exchange for the Negro vote would be a very good trade" since it was apparent that "so far as objectives are concerned there is no doubt that such New Dealers as Senator Guffey and Governor Earle of Pennsylvania, Senator Wagner of New York, *Senator Minton of Indiana* and *Governor Murphy of Michigan* [both future Supreme Court justices] have more objectives in common with their Negro supporters than with many of their southern Democratic colleagues. *That, I think, could also be said of*

Mr. Roosevelt."[138] To be sure, the president did not endorse the idea of disregarding the South after his 1936 victory. Nevertheless, as discussed in the following chapters, the fact that southern voters were "captives" of the Democratic Party did allow his administration to construct a judicial policy that was increasingly unfriendly to the defenders of southern democracy.[139]

Conclusion

The events of Roosevelt's first term display a period of transition within the White House, a period when the demands of legislative coalition-building initially dominated before giving some ground to electoral concerns. As the New Deal began, realists and rights-centered liberals (at times, one and the same) expected their ideas to have an immediate and significant impact on the workings of the federal government. Yet their alliance with the Roosevelt administration did not have sufficient presidential support until the legislative session of 1935. At that point, it became clear to FDR that a more progressive, rights-centered path — one that increasingly challenged the preexisting legal order — could be politically beneficial to him in the short and long term. In other words, it could help him meet his immediate goals of recovery and reelection, while also aiding in his more distant desire of creating an executive-dominated, nationally concentrated, progressive polity. In this period, then, the Roosevelt administration developed an essential foundational structure to support its later commitment to more extensive rights expansion. In this sense, labor's successes in the mid-1930s provided an important pathway for the inclusion of African Americans into the circle of federal rights protection. As black voters joined the Roosevelt coalition, the president sought to employ the opportunity their support provided to diminish the influence of the South and move forth with the implementation of his constitutional vision. Indeed, even as the 1936 election grew near, FDR encouraged reforms in the Democratic Party designed to lessen the power of the South by expanding his own. These reforms signaled his desire to pursue a program that would eventually seek to transform southern politics by weakening state party structures, mobilizing first-time voters, and enhancing the centrality of the presidency in electoral politics. This program fit well with the Roosevelt administration's increasing reliance on realist-style criticisms of law's certainty, and its simultaneous pursuit of progressive policies designed to ensure recovery by augmenting rights and regulating market forces.

THREE   FDR's Constitutional Vision and the
Defeat of the Court-Packing Plan

*The Modern Presidency and the Enemies of
Institutional Reform*

Perhaps because it is one of those rare moments in history when the losers end up winning, it has become common — far too common — for scholars to tell the tale of the Court-packing conflict as a battle lost in a war FDR eventually won; a battle lost, moreover, largely because of the president's failure in leadership. In this chapter, I examine the Court-packing episode from an alternative standpoint, focusing less on FDR's much-discussed "mistakes" and more on the opponents of his plan. In doing so, I make three arguments that either highlight previously underappreciated aspects of the plan or challenge traditional accounts of the episode. With each, I hope to reveal a deeper significance of FDR's confrontation with the Court than is commonly understood and to explore its contribution to the rise of rights-centered liberalism generally and the expansion of judicially protected African American rights specifically. In this sense, I assess the importance of the plan beyond the events that ended in its undoing by considering the extent to which the work of the Roosevelt Court reflected the battle lines of the Court-packing conflict.

First, I suggest that the Court-packing plan represented a criticism of the law that was inspired by realist thought. I do so by explaining how FDR's plan to add six new justices to the Court — one for every sitting member over the age of seventy who had served ten years — carried forward the realist cause. I argue that, viewed in this light, Roosevelt's objective in seeking to reform the judiciary was more expansive than traditionally thought. More than an attempt to tame the apparent carnivorous conservatism of the Court, the plan signified an effort to implant realist ideas into the federal judiciary's decision-making process.

Second — and closely related to the former point — I suggest that despite FDR's much discussed war against the Court, previous accounts of the episode often fail to consider what the war was really about. I argue that the intent of the Court-packing plan was not to simply "constitutionalize" the New Deal, but to revolutionize the judiciary as an institution. Specifically,

FDR did not merely seek to carry out a substantive constitutional revolution by reconstituting the High Court so that it advanced a set of values more sympathetic to his own. Rather, he hoped to transform the judiciary into an agent of the modern presidency, deferring to the expertise of the newly enhanced administrative state. This development, as noted in previous chapters, was essential in the Court's ultimate decision to remake civil rights law, as it developed this line of doctrine with the encouragement of the Justice Department.

Third, I suggest that we cannot appropriately understand the plan without locating its introduction as the breakpoint—the critical juncture—in the New Deal struggle against the preexisting legal order and appreciating how it fit into FDR's larger institutional program and advanced his constitutional vision. More than a failed effort with quickly evaporating relevance, the plan was an essential part of FDR's reconstructive design. Its defeat, moreover, helped define the institutional enemies of reform and shape the contours of the Roosevelt administration's later judicial policy.

In addition to making these three arguments, I examine an event that displayed the Roosevelt administration's willingness to challenge the federal courts and reflected its altered attitude toward the federal protection of rights. Often competing with the Court-packing plan for headline space, the sit-down strike in Flint, Michigan, displayed in compelling terms just how much the federal government had changed course on safeguarding the rights of labor. While seemingly unconnected to the African American cause, the administration's handling of the sit-down strike further strained relations with southern leaders and set in motion a federal machinery that would become highly significant in later efforts to secure the rights of "discrete and insular minorities." In this sense, it is an event that highlights the foundational importance of labor's battle for federally secured rights to the drive to extend federal civil rights to black Americans.

Finally, throughout the chapter, I question the conventional wisdom on the underlying basis for the failure of the Court-packing plan. By most accounts, the plan fell victim to an overconfident president still giddy from a historic landslide victory at the polls and prone to strategic oversights and a parade of errors. Indeed, no U.S. president deemed to have been "great" by history has been so chastised for introducing a single piece of legislation as FDR for his plan to pack the Court. I challenge these analyses about the failure of the plan by placing President Roosevelt's disputed decisions and questioned actions in their institutional context and by exploring the nature of the opposition to the plan. This is not to say that FDR did not make some catastrophic choices in the marshaling of his plan. Clearly, he did. Rather, it is to suggest — through an analysis of his opponents — that the underlying bases of these choices did not lie chiefly, as is traditionally asserted, in the president's personality. In this sense, I advance an understanding of presidential leadership that bridges institutional structure and individual choice. In the following section, I explain the reasoning and value of this approach.

Examining FDR and His Opponents: The Importance of Institutions and History

As soon as word of the Court-packing proposal hit the street on February 5, 1937, critics complained of Roosevelt's misdeed. To William Allen White — the fairly pro–New Deal and widely read Republican columnist — the president's 1936 campaign attack against the "economic royalists" now appeared to be a sham, for he "seemed to have harbored subconsciously a seven-devil lust to become an unconstitutional royalist himself." Monarchy was also on the editorial minds of the *New York Herald-Tribune*, who compared FDR's message to a declaration by Louis XIV: *"L'etat c'est moi"* — "I am the State."[1] Although much time has passed, scholars have been no less forgiving. Kenneth S. Davis suggests that, in attempting to expand the Court's size, Roosevelt was "corrupted by a heady sense of limitless power" based on his "faith in God" and his "own perception" that his electoral mandate was "divine."[2] Michael Nelson relates the actions of FDR to those of the three other presidents with the "largest reelection victories" of the twentieth century. For Nelson, "Roosevelt's Court-packing proposal in 1937, Johnson's unilateral escalation of the Vietnam war in 1965, the cover-up of the Watergate scandal by Richard M. Nixon in late 1972 and 1973, and Reagan's Iran-contra affair in 1985 and 1986," all fall into a category of episodes where second-term presidents, blinded by bouts of postelection arrogance, "instantly breached the bounds of permissible political action in a way that brought down the public's wrath."[3] But is it fair to compare the Court-packing plan to Watergate? To the Iran-contra scandal? In pushing the plan, was Roosevelt really as "brazenly deceitful" as so many have depicted him?[4] More importantly, does such a portrayal accurately explain why judicial reform failed? Does it reveal much about FDR's intent in introducing the plan? Does it tell us how its defeat affected later judicial interpretation?

In looking to Roosevelt as the primary — if not the sole — source of the plan's demise, critics have often overemphasized his shortcomings. In doing so, they have overlooked both how the plan fit into FDR's larger effort to

reshape the nation's institutional arrangement and why congressional opponents understood it as an attack not only on the courts but on their institution as well. In this sense, these critics have failed to appreciate the manner
in which the institution of the presidency helped to shape FDR's decisions
and actions — independent of his personality — and contributed to defining
the plan as a violation of the separation of powers. The result is a portrait of
the presidency that is far too personal, one that allows for significant second-
guessing and better-than-20/20 hindsight.

   With respect to Roosevelt and the Court-packing plan, presidential errors in judgment are said to include: his desire for secrecy in devising the
proposal in the place of consultation with congressional leaders, cabinet
members (except his attorney general), and other legal advisors; his determination to avoid the Court issue during the 1936 campaign; his conclusion
that the election had given him a clear personal mandate; his insensitivity
to America's reverence toward the Supreme Court; his decision to present
the plan in an evasive manner; and his refusal to compromise until it was
too late. Proponents of this view of the Court-packing episode therefore assume that, absent a series of presidential blunders, the Supreme Court
could have been curbed. If FDR had only mastered the skills of the presidency, his effort would have ended in yet another victory rather than his
most stinging defeat. At their best, these critics offer keen insights into one
of Roosevelt's greatest disappointments. At their worst, they serve as little
more than late-day Monday morning quarterbacks. Nevertheless, in examining the presidency in a fashion guided by "personality and circumstance"
and unconcerned with the institutional context in which particular presidents lead, their analyses are inevitably limited.[5]

   In discussing the failure of the Court-packing plan, Stephen Skowronek's
framework, as outlined in chapter 1, aids in developing an analysis that emphasizes the institutional context of Roosevelt's decision to introduce the
plan (as well as his apparent "mistakes" in pushing for its passage). Recall,
in Skowronek's view,

   The presidency is an *order-shattering* institution in that it prompts each
   incumbent to take charge of the independent powers of his office and to
   exercise them in his own right. It is an *order-affirming* institution in that
   the disruptive effects of the exercise of presidential power must be justified in constitutional terms broadly construed as the protection, preservation, and defense of values emblematic of the body politic. It is an *order-
   creating* institution in that it prompts each incumbent to use his powers

to construct some new political arrangements that can stand the test of legitimacy within the other institutions of government as well as the nation at large.[6]

In this sense, FDR's status as a reconstructive president drove his decision to restructure the judiciary, even if did not determine the form of his reform. Following his decisive 1936 electoral victory, few would have expected FDR — as an overwhelmingly popular president with vast political authority and a desire to uproot an institutional order in ruins — to simply lie down before a Court he had so harshly criticized and his opponents had so steadfastly defended.[7] More centrally, few would expect any similarly situated president to do so. Boldness, after all, is inherent in reconstructive presidents, as they take command of the presidency with a strong sense of legitimacy to foster significant institutional reform.

Yet, in contrast to Skowronek, I pay more attention to the defenders of the order FDR was seeking to shatter. I do so for two reasons. First, the vast historical evidence shows that the nature of FDR's attack on the preexisting governing order corresponded with the design of his institutional program and ultimately defined the judiciary's role in the new order. In other words, those who defended the preexisting order in the face of the Court-packing plan did so based on a fairly accurate perception of Roosevelt's intentions in restructuring the nation's institutions. By analyzing these defenders, we can shed fresh light on the objectives and purposes of the new legal order at its founding and assess how the Court fight helped to shape the institutional norms of the post-1937 judiciary. Before considering FDR's opponents, however, it is essential to discuss the president's constitutional vision and explain how this vision shaped the design of the Court-packing plan, a central component of his larger institutional program.

FDR's reconstructive design, as I have discussed, sought to consolidate power in the presidency and commit the enhanced authority of the national administrative state to a progressive agenda that stressed the aggrandizement of statutory rights and the federal protection of individual rights. As Sidney Milkis writes, "FDR and other ardent New Dealers wanted to overcome the state and local orientation of the party system, which was suited to congressional primacy and poorly organized for progressive action on the part of the national government, and to establish a national, executive-oriented party, which would be more suitably organized for the expression of national purposes."[8] Despite this call for a restructured state, FDR and his New Dealers believed that their brand of democracy was in alliance with the one the founding fathers had envisioned. To them, the Constitution had been written and the political institutions developed during a period when agriculture dominated the social and economic fabric of the nation, and for a time a "nearly perfect democracy" existed. But, as then Assistant Attorney General Robert H. Jackson told a group of Yale Law School alumni in 1937, all of this had been "violently changed by industrialization."[9] To account for this development, FDR proposed to *restore* the principles of American democracy through the creation of the modern presidency. The result would be a progressive democracy consistent with the beliefs of the founders but amended to meet the needs of an industrialized America. To ensure an effective and energetic executive branch, however, the judiciary would have to be prevented from encroaching upon the "expert" actions of administrative agencies via a rigid interpretation of the Constitution. To clear the way for a closer alliance between the modern presidency and the populace, individual rights would have to be secured. With respect to legal doctrine, then, FDR's institutional program required a style of interpretation that protected individual rights and liberties and advanced the theory of judicial deference to the executive branch. In this sense, it drew heavily on the congealing union between rights-centered liberalism and legal realism.

In profound ways, FDR's constitutional vision inspired the design of his proposal to reform the judiciary. Compared to the many alternative measures floating about Washington at that time, Roosevelt chose one of the few that enhanced the powers of the presidency. Most of the others sought to reduce the Court's influence either by altering the size of the vote required for the justices to declare a statute unconstitutional or by expanding Congress's power over the judiciary. For instance in 1936, Senator George Norris of Nebraska, believing that the amendment process he once favored was now "impracticable," asked his colleagues to have the "courage" to approve legislation requiring a unanimous decision to invalidate an act of Congress. As he noted, "it takes twelve men to find a man guilty of murder. I don't see why it should not take a unanimous court to find a law unconstitutional." Another 1936 proposal sponsored by none other than Senator Burton Wheeler of Montana — the leader of the opposition to FDR's plan — called for a constitutional amendment enabling the Congress, following an intervening election, to pass a Court-invalidated law with a three-fourths majority (later revised to two-thirds). For Roosevelt and his advisors, however, each of these plans was flawed. With the Norris bill, they reasoned that the justices would ignore the rule or would simply reach unanimous decisions to preserve the prestige of the Court.[10] They eliminated Wheeler's proposal because it not only required a constitutional amendment—a path they did not wish to take—but returned authority over an "unconstitutional" statute back to Congress. And, by requiring a three-fourths vote to overrule the Court, it increased the power of the president's congressional adversaries.

After much consideration, FDR dismissed the option of a constitutional amendment for three reasons. First, he feared opponents could easily raise enough money to block it. The failure of the Child Labor Amendment provided him with a ready example of what a Court-curing proposal would likely encounter in the states. Second, he did not wish to admit that the Court had been correct all along in its interpretation of the Constitution. Instead, he sought to state in dramatic terms that the makeup of the Court's membership was what needed amending. If, as realism suggested, "the *true* law consists in the behavior patterns of judges," there was no need to alter the Constitution.[11] Finally, he was concerned that even if an amendment passed, a still hostile Court would retain its ability to interpret the Constitution's new language differently than intended. Although "distasteful," the Court-packing option fit best with his larger institutional goals of enhancing the powers of the executive branch, centralizing progressive reform at the national level, and achieving judicial reform through a new statute rather than a constitutional amendment.

Speaking against the amendment option, Harold Ickes also expounded upon the connection between the plan and the protection of civil rights and liberties:

> Never forget that the words of the Constitution will not avail to protect our liberties unless the justices of the Supreme Court give force and effect to those words. Do not forget either that those justices who have been the most responsible for the decisions invalidating social and economic legislation are not the justices who have been the most steadfast in the protection of the civil and religious rights of the individual. . . . Individual liberty is far more likely to be defended from new and subtle forms of encroachment by Justices who are alive to the social and economic needs of the present generation than by Justices who have lost touch with, and who cannot understand, the aspirations of their fellow-men.[12]

Attention to the defenders of the preexisting order also sheds light on the intent of the plan, and should clarify some of Roosevelt's controversial actions. To this day, critics of Roosevelt—particularly those on the political left—express disappointment with his decision to squander so much of his vast stock of political clout on the Court. If they can forgive FDR's original sin of introducing the plan, they are perplexed by his refusal to compromise after the famous "switch in time." In the end, they openly wonder what might have been if Roosevelt had acted differently.[13] They do so, however, based on a common misunderstanding of the plan as exclusively an attempt to "constitutionalize" the New Deal.

I argue that FDR designed the legislation to do more; namely, he sought to transcend the immediate concerns of the second New Deal's constitutionality by "revolutionizing" the judiciary. He did so for clear reasons. As historical institutionalists have written, not only do "institutions shape politics," but "institutions are shaped by history" as well. "History matters because it is 'path dependent': what comes first (even if it was in some sense 'accidental') conditions what comes later. Individuals may 'choose' their institutions, but they do not choose them under circumstances of their own making, and their choices in turn influence the rules within which their successors choose."[14] In considering the notion of path dependency, we should not lose sight of the fact that in the half-century before FDR's presidency the judiciary was the single branch of government most set against change. During this period, numerous pieces of progressive legislation met their end via judicial nullification. The judiciary, moreover, had been the most dominant institution in the policy domains the New Deal was devised to transform. Yet, even after FDR's overwhelming reelection victory, forces set against New Deal liberalism were still allied, at least in part, with the Court and its anti–New Deal doctrine. Significantly, many of these defenders were members of Roosevelt's own party. Many also held positions of power in Congress and therefore commanded a certain amount of electoral legitimacy in their own right. Roosevelt felt that he could not dismantle the previous order and install *his* ideal institutional arrangement by simply waiting for the Court to step aside. While the Court was not the only barrier to the implementation of his constitutional vision, it was the symbolic leader of the opposition to his reconstruction. He had begun to confront the Court with his statements following *Schechter* and with his support of the Wagner Act, but now was the time for him, as a reconstructive president, to implant his authority on both the Court and its defenders in Congress. As he put it in 1941, "change would never have come" without a "frontal attack" upon the philosophy of the Court's majority.[15]

In attempting to revolutionize the judiciary, Roosevelt had a natural ally in the reform movement known as legal realism. As the next section shows, the idea to add new "younger" justices to the Court to keep it abreast of the realities of society was strikingly similar to the notions of realism. In seeking to install a degree of realism in the judiciary, however, Roosevelt no longer confronted only conservative Republicans (and some Democrats) as opponents. Two other substantial forces were — to put it mildly — uninspired by the realism experiment, especially as packaged in the Court-packing plan. For separate and distinct reasons, New Freedom progressives and southern Democratic leaders in Congress, often allies of FDR during his first term, abandoned the president during the Court fight. As explained below, New Freedom progressives, witnessing the fulfillment of many of their legislative objectives during FDR's first term, became more concerned with the power of a centralized government dominated by the presidency than with the Court's exercise of judicial review. Southern Democrats, concerned with the direction the president was taking *their* party and anxious about what a Roosevelt Court might mean for their previously protected system of segregation, bolted from FDR as never before. In the end, these two groups made the difference in the defeat of the plan, as they sought to protect their institutional control over policies important to their interests and constituencies. In introducing his plan, Roosevelt had displayed his intention to reshape the nation's governing institutions in striking fashion. When members of his party balked, it was doomed to failure. This result, then, was due less to strategic errors by the president and more to the fact that the plan was the product of his reconstruction (state-building) project, a project that sought to reduce the power of both the federal judiciary and the Congress by placing a modern presidency at the core of a newly energized and centralized national state.

Legal Realism and FDR's Court-Packing Plan

As detailed in chapter 2, the Court's willingness — even eagerness — to tear down the first New Deal at times elicited strong realist-tinged comments from the president during his first term. While this aggressive attack on the judiciary lessened as the 1936 campaign got underway, the Court-packing plan was a natural progression in Roosevelt's increasing advocacy of realism. In fact, even during the reelection effort, the president's words — while not focused specifically on the Court issue — "were blunt and uncompromising, and they clearly anticipated a decidedly unpragmatic turn."[16] Thus, as realism considered whether all law was politics, once the election was over, FDR — with his second New Deal still in judicial jeopardy — moved forward with a plan that seemed to confirm that suggestion. In some sense, this stance made him the ultimate realist of the day. For FDR, if law was separate and apart from politics, the Court's legitimacy in dismantling his programs was in doubt. As he noted in his second inaugural address, with Chief Justice Hughes looking on: "The essential democracy of our Nation and the safety of our people depend not upon the absence of power, but upon lodging it with those whom the people can change or continue at the stated intervals through an honest and free system of elections. The Constitution of 1787 did not make our democracy impotent." Continuing, he implored that the "men and women" of the "Republic . . . will insist that *every* agency of popular government use effective instruments to carry out their will. Government is competent when all who compose it work as trustees for the whole people. It can make constant progress when it keeps abreast of all the facts."[17]

In this light—even if somewhat cautious with his initial message to Congress on February 5—FDR's Court-packing language suggests that his idea of court reform was not simply about ensuring the constitutionality of the New Deal. After all, it was likely too late for the two pillars of the second New Deal to survive constitutional scrutiny if the Court continued on its past course. Congress would certainly not pass the Court-packing plan before the justices heard arguments on the validity of the Wagner Act on February 8, 1937 (just three days after FDR introduced the proposal). And it was unlikely do so before the Court considered the constitutionality of the Social Security Act three months later. Unless the plan sufficiently frightened the justices or the administration moved to delay the cases, the president could not create a Court of fifteen in time to save either of these two acts. FDR obviously could not expect the first of these possibilities—in fact, many thought his proposal would fortify judicial distaste for his programs. Moreover, he dismissed the idea of delaying the cases soon after the 1936 election. In short, the plan's aim appears to have been grander than merely constitutionalizing the second New Deal. And in some clear ways, it advanced notions of realist thought.

Indeed, even in his much maligned first speech on the Court-packing plan, the president voiced realist views: "Little by little, new facts become blurred through old glasses fitted, as it were, for the needs of another generation; older men, assuming that the scene is the same as it was in the past, cease to explore or inquire into the present or the future." In their place, as Roosevelt put it in his straight-talking "Fireside Chat" of March 9, 1937, he would select "Judges who will bring to the Courts a present-day sense of the Constitution—Judges who will retain in the Courts the judicial functions of a court, and reject the legislative powers which the courts have today assumed." FDR's judges would be "younger men who have had personal experience and contact with modern facts and circumstances under which average men have to live and work." For him, if judges and justices understood the existing conditions of the nation and employed a legal method that allowed these social facts to be taken into account, the New Deal would be understood in its appropriate constitutional fashion. In his view, then, the plan was not an "attack on the Court," but a device "to restore" it "to its rightful and historic place in our system of constitutional government and to have it resume its high task of building anew on the Constitution 'a system of living law.'"[18]

The president and his collaborators designed the plan to accomplish a more realistic jurisprudence by seeking either to add new justices to the Court or to coax current ones into retirement. In this sense, despite common understandings of the Court-packing plan, FDR was not necessarily proposing to expand the size of the nation's highest tribunal. While obviously unthinkable, if all six of the sitting justices over the age of seventy resigned in unison, the Court would remain at nine but would have the updated outlook he desired. Future presidents, moreover, would be ensured that the Court was never too far out of line with the realities of American society. They would be able to add a new justice when, after reaching the age of seventy, an "old" one who had served ten years refused to retire within six months. The Court, however, would be limited to a maximum of fifteen members. Age was also not as prominent in the plan as conventional wisdom recalls. A justice over the age of seventy who had not served ten years could remain on the high bench until he had done so. (Of course, all the sitting justices over seventy had served ten years.) This component of the plan suggested that the age of a justice's tenure was more important than the date on his birth certificate. It also adds credence to the notion that the plan sought to imbue the Court with democratic impulses. As one of FDR's legal realist supporters put it: the "proposal provides a continuous process of rehabilitating the Court's personnel so that the normal processes of constitutional growth will not hereafter be interrupted."[19] Speaking in the third person and in Skowronek's *order-affirming* terms, the president had expressed a similar sentiment in December 1936:

> It is the deep conviction of Franklin D. Roosevelt that the Constitution of the United States was never meant to be a "dead hand," chilling human aspiration and blocking humanity's advance, but the founding fathers conceived it as a living force for the expression of the national will with

respect to national needs. Sincerely, steadfastly, the President refuses to believe that the framers meant to tie the hands of posterity until the end of time, denying future generations freedom of action in meeting the problems presented by one hundred and fifty years of change. The . . . New Deal is Franklin Roosevelt's conscientious, deliberated effort to continue the Constitution as a truth and a hope, not as a mere collection of obsolete phrases. The Laws that he has proposed are frank attempts to gain new objectives in human relations, and nothing is more certain than that he will keep up the drive with all the force of his being and all the power of his office.[20]

To be sure, despite this language, many in the realist camp, excluded from the plan's development, intensely disliked the manner in which the president chose to reform the courts. After all, one of their heroes, Justice Brandeis, was the oldest member on the high bench at eighty-one (with two decades of service). Another, Justice Oliver Wendell Holmes, had remained on the Court well into his ninetieth year (with more than twenty-nine years of service). For instance, Karl Llewellyn of Columbia Law School — Jerome Frank's cofounder in realism — noted that "the President's program is unfortunate from every angle but one. . . . We need action. But the majority of the court have given the sign that they do not propose to let us have the action which we need, or even a reasonable part of it, or even to experiment toward salvation. Primitive peoples, in such conditions, get rid of the priest or the oracle. When rain fails persistently, they act. The President proposes nothing so drastic."[21]

Others joined Llewellyn in viewing the Court-packing proposal through a realist lens. Leon Green, Dean of Northwestern Law School, stressed that "the proposal merely affords a way for the *interpretation* of the Constitution to be kept more nearly abreast with the development of the nation. Anyone who knows anything about constitutions knows that they themselves grow in meaning, in sanctity and in their protective value." Continuing with this theme, Green employed language that likely distressed many formalists: "No interpretation of the Constitution has finality so long as it is not approved by the American people. . . . Reinterpretation is always at hand."[22] Speaking in a similar vein, future justice Robert Jackson noted that "the difficulty with the Court is that it has lost touch with reality, that the actual problems faced by working people, and for that matter by employers as well, come to the Court through books and printed briefs and lawyers' windy arguments. The living currents of thought and action do not penetrate the monastic seclusion of the justices."[23] Comparing the medieval medicinal act of bleeding to the Court's "Roberts' land" interpretation of the Constitution, leading realist Thurman Arnold proclaimed: "We know that institutions become in danger when they do not keep up to date and that no . . . court has ever been destroyed by bringing into it men who were abreast of the times. It is odd that today we understand the middle ages so much better than the times in which we live."[24]

To be sure, these realists were likely less concerned with the age of new justices than with whether they would endorse realism's rule-skepticism and employ social scientific methods to attain the facts of a case (often by deferring to the executive branch). Many opponents, moreover, perceived Roosevelt's own calls to provide the judiciary with "new and younger blood" and with jurists who "understand modern conditions," as simple rhetoric from a president seeking to appoint his own "yes-men."[25] Consequently, much of the legal realist theme was lost in the battle over the Court-packing plan. Nevertheless, as discussed below, in his dealings with the defenders of the preexisting order, the president's words and deeds display a desire for developing a new style of judicial interpretation.

Defending the Preexisting Order

Besides borrowing realist ideas, the Court-packing plan, as a component of FDR's reconstruction program, spoke to the needs of rights-centered liberals. With the plan, FDR sought to replace a Supreme Court that had consistently restricted liberty with one that would accede to the desires of an executive devoted to enhancing statutory rights and protecting individual liberties. In turn, those threatened by FDR's larger institutional program prepared to block the plan in any way possible. Here, I focus on their reasoning and actions. In doing so, I seek to draw conclusions on how the conflict helped to define the institutional norms of the post-1937 judiciary. I also explain why some of the president's decisions — which have led to claims about his incompetence — were reasonable for a leader attempting to reshape the nation's institutions.

The Silence of Conservative Republicans and Liberty Leaguers

For FDR and his New Dealers, the protection of civil liberties was not only necessary for the creation of the modern presidency, it was also vital to the installation of a new industrial-labor relations order. This order promised to end the escalation of strikes and the economic chaos they produced by providing workers with the right to organize. In an area long dominated by authoritarian action on both sides, the Roosevelt administration's labor policy—following the passage of the Wagner Act—emphasized a democratic process for settling conflicts. The administration understood that without such liberties as free speech and assembly, the right to organize would be a vacant right, that without the right to organize and strike, the power of collective bargaining would be a hollow power. Thus, as I have discussed, in keeping with the components of his reconstruction, when Roosevelt defended the Wagner Act he employed concepts of democracy and fairness, referring to it as "an act of both common justice and economic advance."[26]

Not surprisingly, industrialists saw the Wagner Act in a different light. According to the American Liberty League, the new law did not release the worker from the shackles of deprivation. Rather, it constituted an "illegal interference with the individual freedom . . . sanctioned by the Constitution" of a worker "to sell his own labor on his own terms." Even before the president signed the National Labor Relations bill into law in July 1935, a number of industrialists had set out to destroy it in practice and in court. On June 27, Ernest T. Weir of National (Weirton) Steel proclaimed, "I am advised by our general counsel that the Wagner-Connery bill is unconstitutional." In September, a panel of fifty-eight "unbiased" Liberty League lawyers declared that the statute constituted "a complete departure from our constitutional and traditional theories of government." At a press conference announcing their conclusion, Earl F. Reed, Weirton's chief counsel, asserted, "when a lawyer tells a client that a law is unconstitutional, it is then a nullity and he need no longer obey the law." Others followed suit. According to Senator Robert La Follette's Civil Liberties Committee, the combined effort of the Associated Industries of Cleveland, the National Metal Trades Association, and the National Association of Manufacturers to subvert the act represented "one of the greatest campaigns of nullification ever waged against any Federal statute." As Joel Auerbach writes, "although the Wagner Act presumably blanketed American workers with First Amendment guarantees of free speech and assembly, many employers refused to accept the new congressional definition of civil liberty."[27]

In attacking the president's labor program on constitutional grounds, the Liberty League instigated a bitter battle over the meaning of the nation's ruling document and seemingly set up a climactic confrontation over the Court-packing plan. After all, it was with this group in mind that Roosevelt undertook his assault on the "economic royalists" in his acceptance speech at the 1936 Democratic Convention. It was also with the Liberty League in mind that he, in the closing days of the campaign, delivered a speech in Wilmington, Delaware — "the home State of the Du Pont corporations and affiliate companies whose principal owners were instrumental in organizing and financing the League" — in which he simply read the words of Abraham Lincoln to "better describe the kind of liberty" his administration sought to achieve.[28] Thus, while FDR wished to avoid making the Court's anti–New Deal decisions a campaign issue, at times he was not above issuing thinly veiled attacks on the beneficiaries of the justices' doctrine. This antagonism toward the business elite continued during the Court fight. In an April 15, 1937, press conference — three days after the Court unexpectedly upheld the Wagner Act — FDR blasted business groups for the rash of sit-down strikes plaguing the nation. By declaring the Wagner Act unconstitutional on their own, he proclaimed, they had fostered an environment of lawlessness in industry.[29]

But when the president announced his Court plan two and a half months earlier, both Republicans and Liberty Leaguers (often one and the same) had remained surprisingly silent. They did so for two reasons. First, voters had not only returned Roosevelt to the White House with the largest plurality in American history, they had also dramatically altered the makeup of the Congress. In the Senate, there was one fewer conservative Democrat (down to eighteen), and only ten conservative Republicans. In the House, the outcome was similar. The conservative coalition comprised roughly thirty anti–New Deal Democrats and eighty Republicans.[30] The voice of the liberal northern wing of the Democratic Party had grown even louder. As a result, early on many thought that Congress would easily enact the Court proposal. Strategy provided the GOP a second reason for its subdued response. Knowing the president was counting on their vocal opposition to help stir up support for his plan, they thought it best to withhold their expected outburst. In other words, with little power to make a difference, keeping quiet was the most effective way to voice their opposition.

Roosevelt's apparent desire for secrecy before the plan's release was connected to his anticipation of conservative outrage and did not primarily lie, as others have argued, "deep in [his] personality." To the extent that he pursued a "policy of secrecy," it was predicated on the fear that "a leak would tip off [the] opposition and enable them to start [a] hostile build up before he got his plan out."[31] But in fact, FDR did not hold the plan in total secrecy. By mid-January 1937 at least two journalists (George Creel and Raymond Clapper) knew that the president might try to pack the Court. And Creel had published "trial balloon" comments made to him by FDR in the December

26, 1936, issue of *Collier's*. "His face like a fist," Roosevelt had excitedly told Creel, "Congress can *enlarge* the Supreme Court, increasing the number of justices so as to permit the appointment of men in tune with the spirit of the age." Anyone who read this edition of "the nation's weekly" knew the president's position as well. On January 24 FDR explained his specific plan to CIO President John L. Lewis and AFL counsel Charlton Ogburn, both of whom approved.[32] Moreover, his State of the Union Address, delivered on January 6, was full of what Joseph Alsop and Turner Catledge called, "muted thunders against the Court as the chief obstacle in the path of social progress, and big with a muffled warning to the justices that unless they could fall into step their powers would be curbed." His references to the Court included: "The statute of NRA has been outlawed. The problems have not. They are still with us. . . . The vital need is not an alteration of our fundamental law, but an increasingly enlightened view with reference to it. . . . Means must be found to adapt our legal forms and our judicial interpretation to the actual present national needs of the largest progressive democracy in the modern world. . . . The judicial branch also is asked by the people to do its part in making democracy successful. . . . The process of our democracy must not be imperiled by the denial of essential powers of free government."[33] Some heard these remarks as a rejection of the amendment route, others as an indication that the president would wait to see whether the Court followed the election returns, and still others as a "mysterious" signal that he would try to pack the nation's highest tribunal.[34] Nevertheless, taken as a whole, FDR's words and deeds do not seem consistent with a man interested in displaying his childlike cleverness, as some have alleged.[35] Rather, they show a strategic attempt to lay the groundwork for the introduction of a controversial plan without revealing its content.

In hindsight, Roosevelt implicitly included the Supreme Court in his attack on the "economic royalists" and interpreted the election results as a partial rejection of Republican platform pledges to "resist all attempts to impair the authority of the Supreme Court." As Roosevelt advisor Rex Tugwell explained: "The Court, as [the GOP] represented it, was the bulwark of liberty; in Franklin's reference it was the protector of privilege. The third branch of government was unreformed. It was, Franklin had said, 'out of step.' But it was not he who insisted on the issue during the campaign."[36] While the GOP's conspiracy of silence did mute popular support for the plan and hamper the president's effort, with only sixteen votes in the Senate, conservative Republicans could do little else but keep quiet. The Democratic rout of 1936 meant that those who mattered most were members of FDR's own party.

New Freedom Progressives' Fear of the Modern Presidency

Of all the criticisms concerning Roosevelt's handling of the Court-packing proposal, perhaps the most convincing relate to his failure to consult with congressional leaders and his initial explanation of the plan's intent. Given the size of the Democratic majority in Congress, many have argued that Roosevelt missed a prime opportunity to establish a vibrant form of party government. Instead, he chose to introduce legislation that sharply divided his party. Moreover, despite everything that had come before, in his message to Congress on February 5, he said nothing of the Court's rejection of the New Deal. Unconvincingly, he stated that his purpose was to reorganize the judiciary because of the age and the heavy workload of the justices. His message began with the words: "I have recently called the attention of the Congress to the clear need for a comprehensive program to reorganize the administrative machinery of the Executive Branch of our Government. I now make a similar recommendation to the Congress in regard to the Judicial Branch of the Government, in order that it also may function in accord with modern necessities."[37]

While seemingly unimportant, these two sentences partially reveal FDR's reasons for not pursuing a dialogue with congressional leaders before he unveiled the plan. During the campaign, he had begun to rely more and more on a group of young advisors clustered in the White House and less on the wisdom of seasoned folk on Capitol Hill and regular party stalwarts. He had indicated his intention to move away from the traditions of the Democratic Party in order to create a party in his own image. In this light, his decision to avoid discussions with congressional leaders over the shape of the Court proposal displays his continuing efforts to reposition the presidency in the national institutional arrangement. As Milkis argues, the third New Deal, which included the Court-packing plan, the Executive Reorganization Act, and the "purge" campaign of 1938, was not intended to promote party government, but rather to foster "a program that would help the president and administrative agencies govern in the absence of party government." At the expense of the Congress, the states, the traditional party framework, and a federal judiciary committed to restraining the growth of a progressive national government, FDR sought to install an institutional structure that would eventually "establish a refurbished executive power as the vital center of American politics." But when the president showed the Executive Reorganization bill to a group of congressional leaders in January 1937, they quickly rejected it as an assault on their institution.[38] He did not dare make the same mistake with the Court-packing bill. The president, then, likely did not seek the advice of congressional leaders before the plan's release because its design — coupled with the Executive Reorganization bill — sought to reduce the power of Congress. Given this, he reasonably expected a negative reaction from some leading members of Congress and feared giving these detractors a head start in gaining support. As Vice President "Cactus" Jack Garner noted, "if the President had told any Congressional leader in advance about his court plan, they would have tried to talk him out of it."[39]

Indeed, the increasingly expansive power of the executive and the nationalization of governmental functions — which had been a concern to many in Congress as Roosevelt's first term ended — emerged as the underlying force uniting progressives and conservatives against the Court-packing plan. Thus, when Senator Wheeler, a New Freedom progressive, announced his opposition to the president's bill, he was firm in his position that "the usurpation of legislative functions by the courts should be stopped." However, he also stressed, "to give the Executive the power to control the judiciary is not giving the law-making power back to that branch of the Government to which it rightfully belongs but rather is increasing the dangers inherent in the concentration of power in any one branch of our Government." For him, the issue was not whether the Court was wrong — it was — but how to prevent future "usurpation of the legislative power" by the judiciary. Wheeler's New Freedom progressivism, like that of Republican William Borah of Idaho and other western senators, was based on hostility to centralized power, whether corporate or governmental. Despite their consistent support for many New Deal programs, the president's Court proposal represented far too dramatic a step in the development of an executive-dominated and nationally concentrated polity — what some called a "modern dictatorship" — for them to sit by on the sidelines. In Wheeler's words, "there is nothing democratic, progressive, or fundamentally sound in the proposal advanced by the Administration."[40]

On the other side of the Senate's ideological spectrum, Carter Glass echoed this sentiment in his dissent to the plan. In a long bitter speech delivered to a national radio audience just four days after the Court had seemingly reversed itself in West Coast Hotel v. Parrish, the seventy-nine-year-old Virginia senator denounced the plan in no uncertain terms. Titling his speech "Constitutional Immorality," Glass stressed, "no threat to representative democracy since the foundation of the Republic has exceeded in its evil portents this attempt to pack the Supreme Court of the United States and thus destroy the purity and independence of this tribunal of last resort."[41]

This fear of the modern presidency, then, produced a strange alliance. Although he disagreed with southern conservatives on just about every other matter, Wheeler felt he had to do "every thing he could to fight the plan" and therefore led an opposition that included conservative Republicans and Democrats — his usual foes. Given his impeccable progressive credentials, Wheeler's decision disabled FDR's attempt to link his congressional adversaries with the "economic royalists" he had so successfully maligned during the 1936 campaign. It also helped the plan's opponents secure the cooperation of Chief Justice Hughes and Associate Justice Brandeis in an effort to undermine the president's argument of an overburdened Court.[42]

Strikingly, then, as the opposition expanded in Congress, it increasingly resembled the *Schechter* Court. Old generation progressives, fearful of a strong executive seeking to centralize and nationalize governmental functions, unexpectedly allied with "irreconcilables" who had disagreed with the president every step of the way. Neither apparently saw the modern presidency in the same *order-affirming* sense as the president did. And given the rapid rise of dictators across the globe, their fears convinced many to oppose the plan.

Southerners and the Preservation of Party and White Supremacy

The final and most cryptic component of the opposition to the Court-packing plan came from a small group of influential Senate leaders from the South. If FDR's plan had any chance of moving through the Senate, Majority Leader Robinson, Jimmy Byrnes, Pat Harrison, and their Texan advisor, Vice President Garner, would have to be on board. During his first term, this group of moderately conservative southerners — labeled by the press as the "Big Four" — had been loyal servants to FDR and a vital factor in the success of his legislative agenda. By the end of the Court fight, their working relationship with the president would be in a shambles.

To be sure, when FDR introduced his proposal, Robinson, Byrnes, and Harrison quickly endorsed it, with the first two the most vocal of the three. The majority leader, believing that one of the new justiceships would be his, noted defensively that the president's proposal was "in no sense a violent innovation" and predicted its passage.[43] Byrnes gave the plan a more earnest endorsement, stating on the day of its release: "I do not know that it goes far enough but I am in favor of it." Nearly two weeks later, sounding like the 100 percent New Dealer he had claimed to be during his recent reelection campaign, the future justice made a national radio appeal to arouse support for the plan and to explain, unlike Roosevelt, its expected impact on the judiciary's attitude toward the New Deal: "What [Liberty League lawyers] fear is that the adoption of the proposal would result in the Court's having a different view of the constitutionality of the legislation enacted by the Congress in compliance with the mandate of the people. I think the fear is justified."[44]

Still, to rights-centered New Dealers, the fact that the Big Four were in control of the ultimate fate of the bill was unnerving. In January, Thomas Corcoran — a close liberal advisor to the president — had told Interior Secretary Harold Ickes that Byrnes "has now gone sour. [He] simply went along because he was to be up for reelection last year. Now, with a term extending beyond that of the President, he has jumped over the traces and gone conservative." Robinson, according to Tugwell, "did not like the Court bill when he understood it." He advocated for it out of party loyalty and because FDR had apparently promised to put him on the Court once an opening became available.[45] Thus, few were surprised — following Justice Willis Van Devanter's retirement announcement in May — that "the liberals" were "to a man against" Robinson's appointment to the Court.[46]

These liberal concerns were no doubt real. While the Big Four had been loyal to Roosevelt during his first four years, with their terms presumably extending beyond his, they now figured to be much less reliable in their support for his plans. Moreover, few New Dealers believed that they were totally committed to FDR's increasingly progressive program. Indeed, many thought they had backed the more rights-centered second New Deal because it was constitutionally questionable. And of course, the president's plan would eliminate the security net the anti–New Deal Court represented in his first term.

As southerners, they had also heard what the Court-packing proposal would mean for the sacred institution of segregation. In his March 29 national radio address, Carter Glass, pointing to the "sectional animosity" of the Court's "fierce defamers," issued a vociferous warning to his fellow southerners. Speaking of Harold Ickes — who had been president of the NAACP's Chicago chapter before joining Roosevelt's cabinet and was one of the most vigorous advocates of judicial reform — the senior Virginia senator alleged that he had "recently reproached the South for providing separate public schools for the races" and had "urged repeal of every statute and ordinance of segregation." Continuing, Glass labeled Ickes an "infuriated propagandist for degrading the Supreme Court" and asserted that he "practically proposes another tragic era of reconstruction for the South." Glass, who reveled in being called the "unreconstructed rebel," then issued his strongest warning about the fate of racial policies before a Roosevelt-enlarged Court: "*Should men of his mind have part in picking the six proposed judicial sycophants, very likely they would be glad to see reversed those decisions of the Court that saved the civilization of the South* and in spite of the menace of passionate partisans, with their violent threats to 'reorganize' the Court, prohibited the seizure and confiscation, without pay, of the estates of private citizens. *It was the Supreme Court of the United States that validated the suffrage laws of the South which saved the section from anarchy and ruin* in a period the unspeakable outrages of which nearly all the Nation recalls with shame."[47] While Glass, an early detractor of the New Deal, was an expected critic of the plan, a similar appeal by a more moderate southern senator — Tom Connally of Texas — threatened to expand the opposition.[48] Indeed, the Court-packing plan was the last straw for many congressional southerners who were already unnerved by the elimination of the two-thirds rule, the president's increasingly progressive positions, and the addition of black American voters to the Roosevelt coalition.

Such southern sentiment toward the plan was in stark contrast to that of many African American groups. For example, the National Negro Congress — backed by labor's Non-Partisan League — put out a pamphlet urging black Americans to support the president's plan. Featuring a photograph of Abraham Lincoln, the pamphlet's title page declared in striking captions: "Shall the Supreme Court Continue to Ignore the 14th and 15th Amendments? Join the Fight to Guarantee the Negro People their Rights under the Constitution by supporting the Supreme Court Modernization Plan." Inside the pamphlet, its authors made the case for why African Americans should favor the plan.

> [T]his same Court upheld the right of states to pass Jim-Crow car laws. . . . The Supreme Court by its decisions has enforced schemes to create Jim-Crow residential areas for Negroes. . . . Every major citizenship right guaranteed to Negroes by the 14th Amendment has been crippled by the Court so that in reality Negro people are able to enjoy only a small portion of their legal rights. . . . More than three million qualified Negro voters are denied any effective means of using their vote by the Supreme Court interpretation of the 15th Amendment. . . . The Negro people, joining hands with the forces of progress, with the mighty forces of labor in this country, must see to it that the will of the people is accomplished.[49]

A number of African American newspaper editors agreed. For example, at the *St. Louis Argus*, editors wrote: "We do not know that a change of judges in the Supreme Court means a radical change in the thought of their successors. But at least it gives us hope, yes double hope, in view of the fact that we are living in a new age, and the President of United States has the spirit in keeping with the times." At the *Philadelphia Independent,* editors went further: "Negroes the country over should welcome the liberalization of the Supreme Court. . . . As the Supreme Court is now constituted, it must become blind when reading the portions of our Constitution dealing with the rights of the Negroes of America. Negroes cannot be more unjustly treated under and by the law than they have under the present system, therefore any move that will change the present conditions should be welcomed. Maybe this change is not meant to react favorably for the Negro, but maybe it shall, like the Emancipation Proclamation, prove a boomerang and bowl over some of the antiquated practices of our lawmakers." While not certain FDR's expanded Court would advance the African American cause, editors at several "Negro newspapers" felt, as those at the *St. Louis Argus* put it, that "strong evidence" suggested it would.[50] In turn, they thought "every Negro in the Country should hail" the president's plan "with enthusiasm, as a boon for a brighter future for the race." (Likely connected to such acclaim was FDR's nomination of the NAACP's William Hastie — on the same day he announced the Court-packing plan — to be the first African American federal judge in U.S. history. As Harvard Sitkoff writes, "black leaders of every persuasion proclaimed the selection [of Hastie] . . . as an epochal act by the Chief Executive.")[51]

Such African American advocacy no doubt fanned the fiery complaints some southerners voiced about the Big Four's continued support for FDR. For example, in his national radio address, Senator Glass exclaimed that "it is perfectly obvious that the so-called Democratic party of the North is now the negro party, advocating actual social equality for the races; but most of our Southern leaders seem to disregard this socialistic threat to the South in their eagerness to retain in power a Party which, to use a phrase of Mr. Roosevelt, 'masquerades as Democratic,' but is really an Autocracy."[52]

Yet to the Big Four the outlook was somewhat different. For they, especially Byrnes and Harrison, represented a new generation of southerners. Born after Reconstruction, Byrnes and Harrison entered national politics together as congressmen in 1910 and moved into the Senate in 1930 and 1918, respectively. In the early years of the Roosevelt administration, they had consistently backed the president. In 1936 they both had campaigned — against their more traditional race-baiting challengers — as true New Dealers. While Harrison was more conservative than Byrnes, both sought a new position for the South at the national level. And while their conception of the "new" South was clearly much different from that of progressives like Alabama Senator Hugo Black and Texas Representative Maury Maverick, they could not be pigeonholed into the conventional understanding of the conservative southern senator either. Byrnes, who had risen to the leadership ranks in a very short period, was considered by many to be "the smartest man in the Senate." Harrison, known for his cleverness and his "knowledge of the legislative technique," had earned the nickname "The Old Gray Fox of the Delta."[53]

To these two leaders, along with Robinson and Vice President Garner, the introduction of the Court-packing proposal presented a distressing paradox. If they chose to oppose it, they would surely lose their influence with the president and split the Democratic conference, thereby throwing the Senate's leadership over to the liberals. Their shrewd efforts to work with a nationalizing administration while still holding on to their southern belief in states' rights would come to an end. On the other hand, if they endorsed the plan, they would see one of their own (Robinson) appointed to the Court and another (Harrison) likely take his place as majority leader. They also hoped Garner would drop the word "Vice" from his title following the next election. The plan might add more liberal justices, but by the time they arrived on the bench the Court would have likely declared much of the second New Deal unconstitutional. In addition, nearly all potential appointees preached judicial restraint and presumably would not endanger southern white supremacy to the extent Glass and Connally feared. By supporting President Roosevelt, they would also retain their ability to block or amend any new legislation that threatened their cherished southern institutions. Finally, they would be in a perfect position to take control of the party when FDR made his scheduled return to Hyde Park in January 1941. Thus, to them, the basis for supporting the plan stemmed from a need to persuade the president of their continued allegiance in order to maintain their influence within the Democratic Party, while preparing for their planned ascendance in 1940. As Attorney General Cummings noted on August 1, 1937: "It is generally felt that back of all these various fights, including the Supreme Court fight, there lies the question of 1940, and the incidental control of party destinies."[54]

To be sure, the Big Four suffered for their support of the bill. For example, Byrnes, the most outspoken of the group, faced criticism from a disquieting source as "the Ku Klux Klan began to rise up in opposition to him in South Carolina." As his biographer writes,

A Supreme Court enlarged with six New Deal justices popularly was expected to render decisions more favorable to Negro plaintiffs in civil rights litigation. Editorials and news articles in both northern and southern newspapers interpreted Roosevelt's court plan as an attempt to gain Negro votes from the Republican party. . . . As Byrnes continued to support the court plan through the spring and summer of 1937, a flier was anonymously distributed throughout South Carolina. "Warning!" was reproduced above a drawing of a watchful eye and the letters KKK. *A picture of a hooded night rider carrying a torch was printed in red ink and below the caption "Communism Must Be Destroyed. Hands Off the Supreme Court."*[55]

True enough, the Big Four did not like the original version of the bill, and early on they pushed for an alternative plan. Indeed, their consistent appeals to FDR for a compromise bill and his consistent refusals reveal just how much the two camps differed in their interpretation of the plan's intent. To the southerners, the plan was not about legal reform. Rather, it concerned the validity of the New Deal statutes yet to be ruled on, the constitutionality of future legislation, and the activism of the Court. With a Justice Robinson and one or two others, an appropriate balance could be reached—a Court committed to judicial restraint could be ensured. But the president wanted more. His plan called for a reconstructed federal judiciary designed to support an aggrandized administrative state. Thus, when congressional leaders first met with him about the idea of a compromise, he reportedly "laughed in their faces so loudly that a number of them were exceedingly annoyed."[56]

Undaunted, these leaders continued to push for a weaker alternative. At the same time, FDR maintained his belief that only a radically reorganized Court would satisfy his desires. Despite the president's position, unfolding events quickly began to affect the plan's fate. Most importantly, the Court's "switch-in-time" decisions—first upholding Washington's state minimum wage law for women and children on March 29 and then validating the Wagner Act on April 12—filled the capital with talk of compromise.[57] At this point, with the president clearly losing votes — in part because of his actions on the sit-down strikes — Robinson made another appeal for compromise. He based this one on his reading of the Court's Wagner Act ruling, explaining to one of Roosevelt's advisors that "the whole interpretation of the commerce clause had been immensely broadened; it was now possible to forge ahead with the President's program without worrying about the Court." To be sure, Robinson was right. In a sweeping decision, the Court embraced the view, long employed by New Deal lawyers, that trade in the United States now operated within a national economic system; therefore, it was appropriate for the Congress to prevent nationwide strikes by enacting legislation guaranteeing workers the right to collective bargaining.[58]

Nevertheless, the president was still not interested in a compromise that would give him only "a couple" more justices and feared (even before the Wagner Act ruling) that Robinson, succumbing to Garner's influence, would agree to one without consulting him. FDR's reluctance to modify the plan frustrated Robinson, who believed throughout the episode that a scaled-back version of the bill represented the best solution for ending division within the Democratic Party. Indeed, even Wheeler was amenable to the notion of additional members on the high bench. But to White House liberals, if Robinson were to get one of these new positions as the president had supposedly promised, and he turned out to be as conservative as they believed, the Court's philosophy would not change much. As Alsop and Catledge wrote in 1938, Roosevelt "wanted a Court which would 'co-operate' with the White House. He needed six justices who would be friendly and approachable, men with whom he could confer, as man to man, on his great plans for social and economic reform and experiment."[59] The fact that the president was not willing to compromise in mid-May supports the notion that he had greater ambitions than simply to constitutionalize the New Deal. Instead, he designed the plan to bring a new style of judging to the bench — one that would align with administrative agencies in an effort to produce social change and *restore* a more progressive democracy. In short, his plan would institutionalize the union between realism and rights-centered liberalism in the federal judiciary.

Events, however, continued to alter the political environment. With the combination of Justice Van Devanter's retirement announcement and the Senate Judiciary Committee's negative vote on the plan (both on May 18), and the Court's decision upholding the Social Security Act six days later, Roosevelt could no longer deflect a compromise bill. Accepting the conclusion of many that he did not (assuming he once did) have the votes to pass his original measure and unwilling to risk "public humiliation," he finally relented by agreeing to a new version of the bill. Still, the alternative measure did not abandon the realist principles of the original plan. It authorized the president to appoint one additional justice every year for each member of the Court older than seventy-five (instead of seventy). With four of the sitting justices already past this ripe old age (three of them conservatives), and assuming none retired or died before, FDR would have the opportunity to increase the Court to thirteen members by 1940. Moreover, with the vacancy created by Van Devanter's retirement, the 1937 appointment, and the 1938 appointment, FDR would also be able to make three appointments within seven months.[60]

Although angered by the president's failure to announce his nomination immediately after Van Devanter's resignation, Robinson pushed on in support of the compromise bill. Predicting passage, he nevertheless knew it would be difficult to fend off a likely filibuster. Still, the majority leader felt that, in the end, the Washington heat and the members' eagerness to get home would limit the length of the delay, although another compromise might be necessary.[61] As he pressed for its enactment, the hot humid days of a D.C. summer and the pressure of the fight became too much for the sixty-five-year-old Arkansas native. On the night of July 13, he collapsed on the floor of his apartment. A maid found him dead the following morning. Robinson's death freed his allies, who had so wanted to see him on the Court, from their previous obligations of support. His likely replacement as majority leader, Pat Harrison — who had proclaimed to a friend on the day of Robinson's collapse that "this thing goes deeper than you think, and I won't have any part of it" — could vote as he wished. The Mississippi senator's biographer interpreted these words to mean, at least in part, that "even in the absence of concrete evidence," and more so than other southerners, Harrison "feared that a liberalized court would move to disrupt the state of race relations in the South."[62] As a shrewd observer of the political scene, Harrison was onto something. Nevertheless, he no longer had to worry. Any hope of enacting the president's plan disappeared with Robinson's death.

Moving toward the Federal Protection of Rights: A New Approach to Labor Unrest

By the time Harrison had made his feelings known, the level of progressive suspicion toward the Big Four had grown significantly. Besides their continuous calls for a compromise on the Court bill and their apparent increasing conservatism on other issues, the Big Four had collided with progressives over the shape of the administration's labor policy. In particular, Byrnes and Garner attacked the president for refusing to issue a statement concerning the sit-down strikes in the automobile industry, which shared the headlines with the Court-packing plan in the early part of 1937. The sit-down strikes, which began in earnest in Akron, Ohio, were largely a battle over the legitimacy of the Wagner Act. Real collective bargaining was simply not occurring, as unions (especially the CIO) battled with industrialists — who incorrectly assumed that the act would soon be cast into the Court's constitutional wastebasket — over its implementation. As John L. Lewis put it on the day before the new year: "some of the largest and most powerful corporations in this country [refuse] to follow modern labor practice, or to obey the law of the land. They deny the entirely reasonable and just demands of their employees for legitimate collective bargaining, decent incomes, shorter hours, and for protection against a destructive speed-up system."[63]

In response to these alleged abuses, CIO allied union leaders — the AFL rejected the idea — began employing the sit-down strike. By design, these strikes involved the active takeover of factories by workers until a settlement was reached, thereby preventing such favorite strikebreaking tactics as the use of replacement workers to continue operation and of armed guards or police to attack picket lines. In 1936 and 1937 the primary targets of the CIO sit-down strikes were the automobile and steel industries. The CIO selected these industries because, according to Lewis, "huge corporations, such as United States Steel and General Motors had no right to rule as autocrats over the hundreds of thousands of employees . . . no right to transgress the law which [gave] to the worker the right of self-organization and collective bargaining . . . no right in a political democracy to withhold the rights of a free people."[64] Not surprisingly, one of the first victims of the sit-down strike was General Motors of Michigan, which had rejected the majority rule and exclusive bargaining principles endorsed by the Wagner Act. In addition, GM had refused to "recognize a labor organization as such and would not enter into a written contract with a union on the behalf of company employees." Finally, the auto giant required that any negotiations with employee representatives take place with local plant managers, not with the corporation as a whole. As labor historian Sidney Fine writes, "GM not only construed the representation and bargaining rights of union officials in as narrow terms as possible, but it also discriminated against union workers . . . spied on its workers . . . [and] established company unions in GM plants and favored them over outside unions." In calling the strike, however, leaders of the United Automobile Workers (UAW) also disregarded the proper procedure defined by the Wagner Act by not requesting an NLRB election. They chose not to do so because they feared they might not win. But even if they did, as Fine writes, "GM would [have] contest[ed] an NLRB election order in the courts, and the UAW, like GM and most everyone else, assumed that the [Wagner Act] would be declared unconstitutional."[65] Put another way, the Supreme Court's activist conservatism and the perception of its pending assault on the Wagner Act influenced the sit-down action of UAW members in the GM factories of Flint.

In an effort to end the Flint strikes, then governor of Michigan Frank Murphy intervened. (FDR later named Murphy to the posts of attorney general and then Supreme Court justice). The newly inaugurated governor, who had been persuaded to run by the president, was a strong progressive, a "union man," and committed to ending the strike without the use of force. (In fact, Lewis had asked UAW leaders to delay the strikes until after his inauguration). On January 10, knowing that his decision would likely prolong the dispute, Murphy ordered the state's emergency relief commission to feed the strikers. Moreover, when violence erupted the day after an unsuccessful attempt by Flint police to evict the strikers, the governor took an unusual stance. While he called in the National Guard and the state police, he refused to return to the old style of handling strikes. Instead, he pledged that the troops would be used only "to protect the public interest and preserve peace and order. . . . [U]nder no circumstances . . . [would they] take sides." Although he considered the strikes illegal, the forty-seven-year-old governor was not prepared to support actions that would lead to bloodshed. Notably, both President Roosevelt and Labor Secretary Perkins supported his decision.[66]

Back in Washington, however, Vice President Garner, who thought the strikes were not only blatantly illegal but dangerous to American society, vigorously urged FDR to take steps to halt them. To Garner, the strikes were not about attaining "better wages or working conditions, but a step in the fight of John L. Lewis for personal and political power." Perhaps even more infuriating to the vice president was his view that "Lewis was arrogantly expecting the backing of the Democratic party . . . as a pay-off for his support and campaign contributions."[67] As a southerner, Garner was not alone. "The southern congressional delegations denounced the sit-down almost with unanimity as a violation of the common-law sanctity of private property." To add fuel to this fire, Garner's reference to Lewis's demand of Roosevelt administration support for the CIO-backed strikers also hit the mark. In a January 21 statement, the labor leader stressed: "We have advised the administration that for six months the economic royalists represented by General Motors contributed their money and used their energy to drive their administration out of power. The administration asked labor for help to repel this attack and labor gave its help. The workers of this country expect the administration to help the workers in every legal way, and to support the auto workers in General Motors plants." Asked to respond, the president noted that in the "interest of peace," he would make no comment.[68]

Unwilling to risk his prestige and popularity on the strike, FDR worked for a resolution behind the scenes. While neither side wanted to see the workers forcibly dislodged from the plants, on February 1, the strikers escalated the tension by outwitting a 200-man unit of the GM plant police and expanding the strike into an additional building. The strategic maneuver was designed to limit GM's national production. The next day, GM successfully obtained a court injunction — it made the request on January 28 — calling for the evacuation of all GM property by 3:00 p.m. the following day. This court order appeared to force the governor's hand, seemingly requiring him to eject the strikers. But the events of February 3, 1937, did not conform to practices of the past. Instead, on "the wildest day in Flint's history," the situation nearly "erupted into civil war," as the strikers ignored the injunction, three thousand picketers walked in support of their decision, and seven thousand curious citizens looked on. A "wild confusion" took over the city. To some, it "signaled the complete breakdown of law and order . . . the arrival of mob rule." In turn, the city government mobilized a civilian police reserve with the thought of violently ejecting the strikers. But the unit took no action. It was quickly disbanded after Murphy, the head of the National Guard, and the executive vice president of GM intervened. For its part, the UAW agreed to keep its members and supporters under control. On the same day of the unrest, negotiations involving the interested parties — the governor and officials from the UAW, the CIO, and GM — resumed in Detroit.[69]

On February 5, the day FDR released his Court-packing message, GM lawyers — on the basis that the injunction had been violated — secured a writ of attachment requesting the Genesee County sheriff to arrest the strikers, the picketers, and UAW officials. However, when the sheriff asked for the assistance of the more than three thousand National Guardsmen on hand in Flint to help execute the writ, the governor declined. "Instead, Murphy authorized the Guard, if it deemed the action necessary, to place a cordon guard around [the striker-held buildings] to prevent the sheriff from attacking the plant." As he related to a friend, he was "not going down in history as 'Bloody Murphy.'" Previously, he had even indicated that he would resign before sending in the troops.[70]

Nevertheless, pressure on the governor was mounting. By delaying the enforcement of the court order, Murphy was giving the impression that the strikers, by illegally trespassing, were somehow above the law. With this in mind, Murphy drafted a "law and order" letter on February 9 and read it to

Lewis that night.[71] In it, he stressed that "the time . . . [had] come for all concerned to comply fully with the decision and order of the court and take necessary steps to restore possession of the occupied plants to their rightful owners." It was his duty to enforce the court order. According to one pro-Lewis account, the imposing labor leader responded by calling the governor's bluff. "You talk of the law. It is not law, it is General Motors' law. . . . This is General Motors' strikebreaking law."[72] He then allegedly threatened to join the strikers in the plant.

In the end, it was a threat Lewis did not need to carry out. The two sides reached a settlement on February 11, 1937. GM negotiators, unaware of Murphy's "law and order" letter, apparently felt that the sit-downers would not be forced out of the plants, thereby halting GM's production until an agreement was reached. Among other concessions, GM granted the UAW its most significant demand of exclusive representation for six months, enough time for it to gather sufficient support to win a majority-rule election. As one autoworker told Lewis, "now, we got the sons of bitches." To be sure, a number of additional factors were working against GM. Most notably, Senator La Follette's Civil Liberties Committee's hearings — held a few days before the settlement — linked GM to the Pinkerton agency and labor espionage, thus weakening the company's position. In addition, FDR may have pressured GM to end the strike. As Fine writes, when William Knudsen, GM's executive vice president, "later asserted that 'the Government . . . practically ordered' the settlement of the strike, it may well have been the president to whom he was referring."[73]

Whether or not Roosevelt "practically ordered" an end to the strike, his maneuvering during this tense situation should be seen in the historic terms in which it occurred. The strikers had blatantly violated the court-ordered injunction, yet the president and his lieutenants — Labor Secretary Frances Perkins and Governor Murphy — did not send in the troops as past government officials (whether local, state, or federal) had done. Despite constant calls for the use of force, they were unwilling to see the episode end in bloodshed.[74] Instead, even by tolerating extralegal actions, they encouraged the right of workers to organize and strike. In an area where violence had been a common reaction by both employers and government officials for decades — especially when workers violated court orders — FDR's support of Murphy's "refusal to use force indiscriminately or as a matter of first resort against workers was a radical" step in delegitimizing the previous legal order. The primary point here is not that the administration simply refused to employ violent means in the situation, for the president did endorse Murphy's threat to restore "law and order." Rather, it is to highlight that the resolution of the strike shifted control over the legitimate use of force from the courts to the executive. This, in turn, contributed to the nationalization of workers' rights and the development of realist-influenced labor law. "The faithful execution" of the law, as Murphy later told a Senate Judiciary subcommittee, included "wise administration of the law," not simply its "literal instantaneous application at any cost. . . . [W]hen there is widespread disobedience to law, it is not enough to enforce the law; it is also necessary to discover and eliminate the causes of that widespread disobedience."[75] With the settlement of the strike coming on the heels of the Court-packing plan's release, FDR had signaled his desire to end the old system of court intervention in resolving industrial unrest. In its place, he sought to create a new order based on more humane and democratic principles, stressing the protection of individual rights over the protection of property rights.

As part of this new approach toward labor and the law, the Justice Department sought to prosecute violators of the Wagner Act. Its first object of inquiry was labor unrest in Harlan County, Kentucky. Long part of the social setting, labor violence returned to Harlan County in the mid-1930s, virtually eroding early New Deal era successes in unionizing the county. Even after the passage of the Wagner Act, CIO organizers were repeatedly met with false arrests, threats, and violent attacks. Consequently, organizers retreated to Washington in February 1937. There, they met with members of the La Follette Civil Liberties Committee in an attempt to convince them to investigate the violent antiunion activities taking place in the county. (As noted above, the La Follette Committee's previous investigation of the automobile industry's use of espionage had been a significant factor in the UAW's successful negotiations with GM.) On hearing of the violent campaign against labor in Harlan County, the committee — allegedly John L. Lewis's brainchild — quickly set to work again. On April 14, it began hearings that "sought to show that the Harlan County Coal Operators' Association was continuing to finance and direct a widespread conspiracy to control county politics and to use the sheriff and his deputies to prevent unionization of the county's mines, thereby violating" the Wagner Act.[76]

With the evidence presented during committee hearings (and additional CIO information), Attorney General Homer Cummings announced on May 19 that the Department of Justice would investigate "to determine whether federal criminal laws [had] been violated in Harlan County, Kentucky." To Cummings, the "complaints paint[ed] a sordid picture of violence and terrorism in Harlan County," and he promised "vigorous and prompt prosecution" if the "investigation disclose[d] offenses under federal jurisdiction." While all the acts of violence and intimidation uncovered by the La Follette Committee violated state laws, for the most part offenders went free, as state prosecutors failed to indict or biased juries nullified the application of the law. Indeed, the violent nature of Harlan County had become so routine that "old-timers" considered "death from shooting . . . as 'death from natural causes.'"[77] Moreover, once A. B. "Happy" Chandler, the newly inaugurated governor, entered office, he dismissed previous state charges against the Harlan County sheriff, a political ally.

To give jurisdiction to the federal courts, the Justice Department developed a litigation strategy that connected the Wagner Act to an old Reconstruction statute. Specifically, since the Wagner Act did not contain criminal provisions, Justice Department lawyers sought to employ section 51 of title 18 of the U.S. Code as a device for prosecuting antilabor practices. This section, originating from the Enforcement Act of 1870, was part of a congressional attempt to protect the civil rights of the recently freed slaves, but the government rarely utilized it after Reconstruction's end. As detailed in chapter 5, it outlawed conspiracies "to injure, oppress, threaten, or intimidate any citizen in the free exercise or enjoyment of any right or privilege secured to him by the Constitution or laws of the United States." By linking this law with the Wagner Act's sanction to protect workers' right to organize and bargain collectively, the Justice Department brought forth indictments. Specifically, it indicted "twenty-four mine executives, twenty-three law enforcement officers and twenty-two corporations for conspiring to deprive the miners in Harlan County, of rights guaranteed them under the National Labor Relations Act."[78] If this prosecution proved successful, it would be the first time the national government had tried and convicted any individual or corporation under the act since the end of Reconstruction.

When the case went to trial in the summer of 1938, the *Nation* saw a clear connection between this prosecution and Roosevelt's attack on the existing legal order via his Court-packing plan: "The New Deal, by reviving the 1870 Civil Rights Act [*sic*], is wielding a new weapon against them [the absentee capitalists], and though the Supreme Court once declared the act unconstitutional it is not likely to do so again. Like Harlan's coal operators, the justices, too, have been chastened."[79] Indeed, coupled with the administration's action during the sit-down strikes, this creative legal strategy signaled a new style of federal government involvement in labor relations. No longer would the federal government sanction violence and intimidation toward workers under the auspices of a court order. Instead, the protection of civil rights and liberties would be the cornerstone of a more democratic and well-ordered polity.

This new labor policy — most notably the administration's handling of the sit-down strikes — clearly had a significant impact on the debate over the Court-packing plan, as congressional members feared what law and order might mean under a reorganized judiciary. As Carter Glass, referring to the sit-down strikes, put it in his address to the nation: "With private property seized at will; the courts openly reviled; rebellion rampant against good order and peace of communities; with governments pleading with mobocracy instead of mastering it. . . . This, with other dangerous evils, contrived or connived at, by governments, is the real crisis which faces the Nation and cannot be cured by degrading the Supreme Court of the United States."[80]

The president's failure to denounce the sit-down strikes, as noted above, also worsened his schism with the Big Four.[81] And as a wave of sit-down strikes sprang up throughout Michigan during the Court-packing debate and threatened to spread across the nation, the vice president and his senatorial allies escalated their rhetoric. Seeking to stem the tide of strikes, on April 1 Senator Jimmy Byrnes offered an amendment to a new version of the Guffey Coal Act — the Court declared the first version unconstitutional in 1936 — which in effect banned the sit-down strike in the coal industry. On the Senate floor, Byrnes asserted that "it is not only the people of Michigan who are affected, but throughout the entire Nation men are out of employment and unable to earn a livelihood because of the sit-down strikes." Others have noted that Byrnes's true intentions for introducing the amendment lay elsewhere. As Martha Swain writes, he was "gravely concerned over the filtering of Lewis's textile organizing teams into South Carolina."[82] Thus, when the CIO initiated an organizing drive in the textile industry on April 4 by sending forty-five agents into eight southern states, the fate of the Byrnes amendment brightened. In turn, it became more threatening to the president. If it passed, FDR would face a dilemma. While he would have a new Guffey Coal bill to sign, the legislation would favor the position of Wagner Act–ignoring industrialists. On the other hand, if he vetoed the measure, he risked showing that he approved of the illegal strikes, which would likely foster their expansion.[83] In the end, the Senate rejected the amendment by a vote of 48 to 36 on April 5, thus relieving the president of a difficult decision. In its place, senators overwhelmingly approved a compromise concurrent resolution — not requiring Roosevelt's signature — that condemned both the sit-down strikes and industrial espionage as "illegal and contrary to sound public policy."[84]

Nevertheless, during the course of 1937, it became increasingly clear that, as a group, Robinson, Byrnes, Harrison, and Garner — no longer threatened by an apparent lame-duck president — had declared their independence from the administration. With their criticism of Roosevelt's stance toward the sit-down strikes and their constant calls for a Court-packing compromise, they had confirmed the early 1937 fears of rights-centered liberals. In mid-June their opposition to the president's relief spending package — partially because they believed that too much of it was going to northern African Americans — deepened the split. Following this vote, Vice President Garner left Washington for the first time in his long career while the Congress was still in session, deciding to "vacation" in his hometown of Uvalde, Texas.

The breakup of the alliance between the president and the remaining members of the Big Four, however, did not occur until after Robinson's death, when FDR intervened in the battle to fill the majority leader position. The contest was between Harrison and Alben Barkley of Kentucky. Barkley, who had sharply criticized the Court in his 1936 keynote address to the Democratic convention and had come to the president's rescue to defeat the Big Four on the relief spending legislation, was the clear choice of progressive Democrats. Conservatives favored Harrison, who represented a continuation of Robinson's leadership. The first sign of Roosevelt's intervention into the contest came in the form of a letter to Barkley following Robinson's death. Addressing Barkley as "the acting majority leader in the Senate," the president called on him to continue the Court-packing fight. Most interpreted FDR's "My dear Alben" letter as an obvious signal of White House support for Barkley. In turn, Harrison's allies quickly denounced the president's interference. As the vote drew near, Roosevelt publicly announced his neutrality, but privately he worked hard to give the Kentuckian the victory, telling Jim Farley, "Barkley must win."[85] Apparently disappointed with Harrison's increasing conservatism and his clear lack of enthusiasm toward the Court plan, the president authorized a White House call to Mayor Edward Kelly of Chicago — the boss of the Illinois machine — to pressure Senator William Dieterich to switch his vote. In the end, Dieterich obliged, giving Barkley a single-vote victory.

The Court-packing episode ended a week after Barkley's election. The president asked the vice president to work out a deal, and after little effort, Garner accepted a compromise written by the opposition. To further insult FDR, opposition senators sought a vote to recommit the original compromise bill to the Judiciary Committee. After declining to help the president's attempt to halt the move, Harrison and Byrnes joined sixty-eight of their colleagues to kill the bill. Their votes signaled just how much their relationship with the president had frayed.

Indeed, soon after Barkley's victory, progressives began to regard the president's intervention as a tragic mistake. If he had maintained his neutrality, they believed Harrison would have won easily, and, as with Robinson, FDR could have persuaded him, out of party loyalty, to support most of his progressive policies. Instead, by backing Barkley, Roosevelt had furthered the split between progressives and conservatives and forced Byrnes and Harrison, at least for the time being, into the enemies' camp. Whether it was too late for the president to continue a working relationship with the remaining members of the Big Four is unclear. Given the dramatic events of the 1937 session and the rising hostility between the White House and this group, he likely felt that reconciliation would potentially undermine his agenda and his attempt to install his constitutional vision. Nevertheless, with the future ideological direction of the Democratic Party apparently up for grabs, FDR had cast his lot. And given the extraordinary changes in the Court's constitution from 1937 to 1941, his positioning in this political environment would profoundly influence judicial doctrine for the next generation of American life.

Conclusion

True to their expectations, when the defenders of the preexisting order eventually lost control over judicial interpretation, the Roosevelt Court constructed the style of doctrine they had feared most. When FDR finally did pack the Court with a string of appointments, beginning with Hugo Black in 1937, it was no longer in the business of advancing an economic theory favorable to antiunion industrialists or of undermining the authority of a modernizing presidency. Neither was it interested in continuing to provide constitutional cover for southern white supremacy. Instead, it was eager to defer to the decisions of an energetic executive branch and openly sympathetic toward extending federal protection of individual rights and liberties. Southern conservatives understood the threat that New Deal jurisprudence posed for southern democracy and resisted it. New Freedom progressives sought a more diffuse political order that institutionalized a sedentary federal judiciary and concentrated political action in the "great forty-eight." Liberty Leaguers opposed FDR every step of the way. Consequently, none of these three clusters of opposition benefited from midcentury jurisprudence.[86]

Despite this decidedly pro–New Deal result with regard to the Supreme Court's post-1937 doctrine, critics of Roosevelt still complain about the Court-packing plan. To them, after the "switch in time"—to paraphrase a popular conclusion of this constitutional conflict—the president no longer needed to continue the battle because he had already won the war. And if, as is generally accepted, Justice Roberts decided to switch his vote in December 1936, it is fair to ask whether the battle should have been fought at all.[87] But such speculation misses the importance of the Court fight itself. Indeed, when FDR made his eight appointments and one elevation in a five-and-a-half-year period,[88] one of his main concerns was whether a potential nominee was with him during the Court fight. As historian Robert Harrison has written, "anyone who had deserted [him] on that issue was eliminated from contention."[89]

This great legislative failure, then, became a defining moment in the design of the legal order Roosevelt was creating. As the president noted in 1941, it was "a turning point in our modern history."[90] It was so because the foundational footings for the post-1937 judiciary were developed and defined at this time. With so much reconstructive authority, even in defeat, FDR succeeded in securing a favorable interpretation for the advancement of his constitutional vision. Despite his miscalculations—both real and perceived—the judiciary was radically transformed, emerging as the most progressive branch of government for the next half-century. And even as the Court-packing plan faded into a memory, its influence remained. Its failure served as the last gasp of the preexisting order and helped condition the Supreme Court's decades-long hostility toward the defenders of that order. Put differently, the battle scars and memories of the Court-packing episode—a bloody shirt of sorts—had remarkably strong reverberations.

FOUR "Approving Legislation for the People, Preserving Liberties — Almost Rewriting Laws"

The Politics of Creating the Roosevelt Court

As New Deal scholars have pointed out in the past, the battle over the Court-packing plan rocked FDR's relationship with the Senate and southern Democrats. Most prominently, many have viewed the plan's rejection and the Court's transformation as driving forces in the rise of the conservative coalition in Congress and the president's corresponding decision to undertake his disastrous "purge" campaign in the 1938 Democratic primaries. Less well known is the Roosevelt administration's continuing effort — through its judicial policy — to remake the Supreme Court into a fortress of liberalism, institutionally constructed to buttress the modern presidency and destabilize southern democracy. In this and the next chapter, I more fully develop my reconsideration of the Roosevelt record on race by analyzing the second and third pillars of this policy, namely, the president's appointments to the Supreme Court and his Justice Department's efforts to extend and federally protect the rights of African Americans. In doing so, I challenge traditional thought on the Roosevelt administration's commitment to advancing the rights of black Americans which has been overly bound by the president's legislative record and virtually unconcerned with his policy toward the judiciary. I argue that the combination of these two pillars of policy — driven largely by a distaste for southern politics — profoundly affected the Supreme Court's institutional mission of the post-1937 era, a Court that in short course committed itself to rewriting civil rights law.

In examining these pillars of the Roosevelt administration's judicial policy, it is important to keep two factors in mind. First, the Roosevelt administration's effort to expand the rights of African Americans was clearly constricted in scope. There is good reason why scholars have traditionally given FDR little credit for advances in civil rights that occurred soon after his death. The extent of his administration's actions on race — particularly those that elicited the most publicity — simply did not meet the demands of the African American community. Second, while FDR was certainly at the center of constructing his administration's policy toward the judiciary, in some cases members of his administration likely took his direction further than expected. Thus, in my examination of politics surrounding FDR's Supreme Court appointments — and in my discussion of the Roosevelt Justice Department in chapter 5 — I attempt to highlight the president's specific role in decisions and actions affecting his administration's policy toward the judiciary. In addition, I begin this chapter by devoting extensive attention to outlining the general motivations underlying a Roosevelt administration judicial policy that simultaneously undermined southern democracy and aided in advancing African American rights.

Presidential Motivations: Institutional Designs and Democratic Party Divisions

As noted in chapter 2, during FDR's first term, his administration's judicial policy began on a defensive note, which meant merely doing the minimum of arguing for the constitutional validity of New Deal measures in court. In other words, there was no serious effort to transform judicial interpretation. In 1935 this passivity gave way to the more aggressive stance of challenging the judiciary by backing reconstructive legislation (most importantly, the Wagner Act). In supporting such legislation — the first pillar of its judicial policy — the administration's principal motivation centered on securing a legislative program. To a lesser extent, it helped to consolidate the Democratic Party's electoral coalition and advance the president's developing constitutional vision. (Still, the Roosevelt administration's use of this reconstruction legislation as a judicial policy was a bit unusual. It did not really employ the legislation, as administrations typically do, as a negotiating device to enact the leading items on the president's legislative agenda. Rather, legislative proposals like the Wagner Act were primary concerns themselves.) With the Court-packing plan, FDR took the more confrontational path of proposing reconstructive legislation to another level. While still framed through reconstructive legislation, the administration now formulated its policy toward the judiciary to statutorily save New Deal legislation from the judicial wastebasket and, more importantly, to advance the president's constitutional vision. At this point, the administration's judicial policy still held little value as a legislative bargaining chip.

Once the Congress cast the Court-packing plan aside, the administration focused on constructing its two new pillars of judicial policy (judicial appointments and the Justice Department's rights-expanding effort). With these pillars, the implementation of FDR's constitutional vision played an increasingly fundamental role. Put another way, beginning in Roosevelt's second term and escalating after the 1938 elections, his administration's judicial policy was primarily formulated as part of a larger institutional program — one that sought to supplant the existing institutional arrangement with one better suited to advance the values he endorsed. To be sure, the realization of FDR's constitutional vision was not the sole goal of his administration's judicial policy. Rather, the quest to expand and reformulate his electoral coalition emerged as a leading motivation as well. While of less importance, the use of this policy as a means to ensure the success of his legislative agenda became more traditional, especially after the onset of war.

Recall from previous chapters, the president's ideal institutional order — what some have labeled the modern presidency — called for political authority to be nationalized as never before and concentrated in the executive branch. Along with creating this new institutional structure, FDR sought to commit it to the expansion of new statutory rights and the protection of individual rights. But obstacles, such as those that undermined his Court-packing and executive-reorganization plans, stood in the way. Principal among them was a form of democracy below the Mason-Dixon line that consistently sent representatives to Congress who were more conservative than FDR — given his high level of support in the South — thought appropriate. The result was a level of frustration that paved the way for the president's effort to unseat recalcitrant Democrats — aimed almost exclusively at elected officials from the South — in the 1938 primaries. As he told Georgia voters during the purge campaign, the separation of powers system: "means that if the people of the State of Georgia want definite action in the Congress of the United States, they must send to that Congress Senators and Representatives who are willing to stand up and fight night and day for Federal statutes drawn to meet actual needs — not something that serves merely to gloss over the evils of the moment for the time being."[1]

FDR certainly had reason to be aggravated by the contours of southern democracy and its effect on the nation's policy. During the 1930s, historian Alan Brinkley writes, "the political structure of most southern states was in all essential respects the same structure the South had erected for itself at the end of Reconstruction. Politics in most of the South was oligarchic, reactionary, and myopic. It thrived on rigid control of the franchise by conservative political elites, on a fervent commitment to white supremacy, on deep suspicion of 'outside interference' in its affairs, and on a one-party system that had faced no real challenge since the 1870s."[2]

As the president knew only too well, "most adults did not vote" in the one-party South. Once "women became eligible to vote," according to Earl and Merle Black, "scarcely more than a fifth of adult southerners voted in either general elections or Democratic primaries." This total included "almost no" African Americans.[3] Moreover, as Gunnar Myrdal accurately described in 1944, the oligarchy that the South's one-party system supported consisted "of big landowners, the industrialists, the bankers and the merchants. Northern corporate business with big investments in the region shar[ed] in the political control." None in this group were particularly enamored with the policies of the New Deal and, therefore, southern representatives consistently limited the progressiveness of the president's program and of the Democratic Party. As one New Deal Democrat put it: "Southern Democracy was the ball and chain which hobbled the Party's forward march."[4] These were the forces that formed the impetus for the purge campaign, a bold effort to liberalize the Democratic Party that failed miserably in the end.

But even after the embarrassment of the doomed purge campaign (which I examine below), the obstinacy of southern politics still called for something more. To preview, the administration increasingly employed its policy toward the judiciary to slowly erode the precedential bedrock underlying the constitutionality of one-party politics in the South. Put another way, through its actions, the Roosevelt Justice Department carried on — albeit at a more restrained pace — what the purge campaign had failed to accomplish, namely, the disruption of southern politics to secure a more liberal future. It did so by seeking to create a new legal order that challenged the traditional localized structure of the American party system. In short, as his presidency neared its midpoint, FDR's judicial policy emerged as an essential component in his effort to "reconstruct" the national polity and reshape Democratic Party politics.

The Roosevelt administration's emphasis on securing federally protected rights was not driven solely by long-term institutional concerns. Practical politics underlay this effort as well. Following the 1936 election, it was clear that the president commanded a reformulated electoral coalition. In 1932 FDR had relied on southerners, first, to secure the Democratic Party's nomination and, then, to faithfully provide him with all their electoral votes. In 1936, while southern support remained strong, the rising popularity of the president and his party in the North gave him greater flexibility to govern the nation as he saw fit. Significantly, as noted earlier, African Americans were a central component of Roosevelt's increased electoral strength in the North. In 1932 black voters had virtually ignored Robert L. Vann, the publisher of the largest-selling "Negro newspaper," who had famously called on them to "go turn Lincoln's picture to the wall. That debt has been paid in full."[5] But in the span of four years, FDR and his New Deal had convinced African American voters to heed Vann's call after all. The switch was so profound that a majority of black voters has never again supported a Republican presidential candidate.

The president now led a coalition that included two seemingly incompatible groups — southern whites and northern blacks. Moreover, while the black vote represented only a small percentage of the total tally, many in Washington thought that African Americans could potentially decide upcoming elections. The author of an unsigned 1940 administration memo elaborated on this point: "The Negro vote will be from 5 to 13 percent of the total vote cast in the November elections in the following states: Delaware, Illinois, Indiana, Kansas, Kentucky, Maryland, Michigan, Missouri, New Jersey, New York, Ohio, Pennsylvania, and West Virginia. . . . [It] may well become the decisive factor in the Presidential elections in most of these states." In 1948 Henry Lee Moon, a political strategist for the Political Action Committee of the CIO, confirmed that the memo's author was roughly correct in calculating potential black participation in these states (see table below).[6] Given these numbers, the equation was a simple one; namely, if African Americans continued to vote as a bloc, they could control the balance of power in the years to come.

In the late 1930s, however, the Democrats' hold on the black vote was hardly secure. Diminished support in the African American community from

Percentage of Potential African American Voters in "Swing" States

State	Percentage[a]
Delaware	13.3
Illinois	5.1
Indiana	3.7
Kansas	3.7
Kentucky	8.5
Maryland	15.9
Michigan	4.4
Missouri	6.7
New Jersey	5.5
New York	4.3
Ohio	5.0
Pennsylvania	5.0
West Virginia	6.7

[a]Based on 1940 figures.

1936 was thought to have been a major factor in the significant Democratic losses of 1938, when Republicans gained seventy-five seats in the House (nearly doubling their number) and seven in the Senate.[7] FDR's failure "to speak out in favor of federal anti-lynching legislation and poll tax repeal bills" topped the list of causes of African American discontent. Administration policies that were leading to war and sparking an "increase in anti-democratic tendencies"—a situation where "the Negro as a minority group has most to lose"—were also major concerns. As George Schuyler of the *Pittsburgh Courier* put it in his October 5, 1940, column: "Our war is not against Hitler in Europe, but against Hitler in America. Our war is not to defend democracy, but to get a democracy we never had."[8] At the state level, "New Deal forces in Missouri" were undermined when the Democratic governor signed legislation establishing "a Jim Crow law school . . . a farcical device to evade the effects" of the Supreme Court's decision in *Missouri ex rel. Gaines v. Canada*—the first major victory in the NAACP's legal campaign to end segregation in the schools.[9] Roosevelt was now under pressure to yield to demands of an African American community with escalating electoral clout. Yet southerners still dominated the leadership in a Congress with a revived conservative coalition, and he ignored them at his own peril. This was the paradox the president faced after his purge misfired.

Still, FDR believed that if he could reach those southerners who had never or rarely cast a ballot on election day, southern democracy would be disrupted. In the best-case scenario, a vast pool of potentially progressive voters would be tapped, southern representation in Washington dramatically altered, and his institutional program implemented.[10] Early in his tenure, Roosevelt had felt too constrained by the existing institutional order and by his own brand of pragmatism to emphasize social reform.[11] As he told the NAACP's Walter White in 1934, this was the reason he could not support the organization's leading concern in Congress, antilynching legislation.

After the 1938 elections, however, the increasing importance of the black vote and Roosevelt's intensifying desire to retool the nation's institutional order led him to push for a more radical program. To advance this program he now partially shifted to an indirect approach—a hidden-hand strategy designed to destabilize southern politics by helping to secure the rights of black Americans and disfranchised southern whites. In keeping with this strategy, the president avoided making public declarations knowingly at odds with the racial preferences of southern senators and representatives—most significantly by not announcing his outright support of the NAACP's antilynching legislation—and instead operated mainly through nonlegislative channels. Rather than promoting legislation that would forever destroy his once cordial alliance with powerful southerners and was destined to die in Congress anyway, he sought to reconstitute the federal courts in a manner that would advance the agenda of racial progressives and help him realize his constitutional vision. At this point, his relative silence on race-based matters could be considered more strategic maneuvering than an embarrassment to the progressive cause. With the Congress closed off as a possible channel for action, he pursued a form of politics by other means.[12] Central to this effort was a policy toward the judiciary that encouraged an approach to the law — born out of the alliance between rights-centered liberalism and legal realism — that highlighted the importance of civil rights. Thus, as dictators across the globe were ferociously treading upon the liberties of their subjects, FDR sought to expand the powers of the presidency by bolstering the federal government's role in safeguarding individual rights, essentially in an effort to construct *his* image of a more democratic and well-ordered society.

The "infection of despotism . . . sweeping the world" nevertheless influenced the terms of this discourse on American democracy. On the one hand, writes historian Alexander Keyssar, "many Americans in the 1920s and 1930s remained skeptical (at best) of universal suffrage, and the rise of fascism, as well as the threat of socialism, in Europe only deepened their concern." To them, "an excess of democracy leading to mobocracy in turn would degenerate into dictatorship."[13] Just as Hitler had risen to power through initial success at the ballot box before casting the democratic process aside, an American demagogue could exploit an admiring populace to command for as long as he saw fit. Indeed, some critics viewed FDR's skillful use of his popularity to expand the powers of the presidency in alarming terms, fearful of the impending arrival of a democratic dictatorship at home.[14]

Others, most importantly southern conservatives, articulated positions even more restrictive in outlook, and seemingly at peace with the enemies of democracy abroad. For instance, during the 1938 antilynching bill debate, Mississippi's Theodore "The Man" Bilbo proposed repatriating all black Americans to Africa, telling his Senate colleagues: "Race consciousness is developing in all parts of the world. Consider Italy, consider Germany. It is beginning to be recognized by the thoughtful minds of our age that the conservation of racial values is the only hope for the future of civilization." Such views earned Bilbo the title the "Mussolini of Mississippi." One of his most ardent allies in defending southern white supremacy, Georgia's Governor Eugene Talmadge was tagged in similar terms as the "Fuehrer of Sugar Creek."[15] Labels aside, most southerners espoused views in sharp conflict with the principle of universal suffrage, with some suggesting that the United States had something to learn from the despots of the world.

For a third group, these dissenters of democracy had little to offer such a diverse nation as the America of the 1930s. To them, the rise of dictatorships across the sea only gave credence to calls for a more inclusive and tolerant democracy at home, to show that, in the face of "the vicious cycle of depression and mass insecurity," democracy could not only survive, but by disposing of Nazi-like racial labels, it could thrive. For example, in his letter to the NAACP's twenty-fifth annual conference, President Roosevelt noted — albeit somewhat timidly — that "no democracy can long survive which does not accept as fundamental to its very existence the recognition of the rights of minorities."[16] A full two months before Hitler's invasion of Poland on September 1, 1939, FDR's recently appointed attorney general, Frank Murphy, elaborated on the terms of this democratic vision: "Not Englishmen or Italians alone, or Gentiles or Jews alone, or white people or black alone, or conservatives or progressives alone. You see the children of every race and every nation and every creed under the sun. You see America and America's future. If you are disheartened by what you see, if these people of other races and national origins seem alien to you, then America's future and your own, will not be happy. But if you see them all as being of the stock that built this great nation from a wilderness, if you look at them as fellow servants of democracy, then our future is bright and full of hope."[17]

To fulfill this vision for America, FDR and his New Dealers rejected a purely negative conception of liberty, discarding the founders' notion that the Bill of Rights should serve only to restrain federal action. Rather, to them, the federal government would have to become, to borrow Murphy's phrase, "a powerful bulwark of civil liberty," a goal that would be advanced — as detailed in chapter 5 — by the Justice Department's Civil Rights Section (CRS). As Murphy explained, "The Fourteenth amendment of the Federal Constitution and the Federal Civil Rights statutes, all products of the Civil War, have enabled the Federal Government to take a much more vigorous part than it could formerly under the Federal Bill of Rights alone. We believe the new Civil [Rights Section] of the Department of Justice will make that part more significant than ever before. Today every dweller in our land, no matter how humble, can look to the State for defense of his liberties, and if that should fail, then to the Constitution and laws of the United States." As these words suggest, FDR's second attorney general not only sought to use his position "to protect civil liberties by all means available," he also encouraged the High Court to expand its use of the incorporation doctrine to nationalize the Bill of Rights in order to aid individuals "denied full protection by the courts of [their] state."[18] It was a position he would pursue with more authority once FDR made him a Supreme Court justice. In fact, such thinking was also emerging on the Court. For example, the day after Justice Stone delivered his decision in *Carolene Products,* he wrote to a friend, "I have been deeply concerned about the increasing racial and religious intolerance which seems to bedevil the world, and which I greatly fear may be augmented in this country."[19]

Not surprisingly, southern conservatives fiercely resisted such an expansive reading of the Fourteenth Amendment, anxious about its effect on white supremacy. For instance, in 1936, when Illinois Representative Arthur Mitchell became the first African American ever to address a Democratic convention, Senator "Cotton" Ed Smith left in protest and headed home to South Carolina. As he explained, "I cannot and will not be a party to the recognition of the Fourteenth and Fifteenth Amendments." Smith's words echoed those of one of his cohorts in southern conservatism, Carter Glass. In 1901, at Virginia's constitutional convention, Glass had prominently declared that "discrimination" was the sole goal of the delegates. "That, exactly, is what this Convention was elected for — to discriminate to the very extremity of permissible action under the limitations of the Federal Constitution, with a view to the elimination of every negro voter who can be gotten rid of, legally, without materially impairing the numerical strength of the white electorate."[20] A full generation later, Glass, now one of the Senate's most senior Democrats, did little to suggest he had amended his ways. But while such exclusionary views had made their way into New Deal legislation, they had no place in the Roosevelt administration's postpurge judicial policy, a policy designed to make American democracy more inclusive.

Roosevelt, then, did not employ his policy toward the judiciary primarily to further Democratic interests by undermining Republican interests (as proponents of the political model suggest) or to simply implant a liberal ideology on the Court (as attitudinalists suggest). Rather, when it came to civil rights, he used it as a device to manage intraparty conflict to extend his political authority and, most importantly, to install his ideal institutional order. In this sense, a symbiotic relationship developed between FDR and African American leaders in his second term. In this alliance, both were set to benefit from a policy devoted to creating a new legal order designed to advance civil rights and to aid in developing the modern presidency. Despite their prominent part in the victorious New Deal coalition, under this new order, the defenders of southern white supremacy would suffer the most significant judicial setbacks.

The effort to construct this new order began in earnest with the Court-packing plan and picked up momentum following the failure of the purge campaign. Thus, at the end of 1938 the Roosevelt administration paid increased attention to employing its judicial policy to accomplish this goal. In the sections that follow, I examine the appointment component of this policy. In doing so, I not only consider FDR's choices for the Court but discuss how the purge campaign and the death of antilynching legislation pushed progressives in the administration toward a more court-centered strategy of expanding and protecting the rights of black Americans.

"The Law Catches Up with Life": FDR and the Shape of the Roosevelt Court

FDR's first experience with the Supreme Court and his selection of similarly minded individuals was an unpleasant one. It came in the form of a "Black Monday" decision in which the justices — in evaluating the president's removal power — unanimously rejected FDR's attempt to dismiss William E. Humphrey from the Federal Trade Commission. To the president, *Humphrey's Executor v. United States* was a roundhouse left of a ruling, undercutting his ability to control *his* rapidly expanding administrative state. As journalists Joseph Alsop and Turner Catledge wrote, "the President saw in the decision the most direct of all possible trespasses on his powers as Chief Executive; he was completely infuriated." But in actuality, *Humphrey's Executor* may have been a blessing in disguise for the Roosevelt administration. According to Harold Ickes, in the days following the Court's action, members of the administration — led by none other than Vice President Garner — discussed the need for "a rigid examination of a man's qualifications" in the appointment process. While this conversation centered on presidential appointments to independent commissions, the lesson appears to have been applied to judicial nominees as well.[21]

Put another way, in judicial appointments, FDR's hand is clear. According to historian Robert Harrison — whose detailed work on the president's appointments to the high bench sheds much light on his thinking — "to a remarkable extent" Roosevelt and his justices "shared a great many attitudes and assumptions about the Supreme Court, the judicial function, and the nature of the law." On other judicial appointments, Sheldon Goldman writes that FDR "embraced being at the center of the selection of lower-court judges . . . the dispensing of these relatively scarce and valuable political resources was an activity that [he] apparently relished." In Goldman's analysis of the lower-court appointments of nine presidents, no other combined Roosevelt's "unusually active personal involvement" with his use of the selection process as a means to advance "the substantive policy goals of [his] administration, including its legislative and administrative objectives."[22]

Indeed, beginning with the Court-packing plan, it was obvious to even casual observers that FDR was interested in filling the courts with his type of jurists, in creating his version of a dream Supreme Court. As I argue in chapter 3, with his plan to curb the Court, FDR not only intended to "constitutionalize" the New Deal, he also sought to transform the federal judiciary from a long-time adversary of progressive reform into an ally of it. This desire remained even after the Court-packing plan failed.

Like no other president since Washington, FDR had an opportunity to assemble a High Court consistent with his own preferences. In all, he would choose nine men for that tribunal, virtually remaking it. More importantly, much of this transformation took place in the short space of four years — those following the defeat of the Court-packing plan — when seven of the nine sitting justices either died or retired.[23] Significantly, during this period of exodus, the president was in open conflict with those conservative members of his own party who disdained his policies that concentrated powers in the executive branch and committed the federal government to a progressive rights-expanding agenda.[24] In an effort to secure his institutional ambitions, FDR chose individuals for the Court he thought would cooperate with the executive branch — justices who would help him install his constitutional vision. Put differently, when Roosevelt finally had his chance to shape the Court's constitution, the construction of a modern presidency, wedded to progressivism, played a prominent role in his appointments.

Of the nine men FDR either elevated or appointed to the high bench, eight were unquestionable progressives.[25] The same eight had the support of NAACP head Walter White.[26] All nine had displayed some level of commitment to legal realism. Four of his appointees had played a substantial role in reforming the Justice Department. Seven had held significant positions in either his administration or in Congress or had been important advisors to him. The same seven had little or no judicial experience, spending their careers in the legislative, executive, or academic arenas. Four had won elected office, three in statewide races. Four were also on numerous Democratic Party short lists for the presidency or vice presidency in 1940 and/or 1944. Two were real-life Horatio Algers, rising from bitter poverty to the highest court in the land. Indeed, unlike thirty-two of the previous seventy-five men to serve on the Court (42.6 percent), none of the Roosevelt justices could be classified as a child of wealth. Only one (Stanley Reed), moreover, was reared in a family with a status above the middle class. Of the previous seventy-five justices, fifty-four (72 percent) fit that description.[27] In all, they were an unusual group to sit on the Court, yet their placement there showed the nation that FDR was devoted to creating a court in his image.

As with his Court-packing plan, Roosevelt's desire to transform the nation's highest tribunal represented a presidential snub to the traditional legal profession. Justice William O. Douglas, his fourth appointee, noted years later that the president liked to make appointments that "upset the fat cats" and "made the established order wince."[28] Indeed, on the whole, Roosevelt and his appointees shared a disregard for the preexisting legal order. This was the result of FDR's determination to select jurists committed to transforming the nature of law to meet the needs of a wider segment of the populace, "to crack[ing] the legal profession in the teeth,"[29] and to awarding men who had played an active part in the New Deal and had challenged the status quo during their careers. As Harrison writes, the Roosevelt justices' "attitudes and assumptions" about the law "grew out of their common hostility as liberals to the jurisprudence (and imprudence) of the Old Court, were nurtured and shaped by the insights of the legal realists, and were sharpened and solidified during the Court-packing crisis of 1937. On the subject of what kind of justice ought to sit on the Court, and what kind of justice ought to be dispensed by the Court, the President and each of his nominees tended to think the same thoughts and say the same things."[30]

Despite the apparent lessons of Roosevelt's earlier conflict with the Court, the president and his appointees did not define their legal philosophy in terms of simple judicial retreat. FDR's conception of the Court's future role was clearly one of a somewhat active institution. For example, in a successful attempt to persuade Frank Murphy to join the high bench in late 1939, he (according to Murphy) stressed that neither the president nor the Congress would be able to "save" the nation in the coming years. "It is the Supreme Court, *approving legislation for the people, preserving liberties —* *almost rewriting laws that will do it* . . . you are needed there right now."[31] While Roosevelt likely overstated his belief in the forthcoming importance of the Court to convince Murphy to take the seat, he was nevertheless enthusiastic about staffing the nation's highest tribunal with progressives committed to his institutional design. He had seen the effects of a hostile Court on his first New Deal and was now eager to create one that would collaborate with his modern presidency. As he put it just weeks after the defeat of his Court-packing initiative and in strikingly realist language: "We know it takes time to adjust government to the needs of society. But modern history proves that reforms too long delayed or denied have jeopardized peace, undermined democracy and swept away civil and religious liberties. . . . We will no longer be permitted to sacrifice each generation in turn while the law catches up with life."[32]

This desire to set a new course for the Court led FDR to select individuals who shared in a commitment — to varying degrees — to the union between rights-centered liberalism and legal realism. In turn, this shared commitment suggested that the Roosevelt justices would pursue a fairly coherent course on extending civil rights and civil liberties (although the Court ultimately split sharply on the latter). In 1941 the future Justice Robert Jackson — often labeled a "conservative" Roosevelt justice — explained why activism would be part of the Court's "new position":

> There is nothing covert or conflicting in the recent judgments of the Court on social legislation and on legislative repressions of civil rights. The presumption of validity which attaches in general to legislative acts is frankly reversed in the case of interferences with free speech and free assembly, and for a perfectly cogent reason. Ordinarily, legislation whose basis in economic wisdom is uncertain can be redressed by the processes of the ballot box and the pressures of opinion. But when the channels of opinion and of peaceful persuasion are corrupted or clogged, these political correctives can no longer be relied on, and the democratic system is threatened at its most vital point. In that event the Court, by intervening, restores the processes of democratic government; it does not disrupt them. . . . I am far from suggesting that our civil liberties can be adequately assured by the courts. . . . But to the extent that the courts can serve to vindicate civil liberties, the recent decisions of the Supreme Court show how the job can be done. It is of more than passing interest to observe that a court which is governed by a sense of self-restraint does not thereby become paralyzed. It simply conserves its strength to strike more telling blows in the cause of a working democracy.[33]

The fact that Jackson was the attorney general when he wrote these words should not be overlooked, for it displays the Justice Department's influence in developing the Court's institutional norms. In other words, given the general tendency of FDR's appointees to defer to the executive, the Roosevelt Justice Department was set to play a significant role in the development of institutional norms and commitments for the post-1937 Court. Indeed, given the Roosevelt justices' realist-inspired deferential approach, it is easy to see how the second and third pillars of FDR's judicial policy fit together. As chapter 5 shows, the staff of the Justice Department's Civil Rights Section endeavored — through selective prosecutions and appeals, creative arguments in court and in *amicus curiae* briefs, and cooperation with outside legal reform groups (namely the NAACP and ACLU) — to give new meaning to old law. Without sympathetic jurists, their efforts would have been purely symbolic. The success of the CRS, therefore, hinged on a substantial shift in judicial interpretation. This shift — while significantly shaped by the Roosevelt Justice Department — would of course not arrive until the Court itself was remade.

The Politics of the First Two Appointments: Southern Men

To be sure, the politics of appointment is an old subject. Many scholars have focused on the importance of judicial nominees in transforming legal doctrine. In addition, a great deal of scholarly attention has been paid to the individuals who assume seats on the high bench, with many — even relatively obscure justices — the subject of numerous articles and biographies. Indeed, with the exception of those men who have attained the presidency, no position attracts so much academic attention. With this in mind, I do not intend to retrace the lives of the Roosevelt justices here. Rather, I simply highlight the politics surrounding the appointments of the individual nominees and briefly assess their perceived commitment to the rights/realism union at the time of their nominations. I do so in an effort to understand FDR's role in reconstructing the federal judiciary following the so-called constitutional revolution of 1937 and to display the connection between the legal agenda of the Roosevelt administration and the emerging mission of the Roosevelt Court. I begin with a discussion of FDR's first two choices to sit on the Court. I then consider the selection of the other seven Roosevelt justices. I make this division to mark the 1938 purge campaign and to display the initial reaction from conservative southerners in Congress to FDR's effort to transform the ideological orientation of the Court.

From the "Heart of Dixie" to the Nation's Highest Tribunal

FDR's first real shot across the bow of the southern ship of democracy came with his choice to fill the Van Devanter vacancy on the Court.[34] It was a choice that caused great commotion in the Senate chamber, especially among southerners. Ironically, the nominee who stirred the Senate pot was himself a senator of the South. In seeking to strike back at those Democrats who had abandoned him during the Court-packing fight, the president named Alabama's Hugo L. Black, considered at the time to be "the most radical man in the Senate," as his first choice for the high bench.[35] To Roosevelt, the selection of Black was a checkmate move. Aware that many of Black's colleagues intensely disliked him — particularly his fellow southerners, who detested his progressive politics and abrasive style — FDR nevertheless figured that senators would not break with their honored tradition of approving a sitting senator nominated by a president to a post. While senators saw through Roosevelt's maneuver, viewing the nomination as a presidential "trick to ram the furthest Left-winger available down the Senate's throat," the gamble paid off. Five days after FDR announced his nomination, the Senate confirmed Black by a vote of 63 to 16. Even "Cotton Ed" Smith, who, according to Harold Ickes, "'God-damned' the nomination all over the place . . . didn't have the courage to stand up and vote against a fellow Senator from the Deep South."[36] He joined fifteen other members who did not vote at all.[37] (Of those sixteen who did cast a vote against the nomination, ten were Republicans, six Democrats. Of the six Democrats, two were southerners, specifically, Virginia's tag team of conservatism, Carter Glass and Harry Byrd.)

Black was clearly the type of progressive Roosevelt was looking for on the Court. Perhaps most importantly, he had vigorously lobbied for the Court-packing proposal and supported the president's effort to expand the power of the executive. In his defense of the Court plan, he had also displayed his commitment to the ideas of legal realism: "The time has arrived when those who favor fitting law to modern needs in order to correct and cure social and industrial injustices must face their problems squarely and fairly. . . . Let those who believe the people should have the right to pass laws to accomplish these purposes abandon theories, disregard the old outworn charges of the Liberty League and its Republican allies that your President wants to be a dictator, and join in aiding to pass [the] bill." In addition to his realism, on labor issues, Black was so closely associated with the movement to advance the rights of workers that his selection led one commentator to note in exasperation, "Mr. Roosevelt could not have made a worse appointment if he had named John L. Lewis."[38]

In the end, the fifty-one-year-old Alabama native was almost forced to withdraw from the post after he confirmed allegations that he was once a member of the Ku Klux Klan. He occupied his seat on the Court only after convincing a national radio audience that — as the Washington community already knew — he was a committed defender of civil rights and liberties. Strikingly, the revelations about Black's previous KKK membership also placed NAACP head Walter White in a precarious position. As Black biographer Howard Ball writes, "White and Black had become friends, and the NAACP official knew that Hugo was a decent, vigorous New Deal liberal." In his autobiography, White explained that he genuinely believed Black was a different brand of southerner: "His superiority of intellect and character over most of his colleagues from the South was so apparent that he seemed to me to be an advance guard of the new South we dreamed of and hoped for when that section of the country emancipated itself from the racial, economic, and political bondage which fear, prejudice, and a regional inferiority complex had created." Thus, when the NAACP denounced Black following his disclosure of his past Klan membership, White, secured by "an understanding of Hugo's true liberalism," sought to "minimize" the effects of his organization's condemnation. (While White did approve the telegram that called on Black to resign, according to Ball he did so not out of personal opposition to FDR's first appointee but because he felt "he had to speak for the membership and interests of the NAACP.") Moreover, soon after Black took his seat on the High Court, White — despite displeasure from NAACP members — again spoke words of support, assuring his critics that the new justice "would prove to be one of the most valued and able members of the Court." Black's enduring commitment to rights-centered liberalism during his long tenure on the bench proved that White had not been fooled.[39]

Black's nomination has traditionally been understood as a significant boost to the liberal wing of the Democratic Party and the first step in Roosevelt's effort to confront the conservatism of southern democracy.[40] Yet it is unclear why a president, apparently interested in purging old-style southerners from the political scene, would select a leading "new" southerner from the Senate for a seat on the publicly isolated Supreme Court. In fact, the Black nomination was not the only time Roosevelt made such a move. Despite his difficulties with southern senators, two of the Roosevelt justices were men both of the Senate and of the Deep South (the other was Jimmy Byrnes). Only once before in American history had two jurists from that bastion of slavery and segregation sat on the Court at the same time. Never before had a president appointed two men from the Deep South to the high bench.[41] Moreover, a third Roosevelt appointee called Kentucky — officially a border state but unofficially a southern state — home. A fourth was born and partially raised in Kentucky, spending the remaining years of his youth in North Carolina and Tennessee.[42] FDR's version of the "southern strategy" is striking given the Roosevelt Court's later commitment to exposing the irony of southern democracy and to advancing the rights of African Americans. But when viewed in relation to the president's desire to install a new institutional structure, the nomination of Black and other southerners becomes more understandable. For one, by selecting southerners sympathetic to his vision of an executive-dominated national government devoted to progressive principles, he could transform the Court in the fashion he wished while simultaneously stalling a Senate uprising against his nominees.

In addition, the choice of Alabama's Black as his first nominee and Kentucky's Stanley Reed as his second potentially had consequences — before the purge campaign — for the development of liberalism in the South. FDR's selection of individuals familiar with the inadequacies of Dixieland democracy suggests his emerging realization that the South's political structure would not allow liberalism to blossom there on its own; that change would have to come through outside intervention. In other words, FDR seemed unwilling to wait for the Godot of American politics — the arrival of southern liberalism — any longer. He would instead attempt to provoke its development. This certainly is part of the explanation for his purge campaign. But it also provides early hints of a desire to reconstitute the federal judiciary to aid in the effort to reconstruct southern politics, all with the intention of extending democracy down South and producing a more liberal Congress. Thus, even before the disappointing 1938 elections — which highlighted the feebleness of southern liberalism — the president seemed to be devising a court-based strategy, a strategy he apparently felt would work only if southern liberals who had succeeded in overcoming the constricting conservatism of southern democracy were a party to its destruction. After the 1938 elections, the path of the president's judicial policy is even clearer. As explained in the following chapter, in the month following the 1938 elections, he hired Frank Murphy as his second attorney general. As one of his first major official acts as head of the Justice Department, Murphy — as instructed by the president — created the Civil Rights Section, an institution designed to reshape judicial interpretation, particularly with regard to the rights of African Americans.

The second and third pillars of the Roosevelt administration's judicial policy, then, were largely driven by FDR's continued inability to tame the conservatism of southern politics and by progressive Democrats' growing frustration with a Congress closed off to rights-expanding legislation. This progressive frustration swelled following the "switch in time" decisions, as conservative opponents of the administration — working without the benefit of a consistently conservative Supreme Court — escalated their resistance to the president's legislative agenda. The failure of the NAACP-backed antilynching bill provides a clear example of this legislative environment. It also displays southern concerns about the construction of a Roosevelt Court and the future of a Democratic Party increasingly interested in appealing to the strategically significant black vote, concerns that would have consequences for the politics of appointment.

"A Bill to Destroy the Democratic Party"

Despite the fact that southern senators had for years strenuously and successfully resisted antilynching legislation, some congressional observers predicted its passage in 1938.[43] In the end, such prognostications proved foolish. Despite the dramatic increase in the number of progressive northern Democrats serving in Congress following the 1936 elections, the Wagner–Van Nuys antilynching bill—which sought to protect the most basic of rights—stalled once again in the Senate, the graveyard of racially progressive legislation. Even with Roosevelt's silent support, Senate progressives could not break a southern filibuster. Moreover, with Washington abuzz with talk of conservative Democrats joining Republicans to form a new party, the debate took on new meaning.[44]

Fearing their potential paths, southerners turned the debate over the legislation into a discussion about the dangers of New Deal liberalism and the future of the Democratic Party. And while FDR stubbornly kept quiet about his position on the measure, the fallout of the 1937 congressional session provoked some of his previously silent critics to take center stage. Principal among them was Mississippi's Pat Harrison, one of the three remaining members of the Big Four. Strikingly, Harrison's condemnation of the legislation displayed the strong resentment southern Democrats had about their diminished control over the legislative process and the loss of the Supreme Court's protective barrier. This resentment was no doubt driven by the realization that both of these newly acquired deficiencies in the South's shield of armor had the potential of exposing its institutions to outside interference, possibly even an assault on its system of white supremacy.[45]

Wound up in this southern insecurity, Harrison took to the floor of the Senate to vilify what he termed a "challenge to constitutional government in the South and an insult to [its] people." During his tirade against the antilynching bill, he employed language similar to that of his more "Negrophobic" colleagues, such as fellow Mississippian Bilbo, urging the "majority" of senators "not to tear down the pillars upon which the white civilization of this county was buil[t] . . . in order to get votes elsewhere," not to "open a Pandora's box that will plague you in the future," not to "rape the Constitution" or assault "local self-government and usurp the sovereign rights of people," not to defend "a fiend [who] had committed the foulest crime against the virtue of the fairest flower that grows in my State." He concluded with a prescription for the future, a warning to those who might disregard his message, and a plea to his party. On the first count, he told his fellow senators how he had read that:

> the Negro Representative from Illinois [Arthur Mitchell] had introduced a bill taking away from the States the right to enact Jim Crow car laws and to segregate the races in public places. No doubt that will be followed by an appeal for the enactment of another Federal statute taking away the right of States to enforce laws prohibiting the miscegenation of the races; and when that has been accomplished they will come back here with another demand, and that demand will no doubt seek the help of the majority party to deprive the States of the constitutional right to say who shall vote in their elections. And in that demand they will no doubt seek to have the Federal Government, perhaps under the cover of bayonets, compel every State to permit Negroes to vote in white Democratic primaries of the South.

As we know, Harrison's forecast for the future was not far off, as the NAACP led the campaign to advance the rights of African Americans. Such shrewd insight — endorsed by both more moderate and more conservative southerners — provides an important frame of reference for understanding southern concerns about the NAACP.

On this note, Harrison was also sensitive to the NAACP's efforts to achieve many of its results through the courts, bypassing legislative channels choked off by southern resistance. For example, during his speech against the antilynching bill, he sternly warned senators desirous of a newly vacant seat on the Supreme Court what a vote for the bill would mean for their prospects.

> Those sweet, pliant, amiable gentlemen who answer to their names when the roll of the Senate is called, and who nowadays every time a newspaper correspondent calls you out for an interview experience a fluttering of the heart because you think the news may have come from the White House that your nomination is going to be sent to the Senate to fill the vacancy on the Supreme Court . . . *had better beware.* You do not add to your standing as lawyers or your qualifications for a place on the highest tribunal in this land by voting for such a legislative monstrosity as that

now pending before this body. *By so doing, you give the assurance that you are going upon the court to destroy this dual form of Government and to rob the States of their sovereignty.*

The final portion of Harrison's harangue against the legislation came as an exhortation to his fellow Democrats, whom he felt were selling the South out to secure the black vote in the North:

> With the Democrats in control of every branch of the government, and especially by a large majority in this body, the people of the South for the first time since the days of the Force bill are confronted *with the determined effort of having the Federal Government usurp the rights of their States and destroy the fundamental principles of their government.* Do you believe, my Democratic friends, that by your action you are strengthening the faith of the South in our party? Do you believe that its long and devoted love warrants any such treatment? Then, if you do, I say, "Beware! Beware!"[46]

Harrison was certainly not alone in his defense of the South and of *its* Democratic Party. The day after his speech, another remaining member of the Big Four, South Carolina's Jimmy Byrnes, rose to the Senate floor in a focused attack on the principal agent pushing the legislation. While Byrnes had a reputation in his state for "elevating the public debate . . . above race baiting," on this day—enlivened "by a personal hatred" for his target—he let loose: "One Negro, whose name has heretofore been mentioned in the debate—Walter White, secretary of the Association for the Advancement of the Colored People [*sic*]—has ordered this bill to pass. . . . If [he], who from day to day sits in the gallery, should consent to have this bill laid aside, its advocates would desert it as quickly as football players unscramble when the whistle of the referee is heard." In assailing White, Byrnes was highlighting the diminished capacity of the South to control the party it had once dominated and its inability to appeal to members of the GOP for support. In short, because of the increasing importance of the black vote in the North, the South had become a region without a party.

> Democrats of the South have no justification for an appeal to the Republicans of the North. Southern Democrats have never voted for a Republican candidate. . . . It undoubtedly is true that the unity of the white people in the South in supporting the Democratic Party has been due to the belief that when problems affecting the Negro and the very soul of the South arose, they could depend upon the Democrats of the North to rally to their

support. Mr. President, southern Democrats may as well realize now the change that has taken place. If statements of Democratic Senators on political conditions in their States can be accepted as true, today 90 percent of the Negroes of the North, instead of voting for Republican candidates, are voting for Democratic candidates. *The Negro has not only come into the Democratic Party, but the Negro has come into control of the Democratic Party.*[47]

To be sure, Harrison and Byrnes were not so much notable for the flair of their phrases or the vigor of their stand against federal encroachment into the South. Others were equally if not more articulate, equally if not more dismayed by the prospect of an antilynching law. Perhaps Senator Richard Russell of Georgia summed up southern anger best when he called the legislation a "bill to lynch the last remaining evidence of States' rights and sovereignty." Or perhaps it was "The Man" Bilbo, who, in more graphic terms, declared that the legislation "would open the floodgates of hell in the South." Warning those supporting it, he continued, "upon your garments . . . will be the blood of the raped and outraged daughters of Dixie, as well as the blood of the perpetrators of these crimes that the red-blooded Anglo-Saxon white southern men will not tolerate."[48]

But Harrison's and Byrnes's words did have a special significance, primarily because they were instrumental in transforming the antilynching debate into a discourse on the state of the Democratic Party. Indeed, it was Byrnes who referred to the antilynching legislation as "a bill to destroy the Democratic Party."[49] And joined by other more conservative southerners, Harrison and Byrnes used the filibuster to record an adamant objection to the current course of the Democratic Party, a course charted by its captain, President Roosevelt.

In the end, Harrison's and Byrnes's fortunes on antilynching represented a reverse image of FDR's on Court-packing. They won the battle but lost the war. Unable to break a southern filibuster spanning nearly six weeks, progressives finally abandoned the effort to enact antilynching legislation. In accounting for this southern victory, FDR's decision not to publicly announce his support of the bill is instructive. Significantly, the decision was driven by strategy. Likely already in the planning stages of his purge campaign later that year, he told the bill's backers that a presidential endorsement would be used by conservative southern Democrats — who were blocking key components of his second-term agenda — to "exploit the situation to gain re-election on a campaign of racial prejudice." This, in turn, would likely inflame racial tensions and undermine the effort to elect southern liberals committed to the New Deal. In confronting this paradox of advocacy, he calculated that his continued silence on civil rights would in the long run produce a Congress more committed to progressive policies of all varieties.

But the president did not remain completely silent on the matter. A month later he announced in a press conference, "if the Senate determines not to proceed with the anti-lynching bill . . . the matter ought not to rest there." He then proposed that the Congress should either adopt legislation giving the Justice Department the authority to investigate lynchings or set up a standing committee to carry out such probes.[50] The connection to the La Follette Civil Liberties Committee's investigation of abuses against labor and the Justice Department's indictment of the mine owners of Harlan County was clear. Although civil rights advocates had denounced him for his failure to publicly support the antilynching bill, FDR seemed to be suggesting that, if southern senators continued to thwart social reform legislation, he and his progressive allies would carry forth their effort through executive and judicial action. Thus, it should not be surprising that less than five years later, a top Justice Department official publicly asserted that a "federal civil right not to be lynched" existed within same Reconstruction-era statute employed in the Harlan County case. Of course, in the South, the system of industrial relations was not at the heart of the controversy. Rather, the nature of one-party politics was under assault. Nevertheless, the significance of FDR's proposal lay in the merging of the two movements, the one to protect the rights of workers with the one to safeguard the civil rights of black Americans. The fundamental aspect of this development was the increasingly held view among rights-centered liberals — driven home by a persistent NAACP and the realities of a world at war's edge — that the African American cause was thoroughly consistent with the essence of New Deal liberalism. Only by making a commitment to this cause could New Dealers be true to their grander democratic ideals and secure an electoral alliance for a more progressive future. To do otherwise was simply continuing the practices of the once southern-dominated Democratic Party, forever stalling the fulfillment of liberalism's end goals.

A Nominee Pleasing to All

To be sure, rights-centered liberals did not register a complete victory. Southern threats like Harrison's had an effect on the path of the president's judicial policy. Most prominently, to fill the void created by the retirement of Justice George Sutherland, Roosevelt chose his noncontroversial solicitor general Stanley Reed, who called the southern border state of Kentucky home. Sutherland had announced his retirement on January 6, 1938, merely four days before the Harrison speech warning those senators inclined to vote for the antilynching bill that they had better "beware." While FDR still considered the more ideologically liberal Frank Murphy — many thought selecting the Catholic Murphy would ease tensions created by his previous choice of an ex-Klansman — he apparently feared a confirmation battle exposing the wounds of the 1937 sit-down strikes. After all, at the tail end of the 1937 session, conservative senators had announced their independence from the president by issuing a "manifesto," a statement of principles that included an attack on the sit-down strikes and a call for "the vigorous maintenance of States' rights."[51]

For his part, Reed was a solid candidate with a reputation as a skillful lawyer. Ideologically, most considered him a moderate liberal loyal to the president's program. In fact, he had been one of the few men privy to the planning of the Court-packing proposal. In addition, he had consistently displayed a commitment to legal realism in his arguments before the Court as solicitor general and in his more political speeches. For example, he had once proclaimed, "the Constitution is a guide to our progress, not a jailer to preserve the status quo." Nevertheless, he had never acquired the image of a New Deal "zealot." After the Black nomination, this "center man" image boosted his prospects for a seat on the Court, as Roosevelt was simply unprepared to challenge Senate conservatives with each of his appointments. On January 15, 1938, in the midst of the southern filibuster against the antilynching bill, the president made his choice known to the nation. Senators from both ends of the ideological spectrum conveyed their approval, with many seeking to define Reed in a fashion consistent with their own views. For example, employing realist language, Majority Leader Barkley announced that Reed would bring to the Court a "sympathetic understanding of the problems of modern society." Senator Sherman Minton of Indiana — a man considered by Roosevelt for the high bench but destined to be appointed by President Truman — thought Reed was a "liberal and a good lawyer." In contrast, Tom Connally of Texas, the leader of the antilynching filibuster, labeled FDR's second choice as an "able, accomplished lawyer of the conservative type." In the end, Reed's wide appeal translated into easy approval. The Senate confirmed him by a voice vote just ten days after the president submitted his name for consideration.[52]

The selection of Reed, however, did not turn the tide in FDR's battle with conservative members of his party. It simply represented a smooth patch of pavement on an otherwise bumpy road. Indeed, as the 1938 congressional session wore on, conflict over his executive reorganization plan and the wages and hours bill exasperated tension between the two. In turn, the president sought to use his popularity to alter the situation and, consequently, the ideological makeup of his party. It was a decision that would profoundly affect his administration's policy toward the judiciary.

The Purge Campaign and the Roosevelt Administration's Judicial Policy

On June 24, 1938, FDR informed the nation of his intention to participate in the upcoming midterm elections in order to carry out "the definitely liberal declaration of principles set forth in the 1936 Democratic platform."[53] At first, his involvement was limited, focusing on repelling conservative efforts to purge liberals from the Democratic governing coalition. To this end, the president threw the weight of his administration behind several incumbent New Deal liberals up for reelection. Most prominently, in this first phase of the 1938 primaries, he helped secure the reelection of Senators Claude Pepper of Florida and Alben Barkley of Kentucky. For the administration's judicial policy, both races were significant. In Florida, the results affected the president's view of southern democracy and helped shape the administration's policy toward the judiciary in the postpurge years. In Kentucky, this policy was seemingly employed by the administration to aid the incumbent.

The Florida race actually occurred before FDR's announced intervention in June. And in many ways, Pepper's success drove the president's decision to transform the purge campaign from a defense of liberals into an effort to defeat conservatives. The staunchly liberal Pepper was up against two serious candidates, only one of whom had declared his "independence" from the president. This meant: "He had opposed the President on the Supreme Court measure, the reorganization bill, and the wages and hours bill." In the end, many thought FDR's support for Pepper — through a statement by his son James — made the difference. On the May election day, Pepper won in a rout, besting his conservative opponent 58.4 percent to 26.6 percent. The other pro–New Deal candidate trailed with 12.2 percent of the vote. In Congress, the Florida results were certainly heard loud and clear. Labor's favored wages and hours bill — previously stalled in the House despite the president's strong support — was quickly enacted into law.[54] Up for reelection themselves, Democratic conservatives were simply unwilling to continue to block this presidential proposal once FDR had displayed the power of his popularity in Florida.

But another factor in the Pepper victory suggested a different reason why the New Deal team had carried the day. It concerned the unusually high voter turnout. In contrast to the 1936 presidential (general) election, when 37.8 percent of voters (327,365) went to the polls, the turnout in the 1938 Democratic primary was 47.9 percent (415,293). Significantly, in the space of these two elections, a Pepper-led movement — supported by FDR — to abolish Florida's one-dollar poll tax had succeeded in the state legislature.[55] Writing in 1939, political scientist J. B. Shannon argued that eliminating this vote-constricting tax in 1937 "was probably the most significant factor in [the] exceptional" turnout in the Florida primary. Pepper agreed, noting later that the poll tax repeal "contributed to my very large majority" in the 1938 primary.[56] The conclusion that the poll tax had a destructive effect on liberal candidates was consistent with the widely accepted belief that Huey Long's ability to mobilize throngs of progressive voters in his 1934 senatorial campaign was linked to the Pelican State's abandonment of the tax in the same year. Such views led FDR to incorporate an attack on the tax in the purge campaign. In fact, even before the Pepper victory, the president emphasized in a letter to Alabama's Aubrey Williams, director of the National Youth Administration, his frustration with southern democracy in general and the poll tax in particular: "I think the South agrees with you and me. One difficulty is that three-quarters of the whites in the South cannot vote — poll tax etc." In an August 31 letter to Representative Brooks Hays of Arkansas, FDR went further, endorsing a poll tax repeal movement in the state legislature by referring to the tax as "inevitably contrary to fundamental democracy and its representative form of government." During a September press conference, the president publicly ratcheted up his rhetoric, assailing the suffrage restriction as "a remnant of the Revolutionary Period."[57] Thus, while the Pepper victory was one of the few successes of the purge campaign, the lesson of tax-free election was not ignored. Instead, as explained in chapter 5, the Roosevelt administration sought to incorporate it into its policy toward the judiciary after the 1938 elections.

In Kentucky, Barkley's challenger was the popular governor, A. B. "Happy" Chandler. According to some accounts, Chandler had received financial support from some notable New Deal enemies, such as the Liberty League and Virginia's Senator Harry Byrd.[58] Consequently, the president stepped in to help defend his choice to replace Joe Robinson as Senate majority leader. Here, the administration's assistance was not limited to the standard endorsement and financial support. It reached into the courtroom as well. On May 16, 1938, the Justice Department, seeking to secure rights guaranteed to workers under the Wagner Act, opened its case against the mine owners of Harlan County. For eleven weeks, at the cost of $300,000, Justice Department lawyers brought forth evidence against the sixty-nine defendants — "all of whom belonged to the ruling nucleus of the Harlan oligarchy." In prosecuting the case, the department sought to show how the defendants pursued a terrorist-style campaign against union organizers and sympathizers in violation of a Reconstruction-era civil rights statute and the Wagner Act. Although the Senate's La Follette Committee had already unearthed most of this material, the government made news by subpoenaing some of Governor Chandler's correspondence. To be sure, the effect of the trial on Chandler's campaign is difficult to determine. While it probably helped Barkley solidify union support, it was unlikely a major factor in his victory. Nevertheless, the Justice Department's action did display the extent to which the administration was willing to challenge the atmosphere of fear that existed in this isolated county. In this sense, the case had a larger meaning. If the conspiracy by Harlan's mine owners and political leaders to deny workers their legal rights could be exposed, perhaps the county's violent traditions could be transformed into relics of the past. As the editors at the *Nation* put it, the county had undergone a "Roosevelt Revolution": "In Harlan County, where the coal operators own the government, where tear gas, dynamite, and guns spitting death from ambush so long kept out the union organizer, the U.M.W.A. now has an office. Ten of the forty-two mines in the county have signed contracts with the union. Its field workers travel in comparative safety. The spectacle of sixteen corporations, eighteen mine executives, and twenty-two deputies on trial is one that Harlan will not soon forget. That the charge should be conspiracy to deprive miners of their right to organize is little less than revolutionary change in Harlan." In the end, the New Deal effort in Kentucky succeeded at the polls but not in court. Barkley won the election comfortably, but the trial ended in a mistrial, the result of a "hopelessly deadlocked" jury.[59] Nevertheless, the Harlan trial set an important precedent for later Justice Department efforts to prosecute the inequities of one-party politics and the brutalities of white supremacy deeper south.

In succession, then, FDR's involvement in two major Senate races had paid off. This success inspired a second, more intrusive phase of presidential intervention into the primaries, a phase that gave the "purge" campaign its name. Notably, although Roosevelt sought to unseat a number of insufficiently liberal members of his own party, he directed his "most outspoken and unequivocal opposition" toward "traditional Southern Democracy." To the president, southern members of Congress had been — in the main — the major Democratic retardant in his pursuit of a more liberal agenda during his second term. Since he could hardly expect greater Democratic margins than those of the Seventy-fifth Congress (1937–38), it was clear to virtually all that to remake the Congress into a more progressive body, the South — often represented by thoroughly conservative veteran Democrats — would have to be the bull's-eye of his target.[60]

To accomplish his goal, FDR returned to the rhetoric of democracy. In a March 28, 1938, speech in his "adopted" state of Georgia, he called for the end of the South's "feudal system," which he considered not much different from the "Fascist system." On June 25, 1938 — the day after he announced his planned participation in the primaries — he sent a greeting to the NAACP (quoted above) wishing the organization "success" in "its efforts in advancing the interests of the Negro race" and noting its "constructive efforts . . . not only in behalf of the Negro people in our nation, but also in behalf of the democratic ideals and principles so dear to our entire nation." Five days later, he told members of the National Education Association, "if the fires of freedom and civil liberties burn low in other lands, they must be made brighter in our own." Here, FDR seems to have been participating in the liberal tendency of connecting the fallacy of southern democracy with the destruction of democracies abroad. As early as 1935, Colorado Senator Edward Costigan had highlighted this "Deutschland and Dixieland" link, telling his colleagues during an antilynching legislation debate that the "choice was between Hitler and Mussolini on the one side, and Washington, Jefferson, Lincoln, Henry Grady, Woodrow Wilson, Franklin Delano Roosevelt on the other."[61]

FDR's war of words continued as he campaigned throughout the South. But in speeches there, he focused less on the depravity of democracy in the Southland and more on the virtues of New Deal economics and the need for a more liberal Congress. For example, in his Barnesville, Georgia, speech kicking off the southern part of his purge tour, he quoted liberally from his July 5 letter to his Conference on the Economic Conditions in the South, in which he referred to the region as "the nation's No. 1 economic problem." Indeed, Roosevelt used the purge campaign "to strengthen the national resolve of the Democratic Party on the basis of the issue of economics. Such a national Democratic Party could not leave the South alone; it had to be transformed."[62] In other words, in FDR's view, the South was the "nation's number one economic problem" because it was his number one political problem. In order to solve both, he sought to replace southern conservatives with southern liberals. His primary senatorial targets were Walter George of

Georgia, "Cotton Ed" Smith of South Carolina, and Millard Tydings, who, while representing the border state of Maryland, allied himself to the conservative principles and practices of the Democratic South.

In the end, Roosevelt's chosen candidates failed on all three counts. Their opponents all won by appealing to such divisive issues as the subversion of the Democratic Party by northern agitators, the reformers' drive for an anti-lynching law, the president's intervention into southern elections, and his relationship with the "interracial CIO." In a plea for Georgia's independence, for instance, Senator George, called Roosevelt's campaign, "the second march through Georgia" and another "carpetbag invasion." In addition, journalist Turner Catledge, a Mississippi native, witnessed "the stately and otherwise dignified" George employ "anti-Negro, anti-Semitic, anti-labor, and anti-Yankee" rhetoric, rhetoric that quickly had members of the crowd "on their feet, cheering wildly. Shouts of 'Go to 'em, Walter,' and 'Let 'em have it,' were punctuated by rebel yells." To Catledge, "George had done what he had to do." The senator's tactics reminded him "of what Pat Harrison used to say — that he could be a statesman for five years, but on the sixth" he had to go back "home to 'sling the shit.' "[63] As with Harrison, the strategy worked. George trounced his pro–New Deal opponent by twenty percentage points.

"Cotton Ed" Smith followed a similar path of resistance, highlighting themes of political independence and racial intolerance. For example, under the banner of independence, Smith stressed in one speech, "no man dares to come into South Carolina and try to dictate to the sons of those men who held high the hands of Lee and Hampton." But it was his racially charged "Philadelphia Story" that came to define his campaign. The "Philadelphia Story" centered on Smith's actions at the 1936 Democratic Convention, where he twice walked out the door: first, to protest an African American minister offering the invocation and, second, to protest the presence of black Congressman Arthur Mitchell at the podium addressing the delegates. In Smith's telling of the story, he focused on the former event, relaying his refusal to believe — upon first entering the convention hall — that a black man was about to pray for the Democratic Party. "But then, bless God, out on that platform walked a slew-footed, blue-gummed, kinky-headed Senegambian. And he started praying and I started walking. And as I pushed through those great doors, and walked across the vast rotunda, it seemed to me that old John Calhoun leaned down from his mansion in the sky and whispered in my ear, 'You did right, Ed. . . .' " What South Carolina voters likely did not fully sense in Smith's account of the moment was its remarkable symbolism. Once Reverend Marshall Shepard of Philadelphia — most probably selected by FDR himself — finished the invocation, the band played "Dixie." It was truly an effort by those orchestrating the convention to display the president's desire to expand his coalition while holding on to the votes of the South. Clearly, it was an attempt that didn't work on Smith. But strikingly, when "Cotton Ed" left the hall, a majority of South Carolina's delegates — including Jimmy Byrnes — did not follow.[64]

Smith would take revenge on the New Deal Democratic Party in 1938, reviving his old slogan of "Cotton Is King and White Is Supreme" and re-constituting the Red Shirts of yesteryear to patrol the polling places on pri-mary night. As David Robertson writes, "just as the Red Shirts of 1876 had in-timidated the state's black citizens in order to secure the return of a white supremacist government, so the Red Shirts in 1938 intended through intim-idation to secure the renomination of South Carolina's most vocal opponent of racial equality and the domestic policies of the New Deal in general — Cotton Ed Smith."[65] With such tactics and the allure of his "Philadelphia Story," Smith easily overcame the appeal of FDR's call for economic re-newal. On election night, clad in a red shirt, he sailed to a solid victory.

In Maryland, Senator Tydings ran a less colorful campaign, sticking mainly with themes of state pride and independence and his opponent's de-sire to be a "rubber stamp senator." On the first score, Tydings, linking the purge campaign with the Court-packing bill, proclaimed to voters that FDR's intervention into the election was akin to an "invasion" of the state: "I believe the day will come when President Roosevelt will realize that nei-ther he or [sic] any other Executive, Federal or State, should attack the in-dependence and usefulness of any branch of the government." He contin-ued, "Maryland will not permit her star in the flag to be 'purged' from the constellation of the states." On the second issue, Tydings took advantage of the fact that his opponent shared a last name with the CIO's John L. Lewis, pounding him for his prolabor positions and attempting to tie his politics to the ideals of communism. Such rhetoric carried the day. With only one-third of the voting population casting a ballot, Tydings crushed his oppo-nent, 58.8 percent to 38.5 percent.[66]

In dramatic terms, the failure of the purge campaign exposed the limits of FDR's coattails and the independence of southern voters. Strikingly, as Alan Brinkley writes, "southern liberals reacted with similar hostility and consternation" as their more conservative brethren. "Even those who might otherwise have been inclined to support the challenges to George and Smith retreated in the face of Roosevelt's tactics; acquiescence in the 'meddling' in state politics, they believed, was both politically and ideologically untenable." For example, the relatively progressive *Atlanta Constitution* applauded the voters' decision to return George to the Senate, asserting that the campaign was about "whether the Democratic voters of a state should decide for themselves who was to speak for them at Washington." Race was also part of the southern liberal resistance. While conservative southerners had always used race as a means to disguise a general distaste for New Deal programs, the president's crusade southward provoked real concern among economic liberals there that they might be onto something. To the *Atlanta Constitution*'s editors, FDR's attempt to purge George was part of his effort to enact "the vicious, dangerous and cruel anti-lynching bill. A bill that would forever make the sovereign states but chattels of the central government."[67] Frustrated by the continued poverty of southern liberalism, Roosevelt had sought to impose his principles on his adopted land. But as these accounts and the election results show, presidential intervention was not the answer.

Yet the election results did display another fact. Of the three main southern senatorial elections where Roosevelt had intervened (Florida, Georgia, and South Carolina), his only success came in the one state without a poll tax. While Pepper was also an incumbent, many observers considered the size of his victory — given his reputation as the most liberal southerner in the Senate — and the support voters displayed for the New Deal somewhat stunning. With 49.7 percent of the voting population casting a ballot, more than 70 percent of them chose either Pepper (58.4 percent) or a pro–New Deal third candidate (12.7 percent). To be sure, the poll tax was not a solution to all the difficulties liberals faced in the South. In South Carolina, where state law did not require voters to pay the poll tax to participate in the Democratic primary, the "fairly high" voter turnout had given Senator Smith "one of the largest majorities of his career." Still, the vote had also produced an easy victory for the pro–New Deal Burnet Maybank in the governor's race. And while "Cotton Ed's" victory was a comfortable one, New Dealers couldn't help but speculate that a more aggressive president — FDR had held some of his fire at the request of Byrnes — and an even larger voting pool would have produced a different outcome. Certainly, the results in South Carolina compared favorably to those in Georgia, where low voter turnout had been devastating for the New Deal. There, in the president's "second state," with only 21.4 percent of the voting population going to the polls, the two anti–New Deal candidates received 76 percent of the vote.[68] Thus, even if not a complete solution, the elimination of the archaic poll tax appeared to make a sizable difference for southern liberals.

More importantly, the president now believed that, if he could reach the silent and substantial majority, he could unleash progressive forces in the South. His position caused enough concern that white southerners began to express their dismay. As Turner Catledge reported in an August 28, 1938, *New York Times* article, "quoted assertions of outstanding party leaders, including the president himself, are taken by them in many instances to mean that universal suffrage, including re-enfranchisement of the southern Negro, is part of the goal of those who have set out to modernize the Democratic Party."[69] And while FDR was not nearly as aggressive as many rights-centered liberals would have preferred in federally protecting African American rights, southerners had good reason to be concerned. After the purge campaign, FDR increasingly employed his administration's policy toward the judiciary to undermine southern democracy. Most prominently, following the 1942 election, Roosevelt renewed his earlier criticism of state laws limiting the vote, stressing, for example, that if the Congress didn't pass anti–poll tax legislation, the Justice Department should test the constitutionality of the tax in court. In other words, unable to get what he wanted in Congress, he called for a campaign in the courts — the very institution that had blockaded the products of his electoral success — to assist in the effort to replace the charade of southern democracy with a system that sought to give voice to all citizens.

A Court Remade, A War Won

Beginning in early 1939 and ending early in 1943, FDR would fill six more vacancies on the Court. His maneuvering and decisions on who would occupy these empty seats says as much about Roosevelt's vision for *his* Court as it does about its ultimate direction. Put another way, FDR's choices for the high bench show a president determined to create a Court willing to defer to the executive branch and committed to advancing the ideals of rights-centered liberalism.

A Majority in a Year

FDR's third opportunity to shape the Supreme Court actually came in the midst of the purge campaign, due to the untimely death of Justice Cardozo on July 9, 1938. But the president made no quick decision on who would fill the "scholar's seat." Indeed, he took nearly six months to announce his choice. The delay stemmed in part from FDR's desire to name a western progressive to the post — to give High Court representation to a region that currently had none. But unable to find a candidate of "suitable stature," the president turned to an old friend, Felix Frankfurter of Harvard Law School. During his search for a westerner, the president had consistently said that he would not appoint Frankfurter to fill the Cardozo seat, hoping instead that the distinguished legal scholar and close advisor would soon take over for an aging Justice Brandeis. Yet, in the end, the president gave in to the pressure of a groundswell of support for Frankfurter and the persuasiveness of calls from the likes of Justice Stone to "place excellence over geography."[70]

At the time of his nomination, most observers considered Frankfurter a progressive in the tradition of Holmes and Brandeis. They saw him as a strong critic of judicial activism and a scholar who understood the judicial process thoroughly enough to destabilize Chief Justice Hughes's powerful control over the Court. While FDR had always considered Frankfurter a leading candidate for an appointment to a Roosevelt Court, early in his administration he voiced concerns about how the scholar's background and lifelong commitment to advancing progressive causes might affect his nomination. Specifically, Frankfurter was Jewish, an immigrant, an attorney in the defense of Sacco and Vanzetti, and a condemner of the Bisbee deportations, the Palmer raids, and the irregularities of Tom Mooney's trial.[71] In an attempt to deflect potential objections, the president asked Frankfurter to become his solicitor general in 1933. As FDR explained to him, "I can't put you on the Supreme Court from Harvard Law School." Frankfurter, however, wasn't interested in the position, preferring instead to stay in Cambridge, where his close association with the Roosevelt administration earned him the title "the most influential single individual in the United States."[72]

Nevertheless, during the Roosevelt years, the future justice did take a more cautious approach toward his nongovernmental political activism. He reduced his role in the ACLU, talked about resigning from the NAACP's executive board, and remained publicly silent on the wisdom of the Court-packing plan and the constitutionality of antilynching legislation. These actions, especially his somewhat hypocritical stance on the Court-packing proposal — his public silence and private disapproval did not prevent him from helping the president strategize for the plan's passage (to allegedly ensure his path to the Court) — raised the ire of some New Dealers.[73] Still, his important — though conservative — role in the development of legal realism,[74] his mentorship of numerous influential New Dealers, and his invaluable advice to the president made him difficult to pass over.

In the end, his status as a Jewish immigrant also proved to be a plus. When FDR announced his appointment on January 5, 1939 — in close proximity to that of Frank Murphy as attorney general and Harry Hopkins as secretary of commerce — commentators marveled at the significance of the "symbolic trio." For example, Ernest Lindley of the *Washington Post* thought these three "superb exemplars of liberalism" defined American democracy for a world now on the verge of war: "For one is a Jew who was born in Austria, one is a Catholic of Irish descent and one is a Protestant, the son of an itinerant harness maker. It may have just happened this way. Each of them is eminently qualified for the position to which he has been named. But the President, like several of his lieutenants, must have been aware of the symbolic significance of this trio of appointments, and must have found unusual satisfaction in thus proving to the whole world that the American system draws no distinction or origin, station or creed."[75] While Lindley stressed the ethnic and religious diversity of the president's nominees, others pointed to symbolism of a somewhat different stripe. After surveying FDR's early 1939 appointments to the executive branch and to the Court, William Hastie noted to NAACP head Walter White: "The worst fears of the unregenerate south are being realized. It seems that the U.S. Senate is the last stronghold of the Confederacy."[76]

Lindley and Hastie were not alone in their praise of the president's choices, especially his nomination of Frankfurter. Many thought that, in picking the Harvard scholar, Roosevelt had made the perfect choice, even if some used the selection as a way to continue their criticism of Hugo Black's appointment. Nearly all newspapers noted Frankfurter's qualifications for the position and delighted in highlighting the imagery of contradicting Hitler's ideas.[77] In these times before war, one of Frankfurter's perceived weaknesses as a nominee had become one of his greatest strengths. He became the third Roosevelt justice — by a Senate voice vote — twelve days after FDR announced his nomination.

Just over two weeks after Frankfurter took the oath of office, his mentor, Justice Louis Brandeis, announced his retirement from the Court. After filling the previous vacancy with a Harvard Law School professor originally from central Europe, FDR was even more interested in naming a westerner. At the same time, Brandeis was lobbying hard for the appointment of William O. Douglas, a leading legal realist, chairman of the Securities and Exchange Commission (SEC), and the president's poker buddy. Douglas was also from west of the Mississippi, born in the town of Maine, Minnesota, and raised in Yakima, Washington. Still, FDR "viewed him as two-thirds Easterner." Indeed, after arriving in New York from Washington State riding the train part of the way "hobo" style and with only six cents in his pocket, Douglas had graduated from Columbia Law School and made his career in the East. Following a short stint on Wall Street and an even shorter one as a country lawyer back in Yakima, he became a faculty member at Columbia, where he joined the "realist revolt against formalism."[78] From there, he went to Yale, continuing to develop his reputation as a brilliant scholar and leading realist. In 1936, he moved to Washington, D.C., to oversee the Wall Street-centered financial world, first as a member of the SEC and then as its chairman. Despite his time on the Street, at the time of his appointment most considered him a "dyed in the wool liberal." FDR eventually acceded to the will of Douglas's supporters, apparently influenced by a smear campaign against the nomination of Senator Lewis Schwellenbach of Washington and convinced, as Republican Senator William Borah of Idaho put it, that the SEC chairman was "one of the West's finest and brightest sons." The president made his announcement on March 20, 1939. During the confirmation process, rumors suggested that Douglas's main challenge would come from John L. Lewis, who was growing increasingly frustrated with the president. But in the end, no serious effort to block the nomination materialized.[79] After proving he was truly "a fighting liberal," the Senate confirmed him two weeks later by a vote of 62 to 4.[80] At the age of forty, he became the youngest justice in 128 years.

The end of the old Court was closing in tight now. Before 1939 was over, yet another opening occurred, the result of Justice Pierce Butler's death on November 16. With this appointment, a majority of the Court would be Roosevelt justices. The transformation from no New Deal representation to a Court controlled by New Dealers, moreover, took less than two and a half years. And with this choice, FDR appeared unconstrained by the conservative coalition in Congress, selecting a man well known for his strident liberalism and his defense of civil rights and liberties mere hours after learning of Butler's death. That man was Roosevelt's attorney general, Frank Murphy. Given Murphy's history with the sit-down strikes and his year in office as head of the Justice Department (as detailed in chapter 5), his progressive credentials were unmatched, his capacity to use the law as a tool for social change unquestioned.

To be sure, Murphy also had his detractors. Conservatives were critical of his actions during the sit-down strikes, and liberals objected to his stance toward radicals and unions as attorney general. Many (of all ideological stripes) questioned his skills as a lawyer. Indeed, even Murphy was unsure of his ability to be a justice. Nevertheless, as FDR put it in 1936, he was determined to appoint judges who knew "how the other 90 percent live."[81] "In that department," writes Harrison, "Murphy had no equal."

[During a stint] as Judge of the Detroit Recorder's Court (a police court similar to the one Hugo Black had presided over for eighteen months) . . . Murphy (like Black) learned valuable lessons about how poverty, igno-rance, and racism disadvantage defendants in the criminal justice sys-tem — lessons which eventually were to influence the development of con-stitutional law. In addition, Murphy had been Mayor of Detroit during the years when the Great Depression hit that city like a tornado; although con-servatives and bankers unjustly criticized him for spending Detroit into bankruptcy, the families on relief, the unemployed, the hungry and the homeless knew that Murphy had done more than almost any other mayor in the country to commit the resources of government on their behalf. Later, both as Governor-General of the Philippines and Governor of Michigan, Murphy had sought to implement the kind of economic legis-lation and political reforms which Roosevelt had championed at the fed-eral level in the name of the one-third of the nation most in distress.[82]

Waiting for the Senate to reconvene, FDR announced his fifth justice on January 4, 1940. Although senators did require Murphy to answer some questions about the sit-down strikes and his commitment to the protection of property rights, they greeted his nomination — despite his shortcomings — with "enthusiasm."[83] Eleven days after FDR sent his name down Pennsyl-vania Avenue, the Senate confirmed him by a voice vote. In an unprece-dented move — one that angered Chief Justice Hughes — Murphy took his oath of office at the White House rather than at the Supreme Court. The symbolism was clear. The "Roosevelt Court" — a court that would partially define itself by deference to the executive — was now in place.

In one day short of a year, the president had named three new justices to the Court. None of them confronted any confirmation difficulties. Even though he was closely aligned with progressives and in continuous conflict with the conservative coalition, FDR had managed to place three leading liberals on the Court. Why conservatives allowed such a trio to escape any serious challenge is striking, given the Roosevelt Court's later decisions es-pousing the virtues of liberalism. While it is difficult to decipher this con-servative indifference, three explanations offer some assistance.

First, given Roosevelt's desire to concentrate powers in the executive branch, it is likely that conservatives thought the Court would no longer play an active or significant role in American political life at the national level. Indeed, in 1940 Congress passed the Walter-Logan Act — vetoed by FDR — in an attempt to empower the judiciary by providing it with the authority to review the rules of administrative agencies. In addition, these appointees had been vocal critics of the Hughes Court's activism, and at the time, this record of advocating restraint superficially translated into a belief that they would never become "super legislators" once on the Court.

Second, conservatives simply did not have the votes to reject any of these nominees. While Republicans had picked up seats in the 1938 elections, Democrats still dominated the Senate body with sixty-nine of its members (nearly 72 percent). Conservatives from both parties might have aligned to filibuster a nomination, but in their minds, it was better to expend such political capital to defeat some of the president's more odious proposals.

Finally, each of the men FDR chose was qualified for the Court and had critics on the left. On the latter matter, Frankfurter was criticized for his newfound cautiousness on progressive issues, Douglas for his ties to Wall Street, and Murphy for his aggressive pursuit of subversives as attorney general. With regard to qualifications, both Frankfurter and Douglas were highly regarded legal scholars, each with a reputation for possessing a brilliant mind for the law. While Murphy's ability to tackle the job of justice was certainly more suspect, the Senate had only one year earlier confirmed him by a vote of 78 to 7 to head the nation's law firm, the Justice Department. Moreover, during that year, Murphy had won accolades from some of the staunchest conservative Democrats for his handling of the affairs of justice. In fact, even "the old pirate," as FDR referred to "Cotton Ed" Smith, had exclaimed that Murphy was "a great American." To conservative senators, then, each of the three appointments FDR made between January 1939 and January 1940 could have been worse. Put differently, each was better than Black, who had quickly developed a reputation as a justice who produced some "truly revolutionary" (dissenting) opinions.[84]

The June 12th Trio

With the high bench now "packed" with a majority of Roosevelt justices, FDR would take a detour from his drive to create a liberal Court with his sixth appointment. But he did not do so quickly, taking nearly five months to name his choice. Nor did he make this next nomination alone. Instead, he announced his sixth, seventh, and eighth justices on the same day, June 12, 1941. The politics surrounding the selection of these three men reveals much about FDR's role in forming his Court, and his willingness to make a political appointment to secure legislative success.

The sixth vacancy of the Roosevelt presidency came with Justice James McReynolds's retirement on January 31, 1941. "Unreconstructed and ornery to the end," McReynolds had recently displayed his "unabashed anti-Semitism by refusing to attend the robing ceremony for Frankfurter" and by not signing "the customary retirement letter to Justice Brandeis." The "last and most rabid of the Four Horsemen" had also set a new record for dissenting votes in 1938 with thirty-four, and for solo dissents in 1939 with thirteen.[85] With FDR's reelection to an unprecedented third term the previous November, the old Tennessee Democrat finally decided to call it quits after nearly twenty-seven years on the Court.

To be sure, right from the start in the search for a new justice, Senator Jimmy Byrnes was the leading contender to be the next Roosevelt nominee. On hearing of McReynolds's decision to leave the bench, Senators Harrison, Glass, and Barkley quickly went to see the president about filling the vacancy with the junior senator from South Carolina. FDR responded by saying, "of course, I will appoint him. He is just as much my friend as yours. . . . My only regret in appointing him is that I need him so much in the Senate."[86]

Indeed, Byrnes's greatest appeal did not center on his legal reputation. He was neither a leading legal realist nor a committed rights-centered liberal. Rather, the underlying reasons why FDR even considered him at all centered on his skills and loyalty as a legislator and political ally. During FDR's first two terms, Byrnes had consistently helped the president secure some of his most controversial proposals, perhaps most notably, his 1939 plan to reorganize the executive branch (thereby, codifying the modern presidency). On the political scene, while Byrnes had sided with "Cotton Ed" Smith during the purge campaign — mainly for reasons pertaining to the control of South Carolina politics — he had been an invaluable aide to the president at the 1940 Democratic convention. Despite the fact that FDR had passed him over for the Court vacancy created by Butler's death in 1939 and for the vice presidency in 1940, Byrnes worked the delegates hard to ensure the president got the running mate and the pro-interventionist platform he wanted. (According to Byrnes's biographer, FDR — based on advice from Harry Hopkins — telephoned the South Carolina senator at the convention to tell him that "the issues of civil liberties for Negroes and Byrnes's prior conversion from Catholicism precluded [him] from further consideration on the ticket." Apparently, Byrnes's "political enemies" had raised the same objections to the suggestion that he replace Butler on the Court.)[87]

Indeed, the war in Europe gave FDR another reason to nominate Byrnes. Facing a Congress resistant to his calls for "all possible aid short of war," the president knew that he would have to reestablish ties with conservative southern senators who were sympathetic to his internationalist posturing in order to enact his Lend-Lease plan. Principal among them was Carter Glass. FDR's old nemesis on domestic concerns was nothing of the sort on foreign affairs, articulating an internationalist position in line with the president's own. Glass, moreover, wanted to see Byrnes—a protégé of sorts—on the high bench. In fact, when the "old rebel," as FDR referred to him, recited the president's response to Byrnes about his suggested ascent to the Court, tears welled up in Glass's eyes.[88]

But Byrnes was not the only candidate in the race for the McReynolds vacancy. Liberals expected the president to tap the shoulder of his attorney general—now Robert H. Jackson—once again. Although word quickly spread that Byrnes would be FDR's choice, liberals still held out hope. On February 8, 1941, Harold Ickes wrote in his diary, "the President's intention now is to appoint Jimmy Byrnes to this vacancy but that does not mean that he might not be persuaded to change his mind." And as FDR remained publicly silent on the matter, rights-centered liberals continued to lobby him to choose someone more closely associated with their cause. In April, for example, Harry Hopkins—"who was indeed very close to" FDR—showed Ickes a "very strong" memorandum that attempted to persuade the president not to nominate Byrnes.[89] But in the end, two events appear to have secured Byrnes's placement on the Court.

First, at the behest of Roosevelt, Byrnes agreed to be the floor manager for the Lend-Lease legislation and once again displayed his legislative skills by easily securing its passage (60–31). Indeed, Byrnes's work on Lend-Lease may have sealed the deal for him. Just five days after FDR signed the bill into law on March 11, 1941, he received a desperate telegram from Walter White, who had just learned the president "was determined to appoint Byrnes." To White, especially after the senator's targeted criticism of him during the 1938 antilynching debate, Byrnes would be a terrible choice: "Last night with magnificent eloquence you appealed to Americans to defend Democracy and to put aside all 'divisions of party or section or race or nationality or religion.' But today's newspapers report that you may tomorrow send to the Senate the name of James F. Byrnes of South Carolina as a member of the United States Supreme Court. We beg of you not to do so. If Senator Byrnes at any time in his long public career failed to take a position not inimical to the human and citizenship rights of thirteen million American Negro citizens, close scrutiny of his record fails to reveal it."[90]

While politics and not ideology drove FDR to consider Byrnes for the Court, the president certainly did not share White's view of his eventual nominee. Rather, to the president, Byrnes, although nothing like the radical

Black, was not a typical southern conservative either. Byrnes was a child of poverty who, "like young Bill Douglas, had to come up the hard way." Put differently, he "knew how the other 90 percent live."[91] Though he did eventually join other southerners in calling for a compromise, Byrnes had been an early and vocal supporter of the Court-packing plan. In a 1939 address to the American Bar Association, he had also expressed views consistent with the principles of legal realism, noting that the history of constitutional law was filled with incidents when the document was adapted "to respond to the needs of the people" and that "this flexibility" was "its strength and not its weakness." To him, "any fundamental law must be a law of the living and not of the dead."[92] Moreover, "by FDR's reasoning," writes the future justice's biographer, "a Supreme Court appointment would free Jimmy Byrnes from the constraints of South Carolina's elective politics based on race. The president's friend thus would be encouraged to develop further as a dependable New Deal liberal."[93] In addition, even if Byrnes turned out to be the racial conservative White feared, by this time the president had already placed a majority of liberals on the Court, and it was virtually certain that the South Carolinian would compile a more progressive judicial record than that of his predecessor (Justice McReynolds).

On the other hand, the president had his electoral coalition to consider. While he had already secured another term in the White House, election results showed that the future of a more liberal Democratic Party increasingly depended on the black vote. To be sure, Roosevelt had defeated his Republican challenger, Wendell Willkie, handily, capturing 54.7 percent of the vote and thirty-eight states. Nevertheless, it was the closest of FDR's three victories. And if African Americans had decided to return to their voting behavior of 1932, the president's electoral college victory would have been far from comfortable. Moreover, in the spring of 1941 the Roosevelt White House was growing increasingly concerned with the call from A. Philip Randolph — the head of the Brotherhood of Sleeping Car Porters — for a march on Washington to protest racial discrimination in America's defense effort. A Byrnes appointment would do little to retard Randolph's displeasure with the administration. Thus, despite the news reports White mentioned in his telegram, FDR did not announce the Byrnes nomination in mid-March 1941. Instead, he would wait nearly three more months to do so. To Byrnes, it must have seemed like he was Joe Robinson in a different year — Charlie Brown to FDR's Lucy.

The reason for FDR's continued delay of the announcement is a bit uncertain. It was likely connected to the second factor that ultimately secured for Byrnes — so greatly disappointed over his loss of the vice presidency in 1940 — the consolation prize of becoming the sixth Roosevelt justice, namely, the retirement of Chief Justice Hughes. While rumors about the chief justice's pending retirement had been widespread and persistent since FDR's reelection, in April 1941 "authoritative sources" gave them greater credibility. If correct, FDR could fill the McReynolds vacancy with Byrnes and the imminent Hughes vacancy with a committed rights-centered liberal, thereby diminishing criticisms from his friends on the left. But with the NAACP and other liberal groups up in arms about the possibility of a Byrnes nomination, the president chose not to act on rumor. He waited until the chief justice made his retirement official on June 2, 1941, thereby allowing him "to carry out his plans."[94] Ten days later, FDR finally named Byrnes to the Court. In the end, the new justice would not serve much longer than he had waited.

As noted above, the president did not make the Byrnes nomination alone. Instead, surprising many in terms of his speed and shrewdness, he made two other appointments on that day. First, based in part on advice from the departing Hughes that he promote a sitting member of the Court to be the top judge, FDR announced that Associate Justice Harlan Stone would be elevated to chief.[95] With the nation on the brink of war, the Republican Stone — by virtue of his stinging dissents in support of the New Deal — would lead FDR's decidedly Democratic Court. While New Deal liberals were disappointed that the president did not select Attorney General Jackson — one of their own — to lead the Roosevelt Court, there was little to complain about in Stone. Aside from giving a powerful bench voice to the criticisms of the anti–New Deal majority in the mid-1930s, Stone was a committed civil libertarian, the author of *Carolene Products*, footnote 4.[96]

With Stone's move to the center chair, Roosevelt had another opening to fill. He turned to the liberals' choice for chief, Robert Jackson. Jackson, succeeding Frank Murphy as attorney general, had continued to build on his status as one of the New Deal's greatest advocates. In earlier roles as a leading defender of the Court-packing plan and as solicitor general, he had repeatedly employed legal realist rhetoric, first to denounce the Court and then to argue for the validity of New Deal measures before it. For instance, in his role of defender of the Court-packing plan, he noted that one reason for "the serious lag between public opinion and the decisions of the Court" was "the legalistic doctrine of stare decisis." He added, "A [new] working majority of the Court could shake the fetters of precedents and, within the present language of the Constitution, remove most of the cause of the long-standing conflict with the elective branches of the Government. . . . Justices freshly appointed from the people would bring a more *realistic viewpoint* to the Court." As a New Dealer, Jackson had a reputation for his progressive — even radical — politics and for his fierce criticism of the Hughes Court's activism. In testimony before the Senate Judiciary Committee on the Court-packing plan, he stressed that, while he had "never accepted the theory of abolishing the power of the judicial review," he did think that it was "absolutely necessary" for "that power" to be "applied with great discretion and great care." As he explained, "if a law is passed depriving people of religious or civil rights, I want the Supreme Court to stand against it, as I would if I were on the Court. But when it comes to legislative policy, such as the regulation of utilities, I do not think the Court should stand against it."[97] Such thinking obviously influenced the work of the Roosevelt Court.

As solicitor general, Jackson added further definition to the New Deal's approach toward the law, giving clarity about the meaning of the union between rights-centered liberalism and legal realism. In a 1938 speech, he proclaimed, paraphrasing Holmes, that "if a liberal bar is to help the liberal forces to write their aspirations into law, the task is not alone one of learning and logic but of experience as well . . . lawyers must supply the legal imagination to design institutions, agencies, and rules of law, which will bring social forces under law without devitalizing them." Then, after comparing their New Deal effort to that of lawyers during the American Revolution, he concluded, "We too are founders — founders of what will tomorrow become the tradition of our profession in this day of change. We too are makers of a nation — the nation of tomorrow. We too are called upon to write, to defend and to make live, new bills of right. We too may soberly but bravely advance the frontiers of justice under the law, into economic affairs where heretofore there was not right except strength, no rule except of a master over necessitous men, no order except pauses between conflicts of force."[98] With such words, it was clear why rights-centered liberals — and even the president himself — thought Jackson was the right man to lead the Roosevelt Court. But in the end, FDR gave in to arguments for the selection of Stone, apparently hopeful that the sixty-nine-year-old would soon retire to make way for the much younger Jackson.

Thus, on one day, June 12, 1941, FDR made three appointments, a moderately conservative southerner, a respected Republican justice, and an ardent New Deal liberal. With regard to any potential confirmation difficulties, the combination was a masterstroke for the president. Even if they desired, senators would have difficulty challenging such a diverse set of nominees. In the end, the Senate confirmed each without serious incident, all by voice votes. The Byrnes confirmation was particularly striking. While it had taken the president months to appoint Byrnes to the McReynolds vacancy, the senators acted favorably on his nomination a mere eight minutes after receiving his name from the White House.

With War, One More

Perhaps the rapidity of Byrnes's confirmation predestined the length of his tenure on the Court. With the onset of the war, Byrnes — who the White House had "borrowed" after the attack on Pearl Harbor — decided to vacate his seat on the high bench to aid the president as his director of economic stabilization. In doing so, he ended the second shortest term of any justice in American history, outlasting Washington-appointee Thomas Johnson by one month.[99] For his final justice, FDR made a choice that — save Stone's elevation — was unusual when compared to his other nominees. Wiley B. Rutledge, a judge on the Court of Appeals for the District of Columbia, had never been an active New Dealer — having spent much of his adult life either in academia or on the bench — and was quite "acceptable to the very legal establishment the President detested." FDR had appointed Rutledge to the D.C. Court in 1939 after passing him over for the high bench in favor of Douglas. (He had also considered him for the 1938 Cardozo vacancy he eventually filled with Frankfurter.) There, according to one commentator, Rutledge gained a reputation for his "bold judicial technique" and his eagerness for "keeping the law of the Constitution abreast of the needs of the time." Another put it a bit differently: "On the Court of Appeals [Rutledge] proved his unwillingness to wait for legislatures to change the law. He took a hand in streamlining it from the bench." A third described him as "pro-labor" and a "realist" with "a liberal, cooperative attitude toward administrative agencies." A Justice Department review of Rutledge concluded that he was "a liberal who would stand up for human rights, particularly during a war when they were apt to be forgotten."[100]

Rutledge's main competition for the surprising vacancy came from the greatly respected Judge Learned Hand of the Second Court of Appeals. Conventional wisdom suggests that FDR chose Rutledge over Hand for three reasons: age, geography, and the tenacity of Felix Frankfurter. With regard to age, the president was apparently concerned about appointing a man of seventy when only five years earlier he had used the presence of justices that same age as the reason for his Court-packing plan. Instead, he chose the forty-eight-year-old Rutledge.[101] With geography, FDR had always wanted to put a true westerner on the Court. He had accepted the western-born and college-educated Douglas in 1939, but now had the opportunity to choose someone who had actually studied law and made his career west of the Mississippi. Rutledge, as FDR put it, had "geography." Hand did not. He was from New York, the home of two other Roosevelt justices. Finally, Hand had Felix Frankfurter pushing hard for his nomination. Too hard. As the story goes, Frankfurter put so much effort into lobbying the president that, in the end, he "overplayed his hand." According to Justice Douglas, the Frankfurter barrage exasperated the president. "Do you know how many people asked me today to name Learned Hand?" FDR (rhetorically) asked Douglas during one of their poker games. "Twenty, and every one a messenger from Felix Frankfurter. And by golly, I won't do it."[102]

Each of these points about President Roosevelt's selection of Rutledge no doubt has validity. But as Gerald Gunther explains in his exhaustive biography of Hand, "the more significant meaning of Hand's rejection lies in political-philosophical factors stemming from the internal dynamics of the 1942 Supreme Court. The New Deal appointees were increasingly divided; Frankfurter increasingly found himself in a minority; Hand's appointment would have given another vote to his side, just as the designation of Rutledge instead assured a strengthened opposition to it." The debate between the two warring factions of the Roosevelt Court centered on the extent of their commitment to judicial restraint. Once again, Gunther explains, "All of the New Deal justices agreed that the hands-off attitude was appropriate for economic laws, but they differed sharply about the proper approach to individual-rights cases. The Frankfurter wing insisted that a double standard was inappropriate: judicial deference to majority rule should govern even when the challenged law curtailed personal rights, not only when economic interests were threatened. The opposing side, led by Justices Black and Douglas, argued just as vehemently that a more activist, interventionist role for the Court was appropriate when personal rights sought protection."[103] At the time of Byrnes's resignation, the battle within the Court was coming to a head over the flag salute cases. In 1940 seven of the Roosevelt justices (with Frankfurter writing and only Stone in dissent) had agreed in *Minersville School District v. Gobitis* that local regulations requiring students belonging to the Jehovah's Witness religion to salute the flag did not violate the First Amendment's free exercise clause. But in June 1942 three of the more liberal justices — Black, Douglas, and Murphy — publicly announced that they had changed their minds.[104] Four months later, Byrnes was gone and FDR had another seat to fill. In the end, he chose Rutledge — the candidate Black, Douglas, and Murphy favored — over the Frankfurter-backed Hand.[105] "In all likelihood," concludes Gunther, FDR's "failure to select Frankfurter's candidate in 1942 reflected not only impatience with Frankfurter's maneuvers but also disagreement with his conception of the role of the Supreme Court."[106]

If true, Felix Frankfurter had learned the wrong lesson from FDR's attack against the Court. While deference should certainly be the creed of the Court, the Roosevelt justices should not necessarily defer to state or local officials on matters of civil rights and liberties, especially when federal authorities were advocating activism. Here, the role of the Justice Department — specifically its Civil Rights Section — in the flag salute dispute is of special significance. Almost immediately after the *Gobitis* decision — announced on June 3, 1940 — Justice Department officials noticed a sharp increase in the number of crimes against Jehovah's Witnesses. "Between June 12 and June 20, 1940 hundreds of attacks upon the Witnesses were reported to the Department of Justice. Several were of such violence that it was deemed advisable to have the Federal Bureau of Investigation look into them."[107]

Following these assaults, the CRS moved to indict several state and municipal officers involved in three separate incidents. In each of the cases, however, grand juries refused to cooperate.[108] Restricted from pursuing a more intense campaign by Attorney General Francis Biddle, CRS staff members took to convincing the Court that it had erred in *Gobitis* and should reverse itself. In an attempt to publicize their opinions, the CRS's Victor Rotnem and Fred Folsom wrote an article for the *American Political Science Review* in December 1942. They began their attack on *Gobitis* by first reviewing some history on the freedom of religion and Jehovah's Witnesses, before laying out the decision's violent effect on the group:

> In the two years following the decision, the files of the Department of Justice reflect an uninterrupted record of violence and persecution of the Witnesses. Almost without exception, the flag and the flag salute can be found as the percussion cap that sets off these acts. . . . [This] ugly picture . . . is an eloquent argument in support of the minority contention of Mr. Justice Stone. The placing of symbolic exercises on a higher plane than freedom of conscience has made this symbol an instrument of oppression of a religious minority. The flag has been violated by its misuse to deny the very freedoms it is intended to represent — the freedoms which themselves best engender a healthy 'cohesive' respect for national institutions.

With the story told, Rotnem and Folsom concluded, "it seems probable that a reversal of that ruling would profoundly enhance respect for the flag."

If the justices were not willing to overturn such a young decision, the two CRS staff members offered another way out, an innovative interpretation of a recently enacted federal statute. "Perhaps" they suggested, "Congress has by-passed the constitutional issue here involved and supplied a statutory solution." While Congress — by enacting Public Law No. 623 in 1942 — had seemingly only modified the proper manner in which to give allegiance to the flag, Rotnem and Folsom urged that it had in fact codified a "federal standard." It had done so with language certifying that "civilians will always show full respect to the flag when the pledge is given by merely standing at attention, men removing the headdress." In their eyes, this meant that "state and local regulations demanding a different standard of performance must give way entirely, or at least be made to conform."[109]

In the end, the Court did not rely on the CRS's statutory arguments to overturn *Gobitis* in *West Virginia State Board of Education v. Barnette*, preferring instead to rule on constitutional grounds. Still, the appeal was an important one, foreshadowing future efforts by the CRS to shape the statutory work of the Court. Moreover, when the Court did discard *Gobitis*, the Justice Department's influence — aided by the onset of a war against dictatorship — was clear. With Justice Department evidence available to support his conclusion, Jackson wrote: "Those who begin coercive elimination of dissent soon find themselves exterminating dissenters. Compulsory unification of opinion achieves only the unanimity of the graveyard."[110]

The six-man majority in *Barnette* was significant for another reason. The newly seated Rutledge — whom the Senate had confirmed on February 8, 1943, by voice vote — joined the *Gobitis*-dissenting Stone and the three Roosevelt justices who had altered course (Black, Douglas, and Murphy). Justice Jackson, who was attorney general when the Court decided *Gobitis* in 1940, wrote the majority opinion, concluding that Jehovah's Witness children did not have to salute the flag after all. Well known for its powerful language, it is perhaps more important as a decision that deeply disrupted the unity of the Roosevelt Court. For in response to the dramatic shift by the Court's leading liberals, Justice Frankfurter held nothing back in seeking to discredit their activist path. Quoting from then Associate Justice Stone's 1936 dissent in *United States v. Butler*, he reminded his New Deal brethren, "the removal of unwise laws from the statute books . . . lies, not to the courts, but to the ballot and to the processes of democratic government."[111]

To be sure, the case of *United States v. Korematsu* tells another story with regard to the principles of deference and rights protection, although significantly concerning action at the federal not state or local level. Here, Justice

Department officials' decision to "surrender" to War Department demands for greater security resulted in an executive order to intern American citizens of Japanese descent. Against the strong rights-centered objections of two Roosevelt justices (Murphy and Jackson — Roberts also dissented), the Court majority chose to adhere to the principle of deference and upheld the administration's internment policy. It represented one of those rare times when the Roosevelt Court's deference to the executive clashed with the advancement of civil rights and liberties, although notably not with regard to black Americans. Indeed, given the facts of *Korematsu*, the decision did not negatively affect the campaign to secure the civil rights of African Americans through the courts. In fact, while hardly a victory for civil rights, Justice Black's decision in *Korematsu* marked the beginning of the suspect classification doctrine. Perhaps highlighting the importance of the Justice Department's advocacy, *Korematsu* remains the only case in which the Court has upheld a racially restrictive governmental action under the strict scrutiny test.[112]

Conclusion

As a group, then, the Roosevelt justices — with realism as their guide — were easily more willing to accept new ideas and methods than those justices they replaced. They were also more amenable to endorsing the "expert" opinions — supported by social scientific evidence — of the Justice Department, especially if those opinions were consistent with ideals of rights-centered liberalism. The Roosevelt justices' relative youth and lack of judicial experience further escalated the influence of the Justice Department. Most of these men had spent their previous years active in the everyday details of administering the nation's government. Their criticisms of the law and of the federal judiciary were well known, but they would have to develop their style of interpretation more fully once they settled into their chambers. In the final analysis, these factors gave the department and legal reform groups aligned with it an indispensable opportunity to help shape doctrine.

Thus while there is no clear evidence that FDR nominated jurists with a specific desire to advance African American rights, his nominees' adherence to rights-centered liberalism combined with their devotion to defer to the executive branch ensured that the NAACP would find fertile ground to lay its antisegregation precedential seeds, seeds that would one day — nourished in part by the Justice Department — sprout into *Brown v. Board*. Put

differently, Roosevelt's appointees' general commitment to the union between rights-centered liberalism and legal realism made them intellectually
aligned with legal reform efforts such as the NAACP's campaign to emas-
culate southern segregation, if not openly supportive of them.[113] In the end,
this commitment would have dramatic effects on the cause to extend the
rights of black Americans.

FIVE

A Constitutional Purge

Southern Democracy, Lynch Law, and the
Roosevelt Justice Department

W hile FDR's appointments were unquestionably central to the expansion of civil rights through the courts, they are only part of the
story. Indeed, it was one thing to select jurists receptive to new
ideas, quite another — particularly during this period of judicial transformation — to back up those appointments with an assertive policy designed to reorder the judiciary. As I argue, together with the progressive nature of FDR's
appointments, the institution-building efforts by the Roosevelt Justice Department expressed the administration's desire to forge a rights-expanding
mission on the Supreme Court following the constitutional crisis of the
1930s. In this chapter, I examine those Justice Department efforts — the third
pillar of the Roosevelt administration's judicial policy — with respect to challenges to the white primary, the poll tax, lynching, and police brutality. I do
so by exploring the significance and consequences of Justice Department
arguments and strategies — articulated in internal documents, published articles, and courtroom appeals — made in the course of prosecuting crimes
in these areas, arguments and strategies that I suggest laid the foundational
precedent for later Supreme Court decisions constitutionally undercutting
southern democracy and white supremacy. I begin with a discussion of the
formation of the Justice Department's Civil Rights Section (CRS).

Creating the Civil Rights Section

On February 3, 1939, the president's new attorney general, Frank Murphy,
announced the creation of a Civil Liberties Unit (soon renamed the Civil
Rights Section) within the Justice Department.[1] The attorney general issued
this statement merely three months after the disappointing results of the
midterm purge elections and only six weeks after the Supreme Court provided the NAACP with its initial victory in *Missouri ex rel. Gaines v. Canada*
by reconsidering its previous interpretation of the Fourteenth Amendment's
equal protection clause. Murphy, who had gained fame as Michigan gover-

nor for his willingness to disregard judicial decrees in order to support labor during the 1937 sit-down strikes, had just lost his own reelection bid. While a setback for New Dealers, the loss provided FDR with the perfect person to shake up the Justice Department. As Peter Irons writes, Murphy "brought to the post a crusading spirit and a passionate moralism that reflected his former membership on the NAACP board of directors and his hatred of racial and religious prejudice." By the time he left, he had completely "changed the complexion" of the Justice Department, making it "the most thoroughly New Deal department of the Federal government."[2] The formation of the CRS was no doubt his most lasting achievement as attorney general.

Rights-advocacy groups took little time in hailing FDR's selection of Murphy. Writing to Murphy four days after the formation of the CRS, the NAACP's Walter White noted, "It would warm the cockles of your heart if you only knew how great is the satisfaction among colored people all over the United States at your presence in the . . . post of Attorney General." The ACLU's Roger Baldwin added to the liberal acclaim by telling Murphy, "you don't know how refreshing it is to have a man in your office with [civil liberties] on his mind. . . . I almost believe we should begin to feel that we could go out of business."[3]

In addition to appointing such a rights-centered liberal to head the Justice Department, the president was also closely involved with creating the Civil Rights Section. In a letter to FDR five months after the CRS's formation, Murphy wrote: "It is my personal opinion that the creation of this unit *at your order*, with all the emphasis it places upon protection of the civil liberties of the individual citizen and of minority groups, is one of the most significant happenings in American legal history." In a 1947 memo, Turner Smith, who had been a CRS attorney since 1942 and its head since 1945, confirmed that it was "generally understood" that Murphy formed the unit "at the specific suggestion of President Roosevelt who was concerned with minority problems."[4] In establishing the CRS, FDR and Murphy likely appreciated the power of bureaucratic momentum as well. By installing the CRS with the specific mission of safeguarding civil rights, they created, as Brian K. Landsberg puts it, "a sort of time bomb. Inevitably, as it started investigating and prosecuting civil rights violations, the need for more effective and comprehensive machinery would become evident."[5]

While small (about a dozen lawyers and three assistants) and experimental at its inception, the CRS was nevertheless a striking symbol of the progressive gains of the New Deal years. As Murphy noted six months after its formation, "for the first time in our history the full weight of the Department will be thrown behind the effort to preserve in this country the blessings of liberty, the spirit of tolerance, and the fundamental principles of democracy." Its original function and purpose was "to make a study of the provisions of the Constitution of the United States and Acts of Congress relating to civil rights with reference to present conditions, to make appropriate recommendations in respect thereto, and to direct, supervise and conduct prosecutions of violations of the provisions of the Constitution or Acts of Congress guaranteeing civil rights to individuals."[6] In the end, it became a center for testing creative legal theories that sought to halt lynchings and police brutality; expand voting rights, particularly for African Americans living in the South; stamp out local political corruption; protect religious liberty; punish violators of peonage and involuntary servitude statutes; and safeguard the constitutional and statutory rights of labor.[7] For the vast majority of African Americans, its most important initiatives concerned the white primary, the poll tax, lynching, and police brutality, four pillars of political repression in the segregated South.

The chief sources of the CRS's theories were sections 51 and 52 of title 18 of the U.S. Code (sections 19 and 20 of the U.S. Criminal Code).[8] Section 51, originally part of the Enforcement Act of 1870, allowed for fines and imprisonment when "two or more persons" *conspired* "to injure, oppress, threaten, or intimidate any citizen in the free exercise or enjoyment of any right secured to him by the Constitution or laws of the United States."[9] Although section 51 received some attention in the courts following its passage, the list of statutory rights it had been used to safeguard was, according to Robert K. Carr, the author of the most detailed work on the CRS's early activities (published in 1947) and the staff director of President Truman's Civil Rights Committee, "discouragingly brief." The list of constitutional rights protected by the statute was longer, but its "usefulness" in securing some of the most fundamental rights recently incorporated by the Supreme Court — such as the freedom of speech and press — "remained to be established." To further complicate the CRS's work, the Court, particularly in voting rights cases, "had shown an increasing tendency to restrict the use of the statute, on the ground that Congress had not intended it to be used to protect the rights in question." This narrow range of protected rights — combined with the difficulties of its vague language, conspiracy requirement, and inflexible penalties — led Carr to write that "if section 51 was to have any extraordinary value, as a means of enabling the federal government to protect individual rights against invasion by public officers or private persons — particularly the latter — a considerable task remained . . . in persuading the courts to sanction a broader use of the statute."[10]

Section 52, derived from part of the Civil Rights Act of 1866 and parts of the Enforcement Act of 1870, allowed for fines and imprisonment when someone "under color of any law . . . willfully subject[ed], or cause[d] to be subjected, any inhabitant" to be deprived "of any rights, privileges, or immunities secured or protected by the Constitution or laws of the United States, or to different punishments, pains, or penalties, on account of such inhabitant being an alien, or by reason of his color, or race."[11] Section 52 also had its problems. For instance, CRS lawyers knew that the terms "under color of law" and "willfully" would present future troubles in court. Moreover, since the statute had seen little judicial action, no promising case law existed to support its use. While it appeared "to have a much sounder constitutional basis than section 51, because it protect[ed] civil liberties against governmental action rather than [both] private and public action," it was "largely untested." Still, combined with the fact that it could be utilized against single individuals, did not require the presence of a conspiracy, and protected the rights of "inhabitants" not just "citizens" (as in section 51), CRS lawyers were hopeful that it would be a "more valuable tool" than its companion statute in the protection of constitutional rights.[12]

In the department's policy circular of May 21, 1940—the first official document after the CRS's creation to lay out the basis for prosecuting violations of federally protected rights under sections 51 and 52—officials stressed that the "broad scope" of the Supreme Court's interpretation of the Fourteenth Amendment "over the last fifteen years" made "section 52 a powerful weapon against misconduct of State officer[s]."[13] If, for example, a state deprived an "inhabitant" of his freedom of speech—as secured by the Court in *Gitlow v. New York* (1925)—any officer of that state who participated in such action could be prosecuted for violation of section 52. The U.S. Department of Justice, through criminal prosecutions, was attempting to establish itself as the protector of all rights guaranteed by an increasingly civil-liberties-minded Supreme Court, as the enforcer of the post–*Carolene Products* decisions.[14] As with its companion statute, if section 52 was to be successfully employed to safeguard both statutory and constitutional rights, federal judges and justices would have to interpret it broadly.

Breathing new life into these statutes was sure to be a long and evolutionary process. Nevertheless, the effort had an inspiring beginning. Years later, Francis Biddle—Roosevelt's solicitor general from 1940 to 1941 and attorney general from 1941 to 1945—summed up the situation this way: "Once the [CRS] was established complaints poured in, not only from victims of the illegal acts but from their fellow townsmen, from whites as well as Negroes, often from local law-enforcement officials who found themselves powerless to deal with the situations they reported, and from groups organized to protect civil liberties." Moreover, when World War II began for the United States, attention to the civil liberties effort rose significantly. As Biddle put it: "The denial of the rights — often merely of the right to live in peace — was a tragic mockery after we had entered the war."[15] Indeed, much of the CRS's work took place under the cover of war. First with fighting on the horizon and then in the midst of war, the Justice Department — eager to avoid its abuses of the past war period — sought to use the conflict as a reason for securing democracy at home by arguing that American patriotism ought to be defined by tolerance, not majority tyranny. Attorney General Murphy expressed such sentiment in an October, 13, 1939, speech entitled "The Test of Patriotism":

> The true citizen of America will remember that loyalty to our tradition of civil liberty is as much a part of patriotism, as defense of our shores and a hatred for treason. He will never forget that civil liberty under the American system is a legal right in time of war as well as time of peace — that, whatever the time, it is liberty for all, irrespective of the accident of birth. The true American will remember that whether it be peace-time or wartime, there could be nothing more unpatriotic in this land of many people and many creeds than the persecution of minorities and the fomenting of hatred and strife on the basis of race and religion. He will realize that if, in the atmosphere of war, we allow civil liberty to slip away from us, it may not be long before our recent great gains in social and economic justice will also have vanished. For a nation that is callused in its attitude toward civil rights is not likely to be sensitive toward the many grave problems that affect the dignity and security of its citizens. We must not let this crisis destroy what we have so dearly won.[16]

Perhaps muted by the realities of war or reassured by a criminal justice system defined by all-white juries, southern reaction in Washington to the Justice Department's action was surprisingly still. A review of the *Congressional Record* and hearings before the House and Senate Appropriations Committees reveals little outrage from southern senators and representatives and no major efforts to cut the department's funds because of the CRS's activities. In part, this acquiescence may also have been a consequence of the CRS's creation. In 1939 South Carolina Senator Jimmy Byrnes, as chair of the Committee to Audit and Control the Contingent Expenses, sought to halt the operations of Wisconsin Senator Robert La Follette, Jr.'s Civil Liberties Committee. Beginning in 1936, the La Follette Committee had attracted widespread attention by uncovering many civil liberty and civil rights abuses against labor by industry and was now seeking funding for an investigation of California farm labor. As noted earlier, throughout the 1930s, southern conservatives had successfully bargained to preclude agriculture workers from most relevant New Deal programs, including the Wagner Act. Excluding these workers, many of whom were African American, enabled the continuation of state and private control over the system of farm tenancy. For that reason, many southern senators feared the La Follette Committee's encroachment into agriculture and its attempt to extend "civil liberty" there.

In choosing California instead of a southern state to make its point that the exclusion of farm labor from the Wagner Act was unjustifiable and destructive to civil rights and liberties, the committee attempted to avoid a confrontation with southerners. Most, however, saw through it. For instance, in arguing against funding the California investigation, "Cotton Ed" Smith, warned of the consequences of securing civil liberty by linking such protection to the advancement of the "inferior race": "For miserable political reasons we are ready . . . to inject into the bloodstream of our . . . splendid social and political system the vicious part of a nation that through all the history of the world has never moved a step forward from the dawn of creation."[17] In opposing both the California investigation and a move to establish a permanent civil liberties committee, Byrnes chose a less racially hostile route. By arguing that the La Follette Committee was more executive than legislative in nature, he persuaded the Appropriations Committee to approve even more funds than the Justice Department had requested for its investigations into civil liberties violations. Byrnes, who had failed to stop funding for the La Follette Committee in the previous two years, was clearly attempting to undermine its support in the Senate by advocating for CRS funds.[18] Nevertheless, as an integral component of the southern leadership in Congress, his actions in aiding the CRS's formation may have forestalled later efforts to cut its relatively small budget.

To be sure, not all southerners remained silent about the CRS's activities. In perhaps the most acrimonious assault on the CRS, an alarmed Representative John Rankin of Mississippi strode to the House floor to stress that the Justice Department was "destined to degenerate into a Gestapo for the persecution of the white people throughout the South and for the persecution of white gentiles throughout the country generally and for the stirring up of race hatred and promoting race strife." Speaking about an upcoming federal lynching trial in his home state, Rankin called the indictments "an insult that has not been offered to a sovereign State of this Union since the darkest days of reconstruction, of which all right-thinking Americans are now ashamed."[19] Other southerners in Congress may have agreed with these sentiments, but they saved such rhetoric for more direct legislative attacks on white supremacy, particularly antilynching and anti–poll tax bills. During closing arguments in the Mississippi lynching trial that Rankin assailed on the House floor, the chief defense counsel cited these legislative efforts to explain the significance of the department's decision to prosecute:

> Several months ago, Negroes undertook to pass what was known as the anti-lynching bill. Thanks to the courage and stamina of a few red-blooded southern Senators, it was delayed by filibuster tactics. Then it was that the same crowd sought to pass the nefarious poll tax repeal bill, and that, too, was defeated by this same band of red-blooded Senators. And today in furtherance of this same design we are confronted by this trial at a time when our nation is engaged in a bitter war to determine if the cause of democracy will survive. . . . Interest in this trial has become nation-wide because of the effect it will have on future Federal prosecutions. If a precedent is established by this jury giving sanction to this abortive attempt to deprive us of our rights as a sovereign state, we can then expect many more prosecutions when it meets the pleasure of those who seek to further centralize power in Washington.[20]

Although the CRS was unsuccessful in this particular case, such words display how its creation in early 1939 represented a dramatic transformation for a department that four years earlier the NAACP's executive secretary had called the Department of *White* Justice.[21]

Giving More People the Power of the Vote

Between 1939 and 1945, the Civil Rights Section, at times in cooperation with the NAACP, undertook various initiatives to punish those engaged in election fraud and to secure the right to vote for the disfranchised, especially African Americans. In its greatest success of the period, Justice Department attorneys convinced the Supreme Court in 1941 to significantly weaken the legal basis of the white primary (*United States v. Classic*).[22] Three years later, in *Smith v. Allwright*, the Court, based on *Classic*, ruled that the white primary was no longer constitutionally valid.

The White Primary

United States v. Classic arose out of the indictment of a group of Louisiana anti-Long reformers, a group that had previously been backed by the Justice

Department in its effort to clean up politics in the land where the Kingfish once ruled. In their endeavor to reform Louisiana politics following Huey Long's death, however, Patrick Classic and the other defendants had allegedly aided their candidate in a primary election for the U.S. House of Representatives by counting in his favor ninety-seven ballots originally cast for two other candidates. The local U.S. Attorney — tipped off by the Long faction — not the CRS, discovered the irregularities. On September 25, 1940, two weeks after the disputed primary, the U.S. Attorney in Louisiana indicted Classic and four other "Commissioners of Election," informing officials in Washington that "in view of the recurring demands in this state that the Federal Government do something about these election matters . . . this test case should be brought to a conclusion in order . . . [to] definitely know the extent of Federal jurisdiction."[23] After some delay, newly appointed Attorney General Robert Jackson — by order of President Roosevelt — agreed to pursue the case with the hope of overturning the 1921 *Newberry* ruling.[24] In *Newberry*, the Court had limited the Federal Corrupt Practices Act of 1910 to general elections, on the basis that primaries were not "elections" within the meaning of Section 4, Article 1 of the U.S. Constitution. As a result, they were the province of the parties, not the government. In its *Grovey v. Townsend* decision fourteen years later, the Court had unanimously upheld the white primary on similar grounds, ruling that the Democratic Party in Texas was not an agent of the state but a voluntary private group.[25] It could therefore exclude blacks.

Because no African Americans were involved, CRS lawyers saw *Classic* as an ideal case to undermine racial exclusiveness in primaries, the only significant elections in the South. In other words, this seemingly nonracial case could be a vehicle for extending the right to vote in primaries for national office to African Americans. And after the district court sustained a demurrer to the indictments, the case went to the Supreme Court on an early appeal. In its brief, the government concentrated on the theory that the defendants had first violated section 51 by depriving citizens of their constitutional right to vote (as granted by Article I and the equal protection clause of the Fourteenth Amendment). In other words, if the defendants had not counted ballots as intended, then they had conspired to deny these ninety-seven voters of their federally protected rights. Second, since the defendants were working as election officials, CRS lawyers argued, they were operating under the "color of law" and, in turn, had also violated section 52.[26]

In May 1941, the Court handed down its decision supporting the government's fundamental claim, that the right to vote under Article I of the Constitution included primary elections for federal office and that sections 51 and 52 could be employed to secure this right. In a consummate display of activist interpretation and realist thought, Justice Stone reasoned that although "the framers of the Constitution . . . did not have specifically in mind the selection and elimination of candidates for Congress by the direct primary . . . in setting up an enduring framework of government they undertook to carry out for the indefinite future and in all the vicissitudes of the changing affairs of men, those fundamental purposes which the instrument itself discloses." Moving on to the applicability of section 51, Stone, relying on two early cases, found "no uncertainty or ambiguity in the statutory language, obviously devised to protect the citizen 'in the free exercise or enjoyment of any right or privilege secured to him by the Constitution.' "[27] Joined by Justices Felix Frankfurter, Stanley Reed, and Owen Roberts, the future Chief Justice concluded with a sweeping definition of state action: "Misuse of power, possessed by virtue of state law and made possible only because the wrongdoer is clothed with the authority of state law, is action taken 'under color of' state law." This definition — one that would become significant for future equal protection and due process cases — upheld the federal government's use of section 52 in its indictment of Classic and the other defendants who, "while holding their offices under state law, commit[ted] acts . . . which obviously [were] not authorized or sanctioned by law." It was a decision the NAACP's Thurgood Marshall called "striking and far reaching."[28]

Somewhat surprisingly, three of the Court's most liberal members — William Douglas, Hugo Black, and former Attorney General Frank Murphy — dissented. Given Murphy's role in the creation of the CRS, some explanation of his vote is required. Apparently, Murphy — and Douglas — originally voted with the majority. Both changed their minds and voted with Black based on a concern for the vagueness of the statute and its potential effect on civil liberties.[29] Indeed, it must be emphasized that, in writing the dissent, Douglas — likely influenced by the Justice Department's civil rights and liberties record during and immediately following the First World War — sought to defend individual liberties from an overeager government. It is also important to keep in mind that these three justices were still developing their judicial philosophies at this time. Notably, they had yet to make their switch on the flag-salute dispute, as discussed in chapter 4.

Moreover, despite their decision to dissent — which foreshadows the later "breakup" of the Roosevelt Court — they agreed with Stone's conclusion that Congress had the power to regulate primaries (thereby overruling *Newberry*). Refusing to defer to the executive branch, however, they asserted — through Douglas — that the Court was entering "perilous territory" in allowing the federal government to use section 51 to oversee primary elections. "It is one thing to allow wide and generous scope to the express and implied powers of Congress; it is distinctly another to read into the vague and general language of an act of Congress specifications of crimes." Given that primaries were "hardly known" when section 51 was enacted and that Congress had left it "unmolested for some seventy years," the Court, Douglas asserted, should not now "perform a legislative function" to sustain the indictment. "A crime, no matter how offensive, should not be spelled out from . . . vague inferences."[30] In keeping with his pledge to protect civil liberties and in contrast to Stone's silence, Douglas explained the implications of his decision for the white primary in clear language: Since "discrimination on the basis of race or color is plainly outlawed by the Fourteenth Amendment, [in] cases where state election officials deprive negro citizens of their right to vote at a general election or at a primary . . . there is no reason why [sections 51 or 52] should not be applicable. But the situation here is quite different. When we turn to the constitutional provisions relevant to this case we find no such unambiguous mandate."[31]

When the constitutionality of the white primary next returned to the Court's docket in *Smith v. Allwright*, the action of the Justice Department provoked controversy within the Roosevelt administration. Although the South's racially exclusive electoral system was now under direct attack by the NAACP, Attorney General Francis Biddle rejected CRS arguments that the Solicitor General's Office should file an *amicus curiae* brief in support of the challenge. Biddle's decision attracted even the president's attention: "There is a good deal of howl because the Department of Justice has refused to participate as *amicus* in the Texas Primary case. How about It?" Biddle knew that the "howl" was coming from Walter White, and in his response to Roosevelt he made it clear that the Justice Department had already "established the right to vote in primaries as a federal right enforceable in the federal courts in the *Classic* case." He then cautioned against intervening again because "the South would not understand why we were continually taking sides." Biddle's decision not to file an *amicus curiae* brief seems inspired by Solicitor General Charles Fahy, who told the attorney general that "although the legal questions have difficulties, whether or not to participate is essentially a policy question. We have already assisted the negroes by winning the *Classic* case which gives them their principal ammunition. Should we go further in their behalf and make a gesture which cannot fail to offend many others, in Texas and the South generally, in a case in which we are not a party? I think not."[32]

CRS attorneys appeared to disagree with the attorney general's decision. As one staff member noted, "the *Classic* case gives hope of reversing the holding in *Grovey v. Townsend* and it is hoped that the Solicitor General, when the question is submitted, will approve a brief amicus in the Circuit Court."[33] In the end, the department did not remain silent on the matter. As part of an apparent intradepartmental compromise, Fred G. Folsom of the CRS published an article in the *Columbia Law Review* expressing the department's view of the relationship between *Classic* and the white primary. Most importantly, he asserted that the Court's 1937 unanimous decision in *Grovey v. Townsend* "might be considered as impliedly overruled by the *Classic* decision." Thurgood Marshall and William Hastie of the NAACP were in "total agreement" with this analysis, and they argued so before the Court.[34]

When the justices handed down their near unanimous decision in *Smith v. Allwright* — with only the one non-Roosevelt appointee dissenting (Owen Roberts) — they put the speculation about the scope of *Classic* to rest by relying on it, and on its definition of state action, to strike down the *Grovey* decision. In contrast to Louisiana, the Texas primary was run by the political parties themselves and not by officers of the state. One crucial test for the NAACP, therefore, was to prove that since this system was sanctioned by state law, these officers were nonetheless within the perimeters of "state action" and thus had denied blacks the right to vote in the primary in violation of the Fourteenth and Fifteenth Amendments. The Court agreed, thereby expanding the *Classic* doctrine of state action to include civil claims of equal protection. For Stone, now the "Roosevelt" Chief Justice following his 1941 elevation, the decision was inevitable after *Classic*. As he noted to Justice Stanley Reed, "when I wrote the *Classic* case I was convinced that the Court would one day feel compelled to overturn the ruling that legitimized the white primary."[35] As he had done with the flag-salute cases, Stone had once again displayed his judicial foresight and his leadership as a civil libertarian.

Within the justices' chambers, *Smith v. Allwright* had caused quite a stir. After the case was originally assigned to Felix Frankfurter, Robert Jackson made an appeal to the Chief Justice, questioning the wisdom of having the "jewish" justice "act as the voice of this Court" in this matter: "We deny the entire South the right to a white primary, which is one of its most cherished rights. It seems to me very important that the strength which an all but unanimous decision would have may be greatly weakened if the voice that utters it is one that may grate on Southern sensibilities." As a result, Justice Reed of Kentucky wrote the opinion.[36] The event displays the cautiousness of even a rights-centered Supreme Court, concerned about the South's reaction to such a far-reaching ruling.

While many inside the Justice Department applauded the Court's decision, it actually made prosecuting election officials under sections 51 and 52 more difficult. For example, when South Carolina, just seventeen days after *Allwright*, repealed all of its laws controlling primary elections and turned the conduct of the primary over to the political party, the CRS did not seek prosecutions even though it faced sharp criticism from the NAACP and other rights-advocacy groups for this stance.[37] The CRS feared, according to Carr, that, first, "the Supreme Court would set aside any convictions that might be obtained, on the ground that party officials have not yet received sufficient warning through the *Allwright* decision that their action [was] unlawful." It also believed "that civil action [was] apt to prove more successful than criminal prosecutions, in protecting the right to vote, because of the difficulty of winning convictions in election cases in the South."[38] Finally, Attorney General Biddle apparently accepted the warnings of other members in the administration who cautioned that "such action by the federal government at this time might be the fact which would translate impotent rumblings against the New Deal into actual revolt at the polls . . . [and] would be a very dangerous mistake." Even before the *Allwright* case, the attorney general expressed such concern. In a memo to FDR, Biddle — responding to the president's request "to look informally into the Negro situation, and make suggestions" — noted, "the South is in a state of emotional alarm over a supposed intention of the Government to intervene in every phase of race relationship." Still, troubled with the "widespread discontent among the Negroes" and fearful that "politically . . . the administration [was] losing the support of the Negro population," Biddle recommended that the Fair Employment Practice Committee (FEPC) — created by FDR in June 1941 under pressure from A. Philip Randolph's March on Washington Movement — "be reorganized and strengthened."[39] Consistent with the Court's decision to have Reed write the majority opinion in *Smith v. Allwright*, Biddle's fears display how race relations had been rubbed raw by wartime tensions, including the work of the FEPC, further southern black migration North, and race riots both below and above the Mason-Dixon line. Indeed, even before the *Allwright* decision, one commentator asked: "Will the South Secede?" He then explained the state of affairs in Dixie and their root cause: "[A] portentous factor in Southern politics is the resurgence of racial antagonisms. It has been said by responsible persons that race relations in the South are worse than they have been in fifty years. This time the Southerner is not being told that the Republican Party is the mortal enemy of 'white supremacy.' Instead, he is being told that the enemy is the New Deal in general and President and Mrs. Roosevelt in particular."[40]

As expected, the *Allwright* decision outraged southerners, especially those in the Deep South. As historian Kari Frederickson writes, "While the states of the Upper South acquiesced in the ruling, the decision was a political bombshell in the Deep South. White legislators across the Black Belt exchanged anxious letters hatching schemes to circumvent the decision. Mississippi congressman John Rankin warned legislators in his state to take action against the "communistic drive . . . to destroy white supremacy in the South. The state legislature eventually passed a law requiring voters to swear their opposition to federal anti-lynching and anti–poll tax legislation and the FEPC."[41]

Perhaps with the South's reaction in mind, the Justice Department's disappointing inaction enforcing *Allwright* through criminal prosecution did not end its alliance with the NAACP and other legal reform groups. Instead, CRS attorneys urged that "if no suitable criminal case develops," the NAACP and the ACLU should be conferred with "in order to give them the benefit of our study" and encourage a test of a state law "through civil action" on equal protection grounds.[42] Such cooperation with these "great groups" (as one head of the CRS referred to them) was in display when the NAACP challenged South Carolina's post-*Allwright* statute in 1947,[43] and the CRS's Folsom informally commented on Thurgood Marshall's brief. As Steven Lawson writes, "this interchange suggested that the Department of Justice would provide advice in preparing civil suits when it did not want to risk criminal proceedings."[44] Its willingness to call for judicial activism appears to have influenced a Supreme Court eager to defer to the executive branch.

The Poll Tax

In contrast to the CRS's success in helping to challenge the law of the white primary, its anticipated assault on the poll tax stalled at the idea stage. Although Attorney General Robert Jackson showed strong sympathy for an attack against the tax as solicitor general, later CRS documents display a widespread belief within the Justice Department that the Supreme Court would not grant *certiorari* for a test of a poll tax statute. After all, in 1937, the Court had unanimously ruled in *Breedlove v. Suttles* that Georgia's poll tax was constitutional. Despite this, two years later, then Solicitor General Jackson put forth an optimistic reading of Justice Pierce Butler's opinion. In *Breedlove*, the Court held that Georgia's poll tax "did not prescribe a qualification for the voter but was a method of collecting the tax." In Jackson's estimation, "This is fortunate, if the poll tax were imposed as a qualification of voters it might be sustained under the constitution because the right of prescribing the qualifications has probably been left to the State legislatures. Since it is not a qualification, however, but is a penalty to enforce the payment of a tax, the question comes down to this: whether a denial of the right to vote for Federal officers is a proper penalty for failure to pay a lawful tax."[45] Despite this early excitement, Justice Department officials gave little attention to an assault on the tax after the CRS's creation in 1939. Perhaps they were convinced that the larger political movement in both the Congress and the states would lead to success in the legislative arena. Nevertheless, their predictions about the improbability of the Court reversing *Breedlove* were confirmed in 1941 when *certiorari* was denied for a case challenging Tennessee's poll tax.[46]

New Dealers sought to repeal this suffrage-restricting tax, as detailed earlier, based on convincing evidence that it effectively disfranchised many citizens prone to support progressive candidates. Although eliminating the poll tax would mostly enhance the participation of poor whites, as Steven Lawson writes, "reformers harbored great expectations as to the benefits of an assault on the tax for impoverished members of both races." A leading African American newspaper, the *Chicago Defender,* imagined what politics a successful enfranchisement movement could be expected to create: Unfettered franchise would "hasten the advent of certain white progressive elements to power. With a clear perception of the mandates of a functioning democracy, liberal white southerners would so implement state laws as to usher in a new era of justice and equality to a mass of inarticulate whites and Negroes." Many southern politicians feared the same result and resisted anti–poll tax legislation. But the South was hardly united on this issue.

Along with Florida Senator Claude Pepper, such other liberal southern politicians as Governor Ellis Arnall of Georgia and Congressman Brooks Hays of Arkansas supported a repeal of the tax "chiefly to topple entrenched political machines by expanding the white electorate." Complicating matters, however, even race-baiters, like Mississippi Senator Theodore Bilbo pushed hard for their state legislatures to abolish the tax. Bilbo did so both to advance his own brand of populism and to increase his power in his state. Specifically, he sought to upend the 1940 reelection bid of Pat Harrison, Mississippi's aristocratic senator. In the end, the movement to repeal Mississippi's tax failed and Harrison returned to the Senate. As his biographer Martha Swain notes, like most southern senators, Harrison was a "Bourbon" of the

South, and therefore held on to the poll tax out of fear for the "'uncertainty of a political contest in which thousands of new voters would participate.' "[47]

At the federal level, after four years of delay, due partially to the president's inconsistent leadership on the issue, the House of Representatives finally voted on anti–poll tax legislation on October 13, 1942. Even with only four southerners supporting the ban, the House overwhelmingly approved the measure by a margin of 254 to 84. By this point, in spite of bitter opposition from some southerners, Congress had already passed and the president had signed the Soldier Voting Act.[48] This legislation set up the machinery to allow qualified servicemen to file absentee votes in federal elections without paying a tax, thereby allowing many southern soldiers (including African Americans) to vote for the first time. To most House members, the bill to abolish the tax for all voters was simply another step toward a more inclusive democracy.

When the legislation came to the Senate floor, however, it confronted a southern filibuster. Despite the efforts of its sponsor, Claude Pepper, the measure met a fate similar to that of other racially progressive legislation, as its supporters failed to bring it up for a vote. For his part, Bilbo, who was never interested in national anti–poll tax legislation, anxiously declared to his fellow senators that if this "bill passes, the next step will be an effort to remove the registration qualification, the educational qualification of the negroes. If that is done we will have no way of preventing negroes from voting." Although some criticized the president for not being an outspoken backer of this bill, his support for the measure was well known. Recall, back in 1938, he had proclaimed the tax "a remnant of the Revolutionary Period." In the following year, one of his main detractors on the issue, Mississippi's Senator Harrison, confirmed the president's position by noting that "of course, [the CIO's] John L. Lewis, and the Southern Conference, Mrs. Roosevelt and the President are all against the tax." Five years later, FDR proclaimed, "the right to vote must be open to all our citizens irrespective of race, color, or creed — without tax or artificial restriction of any kind. The sooner we get to that basis of political equality, the better it will be for the country as a whole."[49]

Indeed, as the 1942 bill neared death in the Senate, Roosevelt turned to the Justice Department and the courts for relief. In the memo to his attorney general (cited earlier), the president urged a legal attack on a state poll-tax statute. To FDR, assuming "the Constitution provides, or at least intends to provide, for universal suffrage," the tax was an "unreasonable qualification" by the states. He continued, "Would it be possible, therefore, for the Attorney General to bring an action against, let us say, the State of Missis-

sippi, to remove the present poll tax restrictions? I understand that these restrictions are such that poor persons are, in many cases, prevented from voting through inability either to raise the poll tax or to raise the cumulative tax
which has accrued over a period of years."[50] Biddle, who often questioned
the president's legal abilities, thought the memo—which "was patently
F.D.R.'s own thinking"—represented an unsophisticated approach to the
law. To the attorney general, "the constitution did not, as [the president]
blithely assumed, provide or intend to provide for universal suffrage." Biddle
apparently dismissed the idea of court action after speaking with Nebraska
Senator George Norris as FDR had requested.[51]

In the end, legal complications thwarted a vigorous attack on the poll tax.
Even the Warren Court did not confront the issue until 1966. The 24th
Amendment (concerning federal elections), ratified in 1964, and the Court's
decision in *Harper v. Virginia Board of Elections* (concerning all other elections) two years later finally abolished this restrictive device.[52] Nevertheless,
FDR's memo does display an eagerness by the president to employ creative
legal thinking, similar to other CRS efforts, to advocate court action that
would open up political channels and allow the pursuit of progressive ends.

The general attack on the poll tax was a continuation of other New Deal
efforts to enable the disfranchised to vote. From Agricultural Adjustment
Administration crop-control referenda to National Labor Relations Board
union elections to the Soldier Voting Act, New Dealers had constantly
pushed the envelope on extending the vote to those who had never cast one.
Perhaps to reestablish his congenial relationship with southerners in Congress, who were crucial to his plans for the war effort in 1942, the president
did not press for the passage of anti–poll tax legislation as forcefully as he
might have. Instead, he looked to his compatriots on the Court for a possible
progressive solution to this paradox. Given the *Classic* decision in 1941 and
America's entry into war, he appears to have thought that they would now
be receptive to an attack on the tax. Unconcerned with the constitutional
complications, he simply wanted "universal suffrage" to be finally achieved
and was willing to use the courts to do it. Unfortunately for him and other
advocates, it would take twenty-four more years and a major civil rights
movement to attain this goal.

Toward a More Humane Society: Ending Lynchings and Police Brutality

Dear Mr. President: I am a corporal in the U.S. Army. . . . I am a Negro
with an American heart, and have been doing my duties as an American
soldier. I consider myself as one of the best. . . . I was sent some papers from

the states a few days ago. And I read where colored people in my home, New Iberia, Louisiana, were being beaten up and chased out of town. . . . They are being beaten up because they succeeded in getting a welding school for the colored, so they could build the tanks and ships we need so badly. They forced them to leave their homes, and also beat up the colored doctors and ran them out of town. . . . I thought we were fighting to make this world a better place to live in. . . . I am giving the USA all I got, and would even die, but I think my people should be protected. I am asking you, Sir, to do all in your power to bring these people to justice and punish the guilty ones.[53]

In many ways, the CRS's lynching and police brutality cases were more important than its voting rights cases in allowing black citizens to freely express their views and to participate on election day. As the election registrar of Marengo County, Alabama, pointedly put it in 1939: "There ain't a fuckin' nigger in this end of the country who'd so much as go near a ballot box."[54] With this in mind, the Roosevelt Justice Department used the buildup to and outbreak of war as a practical and moral basis to attack the unrestrained mob violence and vicious police practices which served as the linchpin of southern democracy and white supremacy.

Lynching

Americans were still reeling from the stunning attack on Pearl Harbor and on their belief in the nation's invulnerability when an obscure Midwestern town emerged on the scene of world affairs. In Sikeston, Missouri, in the daylight hours of January 25, 1942, a mob of white citizens seized Cleo Wright, an African American, from the local jail and murdered him. Japanese and German broadcasters hastened to tell how the mob had taken the victim, who lay near death from four gunshot wounds received while resisting arrest on a rape charge, "tied his feet to the rear of an automobile, dragged him through the Negro section" of Sikeston, and after reaching a churchyard, poured gasoline all over his body. Then, as a crowd of men, women, and children looked on, he was set afire and burnt to death. The Sikeston police force had apparently done little to prevent the lynching from occurring.[55]

In his 1941 State of the Union Address, President Roosevelt had outlined his understanding of the principles of democracy and defined the "four essential human freedoms" to be secured by all governments of the existing world order: "freedom of speech and expression . . . freedom of every person to worship God in his own way . . . freedom from want . . . [and] freedom from fear." If the U.S. government could not secure these freedoms in Middle America, however, it was dubious as to whether they would become a creed for uniting nations in the promotion of human rights. And in the days following the "Sikeston Affair," Axis radio reports reaching listeners in India, Malaya, and the Dutch East Indies took advantage of this contradiction. Reports told that "if the democracies win the War, [this] is what the colored races may expect of them."[56]

While the Sikeston affair was just one of a number of wartime lynchings, in its wake and due to increased political pressure from the African American community, the CRS received more attention both within the Justice Department and from the White House. Thus, when a Missouri state grand jury investigating the Sikeston incident concluded that there was not sufficient evidence for an indictment, the Justice Department moved "to secure the freedom from fear — on the home front."[57] Despite failed attempts to pass federal antilynching legislation, U.S. Attorney General Biddle authorized submission of the case to a federal grand jury: "With our country at war to defend our democratic way of life throughout the world, a lynching has significance far beyond the community, or even the state, in which it occurs. It becomes a matter of national importance and thus properly the concern of the federal government."[58]

Even before the Sikeston lynching, CRS officials had decided to revise the 1940 policy circular, which had set the guidelines for use of sections 51 and 52, because of fears of internal unrest following the Japanese attack on Pearl Harbor. In updating the circular, they sought an even broader interpretation of the two sections and an expansion of the CRS program. Such progress was in part considered possible because of Attorney General Robert Jackson's ascent to a seat on the Supreme Court in June 1941 and the choice of Francis Biddle as his replacement. As solicitor general, Biddle had been decidedly more eager than had Jackson to promote the work of the CRS. And as historian Dominic Capeci writes, "When Biddle . . . became the attorney general in 1941, the stage was set for serious federal activity in the field of civil rights. Biddle signified his intentions very early, filing an *amicus curiae* brief in support of Illinois Congressman Arthur Mitchell's suit against segregated interstate transportation. He also seemed ready to go beyond participation in Supreme Court cases and, through the CRS and the FBI, to forge a sword to protect black citizens left defenseless by indifferent, often racist state officials and residents."[59]

At the same time that he placed Biddle in charge of the Justice Department, President Roosevelt also appointed Victor Rotnem as CRS chief. This was a significant choice. A CRS staff member described Rotnem — one of the victims of the AAA purge — as "a crusader who conceived of the Civil Rights Section as a social as well as a legal operation."[60] And once in charge, Rotnem acted quickly and with symbolism. He changed the name from the Civil Liberties Unit to the Civil Rights Section, because he didn't want its work to be confused with the ACLU and thought the term "civil liberties" had radical connotations — something to avoid following the Hitler/Stalin pact of 1939. He then proceeded to publicize the CRS's work through numerous articles in law-related journals written by himself and other members of the CRS's staff.[61] Thus, with the outbreak of fighting, new departmental executives, and louder calls for federal action from civil rights leaders, the position of the CRS — with its new name and revised circular — reached a heightened level of importance within both the Justice Department and the Roosevelt administration as a whole.[62]

The new circular, dated April 4, 1942, advised all U.S. Attorneys that "a further disregard for civil rights can only be viewed as distinctly injurious to national moral [sic] and subversive of the democratic ideals which this nation is seeking to defend." After quoting Justice Holmes's famous *Schenck v. United States* opinion, it went on to assert that "the existence of war must not be permitted to serve as an excuse for the oppression of any racial, religious, economic, or political group. You are directed to employ every facility available to your offices to secure the cooperation of state and local officials to prevent and rectify situations constituting a threat to the Federally secured civil rights." In turn, the revised circular expanded the "color of law" concept in section 52 to include "persons pretending to be officers" and "persons acting under color of a 'custom.'" What the drafters of the statute meant by the term "custom" was admittedly "not clear," but the CRS staff provided some guidelines: "It should undoubtedly embrace *de facto* officers. It should also embrace persons engaging in practices that have official sanction, or are recognized as law. Typical of such practices is the brutal Kangaroo Court that exists in many local jails throughout the country, or the custom of excluding qualified Negroes from juries." The circular took a stronger line on official "inaction" as well, refining the theory to include the prosecution of "some positive act[s] . . . such as refusal to give police protection, or the turning away from an attack when the officer knows that it is going on." To increase its impact, Attorney General Biddle signed and issued the revised circular at the same time regional United States Attorneys' conferences convened across the country.[63]

In the spirit of this enhanced effort, before proceeding with indictments in the Sikeston affair, CRS lawyers returned to their law books in search of further doctrinal support for their antilynching theories. The difficulty for the CRS in the Sikeston case lay in the fact that no local police officers had *willfully* participated in the lynching (even under the revised definition of inaction), a factor required for prosecution under section 52. Fortunately for the CRS, in the course of researching the case law, one of its staff, Irwin L. Langbein, discovered a 1904 case that seemed to allow prosecution of the Sikeston mob that had seized Wright. According to Langbein, in *Ex parte Riggins* the federal district judge had made two relevant rulings: "first, that notwithstanding the Fourteenth Amendment is a limitation only upon state action, *mob violence which prevents the state from giving a man a fair trial causes the state to fail to fulfill an absolute constitutional obligation*; and second, that section [51] is an appropriate way of enforcement of this obligation."[64]

In other words, Langbein was attempting to sidestep the difficulty of proving "state action" in the lynching of Cleo Wright by showing that the mob had prevented the state from providing the victim with his constitutional right to have due process in the form of a fair trial — a right incorporated through the Fourteenth Amendment and therefore also under federal protection. Under this theory, the federal government could prosecute the members of the mob, acting as private individuals, under section 51 for conspiring to deprive Wright of his constitutional rights. As Rotnem put it in an article entitled "The Federal Civil Right 'Not to be Lynched,'" it is "the fault and liability of private persons under a federal statute for preventing completely and forever a person from asserting, first, in the criminal courts of the state and, later, if need be, in the federal courts on review, a right secured to him by the Constitution." One Justice Department official admitted, however, that "the rationale of this theory" was based on a "belief that a forty-year old *per curiam* decision of the Supreme Court (*Powell v. United States*) rejecting it, [could] be reversed or distinguished."[65]

The point here is not to provide a full explanation of the CRS's legal theory regarding mob lynchings, but rather to show the extent to which its staff eagerly and ingeniously interpreted the law to prosecute these crimes. The CRS proceeded with its antilynching campaign under the pretense that the new (that is, Roosevelt) Supreme Court, based on its decision in *Classic*, would reverse previous Court rulings denying the use of section 51 to protect Fourteenth Amendment rights and uphold indictments or convictions based on its theories.[66] According to CRS documents, officials initiated this effort with the idea that it might "retard, or make unnecessary what otherwise appear[ed] . . . [to be an] inevitable filibuster [against the] anti-lynching bill."[67] As with FDR's proposal concerning the poll tax, the Justice Department was attempting to bypass the legislative process by proceeding with imaginative interpretations of antiquated federal laws with clear confidence that they would be accepted by the Roosevelt Court—a court still in the formative stages of its development.

On July 21, 1942, Attorney General Biddle informed President Roosevelt that in his opinion, investigations would show that many lynchings violated existing federal statutes. On the same day, according to Carr, Roosevelt responded by calling for an "automatic" FBI investigation "in all cases of Negro deaths where the suspicion of lynching is present." Despite Biddle's hope, nine days later, after noting that the lynching was "a shameful outrage" and that the town police had "failed completely to cope with the situation," the federal grand jury investigating the Sikeston affair reluctantly concluded that no federal law had been violated.[68] To be sure, the Sikeston grand jury's disagreement with the CRS's theories was a stinging disappointment. However, it was hardly a surprise. Since most lynchings occurred in the South, where all-white grand and trial juries were often unwilling to indict or convict participants in the lynching of African Americans, the CRS's lawyers came to expect defeat. Despite Missouri's status as a border state, the result was the same.

To make matters worse, as various Roosevelt administration reports on race relations showed, the situation in the South was deteriorating. One such report, completed by the future renowned historian Arthur Schlesinger, Jr. noted, "We heard defenses of lynching from people who, I am certain, would not have defended it ten years ago; and it was defended, not on the ground that it achieved a kind of rough justice, but that, whether or not the people actually lynched were guilty, it kept the 'niggra' in his place." Believing "resentment of northern interference . . . [was] deep and widespread," the young Schlesinger put what little hope he had on the "activity [of] southern liberals." Yet he added, "there is no evidence that in the future the South will suddenly show any capacity to deal intelligently with the problem, and this southern failure may in the long run compel the North to interfere for the sake of the nation. . . . Prognosis terrible."[69] Indeed, each time CRS attorneys went into the South to prosecute members of a lynch mob, they returned to Washington without convictions. Undaunted, they pressed on, seeking to achieve some degree of success but knowing that their efforts were designed for the long term.

Nevertheless, at times they did see short-term results. For instance, in the Mississippi case alluded to above, CRS attorneys were able to gain indictments from a federal grand jury involving the lynching of Howard Wash, an African American who had been convicted in state court of murdering his white employer and had been taken from a "mob proof" jail while awaiting sentencing. It was the first time in forty years that a federal grand jury had returned a lynching indictment, and it had occurred in, of all places, the capital of Mississippi — just southeast of "the most southern place on earth." Assistant Attorney General Wendell Berge — known as "a quiet man who did not seek publicity"—called the indictment "a milestone of very great importance . . . in what has always been one of the most hopeless of all federal crusades, the crusade against the barbarities of lynch law."[70]

The jailer, Luther Holder, and four members of the mob were indicted. (The case against two of the four was dismissed midway through the trial after a government witness failed to clearly identify them as participants.) Holder, after limited resistance against the mob's advance, had reportedly said, "Come on, Wash, they want you." In addition, one of the other two defendants had signed a confession admitting his participation in the incident. Indicative of the situation in the South, however, leading officials of the Magnolia State vigorously attacked the Justice Department's decision to prosecute. As noted earlier, on the floor of the U.S. House of Representatives, Congressman John Rankin caustically denounced the department, and "at least two gubernatorial candidates, in opening campaign addresses, attacked the prosecution as an invasion of states' rights."[71] Perhaps with these leaders as his guide, in closing arguments the chief defense counsel challenged the jurors to reject conviction based not on the facts of the case but on a defense of the South, states' rights, white supremacy, and the soul of the Democratic Party:

> We may as well face the truth. This trial is not a trial to vindicate the lynching of Howard Wash, the Negro, nor is it a trial only to convict the three defendants. . . . It is just another effort on the part of the crack-brained interests within the political party of our forefathers to see how much further we of the South will permit invasion of states' rights as guaranteed by the Fourth [sic] amendment of our Federal Constitution. The cause of white supremacy has been indicted. The people of this great Southland are on trial. We were taught by our fathers that we must ever remain Democrats, for only by our continued association with that party could we hope to maintain our cherished heritage of white supremacy and the perpetual preservation of state rights, but now we are in a quandary to know whether we are justified in continuing that attitude of unquestioned loyalty.[72]

These words clearly display the threat felt throughout the South because of FDR's efforts to push to the periphery traditional party leaders by nationalizing politics in an executive-dominated institutional structure. More specifically, they reveal the reactionary forces unleashed by the Justice Department's revival of civil rights prosecutions in its attempt to bring about a more humane society deep within Dixie. Nonetheless, they worked. With several of its members "winking" in the defense table's direction as they returned to the courtroom with their decision, an all-white jury acquitted all defendants. The defense counsel reportedly winked back.

In his summary of the case, Frank Coleman, who aided the U.S. Attorney and a prominent local attorney in the prosecution, admonished the defense counsel's tactics and the judge's actions. According to Coleman, the defense counsel succeeded in persuading the jurors by refighting "The War Between the States" and setting up "the Tenth Amendment . . . in opposition to the Fourteenth." The judge completely failed "to exclude the spirit of the mob from the Federal courthouse. . . . [F]or Judge Mize to permit these arguments to be brought forward in a court of law, was in effect to deny that the institutions of the law have any place at all in the conflicting realities of southern life." Still, the CRS had made its point. And in the following weeks, the local attorney who assisted in the government's case relayed a story to the Justice Department about an incident in another Mississippi town. Despite the fact that two black soldiers had killed a sheriff, "the people of the community got together, agreed that there would be no mob violence, but that the Negroes would have a fair trial." He concluded by noting: "We think the situation is very encouraging.[73]

Following the Mississippi trial, the CRS moved its antilynching efforts north to Illinois. There, an Indiana sheriff, three of his deputies, and a "posse" of nine Illinois farmers were put on trial for hunting down and shooting James E. Person, a discharged African American soldier who "had been wandering about the countryside along the Illinois-Indiana border, seeking food and frightening farm wives." His body was found six weeks later. In comparison to the Mississippi case, CRS prosecutors thought the evidence was rather weak, but they pressed on "to show that the federal program was not directed exclusively against the South." After three years, the Justice Department dropped the charges against the sheriff and his deputies, and the nine other defendants pleaded no contest. They were each fined $200 and court costs — a disparagingly light penalty given the brutality of the crime.[74]

Given the restrictions of sections 51 and 52, however, convictions gained by the CRS usually ended in only mild punishment. Such results confirm conclusions that obtaining something other than punishment inspired the work of the CRS. Through its efforts, it sought to send a signal that unlawful violence against racial minorities could result in prosecution—that no longer would the Justice Department be indifferent to such atrocities, particularly in a time of war against dictatorship. In this sense, the onset of war was an important force driving these prosecutions. Specifically, the amplified protests from an African American community weary of the status quo and the necessities of international alliances made it much more difficult for white supremacist southerners to peddle their wares of resistance. Still, without the presence of rights-centered liberals in the Justice Department eager to use the outbreak of fighting as an opportunity to pursue a vision of a more orderly and democratic society, it is unlikely that the cause of war would have meant as much as it ultimately did. Special Assistant Coleman explained it this way: "The federal government's interest in the problem was not . . . a mere calculated concern for morale. It was primarily a response to an awakened national conscience, demanding that the constitutional paper guarantees be made real in action. War had brought a pressure to substitute the technique of enforcement for that of promise."[75]

With the nation at war, CRS attorneys stepped up their antilynching efforts. By 1944, they had developed a list of theories they believed could lead to prosecutions in at least 60 percent and possibly all lynching cases. Despite Congress's inaction, they were determined to implement their own antilynching legislation by resurrecting sections 51 and 52 and to replace "Judge Lynch" with a reformulated conception of federal justice.[76]

Police Brutality

Closely related to the prosecution of lynch mobs was the CRS's endeavor, again primarily in the South, to reduce the brutality of police conduct. Here, I focus on one case, *Screws v. United States.*[77] *Screws* emerged as a landmark case for the CRS when it reached the Supreme Court in 1945. Yet, as the table below shows, *Screws* simply represented one of a number of cases undertaken during the CRS's unprecedented drive from 1939 to 1945 to protect the rights of African Americans and, to a lesser extent, other political and religious minorities from police brutality. It was a campaign both to send a signal to the South and to test the durability of the civil rights laws.[78] (In fact, the CRS's efforts focused so much on black American victims that many outside the department falsely came to believe that sections 51 and 52 "did not protect whites.")[79]

Screws v. United States was of great significance for the CRS not only

Police Brutality Cases Prosecuted by the Civil Rights Section, 1939–1945

Case	State	Race of Victim(s)	Result
Racial			
United States v. Sutherland	Georgia	Black	Two mistrials
United States v. Culp	Arkansas	Black and White	Convicted
United States v. Erskine	South Carolina	Black	Convicted
United States v. Evans	Alabama	Black and White	Acquitted
United States v. Screws	Georgia	Black	Convicted/acquitted[a]
United States v. Dailey	Georgia	Black	Acquitted
United States v. Seals	Mississippi	Black	Pleaded guilty
United States v. Propst	Mississippi	Black	Pleaded guilty
United States v. Wiggins	Florida	Black	Dismissed
Political			
United States v. Cowan	Louisiana	White (photographer)	Acquitted
Religious			
United States v. Catlette	West Virginia	White (Jehovah's Witness)	Convicted (2nd trial)
Labor			
United States v. Buchanan	Arkansas	White (union organizer)	*Nolo contendere* (no contest)

[a] The United States Supreme Court overturned the original conviction. The second trial ended in acquittal.

because it called into question the constitutionality of section 52, but because it would likely settle whether this civil rights statute could be used to protect rights guaranteed by the Fourteenth Amendment's vague due process clause. As Woodford Howard and Cornelius Bushoven explain, "if the Court would do for due process rights what *Classic* and *Smith* had done for state action and equal protection, federal authorities could protect Negroes with a potent criminal sword as well as with a constitutional shield."[80] *Screws*, then, would be the greatest test for the future use of sections 51 and 52 for prosecuting violations of federally secured rights. In the end, a sharply split Supreme Court gave limited judicial sanction to the CRS's wartime activities while simultaneously weakening its ability to fulfill its most idealistic goals.

The *Screws* case arose out of an incident involving the beating and eventual death of Robert Hall, an African American seeking to recover his personal property. "Bobby" Hall owned a pearl-handled automatic .45 pistol, but the deputy sheriff of Baker County — "reputedly one of the most backward counties" in Georgia — "wanted it and got it." Hall first appealed to the sheriff, M. Claude Screws, for return of the gun, now in Screws's possession. When this failed, he asked a grand jury for relief, but none was offered. Hall then hired a lawyer, who sent a letter to Screws demanding the immediate return of the "blue steel" pistol. Screws received the letter on January 29, 1943. In the late hours of that evening, Screws, the deputy sheriff, and a local police officer arrested Hall for allegedly stealing a tire. Testimony showed that, before the arrest, the three officers "had been drunk for nearly six hours" and had boasted that they were "going to go and get" a "black son-of-a-bitch" who had " 'lived too long,' who had got too smart and gone before a grand jury and employed a lawyer to recover his gun." After the arrest, the three officers handcuffed Hall and took him by car to the courthouse square. In the course of removing him from the vehicle, a struggle ensued. There, in the center of town and in view of numerous witnesses, the three law officers beat Hall with their fists and a two-pound blackjack "for as long as thirty minutes." They claimed he had instigated the attack with insulting language and then, still in handcuffs, by reaching for a gun. Unconscious and near death, Hall was dragged across the concrete walkway of the square and thrown into a jail cell. Eventually someone called an ambulance, but Hall died shortly after arriving at the hospital from severe wounds to the head. The State brought no charges against the officers.[81]

Georgia officials convinced the Justice Department that the existing criminal justice system in the state simply prevented them from acting. In a display of the predominant position county sheriffs held in the South — and the ability of local communities to resist even state government interference — the local state's attorney said he was "powerless" in the matter, since the officers he would depend on for an investigation were "two of the persons we are seeking to indict."[82] With Ellis Arnall, a southern liberal, in the governor's mansion, the CRS hoped to secure cooperation from state authorities. Following its general rule, the CRS did not take any action until it was clear that Georgia would not prosecute. After some early discussion about sending in the FBI to investigate for a state case, Governor Arnall informed CRS chief Rotnem that he was "of the firm opinion that the Department should go forward with [its] case immediately, and . . . promised to give . . . all possible aid and cooperation."[83] Such assistance was an unusual experience for the CRS.

The Justice Department secured indictments on the grounds that the three defendants had violated both sections 51 and 52. The District Court upheld the section 52 charges, but not the one section 51 violation. A jury then convicted the defendants on the two section 52 charges (a general violation and a conspiracy to violate section 52 under the federal general conspiracy statute).[84] Specifically, the government succeeded in convincing the jury that the defendants had deprived Hall, "under color of law," of rights protected by the Fourteenth Amendment: "the right not be deprived of life without due process of law; the right to be tried, upon the charge on which he was arrested, by due process of law and if found guilty to be punished in accordance with the laws of Georgia."[85] The judge punished each with a $1,000 fine and a three-year jail sentence. The "favorable political environment created by Governor Arnall" and the decision to send the CRS's G. Maynard Smith to direct the trial were credited for the CRS's success. Smith, a native Georgian, had previously worked in a nearby city and therefore understood the atmosphere of the setting and the need to lessen the threat of federal intervention.[86]

The defendants appealed and, after the Court of Appeals affirmed the conviction by a vote of two-to-one, the Supreme Court granted *certiorari*. It announced its decision on May 7, 1945, in four separate opinions. In his plurality opinion, Justice Douglas, the author of the *Classic* dissent, confronted the overriding issues central to the future use of sections 51 and 52 for prosecuting crimes against an individual's civil rights. Considering that, in one of the two dissents, Justice Roberts had dismissed section 52 as unconstitutionally vague, Douglas — joined by Chief Justice Stone and Justices Black and Reed — clearly needed to lay the basis for the statute's validity. The difficulty lay in the language of the statute. It protected no specific federal right, but rather spoke of "any rights, privileges, or immunities secured or protected by the Constitution and laws of the United States." During the trial, the judge's instructions to the jury merely noted that if the jurors found that the defendants had used undue force in arresting Hall, "then they would [have] be[en] acting illegally under color of law, as stated by this statute [section 52], and would [have] depriv[ed] the prisoner of certain constitutional rights guaranteed to him."[87] Under the judge's reading of the statute, the jury did not need to find an explicit intent by the officers to deprive Hall of his federally secured rights.

The term "willful" seemed to escape proper notice, partially because the petitioners never contended that they had not acted willfully. They instead argued that, as Douglas wrote, "such a body of legal principles lacks the basic specificity necessary for criminal statutes under our system of government. Congress did not define what it desired to punish but referred the citizen to a comprehensive law library in order to ascertain what acts were prohibited."[88] Section 52's vagueness required a narrower construction in order to preserve it "as one of the sanctions to the great rights which the Fourteenth Amendment was designed to secure." Alluding back to his *Classic* dissent, Douglas noted that without such a construction, "state officials —

police, prosecutors, legislators and judges — would walk" on "treacherous ground" in order to comply with new developments in the judicial inter-pretation of the due process clause: "Those who enforced local law might not know for many months (and meanwhile could not find out) whether what they did deprived some one of due process of law. The enforcement of a criminal statute so construed would indeed cast law enforcement agencies loose at their own risk on a vast uncharted sea."[89]

In short, a broad interpretation of the statute led to a definition of feder-alism the Court was unwilling to write; namely, if state and local officials failed to comply with newly incorporated due process rights, for whatever reason, they might face criminal prosecution. Douglas continued by noting that "the presence of a bad purpose or evil intent alone may not be suffi-cient. . . . [Yet] a requirement of a specific intent to deprive a person of a fed-eral right made definite by decision or other rule of law saves the Act from any charge of unconstitutionality on the grounds of vagueness." "To pre-serve the entire Act and save all parts of it from constitutional challenge," Douglas then sought to construe "willfully" (in section 52) as acting "in open defiance or in reckless disregard of a constitutional requirement which has been made specific and definite." Such a right was present in *Classic* since "the right to vote is guaranteed by Art. I, § 2, and § 4 of the Constitu-tion. . . . Likewise, it is plain that basic to the concept of due process of law in a criminal case is a trial — a trial in a court of law, not 'trial by ordeal.' "[90] But since the judge did not properly submit the question of intent to the jury, a new trial for the defendants — who according to Douglas were clearly acting under the "color of law" — was required.

In dissent, Justice Roberts (joined by Justices Frankfurter and Jackson) wasted little time in expressing his hostility toward the Justice Department's legal inventiveness. Under our federal structure, he wrote, "the United States could not prosecute the petitioners for taking life." So instead, resting on section 52, it pursued a "theory" that "one charged with crime is entitled to due process of law and that that includes the right to an orderly trial of which the petitioners deprived the Negro." For Roberts, the issue before the Court was simple and single: "The only issue is whether Georgia alone has the power and duty to punish, or whether this patently local crime can be made the basis of a federal prosecution. The practical question is whether the States should be relieved from responsibility to bring their law officers to book for homicide, by allowing prosecutions in the federal courts for a relatively minor offense carrying a short sentence. The legal question is whether, for the purpose of accomplishing this relaxation of State responsibility, hitherto settled principles for the protection of civil liberties shall be bent and tortured."[91]

The senior associate justice then took aim at the federal statutes of an entire period: "It is familiar history that much of this legislation was born of that vengeful spirit which to no small degree envenomed the Reconstruction era. Legislative respect for constitutional limitations was not at its height and Congress passed laws clearly unconstitutional." With this background established, the Court's only non-Roosevelt appointee moved on to the prosecution of the defendants, asserting that it was "based on the theory that Congress made it a federal offense for a State officer to violate the explicit law of his State." Such a reading of section 52, he declared, not only "disregards . . . the normal function of language to express ideas appropriately," it also "fails . . . to leave to the States the province of local crime enforcement" that is required by "our federalism . . . [and] clearly evinced even during the feverish Reconstruction days."[92]

In his review of the small body of case law accompanying section 52, Roberts dismissed *Classic*, a decision he and Frankfurter had joined. (Just before the *Screws* decision, Frankfurter told Rutledge that upon "further reflection and with the experience of time," he had "changed [his] view" on *Classic*).[93] In doing so, he stressed that "the views" reached there "ought not to stand in the way of a decision on the merits of a question which has now for the first time been fully explored and its implications for the working of our federal system have been adequately revealed." Strikingly, as Douglas had done in his *Classic* dissent, Roberts next invoked the protection of civil liberties to his cause: "As misuse of the criminal machinery is one of the most potent and familiar instruments of arbitrary government, proper regard for the rational requirement of definiteness in criminal statutes is basic to civil liberties. . . . [Section 52's] domain is unbounded and therefore too indefinite. Criminal statutes must have more or less specific contours. This has none."[94] Finally, Roberts challenged the legitimacy of the CRS itself as well as Justice Department promises that the number of prosecutions under section 52 would be few (due to Congress's curbing powers, the difficulty of gaining local cooperation, and its own policy of rigorously restraining its desire to indict):[95] "Such a 'policy of strict self-limitation' is not accompanied by assurance of permanent tenure and immortality of those who make it the policy. Evil men are rarely given power; they take it over from better men to whom it had been entrusted. There can be no doubt that this shapeless and all-embracing statute can serve as a dangerous instrument of political intimidation and coercion in the hands of those so inclined."[96] Somewhat remarkably, then, the three dissenting justices were calling for judicial activism in the name of preventing future and more extensive action by the executive branch.

Had this view attracted a majority, the Court would have struck down a federal statute for the first time since the Court-packing days of 1937. The victim would have been one of the few civil rights statutes still available for use. And with Congress unlikely to pass any new legislation (something these three justices thought was necessary for the Justice Department to continue its campaign against police brutality), the CRS's hope of undertaking a civil rights campaign in the courts would have been all but extinguished. By undermining Stone's construction of state action in *Classic,* moreover, even the fate of the white primary cases would likely have come into question.[97]

With three justices joining Douglas, and four in dissent (Murphy in a separate opinion), Justice Rutledge wrote an opinion in which he distinguished himself from the others. Nevertheless, he felt obligated to concur with the result of Douglas's opinion in order to break the stalemate. In arguing against the defendants' claim that their acts were beyond the scope of federal law, Rutledge noted the irony of their position:

> In effect, the position urges it is murder they have done, not deprivation of constitutional right. Strange as the argument is the reason. It comes to this, that abuse of state power creates immunity to federal power. Because what they did violated the state's laws, the nation cannot reach their conduct. It may deprive the citizen of his liberty and his life. But whatever state officers may do in abuse of their official capacity can give this Government and its courts no concern. This, though the prime object of the Fourteenth Amendment and [section 52] was to secure these fundamental rights against wrongful denial by exercise of power of the states.[98]

To Rutledge, the answer was clear:

> There was in this case abuse of state power, which for the amendment's great purposes was state action, final in the last degree, depriving the victim of his liberty and his life without due process of law. . . . Ignorance of the law is no excuse for men in general. It is less an excuse for men whose special duty is to apply it, and therefore to know and observe it.

As to the vagueness claim, Rutledge agreed with a 1915 opinion by one of the "Court's greatest judges," Justice Holmes. "It is not open to question that this statute is constitutional. . . . [It] dealt with Federal rights and with all federal rights, and protected them in the lump."[99] Examining sections 51 and 52 together — since "if one falls for vagueness . . . the other also must fall for the same reason" — he concluded that they had withstood tougher vagueness challenges in both *Classic* and *Smith*. Yet, despite his desire to reshape federalism, Rutledge yielded to reach a resolution on the case by siding with Douglas, Stone, Black, and Reed. In a separate dissent, Justice Murphy agreed substantially with Rutledge's argument, calling on the Court to "uphold elementary standards of decency and to make American principles of law and our constitutional guarantees mean something more than pious rhetoric" and dismissing notions of vagueness.[100] With Rutledge already casting the deciding vote, however, Murphy felt little need to compromise his consistently staunch position toward federally protecting the civil rights of African Americans.

Despite its mixed signals, some scholars have remarked that *Screws* was an important step in the advancement of civil rights in the courts. Robert K. Carr, for instance, called it "a distinct victory for the cause of civil liberty."[101] Howard and Bushoven write that

> the refusal of the Court to retreat from the broad interpretation of state action . . . left *Classic* and *Smith v. Allwright* standing as crucial underpinnings for the modern law of equal protection pioneered by the federal judiciary. For all the lament of libertarians over the surgery performed on criminal statutes in *Screws, a retreat along the lines proposed by Justices Roberts, Frankfurter, and Jackson would have made much more difficult the Supreme Court's subsequent plunge into desegregation of public facilities, not to mention its supervision of voting rights and legislative reapportionment.* By adhering to expansive concepts of state action, the *Screws* case *contributed to the gradual consolidation of precedents which supported the Court's constitutional initiatives in the following decades. . . .* Whatever *the price in statutory effectiveness,* the *Screws* case can only be viewed as a major constitutional victory for federal protection of civil rights.[102]

The "price in statutory effectiveness" was nevertheless substantial. The case left the CRS with a rather shaky "sword" and furthered the growing tendency toward civil cases rather than criminal ones. Following *Screws,* the effort to enforce sections 51 and 52 in cases of police brutality became "more routine"; the CRS's role in the advancement of civil rights through the courts became less significant.[103] Within the Justice Department, the Solicitor General's Office was given more responsibility in this campaign, and, of course, outside of government the NAACP continued its efforts to end segregation. Years later, the disappointment felt by one NAACP lawyer remained. When asked, then Justice Thurgood Marshall noted that as "much as he admired William Douglas, he could never forgive him for the *Screws* decision."[104]

Conclusion

The Supreme Court handed down its ruling in *Screws* just short of a month after FDR's death and on the same day World War II ended for the United States in Europe. Despite mixed reviews, the decision ended the Justice Department's ability to be an equal partner with the NAACP in the area of civil rights. With such limited tools, the CRS could take its criminal campaign only so far without the aid of the justices. When they balked in *Screws*, they sentenced the department to a secondary role in the forthcoming civil rights revolution. Instead, in the nine years leading up to *Brown* the Court would rely on civil suits to make its pathbreaking pronouncements.

Still, the activities of the Roosevelt Justice Department did much to shape judicial doctrine in the postwar era. With its calls for activism to federally secure and protect the rights of African Americans, the department helped the Roosevelt Court—informed by its commitment to the principle of deference to the executive branch—to lay the precedential cornerstone of its new civil rights doctrine. In other words, by seeking to instruct an attentive Court on the proper civil rights course it should pursue, the department diminished the democratic dilemma of judicial activism

As noted above, FDR has received little credit for this vital groundwork his administration accomplished in advancing civil rights and civil liberties. Tarred by his failure to support civil rights legislation,[105] by his approval of the World War II Japanese American internment program,[106] and by his lack of aggressiveness in response to the Holocaust,[107] FDR's legacy has suffered from scholarly assessments skewed by examples of passiveness. In fact, they represent one extreme of the president's complex approach toward civil (and human) rights. At other times, FDR provided enthusiastic assistance and employed the powers of the presidency to help achieve the goals of the civil rights cause. To be sure, FDR was neither a consistent nor a vocal proponent of civil rights reform. His pro–civil rights decisions were often buffered by others in which he balked at progressive efforts in order to ease tensions within the Democratic Party. In sum, he displayed what might be described as "fits of courage" in dealing with the challenge to the "southern way of life" and the corresponding drive to secure civil rights. When civil rights proposals appeared to also advance his broader institutional goals of a national government dominated by a progressive presidency or electoral goals of a more liberal coalition, he often supported them energetically. When they did not, he took few public chances, preferring instead to work subtly, which usually meant slowly, behind the scenes or not at all.

Nevertheless, the full story of FDR's successes in civil rights is more elaborate than the one typically told. This conventional story often focuses on the important activities of Eleanor Roosevelt—who one commentator deemed in 1944 "the most hated woman in the South since Harriet Beecher Stowe"—and the president's creation of the FEPC, which Alabama Governor Frank Dixon dismissed as nothing but a "Kangaroo Court . . . dedicated to the abolition of segregation in the South."[108] While this story is certainly significant, after examining the judicial side of events, I suggest that FDR's record on race requires reconsideration. Specifically, I argue that despite the presence of the Dixiecrat-dominated leadership in Congress and the South's significance in the New Deal electoral coalition, the Roosevelt administration was able to help forge the Supreme Court's mission after 1937. In turn, the Roosevelt justices sought to carry out what the president had failed to achieve in the 1938 elections. Southern Democrats survived FDR's purge, but southern democracy would not escape the rulings of the Roosevelt/ Warren Court.

SIX   The Commitment Continues

Truman, Eisenhower, and the Civil Rights Decisions

W ithin a month of FDR's death, the war in Europe was over. The Allies had devastated a Nazi regime intended to last a thousand years in less than six. America still had to finish its war in the Pacific, but in Europe U.S. attention turned to the question of whether the grand alliance would hold now that the fighting had ceased. In the immediate wake of Germany's surrender, British Prime Minister Winston Churchill expressed his deep concern to FDR's successor about the activities of Stalin's Red Army. "An iron curtain is drawn down upon their front," he wrote three days after the signing of the peace. "We do not know what is going on behind."[1] If Churchill's fears were borne out, tension between the West and the Soviet-dominated East would define the postwar world — the principles of democracy versus the ideals of communism. As the newly inaugurated president, Harry Truman would have to tread carefully on the geopolitical landscape this potentiality threatened to create. It was in this political space that he prepared for his first meeting with Churchill and Soviet premier Joseph Stalin at Potsdam, and primed America for its forthcoming role in the formation of the United Nations. It was at this same time that Truman announced his choice for Secretary of State, the man next in line to be president.[2] His name was Jimmy Byrnes.

The former senator and Supreme Court justice was at the center of action once again. In time, his name would become a centerpiece of discussions about the origins of the cold war. And while President Truman may not have foreseen the potential place of America's record on race relations in the ideological confrontation of the cold war in June 1945, his selection of Byrnes nevertheless sent a clear message. Even with the razing of Hitler's racist Third Reich, Truman did not consider Byrnes's southern heritage a liability in U.S. negotiations with the one-party rulers of the Soviet Union. Indeed, he probably did not consider it a burden at all. Within the domain of the Truman foreign policy team, Byrnes — whom one scholar described as a "chronic, absolute, unquestioning believer in the natural inferiority of

the African stock"—was not alone in his beliefs on race. As historian Thomas
Borstelmann writes, "Truman's primary foreign policy advisers all stood to his
right on racial issues. . . . The elite men who ran the State and Defense Departments and the intelligence agencies were profoundly comfortable with
the world they had grown up and succeeded in, a world marked by European
power, Third World weakness, and nearly ubiquitous racial segregation."[3]

   This history is seemingly inconsistent with recent arguments that stress
international pressure as a vital impetus for civil rights advances in postwar
America. For example, according to legal historian Mary Dudziak, "as presidents and secretaries of state from 1946 to the mid-1960s worried about the
impact of race discrimination on U.S. prestige, civil rights reform came to be
seen as crucial to U.S. foreign relations." Political scientist Azza Salama Layton goes even further, stressing that "it was the international dimension of
U.S. racial policies that swung the pendulum" toward the executive branch's
support of civil rights reform in the mid-1940s.[4] The Truman administration's
activism on civil rights does coincide with escalating cold war tensions. Most
prominently, on December 5, 1946, in an unprecedented move, President
Truman created a civil rights committee "to study and report on the problem
of federally secured civil rights, with a view to making recommendations to
Congress." On February 2, 1948, the president called on the Congress to endorse his ten-point civil rights program in order to "correct the remaining imperfections in our practice of democracy."[5] On July 26, 1948, acting alone,
Truman issued two executive orders, one designed to end racial discrimination in federal employment, the other barring segregation in the armed
forces. Adherents to the cold war thesis suggest that in carrying out these initiatives, the president was seeking to close the gap between America's democratic ideals and its political realities in order to forestall the impact of Soviet rhetoric on potential U.S. allies of color in Asia and Africa. But cold war
interpretations of the origins of civil rights advances in postwar America are
not without challenge. Although recognizing the powerful effects of America's new level of influence in geopolitics as an important factor in civil rights
reform, other scholars have highlighted the domestic origins of Truman's
progressive policies on race. In doing so, they have focused on three factors:
the administration's concern over the rise in racial violence, the growing importance of the black vote, and the increasing aggressiveness and effectiveness of civil rights activists.

   In this chapter, I consider the importance of both domestic and international factors in the Truman administration's pursuit of civil rights reform in
all three branches of government but pay special attention to its policy to-

ward the judiciary. By doing so, I seek to answer the following questions. What brought about Truman's dramatic change on civil rights policy in the middle of his first term in office? Aside from his much-discussed executive orders and proposed legislation, how else did the president employ the powers of the executive branch to advance the rights of African Americans? More specifically, given the NAACP's legal campaign to end segregation, did Truman emphasize the civil rights positions of potential nominees in selecting Supreme Court justices? Following *Screws*, to what extent did the Civil Rights Section continue to advance civil rights law on the criminal side? To what extent did the Truman Justice Department aid the NAACP's cause through *amicus curiae* briefs advocating the reconsideration of race-based southern statutes? I then seek answers for similar questions concerning the Eisenhower administration's civil rights policies leading up to the *Brown* decision.

Attention to both administrations' judicial policy is significant because, following Truman's initial flurry of activity, civil rights advances in the political arena slowed to a trickle. During a special legislative session in the summer of 1948, Congress failed to enact meaningful civil rights reform. And despite Truman's triumphant victory later that year, his second term did not produce the kind of progress his reelection rhetoric had promised. Indeed, of all the developments in civil rights that took place in the decade following FDR's death, the most significant did not occur as landmark legislation or dramatic executive orders. Rather, they came in the form of decisions by the U.S. Supreme Court. Beginning in the last full year of FDR's presidency, the Court, with its 1944 ruling in *Smith v. Allwright*, commenced a decade-long constitutional journey of invalidation, rapidly eroding the core of Jim Crow with a series of decisions that culminated in *Brown v. Board of Education*.[6]

In analyzing the judicial policy of these two administrations (with special attention to civil rights), I again employ the presidency-focused approach. Recall from chapter 1, I argue that three motivations drive presidential action in general and presidential judicial policy specifically: (1) the consolidation or expansion of an electoral coalition (2) the achievement of a president's immediate legislative policy preferences and (3) the implementation of a president's "constitutional vision," defined simply as his image of an ideal institutional order. I do so in an attempt to shed new light on the Supreme Court's decision-making process. After all, given the Court's willingness to defer to the executive following the constitutional crisis of the 1930s, understanding these motivations may be essential to revealing the basis of the justices' ultimate action at the midpoint of the twentieth century.

Translating Political Weakness into a Strong Statement on Civil Rights

The Early Symbolism and Tentative Steps of a Border-State President

From Truman's standpoint, two reasons made his selection of a southerner as secretary of state unproblematic in the summer of 1945. The first was driven by the president's apparent need to repair some of the fissures created within the Democratic Party during the extended Roosevelt era. Harry Truman, after all, was the compromise candidate for the vice presidency in 1944, and following FDR's death, many southerners felt the border-state Missourian would provide them some relief from his predecessor's strident liberalism. Unlike FDR, who had publicly embarrassed Byrnes by passing him over twice for the vice presidency (in 1940 and 1944) and then again for secretary of state in early 1945 (which led to Byrnes's resignation as "assistant president"), Truman sought to place the South Carolinian front and center in his administration. As the president later noted, in selecting Byrnes—a decision he made soon after ascending to the presidency—he sought to "balance things up" for what had happened at the 1944 Democratic convention.[7] To be certain, this meant more than simply throwing a bone to southerners. Rather, Truman's selection of Byrnes was consistent with a cautious policy on race that defined the opening year and a half of his administration and largely pleased southern conservatives. As Kari Frederickson writes, until the 1946 election,

> Truman charted a tentative course on civil rights and in general pursued a policy agenda that increasingly alienated his party's left wing. Unwilling to antagonize the conservative bloc in Congress, Truman expended little political capital to save the FEPC from the political axe wielded by Dixie congressmen, and he retreated from his earlier opposition to the poll tax, stating that it "was a matter for the Southern states to work out." NAACP attorney Charles Houston resigned from his position as FEPC commissioner after Truman refused to implement FEPC directives demanding an end to racially discriminatory hiring practices by two transit companies. Truman allowed the FEPC to whither [sic] away, until by 1946 it was, in the words of one historian, "out of money, out of friends, out of luck and life."[8]

Truman's approach was not one-sided. Unlike his predecessor, the new president was more willing to make public statements sympathetic to civil rights groups. For example, while the FEPC did eventually "wither away," early in his tenure Truman openly expressed support for a permanent FEPC, something FDR had never done. In the summer of 1946, Truman again broke free from FDR's taciturn precedent by publicly supporting antilynching legislation.[9] But as Frederickson's words above explain, Truman's willingness to employ powerful rhetoric in support of progressive civil rights positions was often not equaled with clear and direct action. Indeed, at times he seemed to curb the power of his rhetoric by selecting southerners to fill important civil rights related posts in the Justice Department.

The second reason Byrnes's southern stock mattered little — and might even have eased divisions within the Democratic Party — was a consequence of Truman's view of the international scene. Simply stated, in the summer of 1945, the president did not fully buy into Churchill's alarmist rhetoric about the perilous state of the postwar horizon. Instead, Truman thought it possible to maintain the alliance, which was on the verge of winning the war, to ensure the peace. As he noted during his voyage across the sea to meet with Stalin and Churchill at Potsdam, there was "no reason why we should not welcome [the Russians'] friendship and give ours to them."[10] And while race was certainly not a focus of his thought on this trip, if the alliance held, the civil rights of African Americans would not command much attention on the world scene. In short, Truman's cautious policy on race was not inconsistent with America's foreign policy interests in the opening months of his presidency.

As implied above, Truman's balancing approach toward civil rights reform extended beyond his selection of a foreign policy team and his positions on racially progressive legislation. It influenced his administration's policy toward the judiciary as well. At the Justice Department, the president chose an old friend to serve as attorney general. In appearance, Texan Tom Clark, the moderately conservative head of the department's criminal division under Roosevelt, was a world of difference from his predecessor, Francis Biddle. And it can safely be said that Biddle did not recommend Clark for the job.[11] Instead, "Clark had the backing of Robert Hannegan, chairman of the Democratic National Committee, and 'two very influential Democrats from his state, Sam Rayburn, the Speaker of the House, and Senator Tom Connally.'" More importantly, Truman's choice to head the Justice Department did not display a clear desire to aggressively advance the federal protection of African American rights. In overseeing the criminal division, Clark had initially expressed concern about the *Screws* prosecution, questioning the "soundness of the legal position," and the "wisdom of the policy."[12] In compiling his civil rights team, moreover, Clark symbolically looked south for talent, selecting North Carolina's Theron Lamor Caudle as his replacement as assistant attorney general and Georgia's Turner L. Smith as the new Civil Rights Section head.

But perception did not mesh with reality in the Truman Justice Department of 1945. As these new executives confronted the consequences of the *Screws* decision and the war's impending end, they continued down the path of civil rights advocacy cut by the Roosevelt Justice Department. Prodded by the example of their predecessors, pressure from the NAACP and other rights-advocacy groups, the political demands of a divided Democratic Party led by a president who described himself as "hipped" on individual rights, and the flood of mail calling for more federal action, Clark (and his lieutenants) pursued "a liberal stance on civil rights." Indeed, historian Gail Williams O'Brien argues that, "as native southerners," Clark, Caudle, and Smith "were anxious to demonstrate to liberals that they were just as sensitive to civil rights issues as their nonsouthern predecessors."[13] From a political standpoint, Clark was also positioning himself as a possible vice presidential candidate in 1948. Given the role race had played in the demise of Jimmy Byrnes's 1944 bid for that spot, it was clear that as attorney general he could not ignore the civil rights desires of liberal Democrats and still get the nod. Accounting for the ambiguity the *Screws* decision created for the CRS, then, executives in the Truman Justice Department were consistent with those they replaced in working to extend civil rights protection, despite — if not because of — their southern heritage.

This is not to say that many rights-centered liberal groups — particularly the NAACP — did not criticize the new administration for doing too little to protect the rights of African Americans. They did. In a June 1946 address to the Chicago Bar Association, Attorney General Clark demonstrated the standstill mentality liberals found objectionable. Speaking on the anniversary of New Hampshire's ratification of the Constitution — the ninth and final vote necessary for its adoption — the attorney general stressed the Truman administration's difficulty in civil rights enforcement. As he explained, in "the ensuing thirty-five years" after the passage of the Civil War Amendments, the judiciary "emasculated" the five enabling statutes which "seriously penaliz[ed] state officers and private persons" who violated those newly ratified rights. Because of those decisions "only fragments of the original acts" remained. "After seven years of vigorous prosecution under those statutes [sections 51, 52, and an antipeonage section] . . . a substantial body of case law has been built up. Yet almost every case is still a test of a point of law as well as a test of our power to present sufficient evidence to gain a conviction." As Clark concluded, despite the CRS's "painstaking efforts and vigilance . . . Sections 51 and 52 are imperfect statutory authority upon which to ground a comprehensive and consistent civil liberties program."[14] While Clark was certainly correct in his analysis of the department's civil rights efforts, what most bothered rights-centered liberals was what Clark did next. Knowing the difficulties his department faced in protecting civil rights, he stopped short of calling for new legislation. At this point in the Truman presidency, the administration was simply not prepared to make such a commitment to advancing African American rights. Instead, Justice Department officials would have to work within the constrained legal structure set by the Supreme Court in *Screws*.

To that end, the department retried (unsuccessfully) the *Screws* defendants, attempted (unsuccessfully) to indict individuals involved in a race riot in Columbia, Tennessee, and continued to investigate and prosecute (often unsuccessfully) crimes in the areas of police brutality, voting rights, and lynching. Still, led by the NAACP, rights-advocacy groups again criticized the department for not doing more. Following *Screws*, they believed that it was necessary for the department not only to aggressively push for new legislation but also to take full advantage of any sympathetic language in *Screws*. In this regard, the department — deterred by FBI resistance — did not comply.[15] But simply focusing on such criticisms does not capture the continued significance of the CRS's work in helping to advance civil rights law. Indeed, in the first year and a half of Truman's presidency, although limited by *Screws*, his Justice Department did carry on the civil rights commitment established by its predecessor. This is an important point. Even after the disappointment of the *Screws* "victory," the department's continued effort surely aided the NAACP in convincing the Court to reconsider the constitutional validity of Jim Crow.

The president's first two choices to fill Supreme Court vacancies tell a slightly different story. To be sure, Truman's first selection did not harm the Supreme Court's emerging commitment to civil rights reform. On September 19, 1945, he named Republican Senator Harold Burton of Ohio to replace the only non-Roosevelt justice. Owen Roberts, who retired less than three months after FDR's death, had been the most persistent resister of the Court's limited move toward expanding federal civil rights protection once the Roosevelt justices were in place. Most notably, he was the sole dissenter in *Smith v. Allwright*. Truman apparently chose Burton out of "personal and political kinship" and to preserve a "politically balanced court" (Stone was the only remaining Republican justice). In the end, according to political scientist Henry Abraham, Burton's thirteen-year tenure on the Court was "characterized by a combination of uncertainty, deliberate caution, independence, and unpredictability." His record on civil rights, while better than Roberts's, displayed the qualities of a follower — a role he was "far happier" in — not of a leader.[16]

Tragedy soon tested Truman's concern for political balance on the Court when Chief Justice Stone died suddenly on April 22, 1946. Stone, FDR's choice for the center chair, had clearly established himself as a champion of the Court's move toward rights-centered liberalism. In his place, Truman selected his "favorite poker companion" and treasury secretary, Fred Vinson, of the border state of Kentucky. Recommended — apparently without much vigor — by two former members of the Court (Hughes and Roberts), Vinson filled the bill as "peacemaker" for a Court publicly experiencing a bout of internal discord. "But," writes Abraham, Vinson "did not succeed on the Court, and his tenure was an unhappy one."[17] On cases concerning civil rights and liberties, he was no Stone.

While it is certainly not fair to summarize the career of a jurist on the nation's highest court in a few phrases, the point here is not to provide a complete account of the Truman justices. Rather, it is to briefly evaluate their contribution to the cause of rights-centered liberalism. In this sense, with his first two appointments, Truman chose men who did not meet the progressive standards set by his predecessor.[18] At the time these vacancies arrived, he was simply more interested in appealing to the conservatives in his party. Truman's slow start on civil rights, however, took a dramatic turn toward the end of 1946. In the next section, I consider the nature of this shift and the motivations underlying the president's decision to undertake it.

Seeking to Secure Rights: Elections, Party Politics, and the Cold War

On election night 1946, Republicans rejoiced. They had captured the Congress for the first time since the 1920s by picking up fifty-seven House seats and thirteen Senate seats. Congress would be far more conservative once it convened in January 1947, as "Republicans won fifty-seven of the 138 nonsouthern Democratic House seats and seven of the eight Senate seats . . . held by nonsouthern Democrats with clearly liberal legislative records." President Truman knew that if he wanted another term in the White House, he would have to alter course. Indeed, the election news was not all bad for the Democrats. Figures showed that voter turnout was down nearly 20 percent from 1944, from 54 percent to 37 percent, a trend that had continued from the Democratic down years of 1938 and 1942. Put differently, previous Democratic supporters had not abandoned the party in droves to vote for the

GOP. They just didn't show up at the polls.[19] By activating the Democratic base, the election of 1948 might yield more favorable results for the incumbent. If not, Truman would simply be a caretaker president.

Just as the election had altered the makeup of Congress, events after Truman's ascent to the presidency had also changed the shape of the international scene. Less than a year after the war's conclusion in Europe, the president had revised his view of the Soviets. Privately, he now encouraged Churchill to make his "iron curtain" comments public. On March 7, 1946, the British Prime Minister obliged. Traveling to Truman's home state, Churchill delivered an address that set the stage for a new order in international affairs, stressing that "all the capitals of the ancient states of Central and Eastern Europe — Warsaw, Berlin, Prague, Vienna, Budapest, Belgrade, Bucharest and Sofia — . . . and the populations around them lie in . . . the Soviet sphere." To him, this meant, "all are subject in one form or another, not only to Soviet influence but to a very high and, in many cases, increasing measure of control from Moscow."[20] In short, the cold war had begun. As it heated up, the way America treated its people of color would become increasingly important in diplomatic relations.

Lending striking support to the cold war thesis, seven months after Churchill's speech, President Truman created his civil rights committee. International forces, therefore, appear to have been significant in the Truman administration's commitment to civil rights reform. However, the totality of evidence does not support the notion that the emergence of the cold war "swung the pendulum." In fact, the idea for a presidential civil rights committee emanated from a Justice Department dispute between the CRS and the FBI over the usefulness of conducting civil rights investigations following the 1945 *Screws* decision. Shaken by a postwar rise in racial violence and prompted by mounting outside pressure calling for greater federal action,[21] "several Department officials . . . hit upon a solution — creation of a special Presidential committee by executive order."[22] The 1946 election results were also significant in Truman's decision to form the committee. Following the decisive Democratic loss, the president quickly moved his administration's agenda toward the liberal side of the Democratic Party divide. As part of that shift — one that had notable consequence for the rise of rights-centered liberalism generally and for the cause to expand the rights of African Americans specifically — he established his fifteen-member President's Committee on Civil Rights.

Although both domestic and international concerns pushed the Truman administration to extend the executive branch's commitment to civil rights reform, the president's initial shift in this area should not be exaggerated. Substantially, as explained below, the committee was a device to review the weaknesses of the CRS "experiment"—initiated by FDR and (now Justice) Frank Murphy—and to propose new tools to accomplish the same goals. In other words, following *Screws*, the committee's creation should be understood as a natural progression for a president interested in extending and protecting civil rights. In turn, in his December 5, 1946, executive order forming the committee, Truman invoked one of his predecessor's famous four freedoms:

> Freedom From Fear is more fully realized in our country than in any other on the face of the earth. Yet all parts of our population are not equally free from fear. . . . In some places, from time to time, the local enforcement of law and order has broken down, and individuals—sometimes ex-servicemen, even women—have been killed, maimed, or intimidated. . . . The Constitutional guarantees of individual liberties and of equal protection under the laws clearly place on the Federal Government the duty to act when state or local authorities abridge or fail to protect these Constitutional rights. Yet in its discharge of the obligations placed on it by the Constitution, the Federal government is hampered by inadequate civil rights statutes. The protection of our democratic institutions and the enjoyment by the people of their rights under the Constitution require that these weak and inadequate statutes should be expanded and improved. We must provide the Department of Justice with the tools to do the job.[23]

Read with the work of the Civil Rights Section in mind, it is clear that the failures and successes of the Justice Department effort to safeguard civil rights and liberties during the 1930s and 1940s shaped the committee's "assignment." Moreover, if the justices had given the department a total victory in *Screws*, Truman's statement would likely have carried less weight.

After nearly a year of investigation and deliberation, the committee drafted and submitted a sweeping final report to the president. Entitled *To Secure These Rights*, the report carried on the CRS's hostility toward southern democracy, with the committee members openly attacking "the 'separate but equal' failure" and calling for an outright "elimination of segregation, based on race, color, creed, or national origin, from American life." In their review of segregation's history, committee members emphasized the Supreme Court's significant role in its establishment as a legal institution, but also noted—citing *Missouri ex rel. Gaines v. Canada*—that the justices' heightened "insistence upon equal facilities [was] encouraging." In addition, they stressed, in terms similar to those used by Chief Justice Warren in *Brown* seven years later, the inherent difficulty of segregation: "We believe that not even the most mathematically precise equality of segregated institutions can properly be considered equality under the law. No argument or rationalization can alter this basic fact. A law which forbids a group of American citizens to associate with other citizens in the ordinary course of daily living creates inequality by imposing a caste status on the minority group."[24]

In discussing the federal government's responsibility to secure individual rights, committee members — quoting Truman — asserted in typical New Deal fashion, "the extension of civil rights today means not protection of the people against the Government, but protection of the people by the Government." With this in mind, they analyzed the favorable change in the Court's attitude toward federal legislation to secure civil rights, concluding,

> Our Constitution has long been recognized by the Supreme Court itself as a flexible document, subject to varying interpretation and capable of being adapted to the different needs of changing times. . . . The adequate protection of civil rights is not a new problem, but it is a pressing one, and we believe that the Supreme Court will be as statesmanlike in interpreting the powers of Congress to deal with this problem as it has been in its interpretation of the commerce power. No one wishes Congress to exceed its constitutional powers or wishes the Supreme Court to uphold invalid statutes. But when the clauses of the Constitution contain language from which substantial power to protect civil rights may reasonably be implied, we believe the Supreme Court will be as ready to apply John Marshall's doctrine of liberal construction as it has been in dealing with laws in other fields.[25]

Considering their review of the CRS's work as one of their "most important assignments," committee members then assessed the CRS's record, concluding that it was "a remarkable one." The CRS staff, the FBI, and the U.S. Attorneys "deserve the highest praise for [their] imagination and courage." In all, the Justice Department effort during the eight years since the inception of the CRS, went "well beyond anything that had previously been accomplished." Still, committee members felt that "the record is by no means a perfect one." Consequently, they set out to transform the CRS experiment into a well-tooled federal machine of civil rights protection.[26]

Scholars have tended to highlight *To Secure These Rights* for its proposals concerning civil rights legislation and for its role in dividing the Democratic Party in 1948. Yet, along with its numerous recommendations for congressional action, the president's committee also suggested a court-centered strategy to combat racial inequality. In fact, considering that committee members understood the difficulty its legislative recommendations would face in Congress, *To Secure These Rights* may even be read as a call for the Court to act without the benefit of a new statute. Following its release, the Solicitor General's Office certainly pursued a policy consistent with this line of thought, as it replaced the CRS as the lead agency working to develop civil rights case law. Strikingly, the day after the committee released its report, Solicitor General Philip Perlman announced the government would file an *amicus* brief in *Shelley v. Kraemer*, the restrictive covenant case. Philip Elman, the "civil rights man" in the office at the time, elaborates on the effect of *To Secure These Rights*:

> The report . . . was taken very seriously in the Solicitor General's office. It took a strong position urging an end to racial discrimination in all its forms, and we were aware at that time of cases pending in the Supreme Court in which private parties were challenging the constitutionality of judicial enforcement of racially restrictive covenants on real property. . . . In any event I was told by Perlman on extremely short notice, to start drafting an *amicus curiae* brief in *Shelley v. Kraemer*. . . . [It was a] historic brief, the first time the United States had gone on record in the Supreme Court broadly condemning all manifestations of racial discrimination. . . . The Court decided the cases unanimously our way, and after *Shelley v. Kraemer*, the rewards that came were very great. . . . We were now in business looking for Supreme Court civil rights cases in which to intervene as *amicus curiae*.[27]

Significantly, the Solicitor General's Office submitted its *Shelley v. Kraemer* brief to the Court before the 1948 election. As Elman recalls, the upcoming election was of primary importance in the administration's decision to join the case: "Truman's Gallup poll ratings at the time were very low; it looked as though whoever was going to run against him in 1948, probably Dewey, would beat him badly. *Tom Clark was Attorney General, and both he and [Solicitor General] Perlman were political animals, very much aware of the Negro vote*. On the Interior front, [Oscar] Chapman was also talking to people on the White House staff. Well, I don't know exactly what happened. Probably Tom Clark made the decision after checking with Truman."[28]

The importance of the black vote was also very much on the strategic minds of the president's political advisors. Famously, Clark Clifford — in a memo written mostly by FDR leftover James Rowe — asserted to the president in late 1947 that the path to reelection did not run through the South. "As always, the South can be considered safely Democratic. And in formulating national policy, it can be safely ignored." Instead, Clifford (and Rowe) believed that "the independent and progressive voter" held "the balance of power in 1948; he will not actively support President Truman unless a great effort is made." In particular, Clifford (and Rowe) noted that "a theory of many professional politicians is that the northern Negro voter today holds the balance of power in Presidential elections for the simple arithmetical reason that the Negroes not only vote in a bloc but are geographically concentrated in the pivotal, large and closely contested electoral states such as New York, Illinois, Pennsylvania, Ohio, and Michigan." The memo then spelled out the NAACP-instigated bind President Truman faced:

> Under the tutelage of Walter White, of the National Association for the Advancement of the Colored People, and other intelligent, educated and sophisticated leaders, the Negro voter has become a cynical, hardboiled trader. He is just about convinced today that he can better his present economic lot by swinging his vote in a solid bloc to the Republicans. He believes the rising dominance of the Southern conservatives in the Democratic councils of the Congress and of the Party makes it only too clear that he can go no further by supporting the present Administration. Whether his interest lies in a Federal Anti–Poll Tax Statute, in the protection of his civil liberties, or in a permanent federal FEPC, he understands clearly that he now has no chance of success with any of these because of the Southern Senators of the Democratic Party.

It then made the following recommendation:

> It would appear to be sound strategy to have the President go as far as he possibly could go in recommending measures to protect the rights of minority groups. This course of action would obviously cause difficulty with our Southern friends but that is the lesser of two evils.[29]

Largely, the Clifford (and Rowe) memo built on a Democratic strategy that dated back to the Roosevelt administration. As early as 1939, Rowe, FDR's political man in the Justice Department, was writing memos to the president about how best to use the resources of incumbency to attract the black vote. At their convention in 1940, Democrats for the first time adopted a civil rights platform plank, one decidedly judicial in tone. It read in part: "We pledge to uphold due process and the equal protection of the laws for every citizen, regardless of race, creed or color." In the election, the effort to appeal to African

American voters paid off as Roosevelt picked up "a larger percentage of the [black] vote than in 1936." In 1944 Democrats escalated their efforts once again. At the 1944 convention, members of the Roosevelt team not only secured similar civil rights language for the platform, but also actively employed the administration's judicial policy as a means to ensure that a contingent of black American delegates — from the South Carolina Progressive Democratic Party — "did not play into the hands of the Republicans" by contesting the makeup of the Palmetto State's delegation. While some African Americans were certainly critical of administration policies, black voters nevertheless supported the president in strong numbers. In fact, in FDR's final and closest race, the African American vote — while still a means to liberalize the Democratic Party — became of "crucial importance" to his victory.[30]

Four years later, then, Truman pursued a more aggressive version of the same strategy, issuing executive orders, introducing legislation, and approving the Justice Department's litigation campaign in part to attract the black vote. This new level of civil rights commitment, however, was not without significant consequences. Most importantly, Truman's positioning split the Democratic Party into three competing factions. On the left, Truman had hoped that his pursuit of more liberal policies might help to deter Henry Wallace from bolting from the Democratic Party. But doubting the sincerity of the president's commitment to liberal ideals, the former vice president departed to head the Progressive Party ticket. On the right, Truman — based on the Clifford (and Rowe) memo — believed that, despite his call for civil rights reform, disenchanted southern Democrats would nevertheless remain loyal to the party of their forebears. But as with Wallace, they decided to bolt as well, with South Carolina's Governor Strom Thurmond leading the newly created States' Rights Democratic Party.

Even with such Democratic discord, Truman and running mate Senator Alben Barkley of Kentucky pulled out a close victory over their Republican challengers, Governors Thomas Dewey of New York and Earl Warren of California. With all the ballots counted, the president captured 49.6 percent of the vote and twenty-eight states. Dewey trailed with 45.1 percent and sixteen states. The two disgruntled Democrats followed, each with 2.4 percent of the vote and Thurmond with four states. Significantly, the African American vote was essential to the president's victory. As Harvard Sitkoff writes, "Truman's plurality of Negro voters in California, Illinois, and Ohio provided the margin of victory."[31] Without those states, the *Chicago Daily Tribune*'s famous headline would have been correct. Dewey would have defeated Truman by capturing 267 (of 531) electoral votes to the president's 225.

With regard to the impetus of Truman's shift on civil rights, then, two of the three motivations driving presidential judicial policy were at play. First, and most obviously, the president was using his call for civil rights legislation and the Justice Department's litigation campaign as a means to convince black American voters to maintain their allegiance to the Democratic Party and support his bid for the presidency. Truman said as much four years later in a 1952 Harlem campaign speech. Upon receiving the Franklin Roosevelt award for the second time, he referred to both his plea for legislation and his Justice Department's litigation efforts as reasons African American voters should support the Democratic ticket. It may have been one of the few times a president employed *amicus curiae* briefs to secure votes, but Truman took full advantage of his role in the government's decision (discussed below) to join several race discrimination cases, each of which helped lay the precedential groundwork for *Brown*.[32]

Second, the president's constitutional vision — while blurry during his first year and a half in office — was coming into focus because of events on both the domestic and international scene and, in turn, affected his administration's commitment to civil rights reform. To be sure, as a successor to a "reconstructive" president, Truman had neither the capacity nor the desire to advocate the level of change FDR had implemented. Rather, as a president affiliated with the previous regime and committed to its extension, Truman governed during a "politics of articulation." As Stephen Skowronek writes, this "moment in political time" is "when established commitments of ideology and interest are relatively resilient, providing solutions, or legitimate guides to solutions, to the governing problems of the day." Yet "to dismiss presidents in such situations as presiding over a stable, 'normal' period of politics-as-usual is a mistake."[33] Indeed, although Truman could rely on the dominant New Deal principles to guide his domestic policies, the emergence of the cold war required a different modus operandi for foreign policy. While FDR had primarily intended his reconstructive institutional structure to best advance progressive interests domestically, Truman would have to employ the modern presidency to meet the demands of a new world order. In other words, the distinctiveness of Truman's constitutional vision centered on the creation of an international order that successfully responded to the difficulties of the new global reality. While still guided by the Roosevelt administration's policies to counteract anti-American propaganda during World War II, Truman's calls for civil rights reform became a weapon in the new war against the spread of communism, a device to outflank the Soviets and position the United States as the superior superpower on racial equality. Contained within Truman's constitutional vision was an America unburdened by racial violence and African American protesters in the streets shouting demands for full citizenship and genuine democracy. Put differently, just as FDR's efforts to undermine southern democracy were in part a means to accomplish his institutional desires, Truman's calls for civil rights reform were in part a device to advance an international alignment that would contain Soviet influence. Thus, while the quest to advance African American rights may not have been a central focus of these presidential calls for a more democratic order, it nevertheless benefited significantly from them. Driven by these electoral and international concerns, the Truman administration did not employ its judicial policy to advance its leading legislative agenda items. In fact, the plea for civil rights legislation likely diminished the president's ability to enact his primary legislative proposals as his first term ended.[34]

A Return to Normality? The Second Truman Term

Few would disagree with the notion that after the 1948 elections, the center of civil rights activity turned increasingly to the courts. To be sure, President Truman did not give up on civil rights legislation once he had secured his own term in the Oval Office. His calls for action, however, were quickly drowned out by the screeching sound of legislative gridlock. In all practicality, the death of his civil rights proposals came only two months into his second term, the victim of a Senate procedural vote. While Truman continued to revive his appeal for civil rights reform throughout his presidency, the die was cast. No major civil rights law would be forthcoming.[35] Instead, the most significant developments in civil rights during the Truman years came from the Supreme Court. With this in mind, I focus now on the relationship between the Truman administration's judicial policy and the nature of the Court's rulings in this period.

Consistent with its declining role after the *Screws* decision, the CRS continued to take a back seat to the Solicitor General's Office on matters pertaining to the development of racially progressive civil rights doctrine after the 1948 election. While the CRS did continue to employ "considerable ingenuity" with its prosecutions in the opening years of Truman's second term, in 1951 the Supreme Court placed further limits on its ability to employ sections 51 and 52 as a weapon of civil rights protection. In two separate cases, a sharply split Court both upheld the department's use of section 52 (*Williams v. United States*) and restricted its use of section 51 (*United States v. Williams*). These decisions meant that, despite CRS designs to continue its resuscitation of these "dead-letter" laws, a bare majority of the justices would not go along. Once again, the Court—concerned about the weak legislative foundation—had balked at creating a more powerful civil rights prosecuting authority at the federal level. Strikingly, however, its action may have been based on strategy. According to John Elliff, "the Justices who disliked the Civil Rights Section's interpretation of the Reconstruction laws may have been trying to minimize Southern hostility to those civil rights aims both the Court and the Administration wanted to advance."[36] Indeed, at the same time and with the encouragement of the Truman Justice Department, the Court was continuing to construct the civil case precedent necessary to overturn the separate-but-equal doctrine.

As noted earlier, the Truman Justice Department's encouragement came in the form of *amicus curiae* briefs in cases challenging various aspects of racial segregation. While the department—through both the CRS and the Solicitor General's Office—had employed *amicus curiae* briefs in civil rights cases as early as 1941, the Truman administration escalated the import of this strategy and expanded its use. It did so by joining desegregation cases in which the United States was not a party and where there was no strong federal interest. Beginning with its 1947 brief in *Shelley v. Kraemer*, the Truman Justice Department—specifically the Solicitor General's Office—issued a number of briefs explicitly challenging the *Plessy* doctrine. In its 1950 *United States v. Henderson* brief, the department became the first party to argue before the Court that it should terminate its troubling separate-but-equal doctrine: "Under the Constitution every agency of government, federal and state, must treat our people as *Americans*, and not as members of particular groups divided according to race, color, religion, or national ancestry. All citizens stand equal and alike in relation to their government, and no distinctions can be made among them because of race or color or other irrelevant factors. The color of a man's skin has no constitutional significance."[37]

Also in 1950, the Truman Justice Department sought to aid the NAACP's legal campaign to eradicate segregation from the classrooms of America, advocating in two higher education cases—*Sweatt v. Painter* and *McLaurin v. Oklahoma*—that the Court side with the civil rights organization and put an end to *Plessy*. As with its *Shelley* and *Henderson* briefs, the department laced its brief with language that spotlighted the foreign policy implications of racial discrimination at home. But while the justices unanimously decided in the NAACP's favor, they refused to rule on the broader issues. As we know, the Court waited for the *Brown* case to consider these more segregation-shattering concerns. Here, the Truman Justice Department made its views known once again.

In the waning days of the Truman presidency, the Justice Department issued its *Brown* brief. Significantly, the department released the brief on December 5, 1952, just over a month after Dwight D. Eisenhower captured the presidency for the Republicans. Given this timing, scholars have tended to de-emphasize the brief's value as a play for votes. Instead, they — especially advocates of the cold war thesis — have focused on the brief writers' continued emphasis on the difficulty segregation posed in America's struggle against Soviet tyranny.

But such wording does not necessarily tell the whole story. Even Jimmy Byrnes acknowledged that his plan to equalize South Carolina schools was partially inspired by a desire to lessen the ideological embarrassment segregation represented for the nation internationally.[38] Obviously, Byrnes did not think such cold war concerns required the end of segregation, just a more equalized version of it. (Moreover, he regarded the *Brown* decision as a victory for communist forces in the United States.)[39] Indeed, particularly with its earlier briefs, the Truman Justice Department may have chosen to stress international pressures in order to minimize southern reaction.[40] Put another way, with the nation immersed in the cold war conflict, the department may have sought to ease the anticipated anger and resistance of southerners by appealing to their sense of patriotism.

This is not to say that such international factors were unimportant. Indeed, arguments that foreign affairs influenced the Truman administration and might have convinced the Court to act are convincing. As noted above, such factors certainly played a central role in shaping the president's constitutional vision. Nevertheless, the evidence does not support arguments that they were the primary motivation for Truman administration briefs advocating an end to segregation. Most importantly, the Justice Department had been methodically attacking southern institutions since before the beginning of World War II. In addition, the department tempered the international tone of its brief in *Brown* with moderate positioning. Specifically, the department did not insist that the Court shred the *Plessy* doctrine. Rather, sensing the concerns of the justices, the brief writers chose a "gradualist" approach, suggesting that the Court "might prefer to invalidate school segregation in the particular cases before it because equal facilities were not provided for Negro children. If the Court did order desegregation, it could delay issuance of a decree until after a second round of arguments on the questions of implementation. Or the Court might leave to the federal District Courts the task of developing with local officials plans for school de-segregation." The decision to pursue such a course is telling. If America's ideological conflagration with the Soviets was the driving force in the Truman administration's call to end segregated schools, it seems unlikely that the Justice Department would have produced a document that put the brief's main author (Philip Elman) on the "NAACP's shitlist." Even accounting for a desire to balance international factors with domestic concerns, it is unlikely that a cold war-centered Department would have chosen the incremental course, which according to Elman was both "entirely unprincipled" and "simply indefensible."[41] It nevertheless chose this course in order to provide the Court a "middle ground," based on its reading of the justices' positioning. As Elman writes,

> "With all deliberate speed" . . . offered the Court a way out of its dilemma, a way to end racial segregation without inviting massive disobedience, a way to decide the constitutional issue unanimously without tearing the Court apart. For the first time the Court was told that it was not necessarily confronted with an all-or-nothing choice between separate but equal, as urged by the states, and overruling *Plessy* and requiring immediate integration of public schools in all states, as urged by the NAACP. We proposed a middle ground, separating the constitutional principle from the remedy — a proposal that nobody had previously suggested and that, when we made it, both sides opposed.[42]

In other words, for a department committed to the death of Jim Crow but clearly concerned — along with the justices themselves — about the consequences of such action, this was simply the best path to pursue, even though it lengthened the desegregation process and likely lessened the forthcoming decision's international impact.[43]

By approving briefs challenging southern segregation, President Truman positively influenced the Court's development of civil rights law in his second term. However, his choices to fill two high bench vacancies did not. When the Court's two most liberal members — who were "consistently among the strongest supporters of the positions the [NAACP] urged" — died suddenly in the summer of 1949, the president selected two men he hoped would be more conservative than their predecessors. First, after the death of Justice Murphy, Truman chose another one of his poker buddies, Attorney General Tom Clark. The Clark nomination quickly drew liberal fire. To Harold Ickes, Clark was nothing more than a "second-rate political hack." In his eyes, it was "the worst appointment ever made." While Clark did have some supporters among rights-advocacy groups — particularly the NAACP — most liberals voiced a collection of complaints about his past: "He had launched sweeping security checks throughout the federal apparatus, stepped up wiretapping, disseminated lists of allegedly subversive groups that were given no chance to challenge the smear label, turned down many aliens with strong cases for citizenship on the remotest suspicion of Red sympathies, directed the relocation of Japanese-Americans in wartime, and personally argued a major Supreme Court case against the United Mine Workers' right to strike."[44] The president, however, would have none of the liberals' displeasure, choosing instead to focus on Clark's loyalty. Despite liberal resistance to the nomination, the Senate confirmed the attorney general by a comfortable margin (73–8).

Less than a month after the Senate's action, death took another member of the Court's liberal bloc. With the passing of Justice Rutledge, only two (Black and Douglas) of the five most liberal Roosevelt justices remained. To replace Rutledge, Truman once again turned to a friend, his former Senate colleague Sherman Minton. As a senator, Minton had a reputation as leader of the "extreme left wing," but in his current position as a Court of Appeals judge his ability to lead seemed to vanish. "His opinions on the bench were pedestrian and sometimes tended to miss the substantive point of a case. . . . [He] was not exactly a bright ornament of the American judiciary."[45] Nevertheless, he became a justice when forty-eight senators voted to confirm him on October 4, 1949. Sixteen senators thought the former member of the body didn't deserve the seat.

With Minton in place, Truman's contribution to the Court was complete. History has not judged his choices well. They have been widely criticized as political "cronies" who did not belong on the nation's highest tribunal. Nevertheless, when it came to civil rights, the Truman justices' lack of skill and vision was often mitigated by their willingness to defer to the federal government's positions. As noted earlier, this approach made the Justice Department's briefs that much more important — an influence that would extend into the next administration.

A Request from the Court: The Eisenhower Administration and the *Brown* Decision

The history of American presidential elections has shown that it is exceedingly difficult for one political party to capture the White House for six consecutive terms. Only Thomas Jefferson's Democratic-Republicans and Abraham Lincoln's Republicans — aided by the compromise of 1876 — can carry this banner. Franklin Roosevelt's Democrats came close but in the end failed to overcome the popularity of a war hero with five stars on his collar. As he had in war, Dwight D. Eisenhower won the presidency by first dividing his opponents and then conquering them. One of his chief allies in disentangling the Democratic Party's dominance was none other than Jimmy Byrnes, once FDR's friend and now South Carolina's governor. Byrnes, thoroughly displeased with the turn his party had taken under Truman and unable to secure the Democratic nomination for a southerner like Georgia's Senator Richard Russell, had proclaimed his support for the general soon after Labor Day. Byrnes's decision to abandon his party was a clear sign of southern willingness to do the same on election day. Building on the ticket-splitting foundation laid by Strom Thurmond's bolting band of Dixiecrats in 1948, Eisenhower secured four of the eleven states of the old Confederacy and three of the five border states. Since the days of Reconstruction, only one Republican presidential candidate (Herbert Hoover) had accomplished such a feat. Due more to their frustration with the Truman administration's civil rights policies than with Republican pledges of support, southerners had once again declared their independence. And although Eisenhower's southern strategy had been a limited one — focusing on the upper South and border states and never coming close to promising a return to the days of unencumbered white supremacy — the movement of white southerners into the GOP had begun.

For their part, Democrats attempted to stave off such a revolt to the Republicans by choosing the comparatively racially conservative team of Illinois Governor Adlai E. Stevenson and Alabama Senator John Sparkman as their presidential and vice presidential candidates. The decision displayed clear value in the South. Of the nine states Stevenson and Sparkman won, all were either southern or border states, including the four Thurmond captured in 1948.

In a consummate display of the Democrat's dilemma, Stevenson — with President Truman's assistance — also made a hard sell to African Americans to stay within the party's fold. Not to be outdone, Eisenhower, who enjoyed the support of the racially liberal "eastern" wing of the GOP, countered with his own play for this "balance of power" voting bloc. In the end, however, the Republican's plea for black votes was undermined by his decision to court white southerners.[46] As Truman put it in his Harlem speech: "And now, while the Republican candidate is whispering promises to you, he has been touring the South to woo the Dixiecrats into the Republican fold.

What do you think the Republican candidate and a Dixiecrat Governor talk about when they sit down together for lunch? Do you think they talk about civil rights? I think maybe they talk about taking them away."

On election day, most black Americans forgave the Democratic Party's choice of a "coalition-building" ticket, thereby commending Truman's efforts to advance their cause. In fact, more African American voters cast their ballots for Stevenson in 1952 than they had for Truman four years earlier (73 percent to 66 percent, respectively).[47] Even with such black support, Stevenson couldn't overcome the campaign of a man who appealed to such a wide swath of voters, many of whom had never voted for a Republican in their lives. Eisenhower won in a landslide, capturing 55.1 percent of the popular vote and thirty-nine of the forty-eight states.

Dwight Eisenhower therefore entered the White House carrying the mantle of two Republican parties — the party of the Lincoln-led past and the party of the southern-directed future. In the opening months of his administration, he would make one of the most important civil rights decisions of his presidency — a decision made necessary by a request from the Supreme Court.

Although the justices had heard oral arguments in *Brown* in December 1952, the Vinson-led Court decided that it couldn't yet decide, holding the case over for reargument and issuing a list of questions for the parties to answer. In the meantime, Eisenhower took the oath of office, the first Republican in twenty years. Having heard from the Truman Justice Department, the justices agreed that it would be appropriate to ask the incoming administration for its position.[48] Within the Eisenhower administration, the request was considered at the highest level, including the president himself. Although some in the Eisenhower Justice Department thought there might be a way out of submitting a brief — after all, the Court's order invited the attorney general to participate "if he so desires" — in the end the consensus held that the "request was tantamount to a command." This interpretation aside, Eisenhower's choice for attorney general — the man most responsible for the final decision — also made it likely that the Justice Department would not sidestep the Court's invitation to participate. Herbert Brownell, a leading member of the GOP's liberal eastern wing, was clearly ideologically sympathetic to employing the department's resources to help advance civil rights. Moreover, having just successfully guided Eisenhower to the presidency as his campaign manager, Brownell was well aware of the potential electoral impact of saying no to the Court after the Truman administration had spoken in support of overturning *Plessy*. On the other hand, southern governors, including Jimmy Byrnes, were pressuring the president to help maintain segregation's constitutionality. If the Court overturned the doctrine of separate-but-equal, they speculated threateningly, it would be "the death of Republican hopes in the South."[49] Approximately two months after receiving the Court's request, the administration finally decided — a decision delayed by a wavering president — that it would submit a "supplemental" brief.

Before the brief was finished, however, death returned to the Court once more. Chief Justice Vinson became the fourth consecutive justice to leave the bench involuntarily, the victim of heart failure.[50] Unexpectedly, President Eisenhower would have an opportunity to influence the Court's civil rights rulings beyond the submission of a brief. His options, however, were limited. In the course of securing the Republican nomination, members of Ike's team had promised California Governor Earl Warren a prominent position in an Eisenhower administration if he supported their candidate over Senator Robert Taft of Ohio. Warren complied, first instructing his California delegation not to back the Ohio senator and then telling them to cast their votes against a pro-Taft procedural amendment. In the end, Warren's maneuvering virtually secured the nomination for Eisenhower. But when the president-elect's list of cabinet members was complete, Warren's name was not present. Fearing that he might offend the governor, Eisenhower made a call to California, promising Warren that he would fill the "first vacancy" on the high bench. When Vinson died, Eisenhower's debt came due. While the president did not believe his promise included a vacant center chair, he nevertheless decided on Warren once the governor made it clear that he was awaiting an immediate appointment to the Court. Eisenhower still might have elevated a sitting justice to chief and made Warren an associate, but no member of the decidedly Democratic Court met the needs of this Republican president. With Congress in recess, Warren assumed his position as chief without the benefit of the Senate's consent. When senators did vote on his nomination several months later, he was confirmed without dissent.[51]

As Warren settled into his chambers, work on the *Brown* brief continued in the Eisenhower Justice Department. Once the decision to join the case had been made, department officials had to agree on the shape of the brief. Since the Court's reargument order had requested a historical analysis of the original intent of the Fourteenth Amendment with regard to segregation's legality and a discussion about the implementation of a possible desegregation order, they could appropriately respond without making a direct statement about *Plessy*. In other words, they could simply present an objective reading of the historical record and answer the Court's questions about implementation without including a determination about the constitutional validity of separate-but-equal schools. In the end, the department pursued such a conservative course. On the first concern, the brief writers concluded that the historical record was "inconclusive." On the second — largely because Philip Elman was still an attorney in the Solicitor General's Office and oversaw the drafting of the brief — they followed the path cut by the Truman administration, suggesting desegregation should occur only after considering local concerns.[52]

According to one commentator, Brownell and Assistant Attorney General J. Lee Rankin would have preferred to include an anti-*Plessy* statement but "did not believe President Eisenhower would approve it." Still, they did not rest there. Expecting a question about segregation's constitutionality during oral arguments, the two prepared an answer. And when asked by Justice Douglas about the government's position on this fundamental question, Rankin was ready with the predetermined response: "It is the position of the Department of Justice that segregation in the public schools cannot be maintained under the Fourteenth Amendment."[53] The ball was now in the justices' court.

By approving only a narrow "supplemental" brief and by making statements that sought to separate himself from the "legal" work of the Justice Department, President Eisenhower sought to soften southern reaction to his administration's involvement in the case.[54] But in the eyes of the justices, two consecutive administrations — one Democratic, one Republican — had now told them that nothing prevented them from uprooting *Plessy*, even hinting that it might be time for the Court to finally push Jim Crow off the cliff of constitutionality into the gorge of judicial invalidation.

As with the Truman administration, Eisenhower's electoral concerns and constitutional vision drove this commitment to cautiously aid in extending civil rights. On the first concern, Eisenhower — apparently persuaded by his liberal attorney general — hoped to maintain the traditional base of the GOP while simultaneously seeking to erode Democratic support in the South. To placate disaffected southern Democrats, the president sought to paint the *Brown* decision as virtually inevitable and supported a drawn out implementation program to meet some southern concerns. At the same time, by allowing his attorney general to submit a brief in *Brown*, he sought to reassure eastern Republicans of his loyalty to the party's historic principles. This balancing act carried over into Eisenhower's constitutional vision. In many ways, similar to President Truman's, Eisenhower's institutional attention was devoted to the international arena. There he sought to refine the international alliance to better meet U.S. foreign policy concerns as he viewed them. With regard to civil rights, this translated into a continued — although limited — commitment to rights expansion and protection. On the domestic scene, Eisenhower never issued any serious challenge to the inner core of the New Deal legacy, but he nevertheless differed from his predecessor in a fundamental way. Unlike Truman, who continued to expand upon the New Deal's progressive principles, Eisenhower sought to keep them at bay. To advance this brand of conservatism, he could look to the South for support. Thus, while Eisenhower was a "preemptive" president — defined as an "opposition leader in a resilient regime" — he avoided the fate of others in similar straits. As Skowronek writes, "aggressive leaders in a politics of preemption tend to get themselves impeached, de facto if not de jure."[55] Eisenhower easily avoided impeachment by successfully exploiting the divisions within the Democratic Party. For example, he sought to maintain his winning coalition by refusing to endorse the Court's opinion in *Brown* and by agreeing to take federal action to desegregate Little Rock's schools only to enforce a judicial order. With regard to the latter, he hoped — by literally and figuratively "following an order" — to reduce southern discomfort with his position, playing the role of military man once more. His stance on civil rights, therefore, was disappointing to both sides, but nevertheless allowed him to lay the groundwork for a political regime committed to the advance of the conservative principles that defined his political outlook.

Conclusion

Both domestic and international concerns pushed the Truman and Eisenhower administrations to ask the Court to review the legality of Jim Crow. And in both administrations, the Justice Department was the agency leading the charge to challenge segregation. In this regard, the precedent set by the Roosevelt Justice Department should not be overlooked. To a large extent, the reconstructive actions of FDR's judicial policy had set the mark by which the policies of his two immediate successors would be judged. Given that Truman and Eisenhower were also seeking to attract the black vote and combat the rhetoric of a foreign enemy intent on exploiting America's racial divide, it should not be surprising that both approved of racially progressive action by their Justice Departments. In fact, it would have been far more striking had they not done so. The logic of this argument necessarily places the roots of civil rights reform squarely in the Roosevelt administration, beginning with initiatives taken before the beginning of the Second World War and based largely on FDR's electoral and institutional goals. Nevertheless, the ultimate decisions were left to the Court. In the next chapter, I conclude with an analysis of the Court's institutional mission and the civil rights decisions it produced.

SEVEN Conclusion

The Road the Court Trod

Two of FDR's justices were sons of the Deep South. The president plucked each of them directly from the U.S. Senate to serve on the nation's highest tribunal. Both had first run for the Senate in 1924. One swore off the Ku Klux Klan in his race that year. The other had joined the year before. The first lost. The second became a U.S. senator. Six years later, once the political climate in his state grew more hostile to the Klan, the first joined the second in the nation's upper house. Three decades after their 1924 Senate campaigns, the same two men played crucial roles in the *Brown* decision. Consequently, one was deemed a hero in his state. The other feared returning home. Scholars employing the most dominant model of judicial decision making in political science — the attitudinal model — would use the relationship these two men had with the Klan to help predict their behavior on civil rights. But as those who have already guessed who these two men were know, the real story is a version of "bizarro world" — a place where everything is the opposite of what it's supposed to be. The candidate who swore off the Klan in 1924 was Jimmy Byrnes. The one who joined was Hugo Black. Thirty years later, Byrnes was fighting to maintain segregation as governor of South Carolina, while Alabama's Justice Black was leading the charge on the Court to end it. In the eyes of this first Roosevelt justice, southern white supremacy was simply another version of "Hitler's creed — he preached what the South believed."[1]

While Black was clearly more ideologically liberal than Byrnes, I argue that a mixture of individual values and institutional norms shaped the actions of these two men in 1954. After all, "individuals reconstruct themselves, and more particularly their thought process, as members of the institution to which they belong." Indeed, even Byrnes's brief tenure on the Court suggested that he would have behaved differently had he stayed on the bench. As none other than Walter White wrote in 1948: "The only favorable item, as far as Negroes were concerned, in Byrnes's long public career was a unanimous decision of the Supreme Court," which reversed the murder conviction of a black man who had allegedly killed a white man. Byrnes's biographer provides an even more positive spin of the South Carolinian's stint on the high bench, a view clearly connected to the power of institutional norms. As he writes, "Byrnes proved surprisingly liberal in two majority opinions regarding civil rights that he wrote in the Court's 1941–42 term. . . . The import of [his] written opinions on civil rights, and his concurring vote in a 1942 Court decision finding an all-white grand jury to be prima facie evidence of racial discrimination against a black defendant, support Roosevelt's belief that, once on the Court and freed from South Carolina's elective politics based on race, Jimmy Byrnes would become more of a New Deal liberal." Obviously, we do not know whether a hypothetical Justice Byrnes of 1954 would have joined Black and the other justices in *Brown*. (Justice Douglas did label him a "misfit" for the Roosevelt Court.)[2] We know only that once he returned to the environs of South Carolina politics, he did virtually everything he could to prevent the judicial destruction of segregated education.

While such speculation about Byrnes is informative, a thorough attempt to understand the influence of the Court's institutional mission on the sitting justices is beyond the scope of this project.[3] Nevertheless, by drawing on the substantial literature about the development of the *Brown* decision from inside the Court, I do reach conclusions about the effect the judicial policies of the Roosevelt, Truman, and Eisenhower administrations had on the high bench's institutional mission, a mission that drove its decision to constitutionally dismantle southern segregation.[4] I do so by answering the three questions that have framed this book: Why did a supposedly restraintist Supreme Court issue such an activist opinion? Why did it decide against the *Democratic* defenders of southern white supremacy? And why did it employ social science to support its conclusion instead of issuing a pure statement of legal principle? To highlight the distinctiveness of the presidency-focused approach, however, I first describe and analyze how conventional explanations of the origins of the Court's civil rights decisions would answer these same questions. As suggested earlier, each of these models offers much toward understanding the Court's action, but none captures the complete picture of the source of *Brown*. By design, the presidency-focused approach both fills in the gaps and alters the terms of the analysis.

Conventional Explanations

The Current of History

In his controversial book disputing the importance of *Brown* and the Supreme Court's role in producing social change, Gerald Rosenberg asserts that the civil rights decisions were a reflection of "the growing social, political, and economic forces of the time." A combination of "factors — growing civil rights pressure from the 1930s, economic changes, the Cold War, population shifts, electoral concerns, the increase in mass communication — created the pressure that led to civil rights." Quoting Jack Peltason, he argues, "even if the Supreme Court had sustained segregation, such a decision could not have long endured."[5] Few would dispute this view. Most would agree that the progression of society would have inevitably led to segregation's demise. But no one knows how long segregation would have endured and how much destruction a ruling against the NAACP and the Justice Department might have wrought. More importantly, governments do not always respond favorably to such outside forces. At times, they seek to defuse or repress them. The history of the labor movement in America shows that despite strong pressure to advance the rights of workers, a court-led federal government — often in cooperation with state and local governments — resisted change. The result was widespread violence against workers seeking to organize. Social, economic, and political pressures also pushed the United States to constitutionally ban slavery, but not before one in every forty-eight Americans gave their lives in the Civil War. The forces of history are undoubtedly strong, but that does not mean we should ignore individual and institutional action. The greatest weakness of the current of history approach is that it largely does. Political actors and interest groups are understood as mere pawns executing predetermined maneuvers in the march of history. Thus, as Rosenberg admits, his conclusion tells us nothing about the origins of the Court's decisions. He is instead interested in advancing his contention that — given these percolating pressures — a ruling supporting *Plessy* would have been virtually insignificant. My focus is on understanding why the federal government responded favorably to these pressures, why it acted before any sustained civil rights movement developed, and why its response came first from the judiciary (with the executive's encouragement) and not the national legislature.[6]

Rosenberg nevertheless makes an important point. Many combinations of social, economic, or political pressures might have persuaded individual justices to rule against school segregation.[7] In this vein, others have focused on specific factors in an attempt to causally connect them to the Court's decision in *Brown*. Most of these studies — as discussed earlier — have centered on the Court's action in light of a string of civil rights initiatives introduced by President Harry Truman. Mary Dudziak, for example, argues that the cold war's ideological confrontation convinced the Court, spurred on by this administration, to eviscerate the separate-but-equal doctrine.[8] With similar reliance on the persuasiveness of the Truman Justice Department's arguments before the Court, historians have highlighted domestic pressures — such as civil rights activism, racial violence, and the power of the black vote — that inspired this executive commitment to civil rights.[9] Thus, in response to the first two of my southern-inspired questions, these scholars imply that executive branch arguments convinced the Court, notwithstanding its commitment to New Deal restraint, to issue an activist opinion on civil rights. They tend not to deal with the question of why the Court relied on social science to reach its ruling, but they surely would agree that the cited studies displayed to the justices compelling trends in American society.

As detailed in chapter 6, my work does not dispute the importance of cold war and post–World War II domestic pressures in solidifying executive branch support against racial segregation in the South. I suggest, however, that the Roosevelt administration's judicial policy constituted a strong commitment to securing civil rights before World War II even began. The cold war, then, only intensified the executive desire to eliminate segregation. It did not inspire it. Segregation may have tarnished America's image abroad, but absent ideological revolution, nations rarely end a strategic alliance with a superpower because of its domestic policies. And there is no evidence to suggest that any did in the early years of the cold war, especially given the widespread political, religious, and ethnic repression occurring in Stalin's Soviet Union. *Brown*, moreover, may have been a nice piece of propaganda for an otherwise segregated State Department,[10] but it is unlikely that any nation "switched sides" because of it. The greatest international pressure toward the United States on race concerned violence against African Americans, not school segregation. *Plessy*'s end did little specifically to halt this alleged American "genocide." And the Soviets did little to temper their use of America's "race problem" in their post-*Brown* propaganda. Finally, although the government's brief in *Brown* stressed cold war pressures, the Court said nothing about them in its opinion.[11]

While certainly influencing the executive commitment to civil rights, as with World War II, the cold war more importantly provided members of the Truman and Eisenhower administrations with an opportunity to push for segregation's extinction. More than foreign partners, the civil rights advocates in these administrations were trying to convince Americans of the superior quality of a more inclusive democracy. Saying to a nation consumed by the cold war that the end of segregation aided in the ideological battle with the Soviet Union made that task easier to achieve. In this sense, while the cold war confrontation advanced the cause of racial equality, it did not drive the Court to pen *Brown*. Instead, it reinforced — and sharpened — existing attitudes that Jim Crow ought to be a casualty of a post-Depression America.

Similarly, arguments that electoral and domestic pressures instigated action by President Truman on civil rights do not undermine the significance of his predecessor in creating a sympathetic judiciary. As one Truman historian writes, the president's "emphasis on executive action" to change "a racist social structure"—which "included the issuance of executive orders and the drafting of *amicus curiae* briefs"—was "an extension of precedents developed by the Roosevelt administration."[12] Still, these studies differ from the presidency-focused approach because they often neglect the significance of the institutional perspective of the presidency. For example, while civil rights activism and racial violence rose to some extent during the Truman presidency, they certainly did not escalate dramatically from the Roosevelt years. Nor did civil rights activism reach the level of a sustained social movement it would later attain. Thus, such studies tend to leave unanswered the question of why the levels of activism and violence reached in the late 1940s led the Truman administration to take such a political risk by challenging segregation and asking the Court to upset *Plessy*. Similar problems plague studies that put too much emphasis on the black vote as the root of political change. The continuing importance of African American voters certainly played a role in the positioning of both the Truman and Eisenhower administrations on the race issue, but it is questionable that either would have asked the Court to obliterate the separate-but-equal doctrine solely for what amounts to a crass play for political support.

In other words, such studies err by treating the presidency as a reactionary institution without proving that outside pressures forced these administrations into a specific position. Finally, they do not attempt to explain why the Court accepted administration arguments advocating the end of segregation. There is little evidence that the justices were greatly concerned with civil rights activism or with securing the black vote for the party of the president who appointed them. With regard to racial violence, they seemed more concerned about its escalation following a ruling favorable to the NAACP than with one sustaining Jim Crow.[13]

Nevertheless, I agree that the evidence shows that the executive branch significantly influenced the Court on civil rights. However, by using the presidency-focused approach, I also uncover the executive's role in shaping the Court's institutional mission for the middle part of the twentieth century. In doing so, I place both international and domestic forces in the context of the effort to forge this mission. After all, no matter what political, social, or economic pressures may be stirring in American society, the Supreme Court — particularly one rhetorically committed to deference — does not need to respond to them. Using the presidency-focused approach, I suggest why it did on race in the 1940s and early 1950s.

Advocacy and Support Structure

While most scholarly attention has focused on the members of the Court and the emanations they produce, advocacy and support structure scholars highlight the role of legal mobilization efforts in provoking judicial action. Mark Tushnet, for example, plots the NAACP's legal strategy to show its essential role in persuading the Court to act against segregation.[14] Richard Kluger and Jack Greenberg put similar stress on the NAACP's advocacy efforts in producing *Brown*.[15] Charles Epp emphasizes the importance of a support structure to instigate court action. He argues that efforts by rights-advocacy organizations, combined with changes in the legal profession, new sources of financing, and support from the federal government, provided the foundation of the rights revolution in the United States. In the end, this support structure altered the Court's agenda and enabled groups to capitalize on favorable judicial rulings.[16] To be sure, these scholars do not assert that their models explain the full array of factors leading up to landmark Supreme Court decisions. One needs only to examine the history of labor unions before the Court to understand that well-organized and financed groups are not always successful at legal advocacy. The federal judiciary's steadfast resistance to much of labor's agenda in the late nineteenth and early twentieth century forced union leaders to alter their strategy. By the turn of the century, they increasingly responded to the hostile legal environment by abandoning the political arena in favor of a strategy of collective bargaining known as "business unionism."[17] Other research has predictably shown that the NAACP has been less successful before a more conservative Supreme Court and without the support of the Justice Department.[18]

Instead, Epp argues that the support structure is necessary — not sufficient — for success in court. Tushnet, Kluger, and Greenberg document the NAACP's efforts in shaping the civil rights decisions without discounting the makeup of the Court. As a group, they would answer my first two questions by underlining the NAACP's organization efforts and its vital role in convincing the Court to author its activist opinions on civil rights. As Tushnet writes, Thurgood "Marshall and his [NAACP] colleagues painstakingly constructed the foundations for modern civil rights law." Still, Tushnet accepts that "almost all" of "the work [that] had to be done in *Brown* . . . had to be done inside the Court." For him, the "brilliance of Marshall's strategy [was] that he forced [the justices] to a choice, believing — correctly, as it turned out — that once he forced them to choose, they could make only one decision."[19] This conclusion spotlights the importance of institutional mission, but Tushnet does not attempt to explain its development in relation to the political branches. On the third question, Tushnet and other advocacy scholars point out that the use of psychological tests to challenge segregation originated with NAACP attorneys who — inspired by legal realist thought — sought to show Jim Crow's corrosive effects on African Americans.

The presidency-focused approach is not inconsistent with these arguments. The NAACP's legal campaign against segregation was clearly fundamental to the Court's decision to overturn the *Plessy* doctrine in education. It is likely that the Court would not — even could not — have acted on segregated education absent the NAACP's legal mobilization efforts. But these models admittedly do not incorporate the formation of the Supreme Court that heard these claims. With the presidency-focused approach, it is possible to complete the picture by explaining the creation of what became the *Brown* Court. In doing so, it does not devalue the NAACP's efforts, but rather escalates their significance by emphasizing the organization's political alliance with the Roosevelt administration. As I show, the Roosevelt administration constructed its judicial policy partially in response to NAACP pressure and with the organization's legal campaign in mind. And at times, the Roosevelt Justice Department worked closely with NAACP attorneys on precedent-setting civil rights cases. In addition, as noted earlier, the organization's head supported eight of FDR's nine High Court appointees. Put simply, without the NAACP's political activities, the Roosevelt administration's judicial policy would have been less progressive on race. Together with its allies, the NAACP achieved this result by successfully arguing that for New Deal liberalism to be complete, it would have to include a commitment to extending the rights of African Americans. It made this appeal, moreover, at a time when FDR was enhancing federal power and reconstructing the federal judiciary. In this sense, the NAACP's crusade in the courts reaped the rewards of its earlier political efforts, which worked to shape the Supreme Court that its lawyers would successfully argue before.

Political Systems Model

Relying on realignment theory, some scholars have sought to link significant shifts in judicial interpretation to the dominant political alignment of the times. In this "political systems" model, first developed by Robert Dahl, the policies of the three branches fall into place as the Court legitimates the actions of the national governing coalition. As Dahl reasons, given the institutional weakness of courts, the propensity of Supreme Court vacancies (every 22 months on average), and the president's power to fill those vacancies with nominees whose political philosophies are not radically different from both his own and a majority of senators, the Court will not, "for more than a few years at most, stand against any major alternatives sought by a lawmaking majority." To affect judicial doctrine, presidents should concentrate on building "a stable and dominant aggregation of minorities with a high probability of winning the presidency and one or both houses of Congress" since the Court will ultimately endorse "the fundamental policies of the successful coalition." In this vein, Martin Shapiro writes, "the voting realignment of 1932 led to a realignment of constitutional law. . . . The Republican Court had served Republican clients . . . the new Democratic Court was united in its determination to end this service." The Warren Court, Shapiro adds, "received broad support because [it] moved to incorporate service to the New Deal victors into constitutional law." Although it did not act in an "election-oriented way," it "got away with its activism because it was activism on behalf of the winners not the losers of Americans politics."[20]

While this analysis puts the New Deal in its proper place as the impetus of later court rulings on civil rights, it vastly diminishes the importance of institutional action. The presidency and the Court become mere conduits, channeling partisan desires into judicial decisions. And while it answers my first question — all Supreme Courts will be active if it is necessary to legitimize the lawmaking majority — it fails to explain why the biggest losers before the Roosevelt Court were not only Republicans but the staunchly Democratic defenders of southern white supremacy as well. On the third question, proponents of the political systems model are largely unconcerned with the reasoning of court opinions, believing that they represent "the author's policy preferences dressed up in cursory and pro forma legal argument."[21] Still, the main weakness of this model is its inability to answer the second question given its emphasis on realignment theory.

After all, in his four presidential elections, FDR never lost a southern state. He never garnered less than 60 percent of the vote in any of the old

Confederacy's member states, and never less than 80 percent in the Deep South.[22] Partisan realignment theory suggests that such overwhelming electoral support for a successful presidential candidate — especially one leading a critical realignment — should have eventually produced favorable judicial interpretation for the region's voters. Instead, it produced decisions that undermined the Democratic Party's supremacy in the South.[23] Thus, while the "realigning" election of 1932 created an opportunity for legal change, it hardly foretold the fate of the white South before the nation's highest tribunal. Indeed, southern Democrats had fared much better before the pre–New Deal Court, a Court formed in the vast seventy-two year span — interrupted by just sixteen years of Democratic administrations — of Republican presidential dominance. It was that Court that endorsed the separate-but-equal doctrine that legally legitimized southern segregation. No doubt this assessment of the relationship between realignments and Supreme Court decisions will be particularly problematic for scholars who have identified the New Deal as the prototype realignment, but it is essential for understanding the source of judicial interpretation during this period.[24]

By employing the presidency-focused approach, I provide an explanation for why the Court ruled against the Democratic South's system of white supremacy. I argue that more than interparty conflict — or pure ideology as attitudinalists suggest (see below) — FDR's management of intraparty cleavages in conjunction with his pursuit of a new institutional arrangement drove his administration's judicial policy and aligned him with African American interests. This alliance, moreover, occurred at a time of judicial transformation. The result was the creation of a Court hostile to the South's brand of democracy. The members of the Court would work out the timing and details of the decisions, but political and institutional forces forged during the Roosevelt administration had shaped their judicial mission. My analysis, then, builds on the political systems model by bolstering its framework to incorporate institutional action by the presidency and the Supreme Court. In addition, I look to provide an explanation about the nature of court decisions that takes ideas and legal arguments more seriously than do proponents of the political systems model.

Judicial Independence Approaches

Judicial independence is at the center of the most dominant explanations of the Court's civil rights decisions, whether based on the ideology or leadership of individual justices or on the traditional "legalistic" view that the Court sits to protect minorities from majority tyranny.

ATTITUDINAL MODEL   Of all the explanations of the origins of doctrinal change, the attitudinal model places the greatest emphasis on the behavior of the individual justices. Attitudinalists posit that justices — free to act as unconstrained policymakers because of the insulating institutional features of the Supreme Court — will decide cases based on their own "ideological attitudes and values." As Jeffrey Segal and Harold Spaeth write, "Rehnquist votes the way he does because he is extremely conservative; Marshall voted the way he did because he [was] extremely liberal."[25] This does not mean that the Court will be totally out of line with the policies of the other national institutions. The predictability of the appointment process assures that "the Supreme Court will generally support policies passed by the dominant lawmaking coalition."[26] However, "when the values of the justices conflict with the values of the relevant lawmaking coalition, no restraint will be apparent." Thus, in writing about the recent conservative shift in judicial interpretation, Segal and Spaeth note that "the displacement of the liberal Warren Court with increasingly conservative Burger and Rehnquist Courts did not result because of congruence with public sentiment. It resulted because Nixon, Reagan, and Bush populated the judiciary with persons in their own ideological image."[27]

Attitudinalist answers to the first two of my questions, then, seem clear. In *Brown*, the Court issued an activist opinion because, like all Supreme Courts, it was largely free to act on issues of its choosing. It unanimously supported the end of the *Plessy* doctrine because this course was consistent with the policy preferences of all nine justices. In this sense, attitudinalists share a great deal with proponents of the political systems model, often simply replacing the party label with an ideology label.[28] In turn, they offer little new in terms of what political forces produced new attitudes on the Court or how an individual with a particular ideology came to be a Supreme Court justice. Given their comments on the appointment process, they seemingly return to a realignment-dependent answer, believing that even unconstrained justices will most often follow the dictates of a realigning election. "With fixed preferences," writes Keith Whittington about the attitudinal model, "the justices [are] assumed to be unaffected by social movements, political debate, jurisprudential theory, or changing social conditions."[29] A variant of the attitudinal model known as the strategic or rational choice approach does account for some of these concerns, positing that as rational actors justices pursue their policy preferences in relation to the actions of other relevant participants, such as their colleagues, members of Congress, and the president. At this point, however, its proponents appear less concerned with explaining why a particular policy is the object of the Court's pursuit. In turn, they seemingly offer little assistance for understanding why the Roosevelt Court initiated the effort to remake civil rights law.[30]

The main difference between the attitudinal and political systems models is the type of justice produced. One justice is free to vote according to his or her own policy preferences. The other is more in tune with — and according to Dahl (but not Shapiro) constrained by — the dominant national political alignment.[31] But more than the political systems model, the attitudinal model is devoid of both history and nuance. The irony of five Roosevelt justices joining in such an activist opinion seems lost on the attitudinalists. Justice Reed, who was clearly reluctant to join in *Brown*, is lumped together with the eager Justice Douglas.[32] To code for the ideology of Roosevelt and Truman appointees (and all those who followed), the Republican Party is deemed "conservative" despite its more progressive tradition on issues, most importantly civil rights, that ultimately defined the Court's work. In Segal and Spaeth's analysis of judicial behavior, forgettable decisions attract the same attention as the landmark *Brown v. Board of Education.* Much like Shapiro above, attitudinalists want us to believe that in the civil rights cases the justices simply disagreed with the southern stance on segregation. But they do not tell us how such a court came into creation. Dahl and Shapiro at least provide some basis for why the Court came to decide *Brown* in favor of the NAACP (namely, that crucial elements in the New Deal coalition supported an idea whose time had come). Segal and Spaeth do not. Instead, the predictability of the appointment process appears broken. It takes little wonder to understand why. They rely on work that employs four or six newspaper editorials from an admittedly biased press to sum up — in literally a word — a nominee's lifetime of thought and action before occupying a seat on the high bench.[33] Their arguments imply that southern senators who voted to confirm the *Brown* Court justices were closet racial progressives, duped by the appointing presidents or the nominees themselves, or otherwise diverted. Each theory may have shades of truth, but it is essential to put those confirmation votes in an institutional and historical context. Finally, as with proponents of the political systems model, the nature of the *Brown* opinion is unimportant to attitudinalists. They tend to dismiss the content of court rulings as mere legal mumbo jumbo designed to disguise what is really a policy pronouncement. In their eyes, the use of social science must have filled the bill for justices seeking to rationalize their decision to end segregation in the schools. In sum, as Cornell Clayton writes: "Attitudinalists may be right that justices simply vote their policy preferences and use legal principles to mask their true motives. But the only way to know is to return to interpretive and historical approaches that contextualize their decisions into larger fields of meaning and motivation. Counting votes and other positivist methodologies can describe a particular action or behavior, but not the motive, purpose, or meaning of that action or behavior."[34]

While Clayton overstates our ability to know the justices' "true motives," the presidency-focused approach seeks to provide the historical and institutional context necessary to understand most voting behavior on the bench. Admittedly, it cannot explain all such behavior. The attitudinal model is most useful here. The Court often decides cases involving a wide range of issues. In those that are distinct from an institutional mission shaped by political forces, it is reasonable to suggest that individual ideology will be the dominant factor in how a justice votes. Justices, moreover, have the final say. Their institutional setting may define their behavior, but it does not fully determine their choices. They may choose to issue opinions that conflict with the Court's institutional mission of that historical moment (although game theory suggests that they won't).[35] On the civil rights decisions, however, I argue that the justices behaved in a fashion consistent with an institutional mission substantially influenced by FDR's policy toward the judiciary and reinforced by the same policy of his two successors. Those jurists who participated in this "constitutional revolution," therefore, did not do so simply because such conduct was consistent with their own policy preferences, as attitudinal theorists suggest (although at times it certainly was), but because they were part of an institution with an embedded mission that advanced this style of activism. Indeed, even those justices whose background might have predicted otherwise ultimately joined their brethren on the bench as they unanimously supported NAACP arguments against school segregation.[36]

LEGAL MODEL   In formulating their model, Segal and Spaeth note that they are seeking to counter the dominance of a so-called legal model. According to them, this model asserts that the justices make decisions based on one or a mixture of the following four factors: plain meaning, legislative and Framers' intent, precedent, and balancing. While some have criticized this formulation as a straw man,[37] scholars — most often academic lawyers — continue to advance variations of the legal model. In examining this model, I concentrate on the work of Ronald Kahn, a political scientist, since most academic lawyers focus on developing normative theories on how the Court *ought* to interpret the Constitution to be consistent with our democratic values or constitutional traditions.[38] Kahn is instead interested in explaining the modes of interpretation that actually influenced the Court from 1953 to 1993. His "constitutive" approach regards the Court "as primarily a legal, not a policy-making, institution in which the rule of law — the Constitution, precedents, and fundamental rights and legal principles — influences judicial decision-making." This approach "considers that the polity and rights principles held by the justices are central to Supreme Court decision-making." Outside political, social, and economic forces are not ignored, but rather are de-emphasized in favor of concerns specific to the "interpretive community." According to this view, alterations in the Court's personnel and in the attitudes of the interpretive community are the main sources of doctrinal change. A president's influence through the appointment process is limited since "justices, at crucial times, make decisions that are in conflict with their personal policy wants or those of the presidents who selected them. They do so in part because they view the Court as a countermajoritarian legal institution and share a concern for the legitimacy of the Supreme Court and the rule of law."[39] Thus, the Court acts with a great degree of autonomy from the political process.

In *Brown*, according to Kahn, the Warren Court, influenced by the "hegemonic ideas" of the interpretive community, issued an activist opinion on civil rights because its rights and polity principles mandated such action. Its rights principles emphasized equality, and its polity principles highlighted the Court's special role in protecting the disadvantaged from legislative majorities. "In the view of the Warren Court, the Supreme Court had not only the means to limit governmental injustice but also a mandate to eliminate inequalities by requiring affirmative government action."[40] Kahn is also the first court-centered scholar — here I include all models except the advocacy and support structure model — to provide an answer to the social science question that does not dismiss the nature of the *Brown* decision as little more than rationalizing bunk. The Court's use of psychological tests to support its decision in *Brown* is the result of the rise of relativist democratic and legal theories.[41]

Unlike the other models, Kahn argues that ideas are more important than interests in understanding Supreme Court opinions. In doing so, he makes a valuable point. Justices appear to take the task of constitutional and statutory interpretation seriously. In turn, their chosen modes of interpretation inform their decisions in certain cases. In advancing his own theory of the origins of doctrinal change, however, Kahn often goes too far in dis-

counting the usefulness of other models. This flaw is most acute in efforts
to dismiss most outside political influences on judicial interpretation. For
example, he writes, "*Brown v. Board of Education* and the Supreme Court's
antisegregation decisions . . . clearly violated the policy wants of the Eisenhower administration." But he offers no explanation as to why the Eisenhower Justice Department asked the Court — albeit obliquely — to disrupt
Plessy. Kahn also implores us to consider the importance of the interpretive
community in the development of doctrine by arguing that its articulations
play a larger role in the Court's decision making "than do the policy wants
of the majority coalition or of the individual justices."[42] But he apparently
does not consider the interconnectedness of these groups and individuals.
The dominant ideas of the interpretive community do not have to be separate and distinct from the "policy wants" of the majority coalition and the
individual justices. In the 1930s, leading members of the interpretive community were also members of the Roosevelt administration or advisors to the
president. And as Bruce Ackerman shows, such "constitutional moments"
as the New Deal have consistently had a lasting influence on the Court's interpretation.[43]

Indeed, I do not disagree with the notion that "justices draw upon constitutional principles . . . and legal concepts" in their decision making.
However, this does not exclude the influence of political forces or strategic
political action on doctrinal change. For example, Kahn points to the Warren Court's reliance on precedent-setting cases such as *Carolene Products*,
but he fails to offer a basis for what led to that 1938 decision — written by the
future Roosevelt Chief Justice — and its famous footnote. He notes that "the
doctrinal roots" of *Brown* "can be traced to cases from the previous Court
that outlawed segregation in higher education," but he seemingly dismisses
the political forces that might have led to them.[44] I suggest that, during this
particular historical moment (at least), political forces — channeled
through the presidency of Franklin Roosevelt — simultaneously legitimized
and discredited certain modes of interpretation. To put it in Kahn's words,
by constructing a legal order consistent with the president's larger intraparty
and institutional desires, the Roosevelt administration's judicial policy
helped to redefine the Court's polity and rights principles. Under this view,
the source of acceptable modes of interpretation remains primarily political. The Court may employ these modes of interpretation to develop coherent doctrine, but the essence of the constitutional change is a consequence of politics. Ideas are not insignificant, but they are tied to political
and institutional interests.

JUDICIAL LEADERSHIP MODEL Perhaps the most common explanation for the Court's decision in *Brown* focuses on the judicial leadership of Earl Warren, the so-called Super Chief. As the standard story goes, following the first oral arguments in *Brown* in December 1952, the Supreme Court was in a dismal state of deadlock. While a bloc of liberals was ready to decimate the separate-but-equal doctrine, a larger cluster of conservatives was unwilling to go that far. Then, God intervened. Chief Justice Vinson died.[45] Remaining true to a campaign promise made to gain his support, the newly inaugurated President Eisenhower selected former California Governor and 1948 GOP vice presidential candidate Earl Warren as Vinson's replacement. Once in place in the center chair, Warren broke the impasse between the Court's two opposing camps. He then penned an opinion that sought to appeal to all. In doing so, he wrote a clear statement against segregated schools. But for purists of constitutional "craftsmanship," it left much to be desired. This version of the origins of *Brown* provides clear answers to my first two questions by pointing to the force of Warren's personality and his commitment to racial justice as reasons for the Court's activist civil rights ruling. Finally, the chief justice's use of social science was the result of his desire to issue a unanimous decision. His only way to achieve this goal was to, in a sense, take it easy on southerners by not calling them racists but by simply informing them of the negative effects of segregated education on African American children.

Chief Justice Warren's role in *Brown* is undoubtedly significant. Scholars who have adopted this version of events present a convincing portrait of Warren's ability to end the stalemate and unify the Court. Nevertheless, these scholars ignore the importance of institutional mission. As noted earlier, by the time Warren arrived it was clear that the Court was about to strike down *Plessy*. And while he certainly helped to push the Court in that direction, he did not alter its course. His greatest influence, moreover, might have had more to do with his partisan affiliation than his leadership. As a leading member of the GOP, Warren made the decision a bipartisan one. Any concern the Roosevelt and Truman appointees — all but one of whom had been elected to political office, pursued the vice presidency, or held high posts under these two presidents[46] — might have had about the ramifications of their decision on the Democratic Party would have been partially erased when they agreed to join a decision written by a prominent Republican. Finally, absent the deaths of three Roosevelt justices and their replacement with the more conservative Truman appointees, a judgment outlawing segregation might have arrived before Warren did. The presidency-focused approach, then, is designed to explain the complete development of the *Brown* Court while still giving Warren his due.

The Questions Answered

Why a Supposedly Restraintist Supreme Court Issued an Activist Opinion

In the New Deal's darkest days — when the Court was in the midst of its invalidation campaign — the cries of legal realists strongly suggested that a Roosevelt-constituted high bench would avoid the pitfalls of an activist doctrine. However, as noted throughout this work, the union between realism and rights-centered liberalism guaranteed nothing of the sort. Instead, the observed opinion of FDR's nominees predicted that they would be willing to employ their newfound judicial authority to protect the rights of the previously disadvantaged or, as then Associate Justice Stone put it in 1938, the rights of "discrete and insular minorities."

While the Truman appointees lessened the ideological liberalism of the Roosevelt Court, they did not lessen its commitment to an interpretive approach centered on judicial deference. Significantly, as practiced by this Court, this "hands-off" approach had a noticeable hierarchy, with the executive the first to be heard. Consequently, on the issue of race, the position of the Justice Department was vital. Given the lasting memories of the constitutional crisis of the 1930s, the Court was not likely to enter the fray of segregation-eradication without the support of the executive branch. To do otherwise was akin to institutional suicide. Thus, perhaps more than the rights-centered ideology of the individual justices, the encouragement of an active Justice Department on race was essential to the construction of new civil rights law. Put in more dramatic terms, the Roosevelt (and Truman) Court was constructed to be instructed on race.

The Court did not follow the Justice Department in lock step. Instead, it chose civil cases rather than criminal ones to announce its most far-reaching rulings. This decision was no doubt influenced by a concern about the department's repressive action during and immediately following the First World War — the formative years of these jurists — when it used its authority to subvert civil rights and liberties across America, a concern that was exacerbated by the department's questionable actions toward individual liberties during World War II and the cold war. Even those justices most eager to advance the rights of African Americans were noticeably uneasy about aiding the development of a central prosecuting authority based on the judicially damaged legislation of sections 51 and 52. Instead, the Court focused on the NAACP-generated civil cases, secure in the knowledge that the Justice Department had joined the most important of these as a "friend of the Court," and aware that its chosen path offered more constitutional permanence than the alternative statutory route.[47]

Even in these cases, the members of the Court had to reach the conclusion to end separate-but-equal schools on their own terms. In other words, the Court's institutional mission did not determine the justices' choices, but rather guided them in a specific direction. Consequently, if we take the word of the justices for granted, it appears that in 1952 two of the Court's members — the Roosevelt-appointed Reed and the Truman-appointed Vinson — were not prepared to strike down *Plessy*.[48] As we know, soon thereafter Warren replaced Vinson as chief justice and then helped to convince Reed to join the Court's unanimous opinion in *Brown*.

In issuing this opinion, then, the justices did not pervert New Deal principles toward activism. The New Deal attitude toward judicial deference did not preclude activism. Instead, the presence of a democratic imbalance in the South justified the Court's entry into the segregation controversy.

Why the Court Decided against Southern Democrats

FDR did not construct his Court to follow the dictates of a once southern-dominated Democratic Party. Rather, he used his judicial policy as a means to liberalize his party and disrupt the conservative tendencies of southern politics, each in the pursuit of a reformulated electoral coalition and his reconstructive constitutional vision. The result was the development of a civil rights doctrine that undermined southern democracy and white supremacy. This is not to say that the Roosevelt Court was a clone of the president and proceeded as such, but rather to suggest that the actions of this reconstructive president helped to lay the institutional foundation for the justices' subsequent activism on race. As Rogers Smith has written in a slightly different context, "law is indeed a 'product of political conflict,' but it is not simply a mirror or reflex of that conflict."[49]

To be sure, the effectiveness of the Roosevelt administration's judicial policy was limited by the president's uneasiness with open advocacy of civil rights and liberties. This inconsistency, moreover, appears to have been transferred to the Supreme Court in the form of a clear concern about pushing the South too hard or too fast on race. Indeed, before Earl Warren's arrival, a divided Court squabbled and quaked, obviously troubled about taking the ultimate step of destroying *Plessy*, "the South's Magna Carta."[50] Its decisions also displayed this awkwardness toward activism, with the justices unable to assert the leadership rights-centered liberals thought necessary to protect minorities. Warren's addition to the bench certainly settled some of these fears, in part because his presence made it a Republican-led Court. But even *Brown*, which unequivocally outlawed segregation in the schools, was followed by an implementation decision (*Brown II*) that was largely a victory for the white South.[51] Specifically, by giving control over its desegregation order to local school boards and federal district courts — both dominated by unsympathetic native white southerners — and by nebulously calling for "all deliberate speed," the Court enabled effective legal resistance.

The Justice Department no doubt played a role in such a cautious course. As noted earlier, the Truman administration's *Brown* brief originated the notion of "all deliberate speed" by advocating a "middle ground, separating the constitutional principle from the remedy." And while Philip Elman later admitted, "it was just plain wrong as a matter of constitutional law, to suggest that someone whose personal constitutional rights were being violated should be denied relief," the compromise was considered the best option for a Court concerned about the consequences of its pending action. Most prominently, Justice Black "was scared to death" about overruling *Plessy*, "and he scared everybody else on the Court of the political turmoil in the South that would follow from a decision ending racial segregation in public schools."[52] In turn, the Court unanimously accepted what became the *Brown II* compromise, hoping that endorsements from both the Truman and Eisenhower administrations would limit the intensity of the anticipated southern response. In this sense, the two *Browns* displayed the complexity of the New Deal attitude on race, intent on disrupting southern politics but unsure about its effects. In the end, a bargain acceptable to both sides could not be found. And a Roosevelt-influenced Court mission wound up structuring the judicial activism that eventually tore his New Deal electoral alliance asunder, with the white southerners the biggest losers before this *Democratic-constituted* high bench.

Indeed, success in the judicial arena does not necessarily translate into victory at the polls. Instead, the nature of judicial issues — given their tendency to be secondary, crosscutting concerns — virtually ensures that once the Supreme Court comes around to supporting one partner of a partisan coalition, another will likely desert for a different set of allies. This certainly explains the state of affairs in the Democratic Party of the 1950s. As the Court began issuing decisions favorable to African Americans, white southerners — long the Democratic Party's core — began their slow transition into the GOP.

Why the Court Employed Social Science in *Brown v. Board of Education*

In penning the *Brown* decision, Chief Justice Warren understood that he did not need to preach to the choir, crafting instead a short, readable opinion that sought to ease southern unrest. Consequently, Warren's opinion did not include rousing rhetoric about the evils of segregation or the viciousness of its supporters. Rather, in the tradition of legal realism, he let social scientific studies do most of the talking on the vital question of why truly separate-but-equal schools still violated the equal protection clause. This line of argument drew on the work of the NAACP. As Mark Tushnet writes, "The NAACP's litigation during the 1940s centered on restructuring the law so that courts could rely on the social and economic consequences of discrimination as a basis for invalidating state laws. This approach reached its first peak in the attack on racially restrictive covenants, and then was pursued even more fully in the education litigation that ended with *Brown v. Board of Education*. At the deepest intellectual level, the NAACP's lawyers were convinced that social and economic consequences were relevant to the law."[53] The Justice Department pursued a similar path, filing civil rights briefs piled high with evidence about the destructive social, political, and international consequences of southern segregation.[54] In marked similarity with those defending the New Deal, then, both NAACP and Justice Department lawyers sought to show that the Court's *Plessy* doctrine was no longer consistent with the realities of society, that it had become more destructive than constructive. In the end, the justices accepted this realist-inspired appeal, and the significance of *Brown*'s footnote 11 has been debated ever since.

Conclusions about the Presidency-Focused Approach

The presidency-focused approach, then, adds much to our understanding of the origins of the Supreme Court's civil rights decisions of the 1940s and 1950s. It does so not by dismissing the value of other approaches, but rather by asserting the importance of the executive branch in the construction of constitutional and statutory doctrine. Generally, this highlights the power of the presidency to reorder the judiciary at particular historical moments and in particular ways. Specifically, it forces us to reconsider the role of the Roosevelt administration (and less importantly, the Truman and Eisenhower administrations) in the development of the Court's groundbreaking civil rights decisions.

The ability of this approach to explain episodes of judicial transformation, moreover, is not limited to mid-twentieth-century America. For example, an in-depth analysis of the judicial policies of the Nixon (Ford) and Reagan (Bush) administrations would display their influence on the creation of the conservative Supreme Court led by Chief Justice William Rehnquist. As these Republican presidents called for a "new" federalism and criticized the Warren and Burger Courts for their activism on race, religion, the right of privacy, and the rights of the accused, the Rehnquist Court has in turn developed similar stances on such concerns. And while the dynamics of the politics from 1968 to 1992 did not allow these presidents to as effectively transform the Court's makeup and institutional mission as their Democratic predecessors of the 1930s and 1940s, the political origins of the current Court's conservatism are clearly apparent. In turn, an examination employing the presidency-focused approach would uncover the political motivations underlying this transformation in judicial interpretation as well.

The presidency-focused approach, then, enables further exploration and explanation of the outside political and institutional influences on Supreme Court decision making. In doing so, it allows for a fuller understanding of why the Court acts at particular times and on particular issues, and why members of the democratically elected institutions range from fully accepting those decisions to massively resisting them.

NOTES

The following abbreviations are used in the notes:

DHC	Diary of Homer Cummings, University of Virginia
DOJ Files	Justice Department Files, United States National Archives
DOJ Files-FDR	Justice Department Files, FDR Library
DOJCD-FOIA	Criminal Division Files, Department of Justice (Freedom of Information Act request)
FBP	Francis Biddle Papers, FDR Library
FFP-HLS	Felix Frankfurter Papers, Harvard Law School
NAACP Papers	Papers of the National Association for the Advancement of Colored People
POF	President's Official Files, FDR Library
PPF	President's Personal File, FDR Library
PSF	President's Secretary's File, FDR Library
RHJP	Robert H. Jackson Papers, Library of Congress
RWP	Robert Wagner Papers, Georgetown University
TGCP	Thomas G. Corcoran Papers, Library of Congress
WBP	Wendell Berge Papers, Library of Congress
WBRP	Wiley B. Rutledge Papers, Library of Congress

CHAPTER ONE

1. *Brown v. Board of Education*, 347 U.S. 483 (1954).

2. Justice Owen Roberts, who served on the Court from 1930 to 1945, was the other.

3. Some sources report that Byrnes served on the Court for less than one year. The confusion lies in the fact that FDR appointed Byrnes (and the Senate confirmed him) on June 12, 1941. He took the oath of office on July 8, 1941. However, he did not "take his seat on the Court" until October 6, 1941. He resigned on October 3, 1942. After leaving the Court, Byrnes first held the title of Director of Economic Stabilization in the Roosevelt White House. In May 1943, the president promoted him to the newly created position of Director of War Mobilization. Robertson, *Sly and Able*, 301, 4; Epstein et al., *Supreme Court Compendium*, 289, 302, 311.

4. Robertson, *Sly and Able*, 503, 514–15; Kluger, *Simple Justice*, 529, 543.

5. Robertson, *Sly and Able*, 517, 507.

6. *Mitchell v. United States*, 313 U.S. 80 (1941), with a vacancy created by the retirement of Justice James McReynolds on January 31, 1941; Sitkoff, *New Deal for Blacks*, 235; *Morgan v. Virginia*, 328 U.S. 373 (1946), with Justice Robert Jackson not

participating; *Shelley v. Kraemer,* 334 U.S. 1 (1948), with Justices Reed, Jackson, and Rutledge not participating. See also *Lane v. Wilson,* 307 U.S. 268 (1939).

7. Tushnet, *NAACP's Legal Strategy against Segregated Education,* 143. See *Sipuel v. Oklahoma,* 332 U.S. 631 (1948); *Sweatt v. Painter,* 339 U.S. 629 (1950); and *McLaurin v. Oklahoma State Regents,* 339 U.S. 637 (1950). Also see *Missouri ex rel. Gaines v. Canada,* 305 U.S. 337 (1938).

8. *Smith v. Allwright,* 321 U.S. 649 (1944); *Brown v. Board of Education,* 347 U.S. 483 (1954); President's Committee on Civil Rights, *To Secure These Rights,* 36; and Key, *Southern Politics,* 618.

9. Senator Richard Russell of Georgia, who had predicted the ruling seven months earlier (Fite, *Richard B. Russell, Jr.,* 331), led the critics of the Court. To him, the decision was a "flagrant abuse of judicial power" (*Congressional Record,* May 18, 1954, 6750). In an even more defiant tone, Mississippi's Senator James O. Eastland denounced the ruling as a "legislative decision by a political court" and declared, in defense of white supremacy, that the South would "not abide by nor obey" it. On the other end of the spectrum, Senator Russell Long of Louisiana, while deploring the Court's action, stressed that his oath of office required him "to accept it as law" (William S. White, "Ruling to Figure in '54 Campaign," *New York Times,* May 18, 1954). See also Mann, *Walls of Jericho.*

10. Gladstone Williams, "Georgia's Delegation Hits Ruling," *Atlanta Constitution,* May 18, 1954.

11. *Brown v. Board of Education,* 347 U.S. 483, 495 (1954).

12. I use the term "judicial policy" or "presidential judicial policy" in a manner different from what most readers are accustomed to. Here, "judicial policy" does not mean the policy adopted by the courts, but rather the way in which a presidential administration acted toward the judiciary and on "judicial" issues in order to transform legal doctrine. I use it interchangeably with the phrase "policy toward the judiciary."

13. "Southern democracy" is the term used to describe the political system the South developed after reconstruction. In an effort to bar African Americans from participating in the political process, southern white leaders devised various means to limit access to the ballot box to whites only. These devices included the literacy test, the poll tax, the white primary, and the threat and use of violence. In addition, as a legacy of Abraham Lincoln's Republican Party and the North's victory in the Civil War, white southerners rejected the GOP, making the South a land of one-party politics with the Democrats in control.

14. "5 of 9 Justices Named by Roosevelt," *New York Times,* May 18, 1954.

15. Talmadge quoted in John N. Popham, "Reaction of the South," *New York Times,* May 18, 1954; Russell, *Congressional Record,* May 18, 1954, 6750.

16. Robertson, *Sly and Able,* 516

17. On the Truman administration's brief, see Kluger, *Simple Justice,* 558–61. Chief Justice Vinson had rejected the Truman Justice Department's request to participate in oral arguments the first time the Court heard the case (661).

18. Since the Court had asked the parties to respond to specific questions on reargument, the attorney general concluded that the government's brief would answer only those questions. Nevertheless, Philip Elman of the Solicitor General's Office titled the new brief a "Supplemental Brief" to the Truman administration's 1952 submission. While it "did not come out foursquare against segregation," Elman, the

principal author of both documents, "proceeded on the assumption that nothing in the 1953 brief was intended to weaken the unequivocating stand of the earlier one" (ibid., 651–52). See also Elman, "Solicitor General's Office."

19. Quoted in Quint, *Profile in Black and White*, 22.

20. Russell's statement on *Brown*, in *Congressional Record*, May 18, 1954, 6750; southern officials quoted in Quint, *Profile in Black and White*, 22.

21. Cahn, "Jurisprudence," 157–58.

22. William S. White, "Ruling to Figure in '54 Campaign," *New York Times*, May 18, 1954; Russell, *Congressional Record*, May 18, 1954, 6750.

23. See Piven and Cloward, *Poor People's Movements*; McAdam, *Political Process and the Development of Black Insurgency*; and Rosenberg, *Hollow Hope*.

24. See Kluger, *Simple Justice*; and Tushnet, *NAACP's Legal Strategy against Segregated Education*.

25. See Dahl, "Decision-Making in a Democracy"; and Shapiro, "Supreme Court."

26. See the number of judicial biographies that emphasize the role of the individual justices, for instance, Schwartz, *Super Chief*. There is also group of scholars who emphasize, through differing methods, the independent nature of the Court. See, for example, McCloskey, *American Supreme Court*; Segal and Spaeth, *Supreme Court and the Attitudinal Model*; and Kahn, *Supreme Court and Constitutional Theory*.

27. In a variant of the attitudinal model, scholars employing a strategic or rational choice approach do highlight some institutional constraints on the action of the justices. However, according to critics, they "typically adopt the attitudinalist assumption that the driving force beyond judicial decision-making is an interest in promoting personal policy preferences." In addition, by being "preoccupied with questions relating to how judges jockey for position in a potentially risky terrain . . . [their work is] fairly inconsequential for the rest of society" (Gillman, "The Court As an Idea," 75, 77). On the strategic approach, see Epstein and Knight, *Choices Justices Make*, and "Toward a Strategic Revolution in Judicial Politics"; and Maltzman, Spriggs, and Wahlbeck, *Crafting the Law on the Supreme Court*.

28. To be sure, the NAACP did not always believe that the Justice Department— through its Civil Rights Section (CRS)—was working aggressively enough to further the civil rights cause. Indeed, at times when it was constrained by the politics of the time, the Justice Department appeared to be more of a barrier than an ally to NAACP lawyers. See, for instance, Hastie and Marshall, "Negro Discrimination and the Need for Federal Action"; Kluger, *Simple Justice*; and Tushnet, *Making Civil Rights Law* (especially his discussion of the Raymond Carr case, 49–50). Although some viewed the FBI as the major obstacle to a more assertive campaign, in a 1942 article Rotnem agreed that "the development of a body of case law around the Federal statutes applicable to civil rights matters is sometimes tantalizingly slow." He cautioned, however, "that this inertia is due, in no small part, to two rules of law which are themselves safeguards of the liberty of individuals. Firstly, criminal statutes must be strictly construed. Secondly, the government has a very limited right of appeal from adverse results in criminal cases; the safeguard against double jeopardy found in the Bill of Rights being the source of this limitation" ("Clarifications of the Civil Rights' Statutes," 261). On the FBI, see, for example, Carr, *Federal Protection of Civil Rights*, 152–53.

By 1946, criticism from outside groups had clearly created tension within the department. As then CRS head Turner Smith wrote, "the Civil Rights field is a most exacting one and at the same time a thankless job. People we are trying hardest to help are frequently out [sic] bitterest critics. No lawyer enjoys representing dissatisfied clients" (informal memo from Smith to T. L. Caudle, September 18, 1946, 2; document reprinted in Belknap, *Justice Department Civil Rights Policies prior to 1960*). Also see the extensive correspondence between the NAACP and the Department of Justice in the NAACP Papers.

29. Clayton, *Politics of Justice*, 126. See also Elman, "Solicitor General's Office"; Epp, *Rights Revolution*; and Dixon, "Attorney General and Civil Rights."

30. To confess error means to admit to the allegations.

31. *Henderson v. United States*, 339 U.S. 816 (1950); brief of the United States for *Henderson v. United States*, 65–66. The Department of Justice also asked the Court to overturn the *Plessy* doctrine in *amicus curiae* briefs submitted for *Sweatt* and *McLaurin*.

32. Smith, "Still Blowing in the Wind," 271.

33. Ackerman, *We the People*, vols. 1 and 2.

34. Griffin, *American Constitutionalism*, 46.

35. Whittington, *Constitutional Construction*, 207. See also Whittington, *Constitutional Interpretation*.

36. For example, Bickel, *Least Dangerous Branch*; Ely, *Democracy and Distrust*; and Dworkin, *Law's Empire*.

37. Gillman, "Revisiting the Rise of 'Judicial Supremacy,'" 7. See also Clayton and May, "Political Regimes Approach to the Analysis of Legal Decisions"; Gates, "Supreme Court and Partisan Change"; Silverstein, "Bill Clinton's Excellent Adventure"; Whittington, "Oppositional Presidents and Judicial Negotiations."

38. Clayton and Gillman, introduction, 2. On the new historical institutionalism, see also Clayton and Gillman, *Supreme Court Decision-Making*; Ethington and McDonagh, "Polity Forum: Institutions and Institutionalism"; Orren and Skowronek, "Institutions and Intercurrence," "Beyond the Iconography of Order," and "Study of American Political Development"; Pierson and Skocpol, "Historical Institutionalism in Contemporary Political Science"; Smith, "Political Jurisprudence," "If Politics Matters," and "Ideas, Institutions, and Strategic Choices"; and Thelen, "Historical Institutionalism in Comparative Politics."

39. Smith, "Political Jurisprudence," 95.

40. Neustadt, *Presidential Power and the Modern Presidents*, 11.

41. William Rehnquist, "Presidential Appointments to the Supreme Court," speech delivered at the University of Minnesota, October 19, 1984; portions appeared in the *New York Times*, October 20, 1988, 9. See also Rehnquist, *Supreme Court*, especially chaps. 9 and 10; Scigliano, *The Supreme Court and the Presidency*, 147; Peretti, *In Defense of a Political Court*, 111–32; and Cronin and Genovese, *Paradoxes of the American Presidency*, chap. 8.

42. Miller, *Plain Speaking*, 225–26; Eisenhower quoted in Abraham, *Justices, Presidents, and Senators*, 200. Scholars also quote Truman as saying that "packing the Supreme Court simply can't be done. . . . I've tried it and it won't work. . . . whenever you put a man on the Supreme Court, he ceases to be your friend. I am sure of that" (D. O'Brien, *Storm Center*, 84). Years after he left office, Eisenhower also repeatedly noted that the biggest mistake of his presidency was "the appointment of that dumb son of a bitch Earl Warren" (Ambrose, *Eisenhower*, 190).

43. Katznelson, Geiger, and Kryder, "Limiting Liberalism," 297. See also

Katznelson and Pietrykowski, "Rebuilding the American State." For a review of these two articles in relation to other works on the 1940s, see Orren and Skowronek, "Regimes and Regime Building in American Government." For more on the Roosevelt administration's legislative compromise on race, see Quandango, *Color of Welfare*; and Lieberman, *Shifting the Color Line*. See also Davies and Derthick, "Race and Social Welfare Policy."

44. Weiss, *Farewell to the Party of Lincoln*; O'Reilly, *Nixon's Piano*, chap. 3; Irons, "Politics and Principle"; Brinkley, "New Deal and Southern Politics," 97; and Brinkley, *End of Reform*.

45. Sitkoff, *New Deal for Blacks*; Kirby, *Black Americans in the Roosevelt Era*; and Wolters, *Negroes and the Great Depression*. See also Klinkner and Smith, *Unsteady March*; Kryder, *Divided Arsenal*; Tindall, *Emergence of the New South*; and Myrdal, *American Dilemma*.

46. Russell, *Congressional Record*, May 18, 1954, 6750; Fite, *Richard B. Russell, Jr.*, 331.

47. See, for example, Horwitz, *The Warren Court and the Pursuit of Justice*, 56. (Truman's first appointee, Harold Burton replaced the last non-Roosevelt justice, Owen Roberts, who retired in 1945. When Stone died in 1946, Truman named Fred Vinson as Chief Justice. When Murphy and Rutledge both died in 1949, Tom Clark and Sherman Minton succeeded them, respectively).

48. Schubert, *Quantitative Analysis of Judicial Behavior*, 79–99; Pritchett, *Civil Liberties and the Vinson Court*, 177–200.

49. *Fisher v. Hurst*, 333 U.S. 147 (1948); Rutledge quoted in Tushnet, *NAACP's Legal Strategy against Segregated Education*, 122; Kluger, *Simple Justice*, 270.

50. *United States v. Carolene Products Co.*, 304 U.S. 144 (1938). While Stone's footnote 4 is certainly significant, it should not be overemphasized. As Ackerman writes, "the Court was only making tentative suggestions in cases like *Palko v. Connecticut* in 1937 and *Carolene Products* in 1938." The "self-conscious juridical reconstruction of framework values" would occur only when most of the Roosevelt justices were in place ("Revolution on a Human Scale," 2334). After noting that "the footnote rarely appeared in wartime discussions of civil rights," Risa Goluboff concludes: "The apparent inevitability of the footnote's importance to civil rights jurisprudence is thus a product of recent scholarly construction" ("Thirteenth Amendment and the Lost Origins of Civil Rights," 1630–31 n. 70). See also Cover, "Origins of Judicial Activism and the Protection of Minorities."

51. Pritchett, *Roosevelt Court*, 261; Pritchett, *Civil Liberties and the Vinson Court*, 190, 229; Horwitz, *The Warren Court and the Pursuit of Justice*, 56.

52. Shapiro, "APA," 451; Shapiro, "Supreme Court" 190. For those justices committed to the "preferred position" doctrine — judicial activism to defend fundamental Bill of Rights freedoms and protect the civil rights of African Americans — the support of the Justice Department was likely helpful but not essential.

53. Howard Gillman defines such a mission as "an identifiable purpose or shared normative goal that, at a particular historical moment in a particular contest, becomes routinized within an identifiable corporate form as the result of the efforts of certain groups of people" ("The Court As an Idea," 79).

54. To be sure, the presidency-focused approach does not refer only to action taken by the president, but to the entire executive branch — most importantly, the Justice Department — during a particular administration.

55. Moe and Howell, "Presidential Power of Unilateral Action," 136.

56. This framework is drawn from a study that includes an analysis of the judicial policies of the Nixon and Reagan administrations. See McMahon, "Coalition-Building and Constitutional Visions."

57. W. White, *A Man Called White*, 169–70. According to Nancy Weiss, White mistakenly dates the meeting in 1935 (*Farewell to the Party of Lincoln*, 106).

58. Milkis, *The President and the Parties*, 24.

59. Along with their political benefit, many understood individual rights as essential for establishing industrial peace and ensuring economic prosperity.

60. On the democratic nature of the New Deal "Democratic order," see Plotke, *Building a Democratic Political Order*. For an analysis of the role diminishing collective behavior has had on American politics more recently, see Fiorina, "Decline of Collective Responsibility in American Politics."

61. Because of the importance of the seniority rule in the committee system in Congress, those members who returned to Capitol Hill election after election occupied the most sought-after committee assignments and chaired the most powerful committees.

62. Roosevelt, "Address at Gainesville, Georgia," March 23, 1938, *Public Papers and Addresses, 1938*, 399.

63. Biddle, *In Brief Authority*, 197; "Personal and Confidential" memo from FDR to Biddle, November 17, 1942, FBP (the memo also appears in Biddle, *In Brief Authority*, 197–98).

64. Nixon quoted in Valis, "Congress and the Courts," 54; Ehrlichman, *Witness to Power*, 115.

65. Skowronek, *Politics Presidents Make*, 20, 39, 27–28.

66. Skowronek identifies two types of presidents within this first group of presidents with less authority, those entering office during a time of disjunction and those entering during a time of articulation. The second group fits with his category of preemptive presidents (ibid., 39–49).

67. Skowronek, "Order and Change," 94. See also Gillman, "The Court As an Idea"; and Kahn, "Institutional Norms and Supreme Court Decision-Making."

68. The term "rights-centered liberalism" is obviously similar to Alan Brinkley's phrase "rights-based liberalism." I use the different term to distinguish our arguments, but I am certainly informed by his work, *End of Reform*.

CHAPTER TWO

1. Roosevelt, "Campaign Address on Progressive Government at the Commonwealth Club, San Francisco, Calif.," September 23, 1932, *Public Papers and Addresses, 1928–1932*, 754, 752, 755, 753.

2. To be consistent with the general use of "progressive" and "liberal" among New Dealers, I use the two terms interchangeably.

3. Reiter, "Building of a Bifactional Structure," 128. See also Brinkley, *End of Reform*; and Orren and Skowronek, "Regimes and Regime Building in American Government."

4. Katznelson, Geiger, and Kryder, "Limiting Liberalism," 297.

5. Specifically, I am referring to advocates of the political systems model and (to a lesser extent) attitudinalists (see chap. 7).

6. Roosevelt, "Campaign Address at Baltimore, Md.," October 25, 1932, *Public*

Papers and Addresses, 1928–1932, 837; Byrnes, *All in One Lifetime*, 65. Ironically, the four most conservative justices of the Supreme Court were later tagged with the nickname "the four horsemen."

7. Quotes appear in "Roosevelt Accused of 'Slurring' Court," *New York Times*, October 27, 1932; excerpts of Hoover's "Indianapolis Address," in *New York Times*, October 29, 1932.

8. Byrnes, *All in One Lifetime*, 65.

9. Sitkoff, *New Deal for Blacks*, 40–41.

10. Quoted in Daniel, *The ACLU and the Wagner Act*, 21.

11. The narrowest Senate votes for successful chief justice nominees are as follows: Roger Taney in 1836 with 65.9 percent of those voting (29–15); William Rehnquist in 1986 with 66.3 percent of those voting (65–33); Charles Evans Hughes in 1930 with 66.6 percent of those voting (52–26); and Melville Fuller in 1888 with 67.2 percent of those voting (40–21).

12. R. V. Oulahan, "Senate and the Supreme Court: A New Test," *New York Times*, May 11, 1930.

13. Quoted in Goings, *NAACP Comes of Age*, 40–41.

14. *Red Jacket Consolidated Coal and Coke Co. v. Lewis et al.* (1927); Parker quoted in Goings, *NAACP Comes of Age*, 24.

15. Presumably, had one of the opposing senators voted instead to support the nomination, Vice President Charles Curtis would have broken the 40–40 tie in Parker's favor.

16. Two more southerners were also paired in favor of the nominee. Other southerners cast votes against the nominee out of fear that his selection would revive the long stagnant GOP in the one-party south. Not surprisingly, as a group, southerners were much less supportive of Hughes's appointment. Whereas southerners made up 39 percent of the Democrats who opposed Parker, they made up 67 percent of those who opposed Hughes.

17. R. V. Oulahan, "Senate and the Supreme Court: A New Test," *New York Times*, May 11, 1930.

18. "Personal and Confidential" memo from FDR to Biddle, November 17, 1942, FBP (the memo also appears in Biddle, *In Brief Authority*, 197–98). *Screws v. United States*, 325 U.S. 91 (1945); Rotnem, "Enforcement of Civil Rights," 9; *Henderson v. United States*, 339 U.S. 816 (1950). As Philip Elman of the Solicitor General's Office later noted about the *Henderson* case, "we wrote a brief in which—this was in 1949—for the first time, a partner before the Court asked it to overrule *Plessy v. Ferguson*" ("Solicitor General's Office," 821). See also Kennedy, "Colloquy: A Reply to Philip Elman"; and Elman's "Response."

19. Purcell, *Crisis of Democratic Theory*, 74–75.

20. Frank, *Law and the Modern Mind*, 48, 18. See also Llewellyn, *Bramble Bush*, 12. There is a significant literature on legal realism. See, for example, Llewellyn, "Some Realism about Realism," and "Realistic Jurisprudence"; Pound, "Call for a Realist Jurisprudence"; Twining, *Karl Llewellyn and the Realist Movement*; Kalman, *Legal Realism at Yale*; Horwitz, *Transformation of American Law*; Purcell, "American Jurisprudence between the Wars"; Schlegel, *American Legal Realism and Empirical Social Science*; and G. E. White, "From Sociological Jurisprudence to Realism."

21. But see Lovell, "As Harmless as an Infant."

22. Frank, "Realism in Jurisprudence," 1064, 1068 (Frank's emphasis).

23. Leuchtenburg, *Franklin D. Roosevelt and the New Deal*, 84.

24. Frank, "Realism in Jurisprudence," 1067 (Frank's emphasis).

25. Gilmore, "Legal Realism," 1038.

26. Still, since the two were not inherently linked, the attack on legal formalism did not always coalesce with the pursuit of a rights-centered liberalism in New Deal Washington. And the Roosevelt administration's judicial policy—along with the thoughts and deeds of leading realists—often conveyed this tension. To a significant extent, the differences between the two foreshadowed the divisions of New Deal jurisprudence. As many scholars have explained, New Deal jurisprudence stressed that judges and justices should avoid making public policy, leaving the Congress and the executive branch as the primary decision-making bodies. But it was never clear how New Deal advocates of legal reform would behave once they captured control of the courts, and the products of these democratically elected institutions were not properly progressive. To some reformers, if these products were the consequence of a democratically questionable political process, judicial activism might be required to reform representative democracy. To others, unrestrained activism in the name of a different set of goals, such as individual rights, would simply mean repeating the mistakes of vanquished proponents of legal formalism. In other words, to this second group, it was acceptable for legislative bodies to enact new statutory rights, but it would be a whole other matter for the judiciary to aggrandize individual rights via creative interpretation of vague constitutional clauses. For examples of this tension, see *Colegrove v. Green*, 328 U.S. 549 (1946); and Justice Hugo Black's dissent in *Griswold v. Connecticut*, 381 U.S. 479, 522 (1965).

27. Orren and Skowronek, "Regimes and Regime Building in American Government," 690.

28. Johnson and section 7(a) quoted in Schlesinger, *Coming of the New Deal*, 88 and 137, respectively.

29. John L. Lewis and William Green, quoted in Bernstein, *Turbulent Years*, 34.

30. Lewis later elaborated on his role in the passage of section 7(a) in the face of FDR's inconsistent friendship toward labor. See Alinsky, *John L. Lewis*, 69–70.

31. The *United Mine Workers Journal* and union slogans quoted in Schlesinger, *Coming of the New Deal*, 139; Lewis quoted in Hevener, *Which Side Are You On?* 94.

32. Alinsky, *John L. Lewis*, 71. To be sure, not all unions were as eager to organize as the UMW. Leaders of other AFL unions, especially those who represented skilled craft workers, had in many cases already won their members collective bargaining rights. They therefore had little desire to put any great effort behind organizing industrial workers, those workers whom Teamsters head Dan Tobin had once described as "the rubbish at labor's door" (Irons, *New Deal Lawyers*, 203; Dubofsky and Van Tine, *John L. Lewis*, 203). Thus, despite Lewis's wishes, the AFL did not undertake any major initiative to sign up unorganized industrial workers in response to section 7(a)'s enactment. See Irons, *New Deal Lawyers*, 203; Zieger, *John L. Lewis*.

33. Leuchtenburg, *Franklin D. Roosevelt and the New Deal*, 107. As Lewis told Saul Alinsky, "This great friend of organized labor [Roosevelt] repeatedly fought in a most underhanded way against the inclusion of Section 7(a)" (Alinsky, *John L. Lewis*, 70–71).

34. The president seemingly displayed this attitude when he signed the NIRA into law. See his "Presidential Statement on NIRA," June 16, 1933, *Public Papers and Addresses*, 1933, 251–56.

35. As Schlesinger recounts, "in June 1933 the Bureau of Labor Statistics reported 137 new strikes, in July 240, in August 246; by September nearly 300,000 workers were out. As trouble spread, it began to seem as if work stoppages might threaten the recovery program itself" (*Coming of the New Deal*, 145).

36. Bernstein, *Turbulent Years*, 175–77; Irons, *New Deal Lawyers*, 205, 206. For instance, when the Justice Department stalled in prosecuting Ernest Weir of National (Weirton) Steel Company, the board experienced greater difficulty in persuading employers to conduct union representation elections using its guidelines. See Irons's discussion of the case, *New Deal Lawyers*, 208–10.

37. Robert Wagner, "National Labor Relations Bill," NBC Radio address, May 21, 1935, RWP.

38. On March 25, 1934, without consulting members of the board, the president settled an AFL United Automobile Workers strike by allowing all unions representation at the bargaining table. In a press release, FDR noted that the settlement provided "a framework for a new structure of industrial relations — a new basis of understanding between employers and employees" ("Statement by the President," March 25, 1934, POF, 2).

39. Irons, *New Deal Lawyers*, 212.

40. Bernstein, *Turbulent Years*, 217, 218; the quote is from conservative trade unionist John Frey. On the extent of the strikes, see 217, 298. See also Irons, *New Deal Lawyers*, 214; and B. Nelson, *Workers on the Waterfront*.

41. See Bernstein, *New Deal Collective Bargaining Policy*, 76–83.

42. FDR officially created the National Labor Relations Board with Executive Order 6073 on June 29, 1934.

43. By February 1935, Biddle was so frustrated with the Justice Department's conduct that he voiced his concerns to Assistant Attorney General Harold Stephens in a letter tinged with realist language. For excerpts of Biddle's letter and Cummings's response, see Irons, *New Deal Lawyers*, 221, 224.

44. See Cortner, *Wagner Act Cases*, 79.

45. *Schechter Corp. v. United States*, 295 U.S. 495 (1935).

46. Quoted in Irons, *New Deal Lawyers*, 160. See also Hiss, *Recollections of a Life*, 64–65.

47. Cotton Acreage Reduction Contract, quoted in L. Nelson, "Art of the Possible," 420–21; Irons, *New Deal Lawyers*, 165.

48. See *Report of the President's Committee on Farm Tenancy*, POF.

49. Any reading contrary to this realist-inspired one might give "rise to dissatisfaction and unrest . . . [and] interfere with the orderly execution of the cotton adjustment program, perhaps by bringing on strikes or violence among these classes or by leading to the employment of obstructionary tactics." Protecting tenants against eviction would "cause the least possible amount of labor, economic and social disturbance" and maintain "the social peace necessary to the execution of any planned program" (memoranda by the AAA's Robert McConnaughey and Francis Shea, quoted in Irons, *New Deal Lawyers*, 165, 176).

50. Wallace quoted in Schlesinger, *Coming of the New Deal*, 79; Davis quoted in Irons, *New Deal Lawyers*, 175.

51. Costigan to FDR, February 7, 1935, PPF; Tugwell to Marguarite LeHand, February 5, 1935, PSF; Schlesinger, *Coming of the New Deal*, 80. Tugwell thought that the only way to get around this appearance was to give Frank another position as soon as possible (Tugwell to LeHand).

52. In response to Costigan, Roosevelt, who remarkably seems to have been removed from the squabbling within the Agriculture Department, noted that in his experience "sometimes situations arise in an administrative organization where two or more people simply do not seem to get on with each other. In most cases neither is at fault." He added, "I am sorry and have the highest respect for all parties concerned in the case" (FDR to Costigan, "Private and Confidential," February 13, 1935, PPF).

53. Soon after John L. Lewis formed the Committee of Industrial Organizations (CIO) in 1935, Lee Pressman became its general counsel. Gardner Jackson became involved in a number of progressive causes, most importantly the STFU and the CIO, before returning to work for the government later in the Roosevelt administration. Moreover, six years after the purge, when Frank resigned his position as Chairman of the Securities and Exchange Commission to take a seat on the Second Circuit Court in New York, Roosevelt reminisced in a letter to him about his time at Agriculture. As the president wrote, "when I look back I find Jerry Frank in the very early days of the New Deal fighting the good fight." FDR concluded the note by telling Frank, "you have served the Administration well. I know you will serve your country as well on the bench for many years to come" (Roosevelt to Frank, April 14, 1941, PPF).

54. Quoted in L. Nelson, "Art of the Possible," 134 n. 65. For African Americans in agriculture, this attitude had devastating consequences. For instance, as Sitkoff writes, "black critics of the New Deal excoriated the AAA Cotton Section for perpetrating a mass eviction of the black peasantry. Estimates of the number of Negroes driven out of cotton production by the 40 percent reduction in crop acreage ran as high as half a million, one-third of the total number of Afro-Americans engaged in agriculture in 1933." While Sitkoff cautions that "such charges grossly overestimated the damage done" by the AAA, he nevertheless concludes that it "certainly . . . did nothing to lift the Afro-American from the lowest rungs on the agricultural ladder or to insist that black farmers be treated equally with whites" (A New Deal for Blacks, 53).

55. See W. White, A Man Called White, 169–70.

56. For instance, in August of 1933, when the NAACP's Charles Houston, ACLU President Roger Baldwin, and George B. Murphy of the Afro-American attempted to make an appointment with the president to "protest the lynching evil and submit certain proposals looking toward the protection of American citizens," they ran into an unsympathetic White House staff. In a letter to Houston, Stephen Early, assistant secretary to the president, told the NAACP legal head that the president was concentrating his "time and energy on the immediate problems . . . of national recovery" and, therefore, would be unable to meet with their delegation. Houston was so annoyed by the language of the letter and the treatment the group received from the White House staff, he responded to Early by tersely noting that he had "grave doubts" as to "whether our request or our protest received the consideration they deserved." "Incidentally, official courtesy would seem to demand that the White House staff omit such language as 'What do you boys want?' when addressing grown men, albeit Negroes" (Houston to Early, August 16, 1933; Early to Houston, August 17, 1933; and Houston to Early, August 23, 1933, POF).

57. Houston to Early, August 16, 1933, POF. Two years later, Early described Walter White's antilynching letters to the president as "decidedly insulting" and labeled the NAACP head as "one of the worst and most continuous of trouble makers" ("Personal and Confidential" memo from Early to Malvina Scheider, August 5, 1935, PSF).

58. Walter White, "U.S. Department of (White) Justice," *Crisis*, October 1935. In a January 2, 1936, memorandum to FDR, White included a copy of the article (POF).

59. Sam E. Whitaker (Special Assistant to the Attorney General) to Brien McMahon (Assistant Attorney General), June 19, 1936, POF.

60. See, for example, Mauritz A. Hallgren, "Ohio Gang Protects the Bankers," *Nation*, April 19, 1933, 437–38; and Paul W. Ward, "Hacking to Justice with Cummings, *Nation*, July 3, 1935, 14–16.

61. But see Davies and Derthick, "Race and Social Welfare Policy."

62. Sitkoff, *New Deal for Blacks*, 52, 54. To be sure, as Sitkoff writes, "the relief and welfare operations of the New Deal . . . did assist black southerners to a significant extent" ("Impact of the New Deal on Black Southerners," 123).

63. In 1933, Margold accepted the position of Solicitor of the Interior Department. Charles Houston replaced him as head of the NAACP's litigation campaign.

64. *Powell v. Alabama*, 287 U.S. 45, 52 (1932). See also *Guinn v. United States*, 238 U.S. 347 (1915); *Myers v. Anderson*, 238 U.S. 368 (1915); *Nixon v. Herndon*, 273 U.S. 536 (1927); *Nixon v. Condon*, 286 U.S. 73 (1932); *Norris v. Alabama*, 294 U.S. 587 (1935). For a contemporaneous discussion of this point, see Boudin, "Supreme Court and Civil Rights."

65. Throughout this work, I follow the common distinction between "civil rights" and "civil liberties." Civil rights mainly involve positive protections by government, especially equal protection. Civil liberties refer to the negative rights contained mostly within the Bill of Rights, especially the First Amendment. Nevertheless, the two concepts are often interlinked. In addition, the New Deal altered the terms of the "negative" rights associated with civil liberties. On the civil liberties shift, see *Gitlow v. New York*, 268 U.S. 652 (1925); *Fiske v. Kansas*, 274 U.S. 380 (1927); and *Near v. Minnesota*, 283 U.S. 380 (1931).

66. *Grovey v. Townsend*, 295 U.S. 45 (1935). On the poll tax, see *Breedlove v. Suttles*, 302 U.S. 277 (1937).

67. White to FDR, January 2, 1936, 5, POF. See also Houston to FDR, April 26, 1935, POF.

68. *Schechter Corp. v. United States*, 295 U.S. 495 (1935). Along with *Schechter*, the Court invalidated federal relief legislation for farm mortgagors and surprisingly scoffed at FDR's ouster of William E. Humphrey from the Federal Trade Commission (because of its status as an independent regulatory commission) (*Louisville Bank v. Radford*, 295 U.S. 555 [1935]; and *Humphrey's Executor v. United States*, 295 U.S. 602 [1935]).

69. Smith memo and 1977 interview quoted in Irons, *New Deal Lawyers*, 39.

70. Quote from Cummings and Irons's comment in Irons, *New Deal Lawyers*, 40; see also 35–57 in general.

71. *Panama Refining Co. v. Ryan*, 293 U.S. 388 (1935).

72. FDR quoted in Lasser, *Limits of Judicial Power*, 129. The *Gold Clause Cases* were *Norman v. Baltimore & Ohio Railroad Co.*, 294 U.S. 240 (1935); *Nortz v. United States*, 294 U.S. 317 (1935); and *Perry v. United States*, 294 U.S. 330 (1935). The *Gold Clause Cases* involved emergency monetary policy measures undertaken by FDR and the Congress in 1933 to conserve gold reserves in order to prevent the hoarding of gold and a run on the banks.

73. Roosevelt, *F.D.R.—His Personal Letters*, 459–60.

74. *Railroad Retirement Board v. Alton Railroad Co.*, 295 U.S. 330, 375 (1935);

Stone quoted in Leuchtenburg, *Supreme Court Reborn*, 48. See *Lochner v. New York*, 198 U.S. 45 (1905).

75. Irons, *New Deal Lawyers*, 86, 92, 94, 98.

76. *Schechter Corp. v. United States*, 295 U.S. 495, 528, 541–42, 543.

77. For a more extensive discussion of New Freedom or "Decentralist" progressives, see Hurtgen, *Divided Mind of American Liberalism*, chaps. 1 and 2. According to Thomas Corcoran, after Hughes's reading of the decision, the progressive Justice Brandeis enthusiastically announced to him: "This is clear and strong—and marches to the inevitable doom. . . . This is the end of this business of centralization, and I want you to go back and tell the president that we're not going to let this government centralize everything. It's come to an end." For Brandeis, it would be best for the New Dealers to "go home, back to the states" (Schlesinger, *Politics of Upheaval*, 280).

78. Roosevelt, "Address on Constitution Day," September 17, 1937, *Public Papers and Addresses, 1937*, 366.

79. Cummings, DHC, June 20, 1935.

80. Some newspapers and opponents of the administration highlighted the final sentence as the dusk of democracy. For example, Congressman Bertrand Snell announced that "President Roosevelt has come perilously close to what some people call impeachable grounds" (Schlesinger, *Politics of Upheaval*, 336). Editors at the *New York Times* stressed that "most lawmakers would say that the [constitutional] limits had already been sufficiently defined. Price fixing, confiscation of property, disregard of the rights of the States — these and many other suggested 'operations' of the Government have many times been voided by the Supreme Court and doubtless will be again" ("Thoughts for Lawmakers," *New York Times*, July 14, 1935).

81. Shamir, *Managing Legal Uncertainty*, 71. Publisher Paul Brock also "maintained that, in the aftermath of *Schechter*, Roosevelt had hinted to him that he would pack the Supreme Court in order to have his way" (Leuchtenburg, "When the People Spoke, What Did They Say?" 2094).

82. Roosevelt, *Complete Presidential Press Conferences*, 5:328, 336. Of the three issues outlined by Chief Justice Hughes in his opinion, FDR was clearly the most upset with the potential implications of the Court's reading of the commerce clause. After dismissing the issues concerning the emergency doctrine and the delegation question rather quickly, he launched into an uninterrupted tirade against the Court's view of interstate commerce—a view that threatened his vision of a nationally regulated economy. It was during this portion of the press conference that the president twice made his "horse-and-buggy" comment—the only official statement to come out of the meeting. Those words, divorced of Roosevelt's detailed reasoning, sounded like a bitter president eager to attack the Court. But to the reporters present in the room, FDR was surprisingly in command of the particulars and implications of the decision, which to him was "probably . . . more important than any" other decision "since Dred Scott" (Roosevelt, *Complete Presidential Press Conferences*, 5:328, 336, 315).

83. *United States v. Weirton Steel Co.*, 10 F. Supp. 55 (D. Del. 1935). On hearing this verdict, Wagner gave a realist-style response, proclaiming that the judge's "limited concept of interstate commerce, while in line with many early decisions of our highest court, is not responsive to the changing character of our national economic life" ("Plans Quick Appeal of the NRA Rulings," *New York Times*, March 1, 1935).

84. Representative Withrow of Wisconsin, *Congressional Record*, 1935, 9691.

85. The real threat of more labor uprisings clearly influenced the Senate vote, especially since many expected that the Supreme Court would invalidate section 7(a). Already nearly fifty work stoppages had taken place since the start of the year, and many feared another wave like that of 1934 would break out if the Congress did not pass the Wagner bill.

86. The Senate became more progressive with the midterm elections, as the Democrats gained nine seats to add to their previous sixty. Moreover, with one Farmer-Laborite, one Wisconsin progressive, and ten of the twenty-five Republicans calling themselves progressive, the 1935–36 session began with some seventy senators sympathetic to most of the New Deal. The Democrats also added 9 members to their ranks in the House, bringing their total to an astounding 319. Along with this number, there were 3 Minnesota Farmer-Laborites, 7 Wisconsin progressives, and 10 of the remaining 103 Republicans in support of the New Deal cause (Patterson, *Congressional Conservatism and the New Deal*, 32–33).

87. "Report to the President by the National Labor Relations Board for the Period January 10, 1935 to February 9, 1935, Inclusive," in Gross, *Making of the National Labor Relations Board*, 93.

88. Biddle, quoted in Louis Stark, "Says Recovery Act Is Facing 'Nullity,'" *New York Times*, March 14, 1935. The new labor board was needed in part because Biddle and the Wagner Act drafters wanted NLRB lawyers to be free from the Justice Department—free to "appear for and represent the Board in any case in court," because, as NLRB attorney Tom Emerson put it, Justice Department lawyers "had done nothing except lose a case against Weirton Steel Company." The department, he added, was "the most political branch of the administration, and . . . its staff was filled with people who were more or less failures as lawyers or else ancient bureaucratic types. They had no particular interest in the New Deal and were just completely out of sympathy with section 7(a)" (Irons, *New Deal Lawyers*, 228).

89. Irons, *New Deal Lawyers*, 227. See also Gross, *Making of the National Labor Relations Board*, 130–48 generally; and Cortner, *Jones and Laughlin Case*, 59–61.

90. Richberg, *My Hero*, 191.

91. Ickes, *Secret Diary*, 1:363. Along with the progressive senators, Frankfurter, David Niles, and Ickes attended the meeting with the president.

92. *Congressional Record*, 1935, 7676.

93. Bernstein, *Turbulent Years*, 341.

94. *Congressional Record*, 1935, 9694, 9692, 9684.

95. During this meeting, the two southern leaders argued that "if the bill came up for a vote it couldn't pass" and tried to convince the New York senator to withdraw his bill. Wagner responded with a plea to the president, exclaiming, "All I want is a vote" (Gross, *Making of the National Labor Relations Board*, 140–41). Robinson and Harrison also relied on Justice Department objections to the legislation based on the department's exclusion from cases arising under it (Huthmacher, *Senator Robert F. Wagner and the Rise of Urban Liberalism*, 195–96).

96. On the opposition and the constitutional issue, see Bernstein, *New Deal Collective Bargaining Policy*, 106.

97. Indeed, as Patterson writes, the Senate voting figures from the 1930s "do not—and cannot—reveal the inherent conservatism of men such as Robinson or the practice perfected by men such as Harrison of watering down administration bills in committee" (*Congressional Conservatism and the New Deal*, 348).

98. Daniel, *The ACLU and the Wagner Act*, 101, 102, 117.

99. Wolters, *Negroes and the Great Depression*, 185. See also Hill, *Black Labor and the American Legal System*.

100. See, for example, Frymer, "Race, Labor and State Building."

101. Quoted in Wolters, *Negroes and the Great Depression*, 185.

102. Plotke, "Wagner Act, Again," 122 (Plotke's emphasis). See also Plotke, *Building a Democratic Political Order*. On southern support of the New Deal, see Reiter, "Building of a Bifactional Structure."

103. According to James Patterson, the six most conservative southern Democrats were (in order) Carter Glass of Virginia, Harry Byrd of Virginia, Josiah Bailey of North Carolina, Ellison Smith of South Carolina, Walter George of Georgia, and Richard Russell of Georgia (*Congressional Conservatism and the New Deal*, 348–49). Of those six, Byrd and Bailey voted against the act. Glass, Smith, and Russell did not vote (although Byrd indicated that, if present, Glass would have also opposed the measure). Only George voted in favor of the bill (*Congressional Record*, 1935, 7681).

104. Twelve southern senators opposed the Tydings amendment, while four supported it and six did not vote (*Congressional Record*, 1935, 7675). As Melvyn Dubofsky writes, the amendment "sought to legitimate [company unions] through the subterfuge of forbidding intimidation or coercion from any sources, including unions and workers." In the end, "a number of border state and deep South Democrats joined the Republican recalcitrants in the affirmative, but key Southern Democratic leaders joined the majority" (*State and Labor in Modern America*, 128).

105. *Congressional Record*, 1935, 9979, 9693

106. To be sure, as Gareth Davies and Martha Derthick write with regard to the Social Security Act, "to what extent Congress acted proximately out of racial motives is necessarily obscure, because a discriminatory political system artificially suppressed consideration of race. But it is precisely this caveat that should make contemporary social scientists cautious in asserting the primacy of racial motivation in retrospective analysis, the more so since the range and probable weight of nonracial factors become so obvious when one takes the trouble to reconstruct the political debate of 1935" ("Race and Social Welfare Policy," 235).

107. Moreover, once the Court did approve the constitutionality of the Wagner Act in 1937, conservative southern Democrats led efforts to repeal or revise it.

108. Ickes, *Secret Diary*, 1:363. It was in this vein that Stanley High, a political advisor to the president, noted in 1937: "The southern Democrats, who had begun to accept their dominance in the party's national councils as something fixed and permanent, have suffered no end of inner torment during these last, presumably triumphant, Democratic years. It has been plain to them that Mr. Roosevelt had very little in common with either their philosophy or their program. . . . The policies he initiated were a direct blow at the states'-rights conservatism of the Democracy of the South. The manner in which those policies have been administered is an equally serious threat to the system of rigid party regularity by which the Democratic organizations, in both the South and the Northeast, built up and maintained their strength" (*Roosevelt — and Then?* 247–48).

109. Ickes, *Secret Diary*, 1:363; La Follette quoted in letter from Frankfurter to Roosevelt, May 16, 1935, in Freedman, *Roosevelt and Frankfurter*, 271–72. The president's initial lack of sympathy with the Wagner Act seems intertwined with his focus on economic recovery in 1934 and 1935 and his lack of desire to expand the influence of labor leaders; see Schlesinger, *Coming of the New Deal*, 402.

110. Cummings, DHC, May 24, 1935. On the attendees and nature of the meeting, see Gross, *Making of the National Labor Relations Board*, 143.

111. In the days following *Schechter*, concerns about its constitutionality hovered over the Wagner bill, and labor leaders once again worried aloud about the prospect of another delay for American workers' Magna Carta. In response, Wagner asserted, "the *Schechter* case did not limit in any way the application of the National Labor Relations Bill" ("Labor Bill Valid, Wagner Insists," *New York Times*, May 30, 1935). Still, its drafters rushed to revise its declaration of policy, "emphasizing the effect of labor disputes on interstate commerce and de-emphasizing the mere economic effects which had been rejected by the Court" (oral history interview with Phillip Levy quoted in Gross, *Making of the National Labor Relations Board*, 144).

112. FDR's "must" list appeared in the *New York Times*, June 6, 1935, 10.

113. Irons, *New Deal Lawyers*, 231.

114. Cummings, DHC, June 20, 1935.

115. Ickes, *Secret Diary*, 1:372; Tomlins, *The State and the Unions*, 106. In the specific case of the Guffey coal bill, the president was threatened by a UMW strike that would have sent 400,000 miners home and crippled the nation's industrial production, thereby stalling the recovery once again. By deferring all questions of constitutionality to the courts, Roosevelt accomplished three tasks. First, although the number of strikes did remain at a high level in 1935, with the Wagner Act and the Guffey Coal Act, he effectively delayed a massive strike wave until the Court decided (likely a year away). Second, with conservative groups like the American Liberty League aligning with the Court and the GOP and with industrial leaders like Ernest Weir declaring they would ignore the Wagner Act, he was drawing the partisan lines for the electoral conflict of 1936. Third, Roosevelt was building a case for a potential clash with the Court over the future meaning of the Constitution, for if the justices struck down the second New Deal, all the talk of reducing the power of the courts through a constitutional amendment then sweeping the nation would surely develop into a movement to institute such reforms.

116. The questions of the Wagner Act's constitutionality were so serious that the administration had great difficulty in finding interested individuals to serve on the new board. See Gross, *Making of the National Labor Relations Board*, 149, 167.

117. Ickes, discussing the views of Thomas Corcoran, *Secret Diary*, 1:342. Schlesinger offers more examples of progressive concerns in *Politics of Upheaval*, 213. See also a letter from David Niles to Felix Frankfurter, April 22, 1935, in Freedman, *Roosevelt and Frankfurter*, 261–62.

118. Even Cummings noted in his diary on May 28, 1935, "Personally I cannot help but feel that, while in a certain sense they [the Court's decisions] are a set-back for America, they are a God-send to the Administration. The whole scene is shifted. We are no longer on the defensive concerning certain matters that could not well be defined. We are in a position to push forward with an affirmative program" (DHC).

119. To be sure, labor had already made some gains in the early 1930s with the passage of the Norris-LaGuardia Act, which treated unions, using the common law notion of legal persons, like business corporations. In the tradition of business unionism, both "possessed rights to engage in competitive economic struggle, unchecked (within wide limits) by law." The Wagner Act, however, took a different direction by regarding unions "not as entities with rights but as instruments or agents, designated as representatives by employees through the medium of a government-supervised election" (Tomlins, *The State and the Unions*, 102). The switch from voluntarism to

government intervention was significant for judicial review because the NLRB ousted federal district courts from deciding cases involving industrial relations. Moreover, only the board's final orders (interpreted broadly) could be reviewed, and then only by circuit courts (which aided in the enforcement of the orders). Whereas Norris-LaGuardia had the negative element of limiting the federal judiciary's jurisdiction in labor disputes, the Wagner Act provided new institutional support for unions to attain their collective bargaining rights (Gross, *Making of the National Labor Relations Board*, 135).

120. Rosenfarb, "Protection of Basic Rights," 93; Auerbach, *Labor and Liberty*, 212; Daniel, *The ACLU and the Wagner Act*, 14; California state senator quoted in Auerbach, *Labor and Liberty*, 212.

121. Plotke, "Wagner Act, Again," 127–28; Baldwin, "Organized Labor and Political Democracy," 17. For industrialists, the Wagner Act and the rise of unions meant something quite different. They opposed the bill because, as Joel Auerbach writes, they "perceived that unions and the government threatened their principles as well as their profits. Arguing that economic freedom was a natural right, they refused to grant legitimacy to labor unions as social institutions because unions challenged their traditional prerogatives." To be sure, according to the Senate's La Follette Civil Liberties Committee, "the majority of American businessmen . . . acquiesced in the policy enunciated in section 7(a) and in the Wagner Act. But 'an intransigent minority of powerful corporations' still opposed organization and collective bargaining" long after the Wagner bill became law (*Labor and Liberty*, 143, 146).

122. Farley, *Jim Farley's Story*, 250; High, *Roosevelt — and Then?* 277. Farley cites only the first six states. I added New York because Farley noted that, according to the 1935 poll, Long would command 100,000 votes in that state, "and a vote of that size could easily mean the difference between victory and defeat for the Democratic or Republican candidate" (250). See also Brinkley, *Voices of Protest*, 209–15.

123. *New Republic*, quoted in Brinkley, *Voices of Protest*, 198. See Brinkley's definition of the term "lower middle class," 199–200.

124. In January 1936, with its decision in *United States v. Butler*, the Supreme Court continued its attack on the New Deal, this time invalidating the Agricultural Adjustment Act (*Carter v. Carter Coal Co.*, 298 U.S. 238). Next, by a one-vote margin, the Court struck down the Guffey Coal Act and the New York State minimum-wage law (*Morehead v. New York ex rel. Tipaldo*, 298 U.S. 587). Roosevelt responded to the *Tipaldo* decision by angrily asserting that the Court had delivered us into a "'no-man's-land' where no Government — State or Federal — can function" (*Public Papers and Addresses, 1936*, 191–92).

125. Lewis, however, would come to understand this period as a time when FDR co-opted the goals of workers to increase his chances for reelection, expand the powers of the presidency, and constrain the authority of labor's leaders.

126. Milkis, *The President and the Parties*, 68.

127. Walter White, "An Estimate of the 1936 Vote," *Crisis*, February 1936, 46–47 (emphasis added); copy found in TGCP. In discussing the potential southern abandonment of the Democratic Party, White took care to note an obvious exception: "in elections where a religious prejudice, such as was raised against Al Smith in the 1928 elections, supersedes anti-Negro prejudice" ("An Estimate of the 1936 Vote," 46).

128. Milkis, *The President and the Parties*, 70. For a more extensive discussion on how the abrogation of the two-thirds rule fit into FDR's plan for the Democratic Party, see Milkis, *The President and the Parties*, 69–71.

129. Leuchtenburg, "Election of 1936," 2829–30.

130. See, for example, High, *Roosevelt — and Then?* 255–58.

131. Sitkoff, *New Deal for Blacks*, 89. On the concept of "electoral capture," see Frymer, *Uneasy Alliances*. On the 1934 election results, see note 86 above.

132. Joseph Alsop and Robert Kintner describing Pennsylvania Senator Joseph Guffey, quoted in Milkis, *The President and the Parties*, 63. See also Weiss, *Farewell to the Party of Lincoln*, 180–208.

133. See chap. 5 in Sitkoff, *New Deal for Blacks*, 102–38.

134. Reiter, "Building of a Bifactional Structure," 115.

135. The number of Democratic southern and border-state representatives and senators stood steady at 130 and 30, respectively. See Sitkoff, *New Deal for Blacks*, 111.

136. Ibid., 41, 95; FDR quoted in Freidel, *FDR and the South*, 90.

137. High, *Roosevelt — and Then?* 268.

138. Ibid., 210–12 (emphasis added). President Roosevelt would later appoint Murphy to the Supreme Court. President Truman did the same for Minton. On the "closeness" of High's relationship with the president, see Milkis, *The President and the Parties*, 52–53.

139. To some extent, this development coincided with the emergence of what Gary Gerstle describes as a progressive civil nationalism that at once fed more tolerance for difference and devotion to original American ideals (*American Crucible*, chap. 4).

CHAPTER THREE

1. William Allen White, "Adroit," *Emporia Daily Gazette*, February 6, 1937; "Striking at the Roots," *New York Herald-Tribune*, February 6, 1937.

2. Davis, *FDR*, 55–56, 58.

3. M. Nelson, "President and the Court," 293. See also Tom Wicker, "Beware the Mandate," *New York Times*, December 6, 1986.

4. Gerstle, *American Crucible*, 157. Davis calls FDR "deceitful and untrustworthy" (*FDR*, 94). For scholars critical of Roosevelt, see also Burns, *Roosevelt*; Conkin, *New Deal*; and Lasser, *Limits of Judicial Power*. For a more positive analysis, see Leuchtenburg, *Supreme Court Reborn*.

5. Skowronek, *Politics Presidents Make*, 4. This comment is not limited to those scholars who have criticized FDR's leadership; see also Neustadt, *Presidential Power and the Modern Presidents*; and Dallek, *Hail to the Chief*.

6. Skowronek, *Politics Presidents Make*, 20–21 (Skowronek's emphasis).

7. For a discussion of the Court issue in the 1936 campaign, see Leuchtenburg, "When the People Spoke, What Did They Say?"; and Stephenson, *Campaigns and the Court*.

8. Milkis, *The President and the Parties*, 4.

9. Robert H. Jackson, "Foundation of Our Unrest," Yale Law School Alumni Luncheon, June 21, 1937, 4, DOJ Files. For a contemporaneous discussion of the New Deal's deeper constitutional goal, see the work of Edward Corwin, for example, *Court over the Constitution*, and *President*.

10. Norris quoted in Baker, *Back to Back*, 137–38; Patterson, *Congressional Conservatism and the New Deal*, 89; and Leuchtenburg, *Supreme Court Reborn*, 111–12.

11. Fuller, *Law in Quest of Itself*, 57. Solicitor General Stanley Reed and Attorney General Cummings expressed a similar view in the summer of 1936. In the midst

of their secret work on the Court-packing plan, these top Justice Department officials publicly spoke of a need to respect the Court while simultaneously declaring the "uncertainty" of law and the hope for greater judicial success in the near future. The result, as Ronen Shamir explains, was an attempt to "prepare the ideological foundation for the court-packing plan" by establishing "the idea that majority and minority opinions on the bench should enjoy equal normative footing. Packing the Court, according to this logic, could be legitimately viewed as an attempt to preserve the Court's role in providing the necessary legitimation of new constitutional doctrines by simply 'correcting' a contingent, if not accidental, unfortunate 'imbalance' on the bench" (*Managing Legal Uncertainty*, 76). On the amendment route, see also Kyvig, "Road Not Taken."

12. Harold Ickes, *Secret Diary*, 1:495; Ickes's April 10, 1937, speech quoted in National Lawyers Guild press release, April 27, 1937, TGCP.

13. See, for example, Leuchtenburg, *Supreme Court Reborn*, 156–61; and Burns, *Roosevelt*, 315.

14. Putnam, *Making Democracy Work*. On the new institutionalism, also see March and Olsen, "New Institutionalism," and *Rediscovering Institutions*, 1989; and the works listed in note 38 in chap. 1.

15. Roosevelt, introduction to *Public Papers and Addresses*, 1937, lxvi.

16. Skowronek, *Politics Presidents Make*, 303. As Leuchtenburg points out, FDR's opponents and supporters did focus on the Court issue in the 1936 campaign ("When the People Spoke, What Did They Say?" 2088–103).

17. Roosevelt, *Public Papers and Addresses*, 1937, 2, 5 (Roosevelt's emphasis). See also Rosenman, *Working with Roosevelt*, 144.

18. Roosevelt, *Public Papers and Addresses*, 1937, 55, 127–28, 130.

19. Leon Green, "Unpacking the Court," *New Republic*, February 24, 1937, 67.

20. Creel, *Rebel at Large*, 291.

21. Karl N. Llewellyn, "United Front on the Court," *Nation*, March 13, 1937, 288.

22. Leon Green, "Unpacking the Court," *New Republic*, February 24, 1937, 67–68.

23. Robert H. Jackson, "Today, We Have Two Constitutions," delivered at Carnegie Hall in New York City, March 24, 1937, 8–9, RHJP.

24. Thurman Arnold, "Excerpts from Thurman Arnold's Speech on the Court," TGCP.

25. Roosevelt, *Public Papers and Addresses*, 1937, 129.

26. Roosevelt, *Public Papers and Addresses*, 1935, 295.

27. "Steel Lines Plan Wagner Bill Fight," *New York Times*, June 28, 1935; "58 Lawyers Hold Labor Act Invalid," *New York Times*, September 19, 1935; Wolfskill, *Revolt of the Conservatives*, 72–73; Auerbach, *Labor and Liberty*, 148. See also Bernstein, *Turbulent Years*, 349.

28. Roosevelt, *Public Papers and Addresses*, 1936, 557. The first part of this quote is from a note following the speech (558).

29. Roosevelt asserted: "Ever since the Wagner Labor Relations Act went through . . . the Chamber of Commerce of the United States, the National Manufacturers' Association and Liberty League lawyers [have been sending out] pamphlets saying, 'This Act is unconstitutional. Disregard it.' Disregard a Federal statute!" (Roosevelt, *Complete Presidential Press Conferences*, 9:305–6).

30. Patterson, *Congressional Conservatism and the New Deal*, 81–82

31. Burns, *Roosevelt*, 297; M. Nelson, "President and the Court," 285; quote

from the president's press secretary, Stephen Early, appears in Leuchtenburg, *Supreme Court Reborn*, 126. Moreover, when Roosevelt met with congressional leaders and cabinet members on the morning of February 5, 1937, he noted that one of the reasons he chose to pack the Court rather than amend the Constitution was because the Liberty League had already collected "a large sum of money in New York" to block an amendment attempt (quoted in Wolfskill, *Revolt of the Conservatives*, 250).

32. Creel, *Rebel at Large*, 293–94; George Creel, "Roosevelt's Plans and Purposes, *Collier's*, December 26, 1936, 7, 40; Cummings, DHC, January 24, 1937; and Leuchtenburg, *Supreme Court Reborn*, 128–29. Indeed, after documenting the numerous leaks, Leuchtenburg notes that "given all these revelations, it is hard to account for why FDR's message of February 5 came as such a shock" (287).

33. Alsop and Catledge, *168 Days*, 38–40. The next day, the Washington bureau of Scripps-Howard informed its chain: "An increase in the Supreme Court's membership — 'if necessary' — is being considered by the Administration, it was learned today. And President Roosevelt's forthright stand against amendment of the Constitution was interpreted by many as pointing toward an eventual decision to use this big stick" (Leuchtenburg, *Supreme Court Reborn*, 286–87).

34. When the Cabinet members were given a copy of the State of the Union Address the day FDR delivered it, a couple of them asked whether it "did not foreclose the amendment approach to the court problem, *to which the President replied that it did not; that it merely indicated that no amendment was needed, although one could be resorted to.* The men at the cabinet table, on tenterhooks with curiosity, waited for more, but the President stopped there" (Alsop and Catledge, *168 Days*, 39; emphasis added). See also Connally, *My Name Is Tom Connally*, 185; and Leuchtenburg, *Supreme Court Reborn*, 127–28.

35. See, for example, Burns, *Roosevelt*, 297; see also Davis, *FDR*, 61.

36. Republican platform quoted in Baker, *Back to Back*, 45; Tugwell, *Democratic Roosevelt*, 393. See also Patterson, *Congressional Conservatism and the New Deal*, 107; Baker, *Back to Back*, 91; Alsop and Catledge, *168 Days*, 98–99; and Lasser, *Limits of Judicial Power*, 145.

37. Roosevelt, *Public Papers and Addresses*, 1937, 51.

38. Milkis, *The President and the Parties*, 50; see also Stanley High, "Whose Party Is It?" *Saturday Evening Post*, February 6, 1937; Patterson, *Congressional Conservatism and the New Deal*, 216–18.

39. Timmons, *Garner of Texas*, 218.

40. Burton Wheeler, "Press Statement," reprinted in "Supreme Court Controversy," *Congressional Digest*, March 1937, 91–92; Patterson, *Congressional Conservatism and the New Deal*, 116; Alsop and Catledge, *168 Days*, 95. Wheeler put it even more clearly to Thomas Corcoran: "Once [Roosevelt] was only one of us who made him. Now he means to make himself the boss of us all. . . . Well, he's made the mistake we've been waiting for for a long time — and this is our chance to cut him down to size" (quoted in Clarke, *Roosevelt's Warrior*, 219). Even Norris expressed concern about the Court-packing proposal before reluctantly endorsing it in the end (Patterson, *Congressional Conservatism and the New Deal*, 89). On New Freedom progressivism's uneasiness with realism, see G. E. White, "From Sociological Jurisprudence to Realism."

41. *West Coast Hotel Company v. Parrish*, 300 U.S. 379 (1937); Carter Glass,

"Constitutional Immorality," March 29, 1937, PPF, 16; also reprinted in Smith and Beasley, *Carter Glass*, 496–510.

42. Wheeler, *Yankee from the West*, 320. On Hughes's support, see Davis, *FDR*, 76–81.

43. Harrison gave only "lip service" to the plan, stating simply at the outset that "I'm for the proposition." For the remainder of the fight, he remained silent (quoted in Martha H. Swain, *Pat Harrison*, 149). On Robinson, see Ickes, *Secret Diary*, 2:164; Michelson, *Ghost Talks*, 166; and Connally, *My Name Is Tom Connally*, 166, 192.

44. Quoted in Harrison, "Breakup of the Roosevelt Court," 221–22.

45. Ickes, *Secret Diary*, 2:63; and Tugwell, *Democratic Roosevelt*, 401. On Byrnes, see also Michie and Ryhlick, *Dixie Demagogues*, 79. On Robinson, see also Neal, "Biography of Joseph T. Robinson," 444–45.

46. Robert S. Allen, "New Deal Fights for Its Life," *Nation*, July 10, 1937, 35–36; see also Ickes, *Secret Diary*, 2:144–45. For Robinson's reaction, see S. J. Woolf, "Robinson's Last Interview," *New York Times*, July 15, 1937.

47. Glass, "Constitutional Immorality," 4 (emphasis added). See also Harrell, "Southern Congressional Leaders and the Supreme Court Fight of 1937," 158–60.

48. For Connally's statement of opposition, see Baker, *Back to Back*, 83; and *Congressional Record*, vol. 81, App. 493–94.

49. Quoted in High, *Roosevelt — and Then?* 207. New Dealers had also begun to talk about what a Roosevelt Court would mean for the advancement of civil rights and liberties for *all* Americans. See, for example, "President's Plan and Civil Rights and Liberties," (author unknown), TGCP.

50. "Constitution," *St. Louis Argus*, February 19, 1937; "The Negro and the Supreme Court," *Philadelphia Independent*. See also "President Roosevelt and the Supreme Court," *Newport News Star*, February 13, 1937; "Other Reasons for Liberalizing Courts," *St. Louis Argus*; "Why Not Increase the Court?" *Atlanta Daily World*; and Floyd Calvin in *Louisville Leader* and *New York Amsterdam News*, copies in TGCP.

51. "Blowing Hot and Cold," *St. Louis Argus*, March 12, 1937; Sitkoff, *New Deal for Blacks*, 65. The Senate confirmed Hastie to be a U.S. District Court Judge for the Virgin Islands on March 19, 1937.

52. Quoted in Freidel, *FDR and the South*, 91–92.

53. Michie and Ryhlick, *Dixie Demagogues*, 68, 73, 75.

54. Cummings, DHC, August 1, 1937.

55. Robertson, *Sly and Able*, 255 (emphasis added).

56. Alsop and Catledge, *168 Days*, 78.

57. *West Coast Hotel Company v. Parrish*, 300 U.S. 379 (1937); *National Labor Relations Board v. Jones and Laughlin Steel Corporation*, 301 U.S. 57 (1937).

58. Alsop and Catledge, *168 Days*, 152–53. For more discussion of a compromise, see Ickes, *Secret Diary*, 2:108, 125, 126 (April 3, April 25, and May 2); Connally, *My Name Is Tom Connally*, 189. For Byrnes's position on the compromise, see Alsop and Catledge, *168 Days*, 152. For Harrison's position, see Swain, *Pat Harrison*, 152.

59. Alsop and Catledge, *168 Days*, 155, 252.

60. Ibid., 216. See also Weller, *Joe T. Robinson*, 163. On the alternative plan, see Leuchtenburg, "FDR's Court-Packing Plan," 673.

61. Leuchtenburg, "FDR's Court-Packing Plan," 684–87.

62. Alsop and Catledge, *168 Days*, 265; Swain, *Pat Harrison*, 153–54.

63. Lewis, National Radio Address on December 31, 1936; reprinted in "Congress and the Sit-Down Strikes," *Congressional Digest*, May 1937, 157.

64. Ibid.

65. Fine, *Frank Murphy: The New Deal Years*, 289–90, 296. In my discussion of the sit-down strikes, I rely heavily on the work of Fine, especially his chapter on the strikes (289–325). See also Fine, *Sit-Down*; and Alinsky, *John L. Lewis*, 97–147. On the Wagner Act, the confirmation hearings on Murphy's nomination to be attorney general are also relevant. In a statement before a subcommittee of the Senate Judiciary committee, Murphy noted that at this time *"there was no operating legal machinery for settling labor disputes; the Wagner Act was at that time practically out of operation under decisions of lower federal courts. As a Governor faced with the fact of unprecedented strikes which had to be handled, I had to devise ways and means of handling them as I went along"* ("Statement of the Honorable Frank Murphy," January 13, 1939, 2, DOJ Files; Murphy's emphasis).

66. Quoted in Fine, *Frank Murphy: The New Deal Years*, 302. On Roosevelt, see Timmons, *Garner of Texas*, 216.

67. Garner quoted in Timmons, *Garner of Texas*, 216.

68. Robertson, *Sly and Able*, 257; Lewis and Roosevelt quoted in Fine, *Frank Murphy: The New Deal Years*, 306.

69. Fine, *Frank Murphy: The New Deal Years*, 307–11.

70. Ibid., 314.

71. Murphy did not release the letter until FDR nominated him to be attorney general in 1939, requiring Senate confirmation.

72. Quoted in Fine, *Frank Murphy: The New Deal Years*, 318; see also Alinsky, *John L. Lewis*, 144–46.

73. Fine, *Frank Murphy: The New Deal Years*, 313–21; quotes appear on 317, 318, and 321, respectively. Fine, *Frank Murphy: The New Deal Years*, 320. The number of National Guardsmen in Flint reached its peak on February 7, at 3,454 (308). On the Murphy-Roosevelt relationship during the strike, see also "Memorandum for the President," February 8, 1937, POF.

74. "During the strike wave in the summer of 1934," as Arthur Schlesinger notes, "a memorandum from Homer Cummings told [the president] how he might, if necessary, call out federal troops. At the height of the textile strike, six weeks later, Steve Early sent him language for this purpose, recommending a Harding proclamation as 'the most appropriate to follow in the present emergency.' Roosevelt, of course, did not take such drastic action" (*Coming of the New Deal*, 402–3).

75. Plotke, "Wagner Act, Again," 148; Fine, *Frank Murphy: The New Deal Years*, 316. Murphy went on to state that he "conceived it to be [his] duty as the governor of the State not only to see that the writs of the courts were executed but also to see that peace and order were maintained . . . not only to see that the law was enforced after it was broken but to see that the law was observed before it was broken. To safeguard not only the enforcement of the law but its observance, I conceived it my duty to exert every effort to replace industrial strife and unrest which would wreck the economy of my State with industrial peace and order which would preserve the economy of my State" ("Statement of Honorable Frank Murphy," 6).

76. Hevener, *Which Side Are You On?* 101, 136.

77. Justice Department press release, May 19, 1937, DOJ Files. Cummings also

sent a copy of the release to the president. "Old-timers" quoted in Flynt, "New Deal and Southern Labor," 89.

78. Department of Justice press release, April 17, 1938, 1, DOJ Files. The government handed down the indictments on September 27, 1937.

79. "Bloody Harlan Reforms," *Nation*, August 6, 1938, 121; see also "Harlan on Trial," *New Republic*, July 6, 1938, 242–44.

80. Glass, "Constitutional Immorality," 8.

81. "Washington Notes," *New Republic*, July 14, 1937, 280.

82. Byrnes, *Congressional Digest*, 146; Swain, *Pat Harrison*, 150. On the CIO's campaign in the South, see Zieger, *CIO, 1935–1955*.

83. Fortunately for Roosevelt, the Big Four — while united in their opposition to the sit-down strikes — did not join forces in support of this measure. While Garner clearly backed the amendment, Robinson, unwilling to embarrass the president and eager for a seat on the Court, told Byrnes that while he favored the measure, strategically he would have to oppose it. Harrison, who voted against it as well, declared that he had done so "because it dealt exclusively with coal miners; any sense-of-the-Senate condemnation of sit-down strikes should be in the form of a separate resolution applicable to all industries. 'I have no sympathy with sit-down strikes,' he insisted" (Swain, *Pat Harrison*, 150).

84. Patterson, *Congressional Conservatism and the New Deal*, 136–37.

85. Roosevelt quoted in Farley, *Jim Farley's Story*, 125; see also Patterson, *Congressional Conservatism and the New Deal*, 147–48.

86. In the academic debate about the underlying causes of the Supreme Court's doctrinal shift in 1937, my work fits more closely with those who emphasize a politically inspired change as opposed to an internally led alteration. This is not to say, however, that I endorse the idea of a "constitutional revolution of 1937." As I have argued, the change in doctrine was a gradual process that was driven by political forces but certainly informed by the Court's own positions. For the revisionist argument, see, for example, Cushman, *Rethinking the New Deal Court*; and G. E. White, *The Constitution and the New Deal*. For the more traditional account, see Leuchtenburg, *Supreme Court Reborn*. On the debate generally, see Kalman, "Law, Politics, and the New Deal(s)."

87. See, for instance, Hawley, "Constitution of the Hoover and F. Roosevelt Presidency and the Depression Era," 98–100.

88. By 1941 Roosevelt had filled all but one seat on the Court by either appointment or elevation (Stone). In 1943 he made his ninth appointment (Rutledge) to replace his seventh (Byrnes). Harlan F. Stone and Owen Roberts were the only justices to serve through the entire Roosevelt administration.

89. Harrison, "Breakup of the Roosevelt Court," 18. On the requirements for becoming a Roosevelt justice, see Harrison, "Breakup of the Roosevelt Court," 17–21, 296–99.

90. Roosevelt, introduction to *Public Papers and Addresses*, 1937, lxvi.

CHAPTER FOUR

1. Roosevelt, "Address at Barnesville, Georgia," August 11, 1938, *Public Papers and Addresses*, 1938, 466–67.

2. Brinkley, "New Deal and Southern Politics," 97.

3. Black and Black, *Politics and Society in the South*, 175. Morgan J. Kousser writes that "by 1910, almost no Negroes and only about half of the whites bothered to vote in the most hotly contested elections. . . . the Southern political system which was to last through mid-century had been formed" (*Shaping of Southern Politics*, 224, 226).

4. Myrdal, *American Dilemma*, 453; Stokes, *Chip off My Shoulder*, 503.

5. Robert L. Vann, editorial, *Pittsburgh Courier*, September 11, 1932.

6. Unsigned and undated memo, "Statement in Support of Proposed Negro Plank," in RHJP; Moon, *Balance of Power*, 237–38.

7. According to the unsigned "Statement in Support of Proposed Negro Plank": "[I]n the 1938 elections — when the social program of the New Deal may be said to have reached its peak — a swing back to the Republican Party was noticeable among the Negro vote. For example, in Ohio in 5 out of the 7 congressional districts where the Negro vote exceeded 10,000, Republicans *replaced* Democratic Congressmen. The Senatorship was lost, with Negro wards in Columbus, Cincinnati and Cleveland going heavily Republican. In Pennsylvania Robert S. Vann — owner of the *Pittsburgh Courier* (200,000 circulation)—who had managed the campaign among Negro Democrats in 1936 bolted the Democratic Party."

8. "Statement in Support of Proposed Negro Plank." Schuyler quoted in Sitkoff, *New Deal for Blacks*, 301; and in Klinkner and Smith, *Unsteady March*, 148.

9. "Statement in Support of Proposed Negro Plank"; *Missouri ex rel. Gaines v. Canada*, 305 U.S. 337 (1938).

10. On racial progressive activism during the New Deal period, see Sullivan, *Days of Hope*; and Egerton, *Speak Now against the Day*.

11. On FDR's pragmatism, see Skowronek, *Politics Presidents Make*, chap. 7, pt. 1, 288–324.

12. Simultaneously, FDR employed the Executive Reorganization Act of 1939 to institutionalize "a process whereby public expectations and institutional arrangements established the presidency as the center of government activity" (Milkis, *The President and the Parties*, 146).

13. Frank Murphy, *In Defense of Democracy*, 4, DOJ Files. (This pamphlet, which comprised parts of three Murphy speeches, was issued by the American Association for Economic Freedom in cooperation with the American Council on Public Affairs.) Keyssar, *Right to Vote*, 226–27; Murphy, "Keynote Address" at the Attorney General's Conference, April 19, 1939, 9, DOJ Files.

14. To be sure, some believed dictatorship had already arrived by 1936. During the 1936 presidential campaign, for instance, Congressman Bertrand H. Snell condemned the "unconstitutional dictatorship" and "arrogant individualism of Franklin Delano Roosevelt" (quoted in Leuchtenburg, "When the People Spoke, What Did They Say?" 2091). Not surprisingly, as America's involvement in the war grew more likely, cries about the pending arrival of despotism grew louder. Charles Lindbergh, for one, told a Madison Square Garden crowd on May 23, 1941, "if we go to war to preserve democracy abroad, we are likely to end by losing it at home" (Biddle, "Civil Rights in Times of Stress," 15).

15. Klinkner and Smith, *Unsteady March*, 139.

16. Franklin Roosevelt, "Message for the Twenty-ninth Annual Conference of the National Association for the Advancement of Colored People," June 25, 1938, PPF.

17. Murphy, "Meaning of the Bill of Rights," in *In Defense of Democracy*, 14–15.

Murphy initially entitled this speech "Meaning of Civil Liberty" when he delivered it on June 21, 1939. For a detailed discussion of how "the Nazi menace forced at least some white Americans to begin to reexamine the racial inequalities in their midst," before the United States entered the second world war, see Klinkner and Smith, *Unsteady March*, 137, 136–60. Klinkner and Smith also suggest that "given that the New Deal was largely ineffective in forcing the nation to confront Jim Crow, it is hard to escape the conclusion that it was instead the emergence of fascism and Nazism of the 1930s that most set the stage for real transformations" (137). I agree that the destruction of democracies abroad influenced liberal belief in protecting civil rights and liberties. However, I argue that domestic forces were much more significant in this regard. In addition, it is important to clarify that there was apparently little international pressure forcing the United States to live up to the egalitarian terms of its founding charter before World War II. Such pressure would become more important during the war, and especially during the cold war as the United States sought to collect allies in its ideological confrontation with the Soviet Union (see chaps. 5, 6, and 7).

18. Murphy, "Public and Governmental Responsibilities," in *In Defense of Democracy*, 10 (Murphy initially entitled this speech "Civil Liberties and the Cities" when he delivered it on May 15, 1939); Murphy, "Civil Liberties," radio address, March 27, 1939, 8, 7, POF.

19. Klinkner and Smith, *Unsteady March*, 193. For other decisions in which the Court appears to have been affected by the threat of dictatorship, see *United States v. Curtis-Wright*, 299 U.S. 304 (1936); and *Wickard v. Filburn*, 317 U.S. 111 (1942). For a fuller discussion of this point, see Bixby, "Roosevelt Court, Democratic Ideology, and Minority Rights." Also see my discussion of *Carolene Products* in chap. 1, note 50.

20. Smith quoted in Leuchtenburg, "Election of 1936," 2832; Glass quoted in Keyssar, *Right to Vote*, 112.

21. *Humphrey's Executor v. United States*, 295 U.S. 602 (1935); Alsop and Catledge, *168 Days*, 14; Ickes, *Secret Diary*, 1:374.

22. Harrison, "Breakup of the Roosevelt Court," 17; and Goldman, *Picking Federal Judges*, 17, 360, 3. See also Harrison's article, "Breakup of the Roosevelt Supreme Court."

23. This figure includes Van Devanter's retirement on June 2, 1937. The others are as follows: Sutherland's retirement on January 17, 1938; Cardozo's death on July 9, 1938; Brandeis's retirement on January 30, 1939; Butler's death on November 16, 1939; McReynolds's retirement on January 31, 1941; and Hughes's retirement on July 1, 1941.

24. A Roosevelt-southern split was at its widest between the summer of 1937 — with the defeat of the Court-packing plan — and 1940, when international concerns began to take prominence over domestic issues.

25. The nine are as follows: Hugo L. Black (1937); Stanley F. Reed (1938); Felix Frankfurter (1939); William O. Douglas (1939); Frank Murphy (1940); James F. Byrnes (1941); Harlan F. Stone elevated to Chief Justice (1941); Robert H. Jackson (1941); and Wiley B. Rutledge (1943). Rutledge replaced Byrnes, who served for just over a year.

26. Walter White supported all but Jimmy Byrnes. The organization, however, also opposed Hugo Black.

27. Figures were compiled from table 4-2 in Epstein et al., *Supreme Court Compendium*, 180–92.

28. Douglas quoted in Harrison, "Breakup of the Roosevelt Court," 298.

29. Irving Brant, quoted in Harrison, "Breakup of the Roosevelt Supreme Court," 173. According to Harrison, Brant greatly influenced FDR on his Supreme Court nominations (173).

30. Harrison, "Breakup of the Roosevelt Court," 17.

31. Murphy "Notes on Conference with President," December 9, 1939, quoted in Fine, *Frank Murphy: The Washington Years*, 134 (emphasis added).

32. Roosevelt, "Address on Constitution Day," September 17, 1937, *Public Papers and Addresses, 1937*, 365–66. The editors at the *St. Louis Star-Times* noted that FDR's speech "will rank as one of the most notable utterances ever made on our charter of government. . . . it marks the beginning of a campaign to marshal public opinion behind a true interpretation of the Constitution — a public opinion so clear and dominant that no Supreme Court will dare set its will in opposition to the course of history" ("President's Address," September 20, 1937).

33. Jackson, *Struggle for Judicial Supremacy*, 284–85.

34. Recall that Justice Willis Van Devanter announced his retirement from the Court on May 18, 1937. He officially left the Court on June 2, 1937.

35. Alsop and Catledge, *168 Days*, 301.

36. *Time*, quoted in Ball, *Hugo L. Black*, 93; Ickes, *Secret Diary*, 2:196.

37. Smith's and Maryland's Millard Tydings's refusal to vote, however, displayed special significance. Both had just voted on a motion to recommit the nomination to the Judiciary Committee (Tydings in favor, Smith opposed). Thus, while present, neither could bear to vote either for or against Black (*Congressional Record*, August 17, 1937, 9102–3).

38. Black's speech, "Reorganization of the Federal Judiciary," quoted in Harrison, "Breakup of the Roosevelt Court," 95–96; David Lawrence of the *Chicago Tribune* quoted in Leuchtenburg, *Supreme Court Reborn*, 186.

39. Ball, *Hugo L. Black*, 100, 102–3; White quoted in Ball, *Hugo L. Black*, 100–101, 103. See also W. White, *A Man Called White*, 177.

40. Shannon, "Presidential Politics in the South, I," 146, 149; and Leuchtenburg, *Supreme Court Reborn*, 187.

41. The Deep South is traditionally understood as the part of the South where plantation life (and slavery) thrived. Although at times this area crosses state borders, it has historically been defined by the following six states: Louisiana, Mississippi, Alabama, Georgia, South Carolina, and (northern) Florida. However, more recent accounts have excluded Florida since its black population was the smallest of the six, and its politics has been more often shaped by nonsouthern sources than by the consequences of plantation life. See Black and Black, *Politics and Society in the South*, 12–15.

42. Some accounts, among them the U.S. Census, include both Kentucky and Oklahoma as part of the South. See Katznelson, Geiger, and Kryder, "Limiting Liberalism," 284.

43. Zangrando, *NAACP Crusade against Lynching*, 146.

44. See, for example, Ickes, *Secret Diary*, 2:153.

45. As Ickes put it in the midst of the Court-packing battle: "Some southern leaders affect to believe that an enlarged and more liberal Court would lift from the southern Negro some of the weight of oppression that he has carried since the Civil War" (ibid., 153).

46. *Congressional Record,* January 10, 1938, 253–57 (emphasis added).

47. Robertson, *Sly and Able,* 200, 285. Byrnes quoted in *Congressional Record,* January 1, 1938, 310 (emphasis added). For instance, as Senator Harry Truman of Missouri told southerners: "You know I'm against this bill . . . but the Negro vote in Kansas City and St. Louis is too important" (Swain, *Pat Harrison,* 205).

48. Russell, *Congressional Record,* January 11, 1938, 311; Bilbo quoted in Klinkner and Smith, *Unsteady March,* 133.

49. Robertson, *Sly and Able,* 284. For more on the South's attitude toward anti-lynching legislation, see Rable, "The South and the Politics of Antilynching Legislation."

50. Milkis, *The President and the Parties,* 89–90; Roosevelt, *Complete Presidential Press Conferences,* 11:245.

51. Patterson, *Congressional Conservatism and the New Deal,* 205–6.

52. "Reed's Addresses Show Liberal View," *New York Times,* January 16, 1938; Department of Justice colleague quoted in "Stanley Reed Goes to Supreme Court; Known as Liberal," *New York Times,* January 16, 1938; McCune, *Nine Young Men,* 62; Barkley quoted in "Both Parties Join in Praise of Reed," *New York Times,* January 16, 1938; Minton and Connally quoted in "Stanley Reed Goes to Supreme Court." See also "Lewis Wood, "Hard-Working Lawyer Joins the High Court," *New York Times,* January 30, 1938; and Harrison's chapter on Reed, in "Breakup of the Roosevelt Court," 110–33.

53. Roosevelt, *Public Papers and Addresses, 1938,* 399.

54. Shannon, "Presidential Politics in the South, I," 151–52.

55. Ibid., 151; Sitkoff, *New Deal for Blacks,* 134.

56. Shannon, "Presidential Politics in the South, I," 152; Pepper quoted in Lawson, *Black Ballots,* 63. See also Key, *Southern Politics,* 603–8. Moreover, in *To Secure These Rights,* the President's Committee on Civil Rights quotes a speech delivered on the floor of the House of Representatives on July 21, 1947: "In the Presidential elections of 1944, 10 percent of the potential voters voted in the seven poll-tax states, as against 49 percent in the free-vote states. In the congressional elections of 1946, the figures are 5 percent for the poll-tax states as compared with 33 percent for the free-voting states" (*To Secure These Rights,* 39).

57. Quotes appear in Sitkoff, *New Deal for Blacks,* 134; and Lawson, *Black Ballots,* 57. When Mississippi Senator Pat Harrison challenged the president on his statements, however, Roosevelt backtracked, saying that he was speaking only to the state effort, not the national attempt to abolish the tax through an act of Congress.

58. Shannon, "Presidential Politics in the South, I," 159, 164.

59. "Bloody Harlan Reforms," *Nation,* August 6, 1938, 121; see also "Harlan on Trial," *New Republic,* July 6, 1938, 242–44.

60. Milkis, *The President and the Parties,* 87. On FDR's failure to side with more liberal Democrats in northern primaries, see ibid., 87–88.

61. Roosevelt, *Public Papers and Addresses, 1938,* 168, 401, 418; Costigan quoted in Klinkner and Smith, *Unsteady March,* 138.

62. Roosevelt, *Public Papers and Addresses, 1938,* 464; Milkis, *The President and the Parties,* 88.

63. Smith's CIO quote in Milkis, *The President and the Parties,* 91; George quoted in Brinkley, "New Deal and Southern Politics," 108; Catledge, *My Life and the Times,* 104. In at least one speech, George also noted: "When Walter White sat

in the Senate gallery for nearly six long weeks directing the parliamentary maneu-vers on the floor of the Senate, I know you did not want me to follow Walter White's direction" (Moon, *Balance of Power*, 27).

64. Smith quoted in Brinkley, "New Deal and Southern Politics," 108; and in Robertson, *Sly and Able*, 194. Robertson, *Sly and Able*, 193.

65. Robertson, *Sly and Able*, 277, 276.

66. Shannon, "Presidential Politics in the South, II," 293–94.

67. Brinkley, "New Deal and Southern Politics," 108–9 (including quote from *Atlanta Constitution*).

68. Shannon, "Presidential Politics in the South, I," 151; Shannon, "Presidential Politics in the South, II," 289; Robertson, *Sly and Able*, 276; and Shannon, "Presidential Politics in the South, II," 285.

69. Catledge continued: "It cannot be said definitely now that the new manage-ment of the Democratic party has any definite designs toward re-enfranchising Southern Negroes or interfering in the South's segregation laws. It can be reported, however, that the politicians seeking to defend themselves against the 'purge' are shouting the possibilities and citing evidence which, apparently, is carrying convic-tion to many that white supremacy has returned as a political issue in the South" ("'White Supremacy' Issue Revived in the South," *New York Times*, August 28, 1938).

70. Abraham, *Justices, Presidents, and Senators*, 167.

71. Harrison, "Breakup of the Roosevelt Court," 135–36. As Harrison explains, the Bisbee deportations revolved around a strike by copper workers "at mines throughout Arizona in the summer of 1917. In the town of Bisbee, an armed force of vigilantes, backed by mine officials, kidnapped over a thousand strikers and left them in the desert without food or water." Tom Mooney "was convicted of planting a bomb which killed nineteen people who were attending a 'Preparedness Day' parade in July, 1916. After Mooney was sentenced to death, the key witness for the prosecution was found to have perjured himself, and Frankfurter urged President Woodrow Wil-son to bring pressure on state officials to grant Mooney a new trial. Mooney's death sentence was commuted to life imprisonment, but he remained behind bars for twenty-two years until he was pardoned in January, 1939—just two days after Frank-furter's Supreme Court appointment was announced" (136).

72. Frankfurter, *Felix Frankfurter Reminisces*, 246; Hugh Johnson, "Felix Frank-furter," *Fortune*, 12 (1936): 63.

73. See, for instance, Douglas, *Go East, Young Man*, 324–25.

74. Frankfurter was perhaps the most identifiable adherent of the "objective" ap-proach of legal realism. It fit well with his belief that the United States needed to move beyond the settlement of political issues based on "feeling and rhetoric." To Frankfurter, such "blind guides" worked "only [to] distract and confuse." Since the leading political issues of the day were "deeply enmeshed in intricate and technical facts," the decision-making process needed to "be extricated from presupposition and partisanship" (*The Public and Its Government*, 151–52). In this sense, his ap-proach fits under latter-day "big tent" definitions of legal realism. Such a definition, as William Fisher, Morton Horwitz, and Thomas Reed explain, includes those who contributed to the realist agenda by calling into question "three related ideals cher-ished by most Americans: the notion that, in the United States, the people (not un-elected judges) select the rules by which they are governed; the conviction that the institution of judicial review reinforces rather than undermines representative

democracy; and the faith that ours is a government of laws, not men." While some have criticized such broad definitions for including too many legal scholars and reducing realism into mere antiformalism, they are useful for understanding the role of realist ideas in the New Deal (*American Legal Realism,* 26). See also Schlegel, *American Legal Realism and Empirical Social Science;* and Kalman, *Strange Career of Legal Liberalism.*

75. Ernest Lindley, "Symbolic Trio," *Washington Post,* January 8, 1939.

76. Sitkoff, *New Deal for Blacks,* 66.

77. See Harrison, "Breakup of the Roosevelt Court," 164–67.

78. Abraham, *Justices, Presidents, and Senators,* 170; Harrison, "Breakup of the Roosevelt Court," 174.

79. *Newsweek* quoted in Harrison, 452; Borah quoted in Abraham, *Justices, Presidents, and Senators,* 170; Douglas, *Go East, Young Man,* 461–62.

80. Ickes, *Secret Diary,* 2:594. The four Republicans who cast their votes against Douglas's confirmation believed him to be a "reactionary tool of Wall Street" (Abraham, *Justices, Presidents, and Senators,* 171).

81. Quoted in Harrison, "Breakup of the Roosevelt Court," 193.

82. Ibid., 193–94.

83. Fine, *Frank Murphy: The Washington Years,* 138–39. According to Woodford Howard, Jr., "Conservatives and Southern Democrats, showing signs of relief that Roosevelt's fifth appointment was not worse, echoed the line that the independent-prone Murphy was the right man for the right place" (*Mr. Justice Murphy,* 217). See also, U.S. Senate Committee on the Judiciary, *Supreme Court of the United States* (vol. 4 for Murphy).

84. FDR quoted in Robertson, *Sly and Able,* 274; Smith quoted in Howard, *Mr. Justice Murphy,* 193; Harrison, "Breakup of the Roosevelt Court," 160.

85. Harrison, "Breakup of the Roosevelt Court," 216. See also Abraham, *Justices, Presidents, and Senators,* 133–34.

86. Byrnes, *All in One Lifetime,* 130.

87. Robertson, *Sly and Able,* 293–94.

88. Ibid., 295; Byrnes, *All in One Lifetime,* 130.

89. Ickes, *Secret Diary,* 3:417; Abraham, *Justices, Presidents, and Senators,* 174; Ickes, *Secret Diary,* 3:426, 471. Given Ickes's description, it is possible — even likely — that Walter White wrote the memo Hopkins showed him in April 1941. See note 90 below.

90. Robertson, *Sly and Able,* 297, 298–99. White sent several messages to the president protesting a potential Byrnes appointment. See correspondence from White to FDR on March 16, 1941; March 17, 1941; and June 12, 1941, in POF.

91. Harrison, "Breakup of the Roosevelt Court," 217, 193.

92. Harrison, "Breakup of the Roosevelt Court," 226.

93. Robertson, *Sly and Able,* 290.

94. Gerhart, *America's Advocate,* 229; Ickes, *Secret Diary,* 3:542.

95. Hughes also stressed that if the president accepted his advice that he promote from within the Court, he should choose Stone. Frankfurter recommended Stone to FDR as well.

96. *United States v. Carolene Products Co.,* 304 U.S. 144 (1938).

97. Harrison, "Breakup of the Roosevelt Court," 248–49, 262–63 (emphasis added).

98. Robert Jackson, "Call for a Liberal Bar," delivered to the National Lawyers Guild in Washington, February 20, 1938, DOJ Files.

99. Byrnes officially resigned on October 3, 1942. See Epstein et al., *Supreme Court Compendium*, 302.

100. Harrison, "Breakup of the Roosevelt Court," 288, 290–91; Biddle, *In Brief Authority*, 193. See also "Memorandum for the Attorney General," author unknown, November 12, 1942, FBP.

101. Ironically, Hand outlived Rutledge by twelve years. After serving another twenty years on the Court of Appeals and cementing his reputation as one of the great American judges who never made it to the Supreme Court, he died at the age of eighty-nine.

102. FDR, quoted in McCune, *Nine Young Men*, 200; Douglas, *Go East, Young Man*, 329–30.

103. Gunther, *Learned Hand*, 562, 563.

104. *Minersville School District v. Gobitis*, 310 U.S. 586 (1940) (Roberts also joined the majority opinion); *Jones v. Opelika*, 316 U.S. 584, 623–24 (1942).

105. Stone also favored Hand, but not strongly enough to exclude Rutledge from his short list.

106. Gunther, *Learned Hand*, 562.

107. Rotnem and Folsom, "Recent Restrictions upon Religious Liberty," 1061.

108. In the "worst of the three assaults," however, an information was filed resulting in a second trial conviction (ibid., 1061). The Justice Department also successfully prosecuted two West Virginia officers of the law in 1942 for section 52 violations [*Catlette v. United States*, F.2d 902 (4th Cir. 1943)]. On further CRS maneuvering to enhance its activities in this field, see Elliff, "United States Department of Justice and Individual Rights," 183–88.

109. Rotnem and Folsom, "Recent Restrictions upon Religious Liberty," 1062–64.

110. *West Virginia State Board of Education v. Barnette*, 319 U.S. 624, 641 (1943). While abuses against Jehovah's Witnesses did continue immediately after this decision, they ended a short time later. According to David Manwaring, the CRS "must receive almost all of the credit for finally putting an end to the rash of anti-Witness activity" (*Render unto Caesar*, 186).

111. *West Virginia State Board of Education v. Barnette*, 319 U.S. 624, 647 (1943). On the division within the Roosevelt Court, see Hirsch, *Enigma of Felix Frankfurter*, 176; and Simon, *Antagonists*, 118–19.

112. *Korematsu v. United States*, 323 U.S. 214 (1944). On the conflict between the War Department and the Justice Department over Japanese internment, see Irons, *Justice at War*. In chap. 3, Irons discusses Justice's "surrender" during the evacuation debate.

113. As Mark Tushnet writes, "most of the justices who served on the Court in the early 1940s were personally sympathetic, to varying degrees, to the legal positions asserted by the NAACP, and none had strong objections based in constitutional theory to acting in a manner consistent with their inclinations" (*Making Civil Rights Law*, 70). On the Roosevelt administration's close relationship with the ACLU, see Auerbach, *Labor and Liberty*, chap. 9.

CHAPTER FIVE

1. Victor Rotnem, the CRS's wartime chief, changed the name of the Civil Liberties Unit (CLU) to the Civil Rights Section when he became its chief in 1941. For the purposes of consistency, I have retained the name Civil Rights Section (CRS) throughout.

2. *Missouri ex rel. Gaines v. Canada*, 305 U.S. 337 (1938); Irons, "Politics and Principle," 705; Fine, quoting Robert Jackson and *Detroit News*, in *Frank Murphy: The Washington Years*, 16. For a description of some of the individuals in the "new" Justice Department, see "The Cabinet," *Time*, August 28, 1939, 14–17.

3. White and Baldwin quoted in Fine, *Frank Murphy: The Washington Years*, 80, 82 (dates of letters are February 7, 1939, and May 16, 1939, respectively). Years later, Roger Baldwin noted: "The ACLU's golden era was during the Roosevelt administration. No question about it. The office was stacked with our friends and supporters. Frank Roosevelt was very much aware of civil rights and civil liberties and the kind of staff he picked was too. . . . Name them, they were our friends" (Lamson, *Roger Baldwin*, 255–56).

Members of labor and their allies also noted their approval. The CIO's Lee Pressman called the creation of the CRS a "momentous step" (Fine, *Frank Murphy: The Washington Years*, 80). Editors at the *New Republic* noted: "To those of us who remember Attorney General A. Mitchell Palmer and his Red-hunts, it will be a novel and pleasing sight to watch federal agents tracking down anti-union employers" (*New Republic*, March 8, 1939, 129).

4. Murphy to Roosevelt, July 7, 1939, DOJ Files (emphasis added); memo from Turner Smith to Douglas McGregor, Assistant to the Attorney General, June 3, 1947, reprinted in Belknap, *Justice Department Civil Rights Policies prior to 1960*, 110–12. After interviewing Murphy in 1945, Robert K. Carr concluded, "the creation of a civil liberties unit at that particular moment was [Murphy's] idea and his alone" (*Federal Protection of Civil Rights*, 25). Given Murphy's penchant as a self-promoter, however, it would have surprised few in Washington if he took for full credit for a development where only partial credit was due; see, for example, Howard, *Mr. Justice Murphy*, 187, 225–28.

5. Landsberg, *Enforcing Civil Rights*, 9.

6. Murphy to Roosevelt, July 7, 1939, DOJ Files, 7; second Murphy quote appears in Carr, *Federal Protection of Civil Rights*, 24.

7. On the importance of the CRS's efforts with regard to peonage and involuntary servitude, see Goluboff, "Thirteenth Amendment and the Lost Origins of Civil Rights." See also McMahon, "Coalition-Building and Constitutional Visions." While Goluboff's more recent work focuses on the Thirteenth Amendment, she reaches conclusions similar to mine about the importance of the "developments of the 1940s" to "understanding *Brown's* meaning" and of the Civil Rights Section "to understanding emerging conceptions of civil rights in the 1940s" (1613).

8. Sections 51 and 52 are now sections 241 and 242, respectively, of title 18 of the U.S. Code.

9. In full, section 51 reads: "If two or more persons conspire to injure, oppress, threaten, or intimidate any citizen in the free exercise or enjoyment of any right or privilege secured to him by the Constitution or laws of the United States, or because of his having so exercised the same, or if two or more persons go in disguise on the highway, or on the premises of another, with intent to prevent or hinder his free exercise or enjoyment of any right or privilege so secured, they shall be fined not more than $5,000 and imprisoned not more than ten years, and shall, moreover, be thereafter ineligible to any office, or place of honor, profit, or trust created by the Constitution or laws of the United States."

10. Carr, *Federal Protection of Civil Rights*, 70. For a detailed discussion of the

origins of and court action on sections 51 and 52, see Carr, *Federal Protection of Civil Rights*, 56–77. See also Schweinhaut, "Civil Liberties Section of the Department of Justice"; and Rogge, "Justice and Civil Liberties."

11. In full, section 52 reads: "Whoever, under color of any law, statute, ordinance, regulation, or custom, willfully subjects, or causes to be subjected, any inhabitant of any State, Territory, or District to the deprivation of any rights, privileges, or immunities secured or protected by the Constitution and laws of the United States, or to different punishments, pains, or penalties, on account of such inhabitant being an alien, or by reason of his color, or race, than are prescribed for the punishment of citizens, shall be fined not more than $1,000, or imprisoned not more than one year, or both."

12. Carr, *Federal Protection of Civil Rights*, 71, 76.

13. Department of Justice Circular no. 3356, suppl. no. 1, 17, DOJ Files-FDR, reprinted in Belknap, *Justice Department Civil Rights Policies prior to 1960*, 12–51.

14. *Gitlow v. New York*, 268 U.S. 652 (1925); *United States v. Carolene Products Co.*, 304 U.S. 144 (1938).

15. Biddle, *In Brief Authority*, 154–55.

16. Murphy, "Test of Patriotism," 169–70.

17. In obvious reference to the La Follette Committee and the larger movement seeking to secure civil rights and liberties throughout the nation, Smith also reaffirmed his commitment to a particular view of the Constitution: "May my right arm forget its cunning, and my tongue cleave to the roof of my mouth, if I ever by vote, word, or act cast aspersions upon that instrument, or bow down to the interpretation of it which is now advocated in some quarters" (Smith, *Congressional Record*, August 4, 1939, 11052).

18. In the end, funding for a committee investigation of California farm labor came through only after direct intervention from the president. Writing to Byrnes, Roosevelt asserted: "From the point of view of the preservation of civil liberties, I recommend it [the appropriation for the California investigation] strongly — and from the point of view of good politics, I recommend it equally strongly. Can I make a stronger statement to you?" (Roosevelt to Byrnes, July 26, 1939, POF). The President's recommendation may have saved this investigation, but did not stop Byrnes from cutting the amount from $100,000 to $50,000. The California investigation was the last for the La Follette Committee (Auerbach, *Labor and Liberty* 171–73, 184; Byrnes, *Congressional Record*, July 17, 1939, 12907–8).

19. John Rankin, "Gestapo Practices of the Department of Justice," *Congressional Record*, March 24, 1943, A1396.

20. Chief defense counsel Earle Wingo, quoted in Spencer R. McCulloch, "Last 3 Lynching Trial Defendants Acquitted by Jury in Quick Verdict," *St. Louis Post-Dispatch*, April 24, 1943, 8A.

21. Walter White, "U.S. Department of (White) Justice," *Crisis*, October 1935, 309–10.

22. *United States v. Classic*, 313 U.S. 299 (1941). On suffrage restrictions more generally, see Elliot, *Rise of Guardian Democracy*.

23. Quote appears in Carr, *Federal Protection of Civil Rights*, 86.

24. *Newberry v. United States*, 256 U.S. 232 (1921). On hearing of the situation in Louisiana, where the initial indictments had been dismissed by a judge, FDR scribbled one of his famous short notes. It read: "Jackson, send some men" (Memo from

"Pa" [Edwin M. Watson] to Jackson, October 10, 1940). Jackson responded: "We are testing the matter in the Supreme Court by appealing Judge Borah's decision, but meanwhile until we can reverse the Newberry case, we are at a standstill on primary elections" (Jackson to Roosevelt, October 18, 1940, RHJP).

25. *Grovey v. Townsend,* 295 U.S. 45 (1935).

26. Brief for the United States, March 1941, 46.

27. *United States v. Classic,* 313 U.S. at 316, 321. Stone relied on *Ex parte Yarbrough* (the Ku Klux Cases), 110 U.S. 651 (1884); and *United States v. Mosley,* 238 U.S. 383 (1915).

28. *United States v. Classic,* 313 U.S. at 326; Carr, *Federal Protection of Civil Rights,* 90. Marshall quoted in Hine, *Black Victory,* 206.

29. See Fine, *Frank Murphy: The Washington Years,* 188, 283, 396, 401; see also Carr, *Federal Protection of Civil Rights,* 91–92.

30. *United States v. Classic,* 313 U.S. at 331, 336, 337, 341. On the breakup, see Harrison, "Breakup of the Roosevelt Court"; Pritchett, *Roosevelt Court;* and Urofsky, *Division and Discord.* But also see Shapiro, "Supreme Court," 188–94.

31. *United States v. Classic,* 313 U.S. at 332. After a year's delay, the Justice Department accepted a plea of *nolo contendere* to the section 52 count in the indictment and agreed to drop all other counts. In November 1942, all five defendants were fined a total of $940, given suspended jail sentences, and placed on probation for five years (Carr, *Federal Protection of Civil Rights,* 93).

32. Biddle, *In Brief Authority,* 187; Lawson, *Black Ballots,* 42. Herbert Wechsler, who played a substantial role in writing the government's brief in *Classic* and in arguing the case before the Court, also advised against filing an *amicus curiae* brief (see Kluger, *Simple Justice,* 234–35).

33. Memo from John B. O'Brien to Rotnem, "Matters involving Negro victims handled during the past year," n.d. (received by Rotnem on August 7, 1943), 4, FBP.

34. Folsom, "Federal Elections and the 'White Primary,'" 1033; Lawson, *Black Ballots,* 43; *Brief for Petitioner, Smith v. Allwright,* October Term, 1943. In a December 1, 1944, speech to the National Bar Association, CRS chief Victor Rotnem also commended Marshall's and Hastie's work in *Smith v. Allwright,* noting: "Among your members tonight are found the two men who admittedly made the best presentation of a case before the Supreme Court in the 1943 term. I refer to the argument in the great case of *Smith v. Allwright* which won for Negroes an all important legal victory in their long struggle for the first class citizenship which can belong only to those who have free access to the ballot box." Rotnem added: "[I]t is now my profound hope that these same two gentlemen will be equally convincing in a case now before the court, *Screws v. United States,* in which the constitutionality of one of the most important aspects of the Civil Rights Statutes is being challenged and in which the N.A.A.C.P. has ranged itself at the side of the government in a brief amicus" (Rotnem, "Enforcement of Civil Rights," 1–2).

35. Stone to Reed, April 5, 1944, FFP-HLS.

36. Jackson to Stone, January 17, 1944, FFP-HLS. Frankfurter disagreed with the logic in Reed's opinion, arguing that *Classic* should not be relied on to overturn *Grovey.* Instead, he thought the Court should simply state, "without any pussyfooting," that it had reached a different conclusion based on "a compelling regard for the Constitution as a dynamic scheme of government" (memorandum on *Smith v. All-*

wright; concurring opinion of Frankfurter, 1, FFP-HLS). In the end, however, he decided against issuing his separate one-and-a-half page concurring opinion.

37. The NAACP's campaign to enforce *Allwright* began on the same day the Court handed down its decision. Writing to Attorney General Biddle, Thurgood Marshall urged the department "to enforce the criminal statutes of the United States and to prosecute vigorously persons who deny to others rights guaranteed under the constitution and laws of the United States, especially the right to vote" (Marshall to Biddle, April 3, 1944, 2). See also Marshall to Biddle, May 11, 1944, in which the NAACP attorney urges "prompt action" (NAACP Papers, Legal File, *Smith v. Allwright* [*Texas Primary*]). An internal Justice Department memo noted that "intense pressure has been directed towards the Department by the [NAACP], the March on Washington Movement, the Workers Defense league, the [ACLU], and the Negro press, in order to encourage prosecution by it under the criminal civil rights statutes" ("Memorandum Re Cases Involving Negro Voting and Those Involving the Killing of Negro Soldiers," n.d., 5–6, FFP).

38. Carr, *Federal Protection of Civil Rights*, 177–78.

39. Jonathan Daniels, the North Carolinian advisor to the president on race, speaking of the possibility of similar departmental action in Alabama, quoted in Lawson, *Black Ballots*, 47; Biddle to Roosevelt, January 29, 1943, FBP. According to Lawson, "Biddle said he feared that massive Justice Department intervention on behalf of disfranchised blacks would prompt bigoted whites to ignite a 'terrible conflagration' in the South" (364 n. 97). On the March on Washington Movement, see Bates, *Pullman Porters and the Rise of Protest Politics in Black America*.

40. Carroll Kilpatrick, "Will the South Secede?" *Harper's Magazine*, March 1943, 414–21, 415.

41. Frederickson, *Dixiecrat Revolt and the End of the Solid South*, 39–40.

42. Justice Department document, "Memorandum Re Cases Involving Negro Voting and Those Involving the Killing of Negro Soldiers," n.d., 5–6, FFP.

43. Victor Rotnem, "Statement in the Confidential Proceedings of the President's Committee on Civil Rights, April 3, 1947," reprinted in Belknap, *Presidential Committees and White House Conferences* (quote appears on p. 72 of the document, p. 89 in Belknap).

44. According to Lawson, Folsom "offered a few minor suggestions, but 'on the whole [he] liked the . . . brief'" (*Black Ballots*, 50). The NAACP's arguments convinced District Court Judge J. Waties Waring to grant a black voter, George Elmore, a declaratory judgment against party officials who prevented him from participating in the Democratic primary and to issue an injunction against the future exclusion of African American voters.

45. *Breedlove v. Suttles*, 302 U.S. 277 (1937); Jackson to Aubrey Williams of the National Youth Administration, May 31, 1939, 2, RHJP. Attorney General Frank Murphy, however, disagreed with this interpretation of *Breedlove* in a letter to Eleanor Roosevelt (June 29, 1939, DOJ Files).

46. *Pirtle v. Brown*, 314 U.S. 621 (1942).

47. Lawson, *Black Ballots*, 55, 58; Ralph Bunche quoted in Swain, *Pat Harrison*, 209.

48. When war began, many southern state legislatures decided to loosen their poll tax requirements, while still discriminating against African Americans in the voting process. Georgia abolished its tax in 1945.

49. Quotes appear in Lawson, *Black Ballots*, 70, 55; and Sitkoff, *New Deal for Blacks*, 134. FDR quoted in Sitkoff, *New Deal for Blacks*, 134.

50. The complete version of the memo appears in Biddle, *In Brief Authority*, 197–98.

51. Ibid., 198–99.

52. *Harper v. Virginia Board of Elections*, 383 U.S. 663 (1966).

53. In Biddle, *In Brief Authority* (no name or date given), 155–56.

54. Quoted in Bunche, *Political Status of the Negro in the Age of FDR*, 389.

55. Rotnem, "Federal Civil Right 'Not to Be Lynched,'" 57; "Sikeston Inquiry Seeks to Identify Men in Lynching," *St. Louis Post-Dispatch*, January 26, 1942, 1; Coleman, "Freedom from Fear on the Home Front," 415; see also Capeci, "Lynching of Cleo Wright."

56. Roosevelt, *Public Papers and Addresses, 1940*, 672; radio reports quoted in Rotnem, "Federal Civil Right 'Not to Be Lynched,'" 57.

57. Coleman, "Freedom from Fear on the Home Front," 416. Coleman actually uses a different meaning of the freedom from fear than the president originally articulated. Coleman loosely defines it in the following terms: "the right of individuals to be secure in their persons and to have their liberty, unless taken by due process of law" (416). President Roosevelt said the phrase, "translated into world terms, means a world wide reduction of armaments to such a point and in such a thorough fashion that no nation will be in a position to commit an act of physical aggression against any neighbor—anywhere in the world" (*Public Papers and Addresses, 1940*, 672).

58. Biddle quoted in Rotnem, "Federal Civil Right 'Not to Be Lynched,'" 58. See also Berge to Biddle, February 10, 1942, WBP.

59. Elliff, "United States Department of Justice and Individual Rights," 147; Capeci, "Lynching of Cleo Wright," 872. Biddle also considered "our campaign for the Negroes" as one of his proudest accomplishments as attorney general (*In Brief Authority*, 169).

60. CRS staff member quoted in Elliff, "United States Department of Justice and Individual Rights," 137. There was also a discussion about whether to hire an African American attorney for the CRS (or some other part of the Criminal Division), but nothing ever came of it at the time. The three names proposed were Ben Dyett, Thurgood Marshall, and Charles Houston. (Houston did serve on Roosevelt's FEPC.) As Biddle put it, "I think we talk too much about 'Civil Liberties' and don't carry out when the chance affords" (Biddle to Wendell Berge, March 4, 1942). See also Berge to Clive Palmer, March 7, 1942, WBP; Berge to James Rowe, March 7, 1942, WBP; and Berge to James Rowe, May 21, 1942, WBP; Biddle to James Rowe, November 23, 1942, DOJ Files-FDR; and Rotnem to Rowe, December 8, 1942, DOJ Files-FDR.

61. Along with those quoted throughout this work, see Rotnem, "Criminal Enforcement of Federal Civil Rights," "Federal Criminal Jurisdiction of Labor's Civil Rights," and "Civil Rights during War"; Folsom, "Slave Trade Law in a Contemporary Setting"; and Meyers, "Federal Privileges and Immunities." To be sure, Merl E. Reed cites a document "from Rotnem's desk" that gives the impression he was a sharp critic of the FEPC, concerned that its activities stirred up racial animosity (*Seedtime for the Modern Civil Rights Movement*, 99–101; and Klinkner and Smith, *Unsteady March*, 178). However, the document was undated and unsigned.

62. Elliff also points to the appointment of Wendell Berge—replacing O. John

Rogge — as Assistant Attorney General in charge of the Criminal Division in December 1940, as a turning point for the CRS (Elliff, "United States Department of Justice and Individual Rights," 138). President Roosevelt likely inspired the decision to replace Rogge. On December 3, 1940, he wrote to Attorney General Jackson: "I have been getting a lot of complaints about our friend Rogge — that he is a self-seeker and that he is overbearing" (RHJP).

63. Justice Department Circular no. 3356, suppl. no. 2, April 4, 1942, DOJ Files-FDR, 1, 217–18 (this document is also reprinted in Belknap, *Justice Department Civil Rights Policies prior to 1960*, 64–86); *Schenck v. United States*, 249 U.S. 47 (1919).

64. Langbein quoted in Elliff, "United States Department of Justice and Individual Rights," 152 (emphasis added). See also *Ex parte Riggins*, 134 Fed. 404 (C.C.N.D. Ala. 1904).

65. Rotnem, "Federal Civil Right 'Not to Be Lynched,'" 64; Coleman, "Freedom from Fear on the Home Front," 426; *Powell v. United States*, 212 U.S. 564 (1909).

66. The CRS was also bolstered by an earlier lower court decision which upheld its legal theories in a police brutality prosecution: *United States v. Sutherland*, 37 F. Supp. 344 (N.D. Ga. 1940).

67. "Summary of activity in the field of Civil Rights enforcement," 1942, quoted in Elliff, "United States Department of Justice and Individual Rights," 154.

68. Carr, *Federal Protection of Civil Rights*, 164; Coleman, "Freedom from Fear on the Home Front," 425–26. This "informal" order reaffirmed Attorney General Frank Murphy's 1939 commitment to the NAACP's Walter White to fully investigate all lynchings (Fine, *Frank Murphy: The Washington Years*, 89–90).

69. Quoted in Elliff, "United States Department of Justice and Individual Rights," 154, 155.

70. See Cobb, *Most Southern Place on Earth*. The description of Berge is from Elliff, "United States Department of Justice and Individual Rights," 138; Wendell Berge, "Civil Liberties after a Year of War," delivered at the annual meeting of the Chicago Civil Liberties Committee, January 23, 1943, 12, WBP.

71. Coleman, "Freedom from Fear on the Home Front," 426–27; Spencer R. McCulloch, "Two in Lynching Case Free on Lack of Identification," *St. Louis Post-Dispatch*, April 22, 1943, 1; Holder quoted in Carr, *Federal Protection of Civil Rights*, 170; Coleman's comments on Mississippi leaders quoted in Elliff, "United States Department of Justice and Individual Rights," 157. On the other hand, Coleman noted that in contrast to the *Jackson Daily News*, which "issued bitter editorials condemning the prosecution, . . . the press in other Southern states . . . tended to approve" the federal government's action (Elliff, "United States Department of Justice and Individual Rights," 157).

72. Chief defense counsel Earle Wingo, quoted in Spencer R. McCulloch, "Last 3 Lynching Trial Defendants Acquitted by Jury in Quick Verdict," *St. Louis Post-Dispatch*, April 24, 1943, 8A. To be sure, the U.S. Attorney, Toxey Hall, did not seek to attack white supremacy. Instead, he attempted to use it as an argument: "This is a white man's country, white men ruled the proceedings, a white judge presided, a white jury tried the Negro and a white Sheriff had him in charge." But by refusing to accept the jury's decision not to sentence Wash to death, the lynch mob had "undermine[d] the foundations of civilization" ("Trial for Lynching Goes to the Jury," *New York Times*, April 24, 1943, 28).

73. Coleman quoted in Elliff, "United States Department of Justice and Indi-

vidual Rights," 157–58; Mississippi attorney quoted in Carr, *Federal Protection of Civil Rights*, 171. Biddle did send a letter to Judge Sidney C. Mize commending him on his "charge to the jury" (Biddle to Mize, June 15, 1943; and Mize to Biddle, June 19, 1943, both DOJCD-FOIA).

74. Elliff, "United States Department of Justice and Individual Rights," 158; Carr, *Federal Protection of Civil Rights*, 172–73. See also Capeci, "Lynching of Cleo Wright," 872–73.

75. Carr, *Federal Protection of Civil Rights*, 172–73; Coleman, "Freedom from Fear on the Home Front," 416.

76. Coleman summarized the possibilities of prosecution:

1. *A mob kills a person not in the custody of the state* — No basis for federal jurisdiction.

2. *A mob seizes a prisoner from state custody; state officers are not to blame* — prosecution possible under the theory attempted in the Sikeston Affair (section 51).

3. *A state officer conspires with a mob to lynch a prisoner, or actively assists the mob* — Prosecution possible under section 52.

4. *A state officer willfully, or through cowardice, fails to give his prisoner due protection* — Prosecution possible under section 52.

5. *A mob counsels or seeks to induce or procure a state officer to assist it, or withhold protection from the prisoner* — Section 52 combined with two other sections of the Civil Rights Acts (sections 88 and 550) form the basis of prosecution. This theory should reach practically all public lynchings.

6. *A mob seizes a prisoner from the custody of a federal marshal or other federal officer* — Here section 51 is authoritatively applicable. Logan v. United States, 144 U.S. 263.

7. *A posse, deputized or led by a state officer, kills its quarry without due process* — Section 52 is adequate. ("Freedom from Fear on the Home Front," 427–28)

77. *Screws v. United States*, 325 U.S. 91 (1945).

78. In this sense, as Elliff writes, "the decisions made by the [CRS] not to prosecute were as revealing as the cases prosecuted. Two policies guided the Section's choices. . . . [First,] certain *factual* requirements: a verified complaint from the victim [a change from the policy of initiating an investigation with only a written complaint], an 'aggravated' case, and a victim with a good record. . . . [Second,] the rule that it would not prosecute if *state or local authorities* acted" (Elliff, "United States Department of Justice and Individual Rights," 160–162, Elliff's emphasis).

79. Ibid., 287. See also Rotnem, "Enforcement of Civil Rights," 8.

80. Howard and Bushoven, "*Screws* Case Revisited," 624.

81. The facts of the case were compiled from the transcript of the trial that was submitted as part of the petition for *certiorari*, March 18, 1944, and from Carr, *Federal Protection of Civil Rights*; and Coleman, "Freedom from Fear on the Home Front." Quotes appear in Carr, *Federal Protection of Civil Rights*, 106; Coleman, "Freedom from Fear on the Home Front," 424; "Transcript of Record," 37; Coleman, "Freedom from Fear on the Home Front," 424; "Transcript of Record," 46; Coleman, "Freedom from Fear on the Home Front," 424; and "Transcript of Record," 83–84.

82. T. Hoyt Davis, United States Attorney, n.d. Georgia, letter to Rotnem, March 9, 1943, quoted in Elliff, "United States Department of Justice and Individual Rights," 163.

83. Wendell Berge, "Memo for the Attorney General," March 20, 1943, quoted in Elliff, "United States Department of Justice and Individual Rights," 163.

84. Section 88 of title 18 of the U.S. Code was at the time the general federal conspiracy statute. It read as follows: "If two or more persons conspire either to commit any offense against the United States, or to defraud the United States in any manner or for any purpose, and one or more of such parties do any act to effect the object of the conspiracy, each of the parties to such conspiracy shall be fined not more than $10,000, or imprisoned not more than two years, or both."

85. Quoted in Carr, *Federal Protection of Civil Rights*, 108–9.

86. Elliff, "United States Department of Justice and Individual Rights," 167.

87. *Screws v. United States*, 325 U.S. at 94.

88. Douglas added: "To enforce such a statute would be like sanctioning the practice of Caligula who 'published the law, but it was written in a very small hand, and posted up in a corner, so that no one could make a copy of it'" (ibid., 96).

89. Ibid., 97, 98, 97–98.

90. Ibid., 103, 105, 106.

91. Ibid., 138, 139.

92. Ibid., 140, 142.

93. Frankfurter to Rutledge, May 10, 1945, WBRP.

94. *Screws v. United States*, 325 U.S. at 147, 149–150.

95. As evidence of restraint, the Justice Department submitted the following figures: "Since 1939, the number of complaints received annually by the [CRS] has ranged from 8,000 to 14,000, but in no year have prosecutions under both sections [51 and 52] . . . exceeded 76. In the fiscal year 1943, for example, 31 full investigations of alleged violations of section [52] were conducted, and three cases were brought to trial. In the following fiscal year there were 55 such investigations, and prosecutions were instituted in 12 cases" (ibid., 159).

96. Ibid., 160.

97. See Howard and Bushoven, "*Screws* Case Revisited," 624–25.

98. *Screws v. United States*, 325 U.S. at 114.

99. Ibid., 117, 129, 119; *United States v. Mosley*, 238 U.S. at 386, 387.

100. *Screws v. United States*, 325 U.S. at 119–131, 137.

101. Carr, "*Screws v. United States*," 64.

102. Howard and Bushoven, "*Screws* Case Revisited," 633–34 (emphasis added). See also Cohen, "*Screws* Case."

103. Elliff, "Aspects of Federal Civil Rights Enforcement," 629–40. The new standard led to an acquittal in the second *Screws* trial, and Sheriff Screws went on to win election to the Georgia State Senate in 1958.

104. Urofsky, *Division and Discord*, 104. The NAACP had submitted an *amicus curiae* brief. See also, note 34 above.

105. Of the more than 150 civil rights bills that came before the Congress from 1937 to 1946—most dealing with the issues of lynching, the poll tax, and fair employment practices—not one passed. Many scholars and commentators point to FDR's failure to publicly support them as the chief reason for their demise.

106. As Peter Irons writes: "No single episode more dishonored the civil rights and

liberties record of the Roosevelt administration than the forced evacuation from the West Coast of 110,000 Americans of Japanese ancestry. The travail of this friendless and frightened minority began eleven weeks after the Japanese attack on Pearl Harbor, when Roosevelt signed Executive Order 9066 on February 19, 1942" ("Politics and Principle," 716). See also Irons, *Justice at War*; Robinson, *By Order of the President*.

107. See Morse, *While Six Million Died*; and Wyman, *Abandonment of the Jews*.

108. David L. Cohn, "How the South Feels," *Atlantic Monthly*, June 1944, 47–51, 49; Dixon quoted in Carroll Kilpatrick, "Will the South Secede?" *Harper's Magazine*, March 1943, 419.

CHAPTER SIX

1. Quoted in McCullough, *Truman*, 383.

2. As Truman writes in his memoirs: "Under the law, as matters now stood, the next man in line after me was the Secretary of State, Edward R. Stettinius, Jr. Stettinius, however, had never been a candidate for any elective office, and it was my feeling that any man who stepped into the presidency should have held at least some office to which he had been elected by a vote of the people. . . . Pending a change in the law, I felt it my duty to choose without too much delay a Secretary of State with proper qualifications to succeed, if necessary, to the presidency. At this time I regarded Byrnes as the man best qualified" (*Memoirs*, 1:22–23).

3. Egerton, *Speak Now against the Day*, 576–77; Borstelmann, "Jim Crow's Coming Out," 551–52. See also Borstelmann, *The Cold War and the Color Line*.

4. Dudziak, *Cold War Civil Rights*, 6; Layton, *International Politics and Civil Rights Policies in the United States*, 8.

5. Truman's 1947 State of the Union Address, January 6, 1947, *Public Papers of the Presidents, 1947*, 9; Truman's Special Message to the Congress on Civil Rights, February 2, 1948, *Public Papers of the Presidents, 1948*, 126.

6. *Smith v. Allwright*, 321 U.S. 649 (1944); *Brown v. Board of Education*, 347 U.S. 483 (1954). See also *Morgan v. Virginia*, 328 U.S. 373 (1946); *Shelley v. Kraemer*, 334 U.S. 1 (1948); *Sipuel v. Oklahoma*, 332 U.S. 631 (1948); *Sweatt v. Painter*, 339 U.S. 629 (1950); and *McLaurin v. Oklahoma State Regents*, 339 U.S. 637 (1950).

7. Truman, quoted in Robertson, *Sly and Able*, 388. On the selection of Truman as vice president, see Jonathan Daniels, "How Truman Got to Be President," *Look*, August 1, 1950, 29–33.

8. Frederickson, *Dixiecrat Revolt and the End of the Solid South*, 39.

9. On Truman's June 5, 1945, letter to Illinois Congressman Adolph J. Sabath regarding the FEPC, see Garson, *Democratic Party and the Politics of Sectionalism*, 137; Elliff, "Aspects of Federal Civil Rights Enforcement," 620.

10. Truman, quoted in McCullough, *Truman*, 403.

11. In his memoirs, Truman suggests that Biddle in fact supported the Clark appointment (*Memoirs*, 325).

12. Elliff, "United States Department of Justice and Individual Rights," 210; Clark quoted in Elliff, "Aspects of Federal Civil Rights Enforcement," 619.

13. Truman, *Memoirs*, 326; Elliff, "United States Department of Justice and Individual Rights," 211; G. O'Brien, *Color of Law*, 184.

14. Tom C. Clark, "Civil Rights," address to the Chicago Bar Association,

Chicago, Illinois, June 21, 1946, papers of Philleo Nash; reprinted in Merrill, *Truman Administration's Civil Rights Program*, vol. 11 of *Documentary History of the Truman Presidency*, 75–90, quotes appear on 78–80, 82, 85 (pages 3–5, 7, 10 in the original document). See also T. C. Clark, "Federal Prosecutor Looks at the Civil Rights Statutes."

15. On the FBI's attitude and actions, see Elliff, "United States Department of Justice and Individual Rights," 208–46.

16. Abraham, *Justices, Presidents, and Senators*, 182; Yalof, *Pursuit of Justices*, 23; Abraham, *Justices, Presidents, and Senators*, 182–83.

17. Yalof, *Pursuit of Justices*, 30; Abraham, *Justices, Presidents, and Senators*, 183. On the recommendations, see Yalof, *Pursuit of Justices*, 30–31.

18. See Pritchett, *Roosevelt Court*, 131.

19. Savage, *Truman and the Democratic Party*, 103.

20. Quoted in McCullough, *Truman*, 489.

21. The most notable outside pressure came in the fall of 1946 when "A National Emergency Committee Against Mob Violence, inspired by the NAACP and including labor and religious groups, visited the White House to urge President Truman to call Congress into special session to protect minority rights against violence and 'to initiate a study of the state of race relations in the country'" (Elliff, "Aspects of Federal Civil Rights Enforcement," 626).

22. According to Elliff, "David Bazelon, then Assistant Attorney General for the Lands Division, and Maceo Hubbard, the Section's first Negro attorney and a former member of the wartime FEPC staff" developed the idea. The CRS connection, however, did not end there. The committee's "staff director was to be Professor Robert K. Carr, who was completing his book [cited above] about the CRS based on an examination of Department files . . . [and was therefore] thoroughly familiar with the problems caused by the FBI's need to maintain good relations with local police" (Elliff, "Aspects of Federal Civil Rights Enforcement," 626–27).

23. President's Committee on Civil Rights, *To Secure These Rights*, vii.

24. Ibid., 79, 166, 82.

25. Ibid., 99, 106–7.

26. Ibid., 114. According to the committee, the CRS had at least six "imperfections": (1) "weak statutory tools," (2) "insufficient personnel," (3) "adequacy of cooperation by United States Attorneys," (4) "dependence upon the FBI for its investigative work," (5) "hostility of local officers and local communities," and (6) its "position in the Department of Justice" (114–25).

27. Elman, "Solicitor General's Office," 817–20. See also Kennedy, "Colloquy: A Reply to Philip Elman"; and Elman, "Response."

28. Elman, "Solicitor General's Office," 818 (emphasis added). Along with the influence of electoral politics, a flood of letters also helped persuade the administration file an *amicus curiae* brief in *Shelley v. Kraemer*. Elman explains:

Phineas Indritz, one of the unsung heroes of the civil rights movement [employed in the Department of the Interior, interested in moving "against discrimination against Indians" and "in his spare time doing research for the lawyers in the Supreme Court covenants cases"], . . . [and I] cooked up the idea that [Secretary of the Interior Oscar] Chapman should write to the Attorney General requesting the Department of Justice to file an *amicus* brief in

these cases. Indritz drafted the letter, Chapman signed it. . . . I had friends
working with the NAACP, the American Civil Liberties Union, the American
Jewish Congress, the American Jewish Committee, and other organizations.
Indritz and I got them to write letters to the President and Attorney General
urging the government to intervene in the Supreme Court. All of these letters
eventually came to me . . . it was a large impressive number. I also succeeded
in getting the State Department to send a letter to the Attorney General expressing concern over racial discrimination in the United States, how it im-
paired our foreign policy, and so on. These letters all came pouring in, and as
each came in I would show it to the Solicitor General, Philip Perlman. I then
wrote a formal memorandum recommending that the United States file an
amicus brief. (818)

29. Clark M. Clifford, "Confidential Memorandum for the President," November 19, 1947, papers of Clark M. Clifford; reprinted in Merrill, *Running from Behind*,
vol. 14 of *Documentary History of the Truman Presidency*, 62–104, quotes appear on
64, 67, 72, 73, 101 (on 3, 6, 11, 12, 40 in the original document).

30. "Democratic Platform," in Schlesinger, Israel, and Hansen, *History of American Presidential Elections, 1789–1968*, 4:2956; Moon, *Balance of Power*, 32; Frederickson, *Dixiecrat Revolt and the End of the Solid South*, 45; Moon, *Balance of Power*,
31. On the possibility of black voters switching back to the GOP, see Earl Brown,
"Negro Vote, 1944: A Forecast," *Harper's Magazine*, July 1944, 152–54.

31. Sitkoff, "Harry Truman and the Election of 1948," 613.

32. Truman, "Address in Harlem," October 11, 1952, *Public Papers of the Presidents, 1952–53*, 799.

33. Skowronek, *Politics Presidents Make*, 41.

34. But see Elliff, "United States Department of Justice and Individual Rights," 280.

35. See generally Berman, *Politics of Civil Rights in the Truman Administration*.

36. Elliff, "United States Department of Justice and Individual Rights," 275;
United States v. Williams, 341 U.S. 70 (1951); *Williams v. United States*, 341 U.S. 97
(1951); Elliff, "United States Department of Justice and Individual Rights," 294. See
also Putzel, "Federal Civil Rights Enforcement."

37. Quoted in Elliff, "United States Department of Justice and Individual Rights,"
326 (emphasis in original).

38. To help get his school equalization package through the South Carolina
state legislature, he told its members how as Secretary of State he had been "needled"
by Soviet Foreign Minister Vyacheslav Molotov "about racial trouble in Georgia
when the United States was protesting Soviet high-handedness and ruthlessness in
Eastern Europe" (quoted in Kluger, *Simple Justice*, 335).

39. See W. A. Clark, "An Analysis of the Relationship between Anti-
Communism and Segregationist Thought in the Deep South."

40. Elman, a major contributor to the civil rights briefs, certainly makes light of
the language. In discussing the *Shelley* case, he notes, "the brief we wrote contained
a lot of high-blown rhetoric about liberty and equality and so on, but it was also a
solid, lawyerlike job" ("Solicitor General's Office," 819).

41. Elliff, "United States Department of Justice and Individual Rights," 331;
Elman quoted in Kluger, *Simple Justice*, 560; Elman, "Solicitor General's Office,"
827, 828.

42. "Solicitor General's Office," 827. Elman continues: "This idea did not come . . . from Frankfurter . . . but it did grow out of my many conversations with him over a period of many months. He told me what he thought, what the other Justices were telling him they thought. I knew from him what their positions were" (828).

43. At least according to Frankfurter, "if the issue was inescapably presented in yes-or-no terms, he could not count five votes on the Court to overrule *Plessy*" (ibid., 828).

44. Tushnet, *Making Civil Rights Law*, 69; Ickes quoted in Abraham, *Justices, Presidents, and Senators*, 186; Kluger, *Simple Justice*, 269.

45. The comment on Minton's legislative career is from Henry A. Wallace, quoted in Yalof, *Pursuit of Justices*, 35; Kluger, *Simple Justice*, 269.

46. Truman, *Public Papers of the Presidents, 1952–1953*, 800.

47. Berman, *Politics of Civil Rights in the Truman Administration*, 231.

48. The Truman Justice Department joined the case on its own initiative.

49. Kluger, *Simple Justice*, 650; Burk, *Eisenhower Administration and Black Civil Rights*, 135.

50. This streak would stretch to five with Justice Jackson's death on October 9, 1954.

51. While many have told the story of Warren's appointment to the Court, I have relied most on Yalof's version, *Pursuit of Justices*, 44–50. The quote appears on 46.

52. Elman, "Solicitor General's Office," 835.

53. Anthony Lewis and Rankin quoted in Elliff, "United States Department of Justice and Individual Rights," 393. The Eisenhower Justice Department's participation in *Brown* must also be read in conjunction with the new administration's attitude toward the Civil Rights Section. Unlike its predecessor, which had increasingly diminished the CRS's role in advancing civil rights law (in favor of the Solicitor General's Office), the Eisenhower administration sought to provide the CRS a new vigor for enforcement. From 1953 to 1954, the CRS not only "developed a systematic outline of its broad policies — still within the legal limits of the *Screws* and *Williams* cases — for the first time in six years, but "began significantly more prosecutions than ever before, even though convictions and indictments were as difficult to win as ever" (341). In short, the CRS was no longer the "orphan" it had become in the final years of the Truman administration. Thus, while political pressures had clearly constrained the content of the *Brown* brief, Attorney General Brownell's commitment to reviving the CRS made a significant statement about the Eisenhower administration's interest in extending civil rights protection (the orphan quote is from Shad Polier, the spokesperson for a group of rights advocates who met with executives of the Eisenhower Justice Department; quoted by Elliff, 353.)

54. See Burk, *Eisenhower Administration and Black Civil Rights*, 137–40.

55. Skowronek, *Politics Presidents Make*, 43, 44.

CHAPTER SEVEN

1. Black, quoted in Tushnet, *Making Civil Rights Law*, 142.

2. Feeley and Rubin, *Judicial Policy Making and the Modern State*, 229; Walter White discussing *Ward v. Texas*, 316 U.S. 547 (1942), in *A Man Called White*, 267 (White mistakenly reports it as a rape rather than a murder case); Robertson, *Sly and Able*, 302. Along with *Ward v. Texas*, Byrnes authored *Edwards v. California*, 314 U.S.

160 (1941). The grand jury case Robertson discusses is *Hill v. Texas*, 316 U.S. 400 (1942). Douglas quoted in Robertson, *Sly and Able*, 303.

3. Such an analysis would no doubt be a difficult undertaking. As Malcolm M. Feeley and Edward L. Rubin write with regard to the creation of judicial doctrine concerning prison reform: "On the one hand, institutional action, including action based on ideas, must be located within the minds of the individuals. On the other hand, those individuals cannot be treated as generic persons with undifferentiated motivations like self-interest, but must be recognized as highly contextualized beings acting in accordance with their institutional positions. What is required, in other words, is a phenomenology of institutional thought. This would provide a way of understanding how individual human beings, on the basis of their own thoughts and actions, are shaped by their institutional context, and how, in turn, they shape that context in response to changing circumstances or conceptualizations" (*Judicial Policy Making and the Modern State*, 212).

4. Most importantly, Kluger, *Simple Justice*; Hutchinson, "Unanimity and Desegregation"; and Tushnet, *Making Civil Rights Law*.

5. Rosenberg, *Hollow Hope*, 169; Peltason, *Fifty-eight Lonely Men*, 249. On the forces pressuring governmental action on civil rights, also see Piven and Cloward, *Poor People's Movements*; and McAdam, *Political Process and the Development of Black Insurgency*.

6. While seemingly minor, this third inquiry makes an important distinction. In the United States, court action on constitutional grounds is more significant than legislative action since constitutional rights command a higher authority than statutory rights. For example, when the Supreme Court found that segregation violated the constitutional right to equal protection in *Brown*, to overturn the decision, opponents needed to negotiate the difficult process of ratifying a constitutional amendment. If Congress had outlawed segregation, defenders of the old South could have directly tied their anger to the 1954 elections and sought to change the law. In addition, the Court's decision was a clear statement rejecting the constitutional validity of segregated schools. Legislation emanating from Congress has historically been a product of compromise, filled with enough ambiguity to make implementation long and arduous. The Court faced similar implementation difficulties with *Brown*, but shielded from the public's wrath — most obviously from the South — it did not back down. Given electoral uncertainties, members of Congress and the president might have. Their behavior following *Brown* certainly suggests the probability of such maneuvering. Finally, civil rights legislation would have faced legal challenges and a brier patch of precedent from which unsympathetic jurists could pluck. To be sure, judicial action comes with its own set of difficulties. The fact that the justices sought to settle such a controversial issue provoked questions of legitimacy, with many claiming that the decision rattled the bedrock of democracy — that the people decide. Lack of clear support from either of the other two branches also enabled opponents to massively resist the Court for over a decade. The wisdom of court action on constitutional grounds aside, the distinction between it and legislative action is nevertheless highly significant. And the fact that the judiciary was the branch to outlaw segregation has had a lasting impact on the politics of civil rights in America.

7. See, for example, Bell, "Brown v. Board of Education and the Interest-Convergence Dilemma."

8. Dudziak, "Desegregation as a Cold War Imperative"; Dudziak, *Cold War*

Civil Rights; Layton, *International Politics and Civil Rights Policies in the United States*; Skrentny, "Effect of the Cold War on African-American Civil Rights."

9. See, for example, Berman, *Politics of Civil Rights in the Truman Administration*; Dalfiume, *Desegregation of the U.S. Armed Forces*; Hamby, *Liberalism and Its Challengers*; McCoy and Ruetten, *Quest and Response*; and Sitkoff, "Years of the Locust." On both international and domestic pressures, see Klinkner and Smith, *Unsteady March*. For an interesting discussion of the influence of the party system, see Valelly, "Party, Coercion, and Inclusion."

10. Borstelmann, "Jim Crow's Coming Out," 553.

11. Dudziak, "Desegregation as a Cold War Imperative," 95–99, 113, 114.

12. Berman, *Politics of Civil Rights in the Truman Administration*, 239–40.

13. See, for example, Kluger, *Simple Justice*, 593–94.

14. Tushnet, *NAACP's Legal Strategy against Segregated Education*, and *Making Civil Rights Law*.

15. Kluger, *Simple Justice*; Greenberg, *Crusaders in the Courts*.

16. Epp, *Rights Revolution*. For a discussion of dispute-centered analysis, see McCann, "Reform Litigation on Trial," and *Rights at Work*.

17. See Hattam, *Labor Visions and State Power*, and Forbath, *Law and the Shaping of the American Labor Movement*.

18. Tauber, "NAACP Legal Defense Fund and the U.S. Supreme Court's Racial Discrimination Decision Making."

19. Tushnet, *Making Civil Rights Law*, vii, 215, 216.

20. Dahl, "Decision-Making in a Democracy," 285, 294; Shapiro, "Chief Justice Rehnquist and the Future of the Supreme Court," 145; Shapiro, "Supreme Court," 194, 181, 194. See also, among a vast literature, Burnham, *Critical Elections and the Mainsprings of American Politics*; Adamany, "Law and Society"; Funston, "Supreme Court and Critical Elections"; Casper, "Supreme Court and National Policy Making"; Lasser, "Supreme Court in Periods of Critical Realignment"; Gates, *Supreme Court and Partisan Realignment*; and Graber, "Nonmajoritarian Difficulty."

21. Shapiro, "Supreme Court," 209.

22. On voting results, see Congressional Quarterly's *Presidential Elections, 1789–1996*.

23. To be sure, the Roosevelt administration did undertake its judicial policy with the intent of unifying behavior throughout the political system (as indicated by realignment theory), but the reality of the situation ensured institutional conflict for the foreseeable future, not institutional consensus. This may suggest that "multiple orders" more accurately explain the origins of the Court's activism on civil rights. Under the multiple order framework, periodization schemes such as realignment theory "remain essential parts" of the equation, but, as Karen Orren and Stephen Skowronek write, "the overall view of politics is no longer that of an integrated order punctuated periodically by radical change. Rather, it is one of multiple and disjointed orderings that overlay one another, with the interplay among them breaking down the period-bound distinction between order and change" ("Institutions and Intercurrence," 117).

24. To be sure, Dahl and Shapiro did notice the limitations of realignment theory in predicting doctrinal change. After concluding that "in the absence of substantial agreement within the [national governing] alliance, an attempt by the Court to make national policy is likely to lead to disaster," Dahl speculated that the civil

rights decisions were "exceptions to this generalization" ("Decision-Making in a Democracy," 293). In arguing that the Warren Court independently articulated values and ideals consistent with the New Deal coalition, Shapiro notes, "the only significant element in the . . . coalition that [it] did not serve was conservative southern whites." Shapiro's answer for why the Court could exclude this constituency from its "service" is because "nobody in the New Deal was really fond of them anyway" ("Chief Justice Rehnquist and the Future of the Supreme Court," 146). *Brown*, then, is seemingly the result of a combination of the Court's two main functions, its role as a partner in the national governing coalition and its role as the "enunciator of diffuse values." Desegregation not only appealed to an element of the New Deal coalition, it also was an "idea whose time had come" (Shapiro, "Supreme Court," 181–84). Dahl apparently agrees. Speculating about the Court's civil rights decisions, he writes that they "probably" represent cases in which the Court can "succeed only if its action conforms to and reinforces a widespread set of explicit or implicit norms held by the political leadership" ("Decision-Making in a Democracy," 294). Besides the dislike of southerners, however, neither Shapiro nor Dahl provides an explanation for the limitations of realignment theory. In other words, although a product of the 1932 realignment, each fails to show convincingly why the Court would have agreed to reach decisions—even if the time was ripe—that ultimately tore the New Deal coalition asunder.

25. Segal and Spaeth, *Supreme Court and the Attitudinal Model*, 65.

26. Ibid., 304. As Segal and Spaeth write, "we can predict [that] the ideology of the President's choice . . . will be a function of the President's ideology, the ideological composition of the Senate, and the ideological makeup of the Supreme Court" (159).

27. Ibid., 304–5, 332.

28. Ibid., 332. In an earlier work Spaeth and coauthor David Rohde focused exclusively on ideology and party affiliation and assumed that "Republican Presidents wanted their appointees to be moderate to conservative, and that Democratic Presidents wanted their appointees to be moderate to liberal." Thus, if a Republican president appointed a justice who turned out to be a liberal once on the bench, the appointment was considered a "failure." Rohde and Spaeth showed that presidents were successful over 79 percent of the time in selecting justices supportive of their policy positions (*Supreme Court Decision Making*, 107). As John B. Gates and Jeffrey E. Cohen argue, however, "the assumption that presidential party adequately gauges presidential policy preferences is dubious at best" ("Presidents, Supreme Court Justices, and Racial Equality Cases," 24). See also Meinhold and Shull, "Policy Congruence between the President and the Solicitor General."

29. Whittington, "Once More unto the Breach," 618.

30. See Epstein and Knight, *Choices Justices Make*; and Maltzman, Spriggs, and Wahlbeck, *Crafting the Law on the Supreme Court*.

31. Here, the strategic model is obviously more consistent with Dahl's analysis.

32. See Kluger's discussion of Justice Reed's decision to join his colleagues in *Brown, Simple Justice*, 655–56, 680, 683, 691–93, 698.

33. See Segal and Cover, "Ideological Values and the Votes of U.S. Supreme Court Justices"; Segal et al., "Ideological Values and the Votes of U.S. Supreme Court Justices Revisited"; and George and Epstein, "On the Nature of Supreme Court Decision Making."

34. Clayton, "Supreme Court and Political Jurisprudence," 27.

35. Here, I attempt to avoid one of the primary potential problems of new institutionalism, namely, the tendency "to neglect the significance of individual choice (particularly in favor of 'the state')." As Smith continues, "the new institutionalism requires us only to stress how background structures *shape* values and interests, not to speak as if they have interests of their own" ("Political Jurisprudence," 100–101). On game theory, see, for example, Bates et al., *Analytic Narratives*.

36. The Court issued unanimous opinions in the four major school desegregation cases: *Sipuel v. Oklahoma*, 332 U.S. 631 (1948); *Sweatt v. Painter*, 339 U.S. 629 (1950); *McLaurin v. Oklahoma State Regents*, 339 U.S. 637 (1950); and *Brown v. Board of Education*, 347 U.S. 483 (1954). Again, Justice Reed is a good example.

37. Segal and Spaeth, *Supreme Court and the Attitudinal Model*, 33–53. See, for example, Clayton, "Supreme Court and Political Jurisprudence," 26–28.

38. For example, Bickel, *Least Dangerous Branch*; Ely, *Democracy and Distrust*; and Dworkin, *Law's Empire*.

39. Kahn, *Supreme Court and Constitutional Theory*, 18, 4. Here, polity principles are defined as "justices' deeply held ideas about where decision-making power should be located when deciding questions of constitutional significance. Polity principles involve beliefs about whether courts or electorally accountable political institutions are the more appropriate forum for constitutional decision-making. They also include beliefs about whether state, local, or national levels of government are proper forums for making such decisions. . . . Rights principles are defined as beliefs (held by justices, as well as judicial advocates and constitutional scholars) about legally enforceable claims for individual powers, privileges, or immunities guaranteed under the Constitution, statutes, and law" (21–23).

40. Ibid., 101, 33

41. Ibid., 67–82.

42. Ibid., 56–57, 67.

43. Ackerman, *We the People*, vols. 1 and 2.

44. Kahn, *Supreme Court and Constitutional Theory*, 18, 38–39.

45. On hearing of Vinson's death, Frankfurter reportedly said, "This is the first indication I have ever had that there is a God"; see Kluger, *Simple Justice*, 656. On the importance of Warren, see Schwartz, *Super Chief*; and Ulmer, "Earl Warren and the *Brown* Decision."

46. Frankfurter, although an important advisor to FDR, was the exception. Both Douglas and Jackson were considered for the vice presidency in 1944. See also Epstein et al., *Supreme Court Compendium*, 242–50.

47. For more discussion on this latter point, see note 6 above.

48. Kluger, *Simple Justice*, 614. As Tushnet points out, conclusions (by Justices Douglas and Frankfurter) that the decision would have been 5–4 if the Court decided the case in 1952 "seem seriously overstated" (*Making Civil Rights Law*, 194).

49. Smith, quoting Gordon, "Political Jurisprudence," 98; see Gordon, "Critical Legal Histories."

50. Powe, *Warren Court and American Politics*, 21.

51. *Brown v. Board of Education*, 349 U.S. 294 (1955).

52. Elman, "Solicitor General's Office," 827, 825. Elman even suggests that Black would have preferred to be in dissent, writing an opinion to further liberalism in the South rather than one that virtually destroyed it (825, 828).

53. Tushnet, *Making Civil Rights Law*, 81.

54. To be sure, the realist-inspired reliance on social science did not dominate the entirety of the Court's civil rights work. In the D.C. case of *Bolling v. Sharpe*, Warren echoed the tone of rights-centered liberalism, forcefully concluding that since "segregation in public education is 'not reasonably related to any proper governmental objective,' it is an arbitrary deprivation of liberty" (Powe, *Warren Court and American Politics*, 32; *Bolling v. Sharpe*, 347 U.S. 497 [1954]).

WORKS CITED

MANUSCRIPT COLLECTIONS

Note: I list only those collections from which I have quoted a document.

Criminal Division Files, Department of Justice, Freedom of Information Act request
Diary of Homer Cummings, University of Virginia
Felix Frankfurter Papers, Harvard Law School
Francis Biddle Papers, FDR Library
Justice Department Files, Franklin D. Roosevelt Presidential Library
Justice Department Files, United States National Archives
NAACP Papers
President's Official Files, FDR Library
President's Personal File, FDR Library
President's Secretary's File, FDR Library
Robert H. Jackson Papers, Library of Congress
Robert Wagner Papers, Georgetown University
Thomas G. Corcoran Papers, Library of Congress
Wendell Berge Papers, Library of Congress
Wiley B. Rutledge Papers, Library of Congress

NEWSPAPERS AND PERIODICALS

Note: Specific citations appear in the endnotes.

Atlanta Constitution
Atlanta Daily World
Atlantic Monthly
Chicago Defender
Chicago Tribune
Collier's
Congressional Digest
Crisis
Detroit News
Emporia Daily Gazette
Fortune
Harper's Magazine
Jackson Daily News
Look
Louisville Leader

Nation
Newport News Star
New Republic
Newsweek
New York Amsterdam News
New York Herald-Tribune
New York Times
Philadelphia Independent
Pittsburgh Courier
St. Louis Argus
St. Louis Post-Dispatch
St. Louis Star-Times
Saturday Evening Post
Time
United Mine Workers Journal
Washington Post

BOOKS, JOURNAL ARTICLES, DISSERTATIONS,
THESES, AND PAPERS

Abraham, Henry J. *Justices, Presidents, and Senators: A History of the U.S. Supreme Court Appointments from Washington to Clinton*. New York: Rowman & Little-field, 1999.

Ackerman, Bruce A. "Revolution on a Human Scale." *Yale Law Journal* 108 (1999): 2279–349.

———. *We the People*. Vol. 1, *Foundations*. Cambridge, Mass.: Harvard University Press, 1991.

———. *We the People*. Vol. 2, *Transformations*. Cambridge, Mass.: Harvard University Press, 1998.

Adamany, David. "Law and Society: Realigning Elections and the Supreme Court." *Wisconsin Law Review* 3 (1973): 790–846.

Alinsky, Saul. *John L. Lewis: An Unauthorized Biography*. New York: Putnam, 1949; New York: Vintage, 1970.

Alsop, Joseph, and Turner Catledge. *The 168 Days*. Garden City, N.Y.: Doubleday, Doran & Co., 1938.

Ambrose, Stephen E. *Eisenhower: The President*. New York: Simon & Schuster, 1984.

Auerbach, Jerold S. *Labor and Liberty: The La Follette Committee and the New Deal*. New York: Bobbs-Merrill, 1966.

Baker, Leonard. *Back to Back: The Duel between FDR and the Supreme Court*. New York: Macmillan, 1967.

Baldwin, Roger N. "Organized Labor and Political Democracy." In *Civil Liberties and Industrial Conflict*, by Roger N. Baldwin and Clarence B. Randall. Cambridge, Mass.: Harvard University Press, 1938.

Ball, Howard. *Hugo L. Black: Cold Steel Warrior*. New York: Oxford University Press, 1996.

Bates, Beth Tomkins. *Pullman Porters and the Rise of Protest Politics in Black America, 1925–1945*. Chapel Hill: University of North Carolina Press, 2001.

Bates, Robert H., Avner Greif, Margaret Levi, Jean-Laurent Rosenthal, and Barry R.

Weingast. *Analytic Narratives*. Princeton, N.J.: Princeton University Press, 1998.

Belknap, Michal R., ed. *Justice Department Civil Rights Policies prior to 1960: Crucial Documents from the Files of Arthur Brann Caldwell*. Vol. 16 of *Civil Rights, The White House, and the Justice Department, 1945–1968*. New York: Garland, 1991.

———. *Presidential Committees and White House Conferences*. Vol. 2 of *Civil Rights, The White House, and the Justice Department, 1945–1968*. New York: Garland, 1991.

Bell, Derrick. "*Brown v. Board of Education* and the Interest-Convergence Dilemma." *Harvard Law Review* 93 (1980): 518–29.

Berman, William C. *The Politics of Civil Rights in the Truman Administration*. Columbus: Ohio State University Press, 1970.

Bernstein, Irving. *The New Deal Collective Bargaining Policy*. Berkeley: University of California Press, 1950.

———. *Turbulent Years: A History of the American Worker, 1933–1941*. Boston: Houghton Mifflin, 1969.

Bickel, Alexander M. *The Least Dangerous Branch: The Supreme Court at the Bar of Politics*. New York: Bobbs-Merrill, 1962.

Biddle, Francis. "Civil Rights in Times of Stress." *Bill of Rights Review* 2, no. 1 (1941): 13–22.

———. *In Brief Authority*. Garden City, N.Y.: Doubleday, 1962.

Bixby, David M. "The Roosevelt Court, Democratic Ideology, and Minority Rights." *Yale Law Journal* 90 (1981): 741–815.

Black, Earl, and Merle Black. *Politics and Society in the South*. Cambridge, Mass.: Harvard University Press, 1987.

Borstelmann, Thomas. "Jim Crow's Coming Out: Race Relations and American Foreign Policy in the Truman Years." *Presidential Studies Quarterly* 29 (1999): 549–69.

———. *The Cold War and the Color Line: American Race Relations in the Global Arena*. Cambridge, Mass.: Harvard University Press, 2001.

Boudin, Louis B. "The Supreme Court and Civil Rights." *Science and Society* 1, no. 3 (spring 1937): 273–309.

Brinkley, Alan. "The New Deal and Southern Politics." In *The New Deal and the South*, edited by James C. Cobb and Michael V. Namorato. Jackson: University Press of Mississippi, 1984.

———. *Voices of Protest: Huey Long, Father Coughlin, and the Great Depression*. New York: Vintage, 1982.

———. *The End of Reform: New Deal Liberalism in Recession and War*. New York: Vintage, 1995.

Bunche, Ralph. *The Political Status of the Negro in the Age of FDR*. Chicago: University of Chicago Press, 1973.

Burk, Robert Fredrick. *The Eisenhower Administration and Black Civil Rights*. Knoxville: University of Tennessee Press, 1984.

Burnham, Walter Dean. *Critical Elections and the Mainsprings of American Politics*. New York: W. W. Norton, 1970.

Burns, James McGregor. *Roosevelt: The Lion and the Fox 1882–1940*. New York: Harcourt Brace Jovanovich, 1956.

Byrnes, James F. *All in One Lifetime*. New York: Harper & Brothers, 1958.

Cahn, Edmond. "Jurisprudence." *New York University Law Review* 30 (1955): 150–69.

Capeci, Dominic J., Jr. "The Lynching of Cleo Wright: Federal Protection of Constitutional Rights during World War II." *Journal of American History* 72 (1986): 859–87.

Carr, Robert K. "*Screws v. United States*: The Georgia Police Brutality Case." *Cornell Law Quarterly* 31 (1945): 48–67.

———. *Federal Protection of Civil Rights: Quest for a Sword*. Ithaca, N.Y.: Cornell University Press, 1947.

Casper, Jonathan. "The Supreme Court and National Policy Making." *American Political Science Review* 70 (1976): 50–63.

Catledge, Turner. *My Life and the Times*. New York: Harper & Row, 1971.

Clark, Tom C. "A Federal Prosecutor Looks at the Civil Rights Statutes." *Columbia Law Review* 47 (March 1947): 175–85.

Clark, Wayne Addison. "An Analysis of the Relationship between Anti-Communism and Segregationist Thought in the Deep South, 1946–1964." Ph.D. diss., University of North Carolina, 1976.

Clarke, Jeanne Nienaber. *Roosevelt's Warrior: Harold L. Ickes and the New Deal*. Baltimore: Johns Hopkins University Press, 1996.

Clayton, Cornell W. *The Politics of Justice: The Attorney General and the Making of Legal Policy*. Armonk, N.Y.: M. E. Sharpe, 1992.

———. "The Supreme Court and Political Jurisprudence: New and Old Institutionalisms." In *Supreme Court Decision-Making: New Institutionalist Approaches*, edited by Cornell W. Clayton and Howard Gillman. Chicago: University of Chicago Press, 1999.

Clayton, Cornell W., and David May. "A Political Regimes Approach to the Analysis of Legal Decisions." *Polity* 32 (winter 1999): 233–52.

Clayton, Cornell W., and Howard Gillman, eds. *Supreme Court Decision-Making: New Institutionalist Approaches*. Chicago: University of Chicago Press, 1999.

———. Introduction to *The Supreme Court in American Politics: New Institutionalist Interpretations*, edited by Howard Gillman and Cornell Clayton. Lawrence: University of Kansas Press, 1999.

Cobb, James C. *The Most Southern Place on Earth: The Mississippi Delta and the Roots of Regional Identity*. New York: Oxford University Press, 1992.

Cohen, Julius. "The Screws Case: Federal Protection of Negro Rights." *Columbia Law Review*, 46 (1946): 94–106.

Coleman, Frank. "Freedom from Fear on the Home Front." *Iowa Law Review* 29 (1944): 415–29.

Conkin, Paul. *The New Deal*. New York: Crowell, 1967.

Connally, Thomas Terry. *My Name Is Tom Connally*. As told to Alfred Steinberg. New York: Thomas Y. Crowell Co., 1954.

Cortner, Richard C. *The Jones and Laughlin Case*. New York: Knopf, 1970.

———. *The Wagner Act Cases*. Knoxville: University of Tennessee Press, 1964.

Corwin, Edward S. *Court Over the Constitution: A Study of Judicial Review as an Instrument of Popular Government*. Princeton, N.J.: Princeton University Press, 1938.

———. *The President: Office and Powers*. New York: New York University Press, 1940.

Cover, Robert M. "The Origins of Judicial Activism and the Protection of Minorities." *Yale Law Journal* 91 (1982): 1287–316.

Creel, George. *Rebel at Large: Recollections of Fifty Crowded Years*. New York: G. P. Putnam, 1947.

Cronin, Thomas E., and Michael A. Genovese. *The Paradoxes of the American Presidency*. New York: Oxford University Press, 1998.

Cushman, Barry. *Rethinking the New Deal Court: The Structure of a Constitutional Revolution*. New York: Oxford University Press, 1998.

Dahl, Robert A. "Decision-Making in a Democracy: The Supreme Court as a National Policy-Maker." *Journal of Public Law* 6 (1957): 279–95.

Dalfiume, Richard M. *Desegregation of the U.S. Armed Forces: Fighting on Two Fronts, 1939–1953*. Columbia: University of Missouri Press, 1969.

Dallek, Robert. *Hail to the Chief: The Making and Unmaking of American Presidents*. New York: Hyperion, 1996.

Daniel, Cletus E. *The ACLU and the Wagner Act: An Inquiry into the Depression-Era Crisis of American Liberalism*. Ithaca, N.Y.: Cornell Studies in Industrial and Labor Relations, 1980.

Davies, Gareth, and Martha Derthick. "Race and Social Welfare Policy: The Social Security Act of 1935." *Political Science Quarterly* 112, no. 2 (1997): 217–35.

Davis, Kenneth S. *FDR, into the Storm, 1937–1940: A History*. New York: Random House, 1993.

Dixon, Robert G., Jr. "The Attorney General and Civil Rights, 1870–1964," In *Roles of the Attorney General of the United States*, edited by Luther A. Huston, et al. Washington, D.C.: American Enterprise Institute, 1968.

Douglas, William O. *Go East, Young Man: The Early Years: The Autobiography of William O. Douglas*. New York: Random House, 1974.

Dubofsky, Melvyn. *The State and Labor in Modern America*. Chapel Hill: University of North Carolina Press, 1994.

Dubofsky, Melvyn, and Warren Van Tine. *John L. Lewis: A Biography*. New York: Quadrangle/New York Times Books, 1977.

Dudziak, Mary L. *Cold War Civil Rights: Race and the Image of American Democracy*. Princeton, N.J.: Princeton University Press, 2000.

———. "Desegregation as a Cold War Imperative." *Stanford Law Review* 41 (1988): 61–120.

Dworkin, Ronald. *Law's Empire*. Cambridge, Mass.: Harvard University Press, 1986.

Egerton, John. *Speak Now against the Day: The Generation before the Civil Rights Movement in the South*. New York: Knopf, 1994.

Ehrlichman, John. *Witness to Power: The Nixon Years*. New York: Simon & Schuster, 1982.

Elliff, John T. "Aspects of Federal Civil Rights Enforcement: The Justice Department and the FBI, 1939–1964." *Perspectives in American History* 5 (1971): 605–73.

———. "The United States Department of Justice and Individual Rights, 1937–1962." Ph.D. diss., Harvard University, 1967.

Elliot, Ward. *The Rise of Guardian Democracy: The Supreme Court's Role in Voting Rights Disputes, 1845–1969*. Cambridge, Mass.: Harvard University Press, 1974.

Elman, Philip. "Response." *Harvard Law Review* 100 (1987): 1949–57.

———. "The Solicitor General's Office, Justice Frankfurter, and Civil Rights Litigation, 1946–1960: An Oral History." *Harvard Law Review* 100 (1987): 817–52.

Ely, John Hart. *Democracy and Distrust: A Theory of Judicial Review*. Cambridge, Mass.: Harvard University Press, 1980.

Epp, Charles R. *The Rights Revolution: Lawyers, Activists, and Supreme Courts in Comparative Perspective*. Chicago: University of Chicago Press, 1998.

Epstein, Lee, and Jack Knight. *The Choices Justices Make*. Washington, D.C.: Congressional Quarterly Press, 1998.

———. "Toward a Strategic Revolution in Judicial Politics: A Look Back, a Look Ahead." *Political Research Quarterly* 53, no. 3 (September 2000): 625–61.

Epstein, Lee, Jeffrey A. Segal, Harold J. Spaeth, and Thomas G. Walker. *The Supreme Court Compendium: Data, Decisions, and Developments*. Washington, D.C.: Congressional Quarterly, 1994.

Ethington, Philip J., and Eileen L. McDonagh, eds. "Polity Forum: Institutions and Institutionalism." *Polity* 28 (fall 1995): 84–140.

Farley, James A. *Jim Farley's Story: The Roosevelt Years*. New York: Whittlesey House, 1948.

Feeley, Malcolm M., and Edward L. Rubin. *Judicial Policy Making and the Modern State: How the Courts Reformed America's Prisons*. New York: Cambridge University Press, 1999.

Fine, Sidney. *Frank Murphy: The New Deal Years*. Chicago: University of Chicago Press, 1979.

———. *Frank Murphy: The Washington Years*. Ann Arbor: University of Michigan Press, 1984.

———. *Sit-Down: The General Motors Strike of 1936–1937*. Ann Arbor: University of Michigan Press, 1967.

Fiorina, Morris P. "The Decline of Collective Responsibility in American Politics." *Daedalus* 109, no. 3 (summer 1980): 25–45.

Fisher, William, Morton Horwitz, and Thomas Reed. *American Legal Realism*. New York: Oxford University Press, 1993.

Fite, Gilbert C. *Richard B. Russell, Jr., Senator from Georgia*. Chapel Hill: University of North Carolina Press, 1991.

Flynt, Wayne. "The New Deal and Southern Labor." In *The New Deal and the South*, edited by James C. Cobb and Michael V. Namorato. Jackson: University Press of Mississippi, 1984.

Folsom, Fred G. "Federal Elections and the 'White Primary.'" *Columbia Law Review* 43 (1943): 1026–35.

———. "A Slave Trade Law in a Contemporary Setting." *Cornell Law Quarterly* 29 (1943): 203–16.

Forbath, William E. *Law and the Shaping of the American Labor Movement*. Cambridge, Mass.: Harvard University Press, 1991.

Frank, Jerome. *Law and the Modern Mind*. New York: Brentano's Publishers, 1930.

———. "Realism in Jurisprudence." *American Law School Review* 7 (1934): 1063–69.

Frankfurter, Felix. *Felix Frankfurter Reminisces*. As recorded by Harlan B. Philips. New York: Reynal & Co., 1960.

———. *The Public and Its Government*. New Haven, Conn.: Yale University Press, 1930.

Frederickson, Kari. *The Dixiecrat Revolt and the End of the Solid South, 1932–1968*. Chapel Hill: University of North Carolina Press, 2001.

Freedman, Max, annotator. *Roosevelt and Frankfurter: Their Correspondence, 1928–1945*. Boston: Little, Brown, 1967.

Freidel, Frank. *FDR and the South*. Baton Rouge: Louisiana State University Press, 1965.

Frymer, Paul. "Race, Labor and State Building: Marrying the Disciplines to Understand the NLRB." Paper presented at the annual meeting of the Western Political Science Association, San Jose, Calif., 2000.

———. *Uneasy Alliances: Race and Party Competition in America*. Princeton, N.J.: Princeton University Press, 1999.

Fuller, Lon. *The Law in Quest of Itself.* Chicago: Foundation Press, 1940.

Funston, Richard. "The Supreme Court and Critical Elections." *American Political Science Review* 69 (1975): 795–811.

Garson, Robert A. *The Democratic Party and the Politics of Sectionalism*. Baton Rouge: Louisiana State University Press, 1974.

Gates, John B. "The Supreme Court and Partisan Change: Contravening, Provoking, and Diffusing Partisan Conflict." In *The Supreme Court in American Politics: New Institutionalist Interpretations*, edited by Howard Gillman and Cornell Clayton. Lawrence: University Press of Kansas, 1999.

———. *The Supreme Court and Partisan Realignment: A Macro- and Microlevel Perspective*. Boulder, Colo.: Westview Press, 1992.

Gates, John B., and Jeffrey E. Cohen. "Presidents, Supreme Court Justices, and Racial Equality Cases: 1954–1984." *Political Behavior* 10 (1988): 22–36.

George, Tracey E., and Lee Epstein. "On the Nature of Supreme Court Decision Making." *American Political Science Review* 86 (June 1992): 323–37.

Gerhart, Eugene C. *America's Advocate: Robert H. Jackson*. New York: Bobbs-Merrill, 1958.

Gerstle, Gary. *American Crucible: Race and Nation in the Twentieth Century*. Princeton, N.J.: Princeton University Press, 2001.

Gillman, Howard "The Court As an Idea, Not a Building (or a Game): Interpretive Institutionalism and the Analysis of Supreme Court Decision-Making." In *Supreme Court Decision-Making: New Institutionalist Approaches*, edited by Cornell W. Clayton and Howard Gillman. Chicago: University of Chicago Press, 1999.

———. "Revisiting the Rise of 'Judicial Supremacy' in the United States: The Federal Judiciary and Regime Politics, 1863–1895." Paper presented at the annual meeting of the Western Political Science Association, San Jose, Calif., 2000.

Gillman, Howard, and Cornell Clayton, eds. *The Supreme Court in American Politics: New Institutionalist Interpretations*. Lawrence: University Press of Kansas, 1999.

Gilmore, Grant. "Legal Realism: Its Cause and Cure." *Yale Law Journal* 70 (1961): 1037–48.

Goings, Kenneth W. *The NAACP Comes of Age: The Defeat of Judge John J. Parker.* Indianapolis: Indiana University Press, 1990.

Goldman, Sheldon. *Picking Federal Judges: Lower Court Selection from Roosevelt Through Reagan*. New Haven, Conn.: Yale University Press, 1997.

Goluboff, Risa L. "The Thirteenth Amendment and the Lost Origins of Civil Rights." *Duke Law Journal* 50 (2001): 1609–85.

Gordon, Robert. "Critical Legal Histories." *Stanford Law Review* 36 (1984): 57–125.

Graber, Mark A. "The Nonmajoritarian Difficulty: Legislative Deference to the Judiciary." *Studies in American Political Development* 7 (spring 1993): 35–73.

Greenberg, Jack. *Crusaders in the Courts: How a Dedicated Band of Lawyers Fought for the Civil Rights Revolution*. New York: Basic Books, 1994.

Griffin, Stephen M. *American Constitutionalism: From Theory to Politics.* Princeton, N.J.: Princeton University Press, 1996.

Gross, James A. *The Making of the National Labor Relations Board.* Albany: State University of New York Press, 1974.

Gunther, Gerald. *Learned Hand: The Man and the Judge.* Cambridge, Mass.: Harvard University Press, 1994.

Hamby, Alonzo L. *Liberalism and Its Challengers: FDR to Reagan.* New York: Oxford University Press, 1985.

Harrell, Kenneth E. "Southern Congressional Leaders and the Supreme Court Fight of 1937." Master's thesis, Louisiana State University, 1959.

Harrison, Robert. "The Breakup of the Roosevelt Court: The Contribution of History and Biography." Ph.D. diss., Columbia University, 1987.

———. "The Breakup of the Roosevelt Supreme Court: A Contribution of History and Biography." *Law and History Review* 2 (1984): 165–221.

Hastie, William H., and Thurgood Marshall. "Negro Discrimination and the Need for Federal Action." *Lawyers Guild Review* 2, no. 6 (November 1942): 21–23.

Hattam, Victoria C. *Labor Visions and State Power: The Origins of Business Unionism in the United States.* Princeton, N.J.: Princeton University Press, 1993.

Hawley, Ellis W. "The Constitution of the Hoover and F. Roosevelt Presidency and the Depression Era." In *The Constitution and the American Presidency,* edited by Martin Fausold and Alan Shank. Albany: State University of New York Press, 1991.

Hevener, John W. *Which Side Are You On? The Harlan County Coal Miners, 1931–1939.* Urbana: University of Illinois Press, 1978.

High, Stanley. *Roosevelt — and Then?* New York: Harper & Brothers, 1937.

Hill, Herbert. *Black Labor and the American Legal System: Race, Work, and the Law.* Washington, D.C.: Bureau of National Affairs, 1977; Madison: University of Wisconsin Press, 1985.

Hine, Darlene Clark. *Black Victory: The Rise and Fall of the White Primary in Texas.* Millwood, N.Y.: KTO Press, 1979.

Hirsch, H. N. *The Enigma of Felix Frankfurter.* New York: Basic Books, 1981.

Hiss, Alger. *Recollections of a Life.* New York: Seaver Books/Henry Holt, 1988.

Horwitz, Morton J. *The Transformation of American Law, 1870–1960: The Crisis of Legal Orthodoxy.* New York: Oxford University Press, 1992.

———. *The Warren Court and the Pursuit of Justice: A Critical Issue.* New York: Hill & Wang, 1998.

Howard, J. Woodford, Jr. *Mr. Justice Murphy: A Political Biography.* Princeton, N.J.: Princeton University Press, 1968.

Howard, Woodford, and Cornelius Bushoven. "The *Screws* Case Revisited." *Journal of Politics* 29 (1967): 617–36.

Hurtgen, James R. *The Divided Mind of American Liberalism.* New York: Lexington Books, 2002.

Huston, Luther A., Arthur Selwyn Miller, Samuel Krislov, and Robert G. Dixon Jr. *Roles of the Attorney General of the United States.* Washington, D.C.: American Enterprise Institute for Public Policy Research, 1968.

Hutchinson, Dennis J. "Unanimity and Desegregation: Decisionmaking in the Supreme Court, 1948–1958." *Georgetown Law Review* 68 (1979): 1–96.

Huthmacher, J. Joseph. *Senator Robert F. Wagner and the Rise of Urban Liberalism.* New York: Atheneum, 1968.

Ickes, Harold L. *The Secret Diary of Harold L. Ickes.* 3 vols. New York: Simon & Schuster, 1953–54.

Irons, Peter H. *Justice at War: The Story of the Japanese American Internment Cases.* Berkeley: University of California Press, 1983.

———. *The New Deal Lawyers.* Princeton, N.J.: Princeton University Press, 1982.

———. "Politics and Principle: An Assessment of the Roosevelt Record on Civil Rights and Liberties." *Washington Law Review* 59 (September 1984): 693–722.

Jackson, Robert H. *The Struggle for Judicial Supremacy: A Study of a Crisis in American Power Politics.* New York: Vintage, 1941.

Kahn, Ronald. "Institutional Norms and Supreme Court Decision-Making." In *Supreme Court Decision-Making: New Institutionalist Approaches,* edited by Cornell W. Clayton and Howard Gillman. Chicago: University of Chicago Press, 1999.

———. *The Supreme Court and Constitutional Theory, 1953–1993.* Lawrence: University Press of Kansas, 1994.

Kalman, Laura. "Law, Politics, and the New Deal(s)." *Yale Law Journal* 108 (1999): 2165–213.

———. *Legal Realism at Yale, 1927–1960.* Chapel Hill: University of North Carolina Press, 1986.

———. *The Strange Career of Legal Liberalism.* New Haven, Conn.: Yale University Press, 1996.

Katznelson, Ira, and Bruce Pietrykowski. "Rebuilding the American State: Evidence from the 1940s." *Studies in American Political Development* 5 (1991): 301–39.

Katznelson, Ira, Kim Geiger, and Daniel Kryder. "Limiting Liberalism: The Southern Veto in Congress." *Political Science Quarterly* 108, no. 2 (1993): 283–306.

Kennedy, Randall. "Colloquy: A Reply to Philip Elman." *Harvard Law Review* 100 (1987): 1938–48.

Key, V. O. *Southern Politics.* New York: Vintage, 1949.

Keyssar, Alexander. *The Right to Vote: The Contested History of Democracy in the United States.* New York: Basic Books, 2000.

Kirby, John B. *Black Americans in the Roosevelt Era: Liberalism and Race.* Knoxville: University of Tennessee Press, 1980.

Klinkner, Philip A., with Rogers M. Smith. *The Unsteady March: The Rise and Decline of Racial Equality in America.* Chicago: University of Chicago Press, 1999.

Kluger, Richard. *Simple Justice: The History of* Brown v. Board of Education *and Black America's Struggle for Equality.* New York: Vintage, 1975.

Kousser, Morgan J. *The Shaping of Southern Politics: Suffrage Restriction and the Establishment of the One-Party South, 1880–1910.* New Haven, Conn.: Yale University Press, 1974.

Kryder, Daniel. *Divided Arsenal: Race and the American State during World War II.* New York: Cambridge University Press, 2000.

Kyvig, David E. "The Road Not Taken: FDR, the Supreme Court, and Constitutional Amendment." *Political Science Quarterly* 104, no. 3 (1989): 463–81.

Lamson, Peggy. *Roger Baldwin: Founder of the American Civil Liberties Union.* Boston: Houghton Mifflin, 1976.

Landsberg, Brian K. *Enforcing Civil Rights: Race Discrimination and the Department of Justice.* Lawrence: University Press of Kansas, 1997.

Lasser, William. *The Limits of Judicial Power: The Supreme Court in American Politics.* Chapel Hill: University of North Carolina Press, 1988.

————. "The Supreme Court in Periods of Critical Realignment." *Journal of Politics* 47 (1985): 1174–87.

Lawson, Steven. *Black Ballots: Voting Rights in the South, 1944–1969.* New York: Columbia University Press, 1976.

Layton, Azza Salama. *International Politics and Civil Rights Policies in the United States, 1941–1960.* New York: Cambridge University Press, 2000.

Leuchtenburg, William E. "Election of 1936." In *History of Presidential Elections,* vol. 3, *1900–1936,* edited by Arthur M. Schlesinger Jr. and Fred L. Israel. New York: Chelsea House, 1971.

————. "FDR's Court-Packing Plan: A Second Life, A Second Death." *Duke Law Journal* (1985): 673–89.

————. *Franklin D. Roosevelt and the New Deal, 1932–1940.* New York: Harper & Row, 1963.

————. *The Supreme Court Reborn: The Constitutional Revolution in the Age of Roosevelt.* New York: Oxford University Press, 1995.

————. "When the People Spoke, What Did They Say? The Election of 1936 and the Ackerman Thesis." *Yale Law Journal* 108 (1999): 2077–114.

Lieberman, Robert C. *Shifting the Color Line: Race and the American Welfare State.* Cambridge, Mass.: Harvard University Press, 1998.

Llewellyn, Karl N. *The Bramble Bush.* 1930. New York: Oceana Publications, 1960.

————. "A Realistic Jurisprudence—the Next Step." *Columbia Law Review* 30 (April 1930): 431–65.

————. "Some Realism about Realism—Responding to Dean Pound." *Harvard Law Review* 44 (1931): 1222–56.

Lovell, George I. "'As Harmless as an Infant': Deference, Denial, and *Adair v. United States.*" *Studies in American Political Development* 14 (2000): 212–33.

Maltzman, Forrest, James F. Spriggs II, and Paul J Wahlbeck. *Crafting the Law on the Supreme Court: The Collegial Game.* New York: Cambridge University Press, 2000.

Mann, Robert. *The Walls of Jericho: Lyndon Johnson, Hubert Humphrey, Richard Russell, and the Struggle for Civil Rights.* New York: Harcourt Brace, 1997.

Manwaring, David. *Render unto Caesar: The Flag-Salute Controversy.* Chicago: University of Chicago Press, 1962.

March, James G., and Johan P. Olsen. "The New Institutionalism: Organizational Factors in Political Life." *American Political Science Review* 78 (1984): 734–49.

————. *Rediscovering Institutions: The Organizational Basis of Politics.* New York: Free Press, 1989.

McAdam, Doug. *Political Process and the Development of Black Insurgency, 1930–1970.* Chicago: University of Chicago Press, 1982.

McCann, Michael W. "Reform Litigation on Trial." *Law and Social Inquiry* 17 (1992): 715–43.

————. *Rights at Work: Pay Equity Reform and the Politics of Legal Mobilization.* Chicago: University of Chicago Press, 1994.

McCloskey, Robert. *The American Supreme Court.* Chicago: University of Chicago Press, 1960.

McCoy, Donald R., and Richard T. Ruetten. *Quest and Response: Minority Rights and the Truman Administration.* Lawrence: University Press of Kansas, 1973.

McCullough, David. *Truman.* New York: Simon & Schuster, 1992.

McCune, Wesley. *The Nine Young Men.* New York: Harper & Brothers, 1947.

McMahon, Kevin J. "Coalition-Building and Constitutional Visions: Presidents, Parties, and the Origins of Judicial Interpretation." Ph.D. diss., Brandeis University, 1997.

———. "Constitutional Vision and Supreme Court Decisions: Reconsidering Roosevelt on Race." *Studies in American Political Development* 14 (spring 2000): 20–50.

Meinhold, Stephen S., and Stephen A. Shull. "Policy Congruence between the President and the Solicitor General." *Political Research Quarterly* 51 (1988): 527–37.

Merrill, Dennis K., ed. *Running from Behind: Truman's Strategy for the 1948 Presidential Campaign.* Vol. 14 of *Documentary History of the Truman Presidency.* Bethesda, Md.: University Publications of America, 1996.

———. *The Truman Administration's Civil Rights Program: The Report of the Committee on Civil Rights and President Truman's Message to the Congress of February 2, 1948.* Vol. 11 of *Documentary History of the Truman Presidency.* Bethesda, Md.: University Publications of America, 1996.

Meyers, S. P. "Federal Privileges and Immunities: Application to Ingress and Egress." *Cornell Law Quarterly* 29 (1944): 489–513.

Michelson, Charles. *The Ghost Talks.* New York: G. P. Putnam's Sons, 1944.

Michie, Alan, and Frank Ryhlick. *Dixie Demagogues.* New York: Vanguard Press, 1939.

Milkis, Sidney. *The President and the Parties: The Transformation of the American Party System since the New Deal.* New York: Oxford University Press, 1993.

Miller, Merle. *Plain Speaking: An Oral Biography of Harry S. Truman.* New York: Berkeley, 1974.

Moe, Terry M., and William G. Howell. "The Presidential Power of Unilateral Action." *Journal of Law, Economics, and Organization* 15, no. 1 (1999): 132–79.

Moon, Henry Lee. *Balance of Power: The Negro Vote.* Garden City, N.Y.: Doubleday, 1948.

Morse, Arthur D. *While Six Million Died: A Chronicle of American Apathy.* New York: Random House, 1968.

Murphy, Frank. *In Defense of Democracy.* Washington, D.C.: American Council on Public Affairs, 1940.

———. "The Test of Patriotism." *National Lawyers Guild Quarterly* 2 (October 1939): 165–70.

Myrdal, Gunnar. *An American Dilemma: The Negro Problem and Modern Democracy.* New York: Harper & Brothers, 1944.

Neal, Nevin Emil. "A Biography of Joseph T. Robinson." Ph.D. Diss., University of Oklahoma Graduate School, 1958.

Nelson, Bruce. *Workers on the Waterfront: Seamen, Longshoremen, and Unionism in the 1930s.* Urbana: University of Illinois Press, 1988.

Nelson, Lawrence J. "The Art of the Possible: Another Look at the 'Purge' of the AAA Liberals in 1935." *Agricultural History* 57 (1983): 416–35.

Nelson, Michael. "The President and the Court: Reinterpreting the Court-Packing Episode of 1937." *Political Science Quarterly* 103 (summer 1988): 267–93.

Neustadt, Richard. *Presidential Power and the Modern Presidents: The Politics of Leadership from Roosevelt to Reagan.* New York: Free Press, 1990.

O'Brien, David M. *Storm Center: The Supreme Court in American Politics.* 5th ed. New York: W. W. Norton, 2000.

O'Brien, Gail Williams. *The Color of Law: Race, Violence, and Justice in the Post-World War II South.* Chapel Hill: University of North Carolina Press, 1999.

O'Reilly, Kenneth. *Nixon's Piano: Presidents and Racial Politics from Washington to Clinton*. New York: Free Press, 1995.

Orren, Karen, and Stephen Skowronek. "Beyond the Iconography of Order: Notes for a 'New Institutionalism.'" In *The Dynamics of American Politics: Approaches and Interpretations*, edited by Lawrence C. Dodd and Calvin Jillson. Boulder, Colo.: Westview Press, 1994.

———. "Institutions and Intercurrence: Theory Building in the Fullness of Time." In *Political Order*, edited by Ian Shapiro and Russell Harden. Nomos 38. New York: New York University Press, 1996.

———. "Regimes and Regime Building in American Government: A Review of the Literature on the 1940s." *Political Science Quarterly* 113, no. 4 (winter 1998–99): 689–702.

———. "The Study of American Political Development." In *Political Science: The State of the Discipline* 3, edited by Ira Katznelson and Helen Milner. New York: W. W. Norton, 2002.

Patterson, James T. *Congressional Conservatism and the New Deal: The Growth of the Conservative Coalition in Congress, 1933–1939*. Lexington: University of Kentucky Press, 1967.

Peltason, J. W. *Fifty-eight Lonely Men: Southern Federal Judges and School Desegregation*. New York: Harcourt, Brace & World, 1961.

Peretti, Terri Jennings. *In Defense of a Political Court*. Princeton, N.J.: Princeton University Press, 1999.

Pierson, Paul, and Theda Skocpol. "Historical Institutionalism in Contemporary Political Science." In *Political Science: The State of the Discipline* 3, edited by Ira Katznelson and Helen Milner. New York: W. W. Norton, 2002.

Piven, Frances Fox, and Richard Cloward. *Poor People's Movements*. New York: Vintage, 1979.

Plotke, David. *Building a Democratic Political Order: Reshaping American Liberalism in the 1930s and 1940s*. New York: Cambridge University Press, 1996.

———. "The Wagner Act, Again: Politics and Labor, 1935–37" *Studies in American Political Development* 5 (1989): 105–56.

Pound, Roscoe. "The Call for a Realist Jurisprudence." *Harvard Law Review* 44 (1931): 697–711.

Powe, Lucas A., Jr. *The Warren Court and American Politics*. Cambridge, Mass.: Harvard University Press, 2000.

Presidential Elections, 1789–1996. Washington, D.C.: Congressional Quarterly, 1999.

President's Committee on Civil Rights. *To Secure These Rights*. New York: Simon & Schuster, 1947.

Pritchett, C. Herman. *Civil Liberties and the Vinson Court*. Chicago: University of Chicago Press, 1954.

———. *The Roosevelt Court: A Study in Judicial Politics and Values, 1937–1947*. New York: MacMillan, 1948.

Purcell, Edward. "American Jurisprudence between the Wars: Legal Realism and the Crisis of Democratic Theory." *American Historical Review* 75 (1969): 424–46.

———. *The Crisis of Democratic Theory: Scientific Naturalism and the Problem of Value*. Lexington: University Press of Kentucky, 1973.

Putnam, Robert D., with Robert Leonardi and Raffaella Y. Nanetti. *Making Democ-*

racy Work: Civic Traditions in Modern Italy. Princeton, N.J.: Princeton University Press, 1993.

Putzel, Henry, Jr. "Federal Civil Rights Enforcement: A Current Appraisal." *University of Pennsylvania Law Review* 99 (1951): 439–54.

Quandango, Jill S. *The Color of Welfare: How Racism Undermined the War on Poverty.* New York: Oxford University Press, 1994.

Quint, Howard H. *Profile in Black and White: A Frank Portrait of South Carolina.* Westport, Conn.: Greenwood Press, 1958.

Rable, George C. "The South and the Politics of Antilynching Legislation, 1920–1940." *Journal of Southern History* 51, no. 2 (May 1985): 201–20.

Reed, Merl E. *Seedtime for the Modern Civil Rights Movement: The President's Committee on Fair Employment Practice, 1941–1946.* Baton Rouge: Louisiana State University Press, 1991.

Rehnquist, William H. *The Supreme Court: How It Was, How It Is.* New York: Morrow, 1987.

Reiter, Howard L. "The Building of a Bifactional Structure: The Democrats in the 1940s." *Political Science Quarterly* 116, no. 1 (2001): 107–29.

Richberg, Donald. *My Hero: The Indiscreet Memoirs of an Eventful but Unheroic Life.* New York: Putnam, 1954.

Robertson, David. *Sly and Able: A Political Biography of James F. Byrnes.* New York: W. W. Norton, 1994.

Robinson, Greg. *By Order of the President: FDR and the Internment of Japanese Americans.* Cambridge, Mass.: Harvard University Press, 2001.

Rogge, O. John. "Justice and Civil Liberties." *American Bar Association Journal* 25 (1939): 1030–31.

Rohde, David, and Harold J. Spaeth. *Supreme Court Decision Making.* San Francisco: W. H. Freeman, 1976.

Roosevelt, Franklin D. *The Complete Presidential Press Conferences of Franklin D. Roosevelt.* 25 vols. New York: Da Capo Press, 1972.

———. *F.D.R.—His Personal Letters, 1928–1945.* Edited by Elliott Roosevelt. New York: Duell, Sloan and Pearce, 1950.

———. *The Public Papers and Addresses of Franklin D. Roosevelt.* Compiled by Samuel I. Rosenman. 13 vols. New York: Random House, 1938–50.

Rosenberg, Gerald N. *The Hollow Hope: Can Courts Bring About Social Change?* Chicago: University of Chicago Press, 1991.

Rosenfarb, Joseph. "Protection of Basic Rights." In *The Wagner Act: After Ten Years,* edited by Louis G. Silverberg. Washington, D.C.: Bureau of National Affairs, 1945.

Rosenman, Samuel. *Working with Roosevelt.* New York, Harper, 1952.

Rotnem, Victor W. "Civil Rights during War: The Role of the Federal Government." *Iowa Law Review* 29 (1944): 409–14.

———. "Clarifications of the Civil Rights' Statutes." *Bill of Rights Review* 2, no. 4 (summer 1942): 252–68.

———. "Criminal Enforcement of Federal Civil Rights." *Lawyers Guild Review* 2, no. 3 (May 1942): 18–23.

———. "Enforcement of Civil Rights." *National Bar Journal* 3 (1945): 1–9.

———. "The Federal Civil Right 'Not to Be Lynched.'" *Washington University Law Quarterly* 28 (February 1943): 57–73.

———. "Federal Criminal Jurisdiction of Labor's Civil Rights." *Lawyers Guild Review* 2, no. 5 (September 1942): 21–24.

Rotnem, Victor W., and F. G. Folsom. "Recent Restrictions upon Religious Liberty." *American Political Science Review* 36 (1942): 1053–68.

Savage, Sean J. *Truman and the Democratic Party.* Lexington: University Press of Kentucky, 1997.

Schlegel, John Henry. *American Legal Realism and Empirical Social Science.* Chapel Hill: University of North Carolina Press, 1995.

Schlesinger, Arthur M., Jr. *The Coming of the New Deal.* Boston: Houghton Mifflin, 1958.

———. *The Politics of Upheaval.* Boston: Houghton Mifflin, 1960.

Schlesinger, Arthur M., Jr., Fred L. Israel, and William P. Hansen, eds. *History of American Presidential Elections, 1789–1968.* 4 vols. New York: Chelsea House, 1971.

Schubert, Glendon A. *Quantitative Analysis of Judicial Behavior.* Glencoe, Ill.: Free Press, 1959.

Schwartz, Bernard. *Super Chief: Earl Warren and His Supreme Court: A Judicial Biography.* New York: New York University Press, 1983.

Schweinhaut, Henry A. "The Civil Liberties Section of the Department of Justice." *Bill of Rights Review* 1, no. 3 (spring 1941): 206–16.

Scigliano, Robert. *The Supreme Court and the Presidency.* New York: Free Press, 1971.

Segal, Jeffrey A., and Albert D. Cover. "Ideological Values and the Votes of U.S. Supreme Court Justices." *American Political Science Review* 83 (June 1989): 557–65.

Segal, Jeffrey A., and Harold J. Spaeth. *The Supreme Court and the Attitudinal Model.* New York: Cambridge University Press, 1993.

Segal, Jeffrey A., Lee Epstein, Charles M. Cameron, and Harold J. Spaeth. "Ideological Values and the Votes of U.S. Supreme Court Justices Revisited." *Journal of Politics* 57 (August 1995): 812–23.

Shamir, Ronen. *Managing Legal Uncertainty: Elite Lawyers in the New Deal.* Durham, N.C.: Duke University Press, 1995.

Shannon, J. B. "Presidential Politics in the South: 1938, I." *Journal of Politics* 1 (1939): 146–70.

———. "Presidential Politics in the South: 1938, II." *Journal of Politics* 1 (1939): 278–300.

Shapiro, Martin M. "APA: Past, Present, Future." *Virginia Law Review* 72 (1986): 447–92.

———. "Chief Justice Rehnquist and the Future of the Supreme Court." In *An Essential Safeguard: Essays on the United States Supreme Court and Its Justices,* edited by D. Grier Stephenson. Westport, Conn.: Greenwood Publishing, 1990.

———. "The Supreme Court: From Warren to Burger." In *The New American Political System,* edited by Anthony King. Washington, D.C.: American Enterprise Institute, 1978.

Silverstein, Mark. "Bill Clinton's Excellent Adventure: Political Development and the Modern Confirmation Process." In *The Supreme Court in American Politics: New Institutionalist Interpretations,* edited by Howard Gillman and Cornell Clayton. Lawrence: University Press of Kansas, 1999.

Simon, James. *The Antagonists: Hugo Black, Felix Frankfurter, and Civil Liberties in Modern America.* New York: Simon & Schuster, 1989.

Sitkoff, Harvard. "Harry Truman and the Election of 1948: The Coming of Age of Civil Rights in American Politics." *Journal of Southern History* 38 (1971): 597–616.

———. "The Impact of the New Deal on Black Southerners." In *The New Deal and the South*, edited by James C. Cobb and Michael V. Namorato. Jackson: University Press of Mississippi, 1984.

———. *A New Deal for Blacks*. New York: Oxford University Press, 1978.

———. "Years of the Locust: Interpretations of the Truman Presidency since 1965." In *The Truman Period as a Research Field: A Reappraisal, 1972*, edited by Richard S. Kirkendall. Columbia: University of Missouri Press, 1974.

Skowronek, Stephen. "Order and Change." *Polity* 28 (fall 1995): 91–96.

———. *The Politics Presidents Make: Leadership from John Adams to George Bush*. Cambridge, Mass.: Harvard University Press, 1993.

Skrentny, John David. "The Effect of the Cold War on African-American Civil Rights: America and the World Audience, 1945–1968." *Theory and Society* 27 (1998): 237–50.

Smith, Rixey, and Norman Beasley. *Carter Glass: A Biography*. New York: Longmans, Green & Co., 1939.

Smith, Rogers. "Ideas, Institutions, and Strategic Choices." *Polity* 28 (1995): 135–40.

———. "If Politics Matters: Implications for a 'New Institutionalism.'" *Studies in American Political Development* 6 (1992): 1–36.

———. "Political Jurisprudence, The 'New Institutionalism,' and the Future of Public Law." *American Political Science Review* 82 (March 1988): 89–108.

———. "Still Blowing in the Wind: The American Quest for a Democratic, Scientific Political Science." *Daedulas* 126 (winter 1997): 253–87.

Stephenson, Donald Grier, Jr. *Campaigns and the Courts: The U.S. Supreme Court in Presidential Elections*. New York: Columbia University Press, 1999.

Stokes, Thomas. *Chip off My Shoulder*. Princeton, N.J.: Princeton University Press, 1940.

Sullivan, Patricia. *Days of Hope: Race and Democracy in the New Deal Era*. Chapel Hill: University of North Carolina Press, 1996.

Swain, Martha H. *Pat Harrison: The New Deal Years*. Jackson: University of Mississippi Press, 1978.

Tauber, Steven C. "The NAACP Legal Defense Fund and the U.S. Supreme Court's Racial Discrimination Decision Making." *Social Science Quarterly* 80 (1999): 324–40.

Thelen, Kathleen. "Historical Institutionalism in Comparative Politics." *Annual Review of Political Science* 2 (1999): 369–404.

Timmons, Bascom N. *Garner of Texas: A Personal History*. New York: Harper & Brothers, 1948.

Tindall, George B. *The Emergence of the New South, 1931–1945*. Baton Rouge: Louisiana State University Press, 1967.

Tomlins, Christopher. *The State and the Unions: Labor Relations, Law, and the Organized Labor Movement in America, 1880–1960*. New York: Cambridge University Press, 1985.

Truman, Harry S. *Memoirs*. Vol. 1, Year of Decisions. Garden City, N.Y.: Doubleday, 1955.

———. *Public Papers of the Presidents: Harry S. Truman, 1947*. Washington, D.C.: U.S. Government Printing Office, 1963.

————. *Public Papers of the Presidents: Harry S. Truman, 1948.* Washington, D.C.: U.S. Government Printing Office, 1964.

————. *Public Papers of the Presidents: Harry S. Truman, 1952–53.* Washington, D.C.: U.S. Government Printing Office, 1966.

Tugwell, Rexford. *The Democratic Roosevelt: A Biography.* New York: Doubleday, 1957.

Tushnet, Mark V. *Making Civil Rights Law: Thurgood Marshall and the Supreme Court, 1936–1961.* New York: Oxford University Press, 1994.

————. *The NAACP's Legal Strategy against Segregated Education, 1925–1950.* Chapel Hill: University of North Carolina Press, 1987.

Twining, William. *Karl Llewellyn and the Realist Movement.* 2d ed. Norman: University of Oklahoma Press, 1985.

Ulmer, S. Sidney. "Earl Warren and the Brown Decision." *Journal of Politics* 33 (1971): 689–702.

U.S. Senate Committee on the Judiciary. *The Supreme Court of the United States: Hearings and Reports on Successful and Unsuccessful Nominations of Supreme Court Justices by the Senate Judiciary Committee.* Compiled by Roy M. Mersky and J. Myron Jacobstein. Buffalo, N.Y.: W. S. Hein, 1977–.

Urofsky, Melvin I. *Division and Discord: The Supreme Court under Stone and Vinson, 1941–1953.* Columbia: University of South Carolina Press, 1997.

Valis, Wayne. "The Congress and the Courts." In *The Future Under President Reagan,* edited by Wayne Valis. Westport, Conn.: Arlington House, 1981.

Valelly, Richard M. "Party, Coercion, and Inclusion: The Two Reconstructions of the South's Electoral Politics." *Politics and Society* 21 (1993): 37–67.

Weiss, Nancy J. *Farewell to the Party of Lincoln: Black Politics in the Age of FDR.* Princeton, N.J.: Princeton University Press, 1983.

Weller, Cecil Edward, Jr. *Joe T. Robinson: Always a Loyal Democrat.* Fayetteville: University of Arkansas Press, 1988.

Wheeler, Burton, with Paul F. Healy. *Yankee from the West: The Candid, Turbulent Life Story of the Yankee-Born Senator from Montana.* Garden City, N.Y.: Doubleday, 1962.

White, G. Edward. *The Constitution and the New Deal.* Cambridge, Mass.: Harvard University Press, 2000.

————. "From Sociological Jurisprudence to Realism: Jurisprudence and Social Change in Early Twentieth-Century America." *Virginia Law Review* 58 (1972): 999–1028.

White, Walter. *A Man Called White: The Autobiography of Walter White.* New York: Viking Press, 1948.

Whittington, Keith. *Constitutional Construction: Divided Powers and Constitutional Meaning.* Cambridge, Mass.: Harvard University Press, 1999.

————. *Constitutional Interpretation: Textual Meaning, Original Intent, and Judicial Review.* Lawrence: University Press of Kansas, 1999.

————. "Once More unto the Breach: PostBehavioralist Approaches to Judicial Politics." *Law and Social Inquiry* 25 (2000): 601–34.

————. "Oppositional Presidents and Judicial Negotiations: Judicial Authority in Political Time." Paper presented at the annual meeting of the American Political Science Association, Boston, Mass., 1998.

Wolfskill, George. *The Revolt of the Conservatives: A History of the American Liberty League, 1934–1940.* Boston: Houghton Mifflin, 1962.

Wolters, Raymond. *Negroes and the Great Depression: The Problem of Economic Recovery.* Westport, Conn.: Greenwood Publishing, 1970.

Wyman, David S. *The Abandonment of the Jews: America and the Holocaust, 1941–1945.* New York: Pantheon Books, 1984.

Yalof, David Alistair. *Pursuit of Justices: Presidential Politics and the Selection of Supreme Court Nominees.* Chicago: University of Chicago Press, 1999.

Zangrando, Robert L. *The NAACP Crusade against Lynching, 1909–1950.* Philadelphia, Pa.: Temple University Press, 1980.

Zieger, Robert H. *The CIO, 1935–1955.* Chapel Hill: University of North Carolina Press, 1995.

———. *John L. Lewis: Labor Leader.* Boston: Twayne Publishers, 1988.

INDEX

AAA. *See* Agricultural Adjustment Administration
Abraham, Henry, 183–84
Ackerman, Bruce, 8, 216
ACLU, 7, 27, 110, 128, 145, 156, 162, 252n. 3, 255n. 37, 261–62n. 28
  and opposition to Wagner Act, 48, 51
  and support of Wagner Act, 55
AFL. *See* American Federation of Labor
Agricultural Adjustment Act, 42, 238n. 124
Agricultural Adjustment Administration (AAA), 38–40, 54, 162, 232n. 54
Agriculture Department, 39, 232nn. 52, 53
Alsop, Joseph, 76, 85, 106, 239n. 132
American Civil Liberties Union. *See* ACLU
American Federation of Labor (AFL), 35, 52, 76, 87, 230n. 32, 231n. 38
American Jewish Committee, 261–62n. 28
American Jewish Congress, 261–62n. 28
American Liberty League, 121, 237n. 115, 240n. 29
  and the Court-packing plan, 74–75, 80, 95, 111, 240–41n. 31
  and the Wagner Act, 74–75
American Political Science Review, 140
amicus curiae briefs, 7, 12, 110, 179, 191, 193, 196, 207, 221, 226n. 31. *See also individual court cases*
antilynching legislation, 128, 134, 181
  FDR and, 15, 40, 102, 106, 117–18
  Justice Department response to filibuster of, 118, 160–67
  Southern distaste of, 22, 103, 114–19, 123–24, 126, 150, 156
  See also Justice Department; lynching
Arnall, Ellis, 157, 169–70
Arnold, Thurman, 73
Associated Industries of Cleveland, 74
Atlanta Constitution, 3, 126

attitudinal model, 6, 105, 203, 211, 212–14, 225n. 27, 228n. 5
Auerbach, Joel, 74

Bailey, Josiah, 58, 236n. 103
Baldwin, Roger, 51, 55, 145, 232n. 56, 252n. 3
Ball, Howard, 112
Barkley, Alben, 133, 190
  and 1938 primary, 120, 121–22
  as Senate majority leader, 94–95
  and support of Reed, 119
Barnette. See West Virginia State Board of Education v. Barnette
Bazelon, David, 261n. 22
Berge, Wendell, 165, 256–57n. 62
Bernstein, Irving, 50
Biddle, Francis, 140, 161–62, 181, 256nn. 59, 60, 257–58n. 73, 260n. 11
  and creation of CRS, 147–48
  and FDR's "universal suffrage" memo, 17, 29, 158–59
  and lynching, 161, 164
  and NLRB, 37, 49, 231n. 43, 235n. 88
  and white primary, 153–55, 255nn. 37, 39
  See also Justice Department
Bilbo, Theodore, 103, 114, 117, 157–58
Bisbee deportations, 128, 249n. 71
Black, Earl, 100
Black, Hugo L., 13, 131, 132, 135, 142, 152, 170, 174, 196, 230n. 26
  as Alabama senator, 83, 203
  and *Brown,* 3, 203–4, 220, 267n. 52
  and flag salute cases, 139, 141, 152
  and Ku Klux Klan, 111–12, 203
  Supreme Court appointment of, 95, 111–13, 119, 129, 246n. 26, 247n. 37
  and Walter White, 111–12
Black, Merle, 100
"Black Monday," 21, 43, 46, 48, 51, 106